D0026224

For Mary Ann Keeler

— I so much enjoyed
and my visit to Grand Valley.
— Thank you for inviting me.
and Happy Christmas 2003.

Best wishes

Stephen Murray
National Humanities Center
December 19 2003.

BEAUVAIS
CATHEDRAL

BEAUVAIS CATHEDRAL

Architecture of Transcendence

STEPHEN MURRAY

PRINCETON UNIVERSITY PRESS

PRINCETON, NEW JERSEY

Copyright © 1989 by Princeton University Press
Published by Princeton University Press, 41 William Street,
Princeton, New Jersey 08540
In the United Kingdom: Princeton University Press, Oxford

All Rights Reserved

Library of Congress Cataloging-in-Publication Data
Murray, Stephen, 1945–
Beauvais Cathedral, architecture of transcendence / Stephen Murray.
p. cm.
Bibliography: p.
Includes index.
ISBN 0–691–04236–5 (alk. paper)
1. Cathédrale Saint-Pierre (Beauvais, Oise, France)
2. Architecture, Gothic—France—Beauvais (Oise)
3. Beauvais (Oise, France)—Buildings, structures, etc. I. Title.
NA5551.B5M87   1989
726'.6'094435—dc19   88–19952
                                                        CIP
ISBN 0-691-04236-5
9 8 7 6 5 4 3 2
Publication of this book has been aided by a grant from
The Millard Meiss Publication Fund
of the College Art Association of America

This book has been composed in Linotron Sabon

Clothbound editions of Princeton University Press books
are printed on acid-free paper, and binding materials are
chosen for strength and durability. Paperbacks, although satisfactory
for personal collections, are not usually suitable for library rebinding
Printed in the United States of America by Princeton University Press,
Princeton, New Jersey

And he that talked with me had a golden reed to measure the city,
and the gates thereof, and the wall thereof.
And the city lieth foursquare, and the length is as large as
the breadth. . . .
And he measured the wall thereof, an hundred and forty and four
cubits, according to the measure of a man, that is, of the angel.
And the building of the wall of it was of jasper: and the city was pure
gold, like unto clear glass.

—Revelation 21:15–18

CONTENTS

LIST OF ILLUSTRATIONS

In order to allow the illustrations to constitute a self-explanatory visual document, I have arranged them in the following sequence: Beauvais Cathedral, plans and drawings, exterior views, starting with the general, and proceeding to details, west to east, lower parts before upper, north before south. Then follow interior views, from west to east, lower parts before upper, north before south. Finally, the comparable monuments are arranged in alphabetical order. Drawings are by the author unless otherwise indicated.

Photographic Sources

Photographs are by the author with the exception of the following:

Caisse Nationale des Monuments Historiques et des Sites, Arch. Phot. Paris: Figs. 20, 23, 160, 169, 170.

Courtauld Institute of Art, London: Figs. 98–100, 115, 118, 122, 123, 129, 159.

Christopher Crockett: Figs. 175–177.

F. Duchenne: Fig. 124.

Institut Géographique National, Paris: Figs. 19, 31–39, 41, 47, 48, 50.

Shirley Prager Branner kindly gave permission to reproduce Robert Branner's section of Bourges Cathedral, Fig. 158.

PREFACE

Entering the city of Beauvais each day to work in the municipal library, the departmental archives, or in the cathedral itself, I would descend from the south side, where the land drops precipitously down into the basin of the river Thérain. My work in the archives or in the cathedral involved me with a mass of bits of evidence relating to chronology or design, but each day the spectacle of the south flank of Saint-Pierre of Beauvais would challenge me to reach toward broader modes of interpretation. The epithet "architecture of transcendence" was coined in order to convey several distinct but related avenues of thought: transcendence, because seemingly by a miracle the cathedral has survived the ravages of time—ravages that have all but obliterated the medieval fabric of the city itself. To be sure, all venerable edifices have this kind of transcendence, but the ability of Saint-Pierre of Beauvais to withstand the vicissitudes of time is particularly striking in the context of the two great structural disasters that took place there (collapse of the choir in 1284, collapse of the crossing tower in 1573) as well as the savageness of the destruction of the city in 1940.

This book is about the way in which the Gothic cathedral of Saint-Pierre of Beauvais was conceived and built. Of particular importance is our ability to relate the architectural vision inherent in the cathedral to the temporal context in which it was conceived. Existing theories concerning the development of "High Gothic" architecture tend to emphasize the importance of Chartres and Bourges cathedrals (1190s) and to group subsequent buildings dependent upon one or the other of those great structures, or with those that rejected their validity altogether. However, it is obvious that such a pattern results more from the inbuilt tendency of the art historian to classify and group objects or monuments by type than from lines of filiation or dependency affecting the medieval master builder or the clerical patron. Moreover, this kind of framework of interpretation tends to reduce our appreciation of the originality of the designers of the decades after 1200.

Was a Gothic cathedral generally conceived and built as the result of a single sublime vision? Whereas such unified visions might be evident at Chartres and Bourges, it will be demonstrated in the following pages that the

Beauvais choir embodies three distinct visions, the first and third of which transcend the authority of any existing prototypes.

The conception of the initial vision at Beauvais (1225) can be related to the initiative and personal agency of Bishop Miles of Nanteuil. This bishop, described in the Chronicle of Reims as being "as proud as Nebuchadnezzar," was simultaneously count of Beauvais, combining secular with spiritual power. This monopoly provided the means to undertake the colossal enterprise of construction. Begun soon after the fourth Lateran Council, the cathedral of Saint-Pierre expresses the power of the church and of the established clergy—Bishop Miles of Nanteuil claimed to owe allegiance to no secular lord, but only to Saint Peter himself. However, in the context of the 1230s this lofty ideal became confused with the petty machinations of the rebel magnates who rose against the regency of Blanche of Castile. Miles of Nanteuil's tenure as bishop ended with the violent confrontation of the 1230s, and the second phase of construction (reduced in mass and ornamentation) expresses the subjugation of the bishop to the king of France.

The third vision at Beauvais, the upper choir, can be associated with the patronage of Bishop William of Grez. This phase of construction allowed the cathedral to attain a height that transcended all existing structures. Notre-Dame of Paris, begun in the mid-twelfth century, was considered at thirty-three meters to be outrageously tall. Then in the decades around 1200 new records were set: Chartres at thirty-four meters, Bourges at thirty-seven, Reims at thirty-eight, and finally Amiens at forty-two. Amiens was not vaulted when Beauvais was begun, and a dialogue seems to have taken place between the two buildings. They ended up with identical proportions (height of central vessel equals three times width) but the greater central span of Beauvais was accompanied by greater height (46.75m). This was the first monument in northern Europe to surpass the Pantheon in height.

Here again we can relate the architectural forms of the cathedral to attendant circumstances. Whereas Bishop Miles had attempted to maintain and express the power of the church in the face of incursions by the king of France, the 1250s saw an intense struggle on the part of the secular clergy to maintain their position in the face of the growing power of the mendicants (Franciscans and Dominicans) whose doctrines tended to undermine the temporal underpinnings of the established church. It is particularly interesting to find a canon of the Beauvais chapter, William of Saint Amour, assuming a leading role in the 1250s in the struggle against the mendicants. Freed from the trammels of material possessions and under the influence of a revived interest in Aristotle, members of the mendicant orders developed new kinds of intellectual framework to reconcile reason and faith. The transcendent superstructure of the Beauvais choir, on the other hand, expresses a more conventional Dionysian hierarchy and a vibration between things spiritual and things temporal. Like the celestial city seen by Saint John, the choir is four square, its height equaling its width. The high wall of the celestial city reached 144 cubits, that of the Beauvais choir 144 (royal) feet.

In my exploration of the various levels on which Beauvais Cathedral may be understood and interpreted, I have received substantial help and encouragement from a variety of institutions and individuals.

My first thanks go to Peter Kidson, with whom I began to look at Gothic architecture.

In 1977–1978, under the tenure of an NEH fellowship, I was able to devote myself to full-time study of Beauvais Cathedral, to survey the choir and to draft an accurate plan. I have also held a summer grant and various travel grants from Indiana University, as well as a grant-in-aid from the American Philosophical Society, and I should like to express my thanks to all these agencies. My work in Beauvais was facilitated through the help and cooperation of Joachim Bardagi, municipal archaeologist; Emile Chami; Philippe Bonnet-Laborderie; Abbé Duchenne; Yves Boiret, departmental architect; Mme Gut, archivist; M. Lemaire, librarian; Mme Crignon; and M. Senn, loyal guardian of the cathedral for almost half a century.

Many colleagues here in the United States have helped me with their encouragement, advice, and criticism. I should particularly like to name and to thank William Clark and Caroline Bruzelius who read and criticized the original manuscript, and Marilyn Schmitt, François Bucher, Walter Leedy, Peter Fergusson, and J. H. Munby. The late Christine Ivusic, fine arts editor at Princeton University Press, helped me transform my original manuscript into its present form, and I remember her encouragement with particular gratitude. Kathleen Groom and Paul Sherbow provided invaluable help in the final stages of the preparation of the manuscript, and Diego Oleas prepared the three axonometric drawings.

From my wife, Grainne, I have received every kind of help in all stages of the preparation of this book. Together with my children, Pippa and Finnian, she bore with me through one of the coldest winters in recent memory at Beauvais, lodged in an unfurnished, semi-heated room in a house attached to the former leper hospital of Saint-Lazare, and it is to my family that I dedicate this book.

ABBREVIATIONS

Arch. Oise   Archives Départementales de l'Oise

Art Bull.   *Art Bulletin*

Bibl. Ecole Chartes   *Bibliothèque de l'Ecole des Chartes*

Bibl. Nat.   Bibliothèque Nationale

Bull. mon.   *Bulletin monumental*

Bull. Soc. arch. Eure-et-Loir   *Bulletin de la Société archéologique d'Eure-et-Loir*

Cong. arch.   *Congrès archéologique*

Gaz. des Beaux-Arts   *Gazette des Beaux-Arts*

GEMOB   Groupe d'Etude des Monuments et Œuvres d'Art du Beauvaisis

J. Brit. Arch. Assoc.   *Journal of the British Archaeological Association*

J. Soc. Arch. Hist.   *Journal of the Society of Architectural Historians*

Mém. Soc. acad. Oise   *Mémoires de la Société academique de l'Oise*

Mém. Soc. ant. Pic.   *Mémoires de la Société des antiquaires de Picardie*

Mém. Soc. nat. ant. France   *Mémoires de la Société nationale des antiquaires de France*

Trav. Acad. nat. Reims   *Travaux de l'Académie nationale de Reims*

BEAUVAIS
CATHEDRAL

INTRODUCTION

The cathedral of Saint-Pierre at Beauvais dominates the central city today much as it did in the Middle Ages. Once surrounded by a maze of pungent narrow streets and wooden houses, however, it now stands amid sterile modern stone and concrete structures like a great whale stranded on some unfriendly shore. In the same way, the historical framework in which this great piece of architecture was created has long since been swept away. Once the seat of one of the wealthiest and most powerful prelates of France, as well as a chapter of some fifty canons, the cathedral now accommodates a congregation of modest size and a flow of summer tourists.

The fabric of the cathedral itself (Figs. 31–39) is incomplete, with a thirteenth-century choir and a sixteenth-century transept, but lacking a nave or western frontispiece. The choir, constructed between 1225 and 1272 (Figs. 122–124), was the tallest structure ever built in northern Europe and was certainly the most ambitious cathedral project of the High Gothic era. However, in 1284, twelve years after its inauguration, a major part of the upper choir collapsed. In the half century that ensued the choir was rebuilt from the ground

level up, with additional supports interposed between the original piers—thus effectively blocking the magnificent spatial vistas envisaged by the original designers. Repairs were finished by the mid-fourteenth century, but the devastation and depopulation caused by the Hundred Years' War and the Black Death prevented the clergy from continuing construction until around 1500. The transept was designed by the greatest master mason of French Late Gothic, Martin Chambiges, who directed construction work until his death in 1532. Directly after the completion of the transept (ca. 1550) a colossal lantern tower was erected over the crossing (Fig. 29). This tower collapsed in 1573, and after the work of repair was completed, halfhearted attempts were made to vault the eastern bay of the nave. These attempts were abandoned around 1600, and the west end of the cathedral was consolidated in a provisional fashion by means of great buttresses constructed between the stumps of the nave piers, and a west wall of rubble and timber covered with slates. The view of Beauvais Cathedral from the west (Fig. 31) provides one of the most moving experiences of medieval architecture. We see the remnants of the nave of the old cathedral, known since the Middle Ages as the *Basse-Œuvre*, dwarfed by the gigantic bulk of the Gothic edifice. Yet the *Basse-Œuvre* itself, constructed in the years around 1000, is not insignificant in size, its wooden roof rising some nineteen meters above pavement level.[1] It is from the west that the beholder can perceive the bones and muscles of the Gothic edifice. The massive stones of the unfinished charges of the vaults and towering uprights of the flying buttresses are a powerful expression of the ambitions of the builders of what was intended to be the greatest Gothic cathedral ever constructed.

The passing of time has been cruel to those ambitions. The city of Beauvais was destroyed by fire bombs in 1940.[2] The cathedral, a stone structure, survived with minor damage, but the stained glass was removed and the windows were fitted with wooden screens. The restoration of the glass has been a lengthy project and remains incomplete. The interior lighting of the edifice has obviously suffered greatly. After forty years of work the lighting of the cathedral is now close to its prewar state. Especially significant has been the recent work on the transept—within the last few years the windows have been reglazed and the sixteenth-century organ loft, heavily damaged in 1940, has been removed from the south transept. The thirteenth-century transept of Beauvais Cathedral (Figs. 75–77), one of the most extraordinary inventions of Gothic architecture, may now be seen as it has not been seen since the sixteenth century.

The framework of this monograph is intended to reflect the variety of different levels on which the cathedral may be understood. On the one hand it may be seen as an all-embracing symbol of its time, expressing the religious and political aspirations of its patrons translated, as far as financial resources would allow, into stone, glass, and wood. As such, the construction of the cathedral was a collective effort, involving the participation of thousands of people and embracing centuries of work. On the other hand, Beauvais, like any Gothic cathedral, may also be seen as the expression of a vision conceived by the master mason within the context of a dialogue with the clerical patrons, the bishop, and chapter. In the case of some cathedrals, abundant resources have allowed the entire structure to be built in a period of decades, and the vision of the initial master planner is easily recognizable throughout the edifice.[3] In other cases, where financial resources were less than adequate, or where some disaster has intervened, protracted campaigns have ensued, and the initial vision might be lost, as a succession of master masons introduced modifications in accord with contemporary taste and their own ideas.[4]

The study of a Gothic cathedral must be undertaken both with a broad vision to embrace the overall characteristics of the monument as a totality, and with a microscope in order to detect the stages of construction and thus to recognize the genius of the successive designers. The totality of the monument is revealed through the analysis and interpretation of plan, elevation, and the organization of space and mass. Three notable architectural historians have each offered their own interpretation of the choir of Beauvais as a totality: Eugène Viollet-le-Duc, Robert Branner, and Jean Bony. It would be as well to provide a sketch of each of these three visions. The greatest nineteenth-century proponent of Gothic, Viollet-le-Duc, praised it in these terms: "It is the Parthenon of French Gothic. It has the misfortune, however, of remaining unfinished and of not being placed in a conserving popu-

---

[1] For the *Basse-Œuvre*, see E. Chami's excavation reports in *Archéologie médiévale*, 1971–1977.

[2] M. Brayet, *Beauvais, ville martyre . . . juin-août, 1940*, Beauvais, 1964; F. Watteeuw, *Beauvais et les Beauvaisiens des années 40*, GEMOB, Paris, 1980.

[3] As, for example, in Bourges Cathedral; see R. Branner, *La Cathédrale de Bourges et sa place dans l'architecture gothique*, Paris, 1962.

[4] Troyes Cathedral provides an excellent example of such delayed construction; see S. Murray, "The Completion of the Nave of Troyes Cathedral," *J. Soc. Arch. Hist.*, XXXIV, pp. 121–139; idem, *Building Troyes Cathedral: The Late Gothic Campaigns*, Bloomington, 1987.

lation, like the ancient Greeks, able to appreciate, respect, and be proud of the great efforts of human intelligence."[5]

Viollet-le-Duc had some difficulties in reconciling his various theories concerning Beauvais Cathedral. On the one hand, this was a building where the intellectual dominated, one incorporating structural refinements of the greatest perfection. Thus, the intermediary flying buttress uprights (Fig. 24) were placed *porte-à-faux*, overhanging the inner aisle so that their alleged tendency to hinge inward would create a force that would help to meet the outward thrust of the high vaults transmitted by the flyers. If Beauvais Cathedral embodied such enlightened structural refinements, why, then, did it collapse? Viollet-le-Duc attributed the collapse of 1284 to the inferior workmanship apparent in the masonry of the upper parts of the building and to a certain faulty detail.[6] He believed that the use of long sticks of detached (*en délit*) shaft in the upper piers of the exterior central vessel caused differential settlement, whereby the coursed masonry would settle to a greater extent than the shafts, leading to dislocation and collapse. Viollet-le-Duc, although he noted that the Gothic choir was founded in 1225, commented that he was unable to see any part of the lower choir, which dated from before the 1240s.[7] He placed the work in a phase of Gothic where, according to his own theories, invention had, to some extent, been replaced by a mechanical repetition of well-established structural and formal elements.

Robert Branner has provided the fullest and most sensitive commentary on the overall qualities of the Beauvais choir.[8] Branner's interest in the links between the elevational system of Beauvais Cathedral and that employed at Bourges, which was begun before 1195, caused him to favor an early date for the commencement of work in the former building: he suggested that work began on the radiating chapels directly after 1225. Thus, work that Viollet-le-Duc had put in the 1240s was now pushed back by fifteen years, and the "master of Beauvais" was depicted by Branner as a true revolutionary, "one who thought in volumes rather than surfaces."[9] Branner characterized this "prodigious meditation" of the master of Beauvais as a revolt against the academic style of Robert of Luzarches, master mason of Amiens Cathedral, and the "classic" qualities of the cathedrals of Chartres, Reims, and Amiens.[10] The peculiar vision of the master of Beauvais, according to Branner, lay in the fusion of the spatial qualities of Bourges, Amiens, and Chartres: by reducing the width of the side aisles and increasing the span of the main arcade in such a way as to allow the viewer's gaze to penetrate into the inner aisle. Branner divided the choir into the work of three successive masters, but he did not, however, attempt to justify his reasoning by means of a thorough-going analysis.

Jean Bony's treatment of the Beauvais choir in his recent book is heavily dependent upon Robert Branner's thesis.[11] Bony accepted Branner's chronology and his commentary on the spatial unity of the choir. Although the concept of the family of Chartres and "resistance to Chartres" does not receive the same emphasis as in his earlier work,[12] Bony stressed the unity of buildings in "the Chartrain series," and found links between Beauvais and these buildings. For example, the cathedral choir plan (Fig. 6) resembles the choir of Longpont (Fig. 161), and the rounded abaci used in the window tracery at Beauvais are

[5] E. Viollet-le-Duc, *Dictionnaire raisonné de l'architecture française*, I, Paris, 1858, p. 71.

[6] Ibid., IV, pp. 177–182.

[7] Ibid., II, p. 336. See also Vol. I, p. 239, where Viollet-le-Duc dated the Beauvais choir to 1240–1250.

[8] R. Branner, "Le Maître de la cathédrale de Beauvais," *Art de France*, II, 1962, pp. 77–92 (hereafter cited as "Maître de Beauvais").

[9] Ibid., p. 80.

[10] Ibid. The concept of rivalry between the designers of

the cathedrals of Beauvais and Amiens had already been expressed by Viollet-le-Duc, *Dictionnaire*, II, p. 336: "L'architecte de la cathédrale de Beauvais avait voulu surpasser l'œuvre des successeurs de Robert de Luzarches."

[11] J. Bony, *French Gothic Architecture of the 12th and 13th Centuries*, Berkeley, 1983, pp. 288–295, 363–364.

[12] J. Bony, "The Resistance to Chartres in Early-Thirteenth-Century Architecture," *J. Brit. Arch. Assoc.*, XX–XXI, 1957–1958, pp. 35–52.

similar to the forms at Reims. Bony found a "kind of concentrated disproportion" in the Beauvais choir and a "contradiction in size between the lower and the upper parts of the structure."[13] The relative elongation of the clerestory at Beauvais led Bony to propose links with the collegiate church of Saint-Quentin—links that are not, however, apparent through a comparison of the details of the two buildings.

Although, as we have said, the study of a great cathedral should embrace a vision of the totality followed by a closer analysis intended to reveal the chronology of construction, it will be readily apparent to the sceptical reader that the writer of an "objective" description will have already formed his or her own opinions concerning the sequence of construction and the genius of the designers. As we describe the plan and elevation of the Beauvais choir and the organization of space and mass, we cannot escape from the conclusion that there are two broadly different architectural modes to be observed in the lower building (Figs. 94, 116). The former mode involves great mass, walls treated in a sculptural fashion, and expansive spaces (transept and outer walls of the choir), and the latter mode brings contracted spaces, brittle two-dimensional compositions, and optical illusion (east end of the choir and central vessel). Were these architectural modes selected simultaneously as the appro-

priate ones for the parts of the building in which they were employed, or do they reflect different mentalities and different phases of execution?[14]

To answer this question we must undertake some detective work, which involves sifting through the written sources, both primary and secondary, and correlating evidence derived from these sources with the building itself. Despite the destruction wrought upon the archive sources relating to Beauvais Cathedral by the French Revolution and the calamitous fire of 1940, a considerable body of primary manuscript sources still exists, as well as numerous published studies of the ecclesiastical and urban history of Beauvais.[15] In the building itself, three kinds of evidence allow us to reconstruct the sequence of construction: breaks in the geometrical regularity of the design; interruptions in the stone coursing or changes in the type of stone used; and development in the form of molding profiles, capital sculpture, tracery, decorative forms, and the like. Such details of style obviously must be interpreted in the light of comparisons with similar details in other monuments.

It might be as well to announce right from the start that the present study embodies a revisionist interpretation of the chronology of the choir of Beauvais Cathedral.[16] Previous writers chose between two alternative options for the start of construction (1225 or 1247),

[13] Bony, *French Gothic Architecture*, pp. 288, 293.

[14] Branner ("Maître de Beauvais") put the two-dimensional mode first and astonished himself with the precosity of his *maître de Beauvais*. He went on to remark on the *retardataire* quality of the work in the transept. F. Salet expressed reservations about Branner's chronology in *Bull. mon.*, CXX, 1962, pp. 78–79.

[15] The following inventories provide an introduction to the primary sources: G. Desjardins and A. Rendu, *Inventaire-sommaire des archives départementales antérieures à 1790: Archives ecclésiastiques, série G*, I, Beauvais, 1878; Vol. II (by E. Rousset and M. J. Estienne), Beauvais, 1942; V. Leblond, *Inventaire-sommaire de la collection Bucquet-aux Cousteaux*, Paris and Beauvais, 1907. General histories of Beauvais can be found in L.-H. Labande, *Histoire de Beauvais et de ses institutions communales jusqu'au commencement du XVe. siècle*, Paris, 1892; P. Louvet, *Histoire et antiquitez du diocèse de Beauvais*, 2 vols., Beauvais, 1631–1635; idem, *L'Histoire de la ville et cité de Beauvais et des antiquitez du pays de Beauvaisis*, Rouen, 1614; A. Loisel, *Mémoires des pays, villes, comté et comtes,*

évesché et évesques, pairrie, commune, et personnes de renom de Beauvais et Beauvaisis, Paris, 1617; D. Simon, *Supplément aux mémoires de l'histoire civile et ecclésiastique du Beauvaisis de M. Anthoine Loisel et de M. Pierre Louvet*, Paris, 1704; E. de la Fontaine, *Histoire politique, morale, et religieuse de Beauvais*, 2 vols., Beauvais, 1840; Abbé F. A. Delettre, *Histoire du diocèse de Beauvais depuis son établissement, au IIIe. siècle jusqu'au 2e. septembre 1792*, 3 vols., Beauvais, 1842–1843; M.-M. Launay, C. Fauqueux, and A. Launay, *Essai d'histoire régionale: Département de l'Oise et pays oui l'ont formé*, Beauvais, 1925. A useful, if somewhat outdated bibliography of sources on the history of Beauvais is provided by E. Vercauteren, *Etude sur les civitates de la Belgique seconde*, Brussels, 1934, pp. 265–286. See also P. Dollinger and P. Wolff, *Bibliographie d'histoire des villes de France*, Paris, 1967.

[16] This theory was first published in my article "The Choir of the Church of Saint-Pierre, Cathedral of Beauvais: A Study of Gothic Architectural Planning and Constructional Chronology in Its Historical Context," *Art Bull.*, LXII, 1980, pp. 533–551.

and where an opinion was expressed on the internal chronology, an east to west sequence was generally favored (Branner, Bony).[17] At a very early stage in his study of the building, this author became convinced that work began in the area of the transept in 1225 and proceeded from west to east, with a hesitation in the 1230s (Figs. 21, 22). To the uninformed this might seem like a petty argument over trivial details. In the following pages, however, it will be demonstrated that this new interpretation is absolutely critical to a correct understanding of the monument within the context of the very significant stylistic and structural changes of the years between the 1220s and the 1260s. Moreover, the character of the two major campaigns of construction of the lower choir of Beauvais Cathedral must be interpreted correctly in order to reach an understanding of the nature of the famous collapse that took place in 1284.

These concerns lie behind the organization of the early chapters of this book. The reader is first presented with a general picture of the cathedral and its historical context. A consideration of the chronology of construction comes next, and a more intensive analysis of the building is undertaken following the sequence proposed for the building campaigns. In this way it is possible to bring together material of a purely historical nature (who was Bishop Miles of Nanteuil?) with the analysis of the parts of the cathedral constructed during the tenure of the bishop, considered in the context of the related monuments.

The opening chapters on the construction of the choir are followed by a discussion of the great collapse that ensued in 1284 and an account of the attempts to complete the cathedral in the later Middle Ages. The rich documentation for the Late Gothic campaigns of construction on the transept allow us to identify the great master who directed work on the transept, Martin Chambiges, and to consider his contribution to the cathedral of Beauvais in relation to his works elsewhere.

[17] A general summary of the various interpretations of the chronology of the construction of the Beauvais choir appears in Chapter III.

CHAPTER I

The Gothic Choir of Beauvais Cathedral

The student of medieval architecture will almost inevitably become familiar with a curious kind of temporal ambiguity affecting his relationship with the monument. We have to look at the great cathedral as it is; simultaneously, however, we will want to be able to control its life at a range of different times during its construction. In other words, we look at it both as absolute idea and as process. This duality (idea and process) has rendered it exquisitely difficult to write a satisfactory history of Gothic architecture since each of the hundreds of monuments to be considered has to be read as a complex stratigraphy of changing artistic intentions.

It is the declared aim of this chapter to explore the choir of Beauvais Cathedral as absolute idea. Yet we cannot escape from a preoccupation with the process of becoming, since the monument that was originally completed in 1272 exists no longer—the rebuilding of the choir after the great collapse of 1284 has transformed it in many different ways. Moreover, it is impossible to describe certain elements of the building, particularly the flying buttresses, without at least raising the question as to whether they should be considered as "ideal" forms, or whether they were the result of the process of finding solutions to problems that had not been fully anticipated at the outset.

This time warp is particularly important when we consider the cathedral in its urban context—hence the image of the stranded whale used in the Introduction. We will therefore begin with a brief introduction to the topography of the city of Beauvais and a discussion of the nature of the site, foundations, and building materials of the Gothic choir. Then will follow an analysis of the plan, elevation, space, and massing of the monument.

Topography, Site, and Foundations

A traveler approaching the medieval city of Beauvais (Fig. 1) would find a mass of wooden houses and a maze of narrow streets enclosed inside walls of silverish gray and dominated by the spires of a dozen or more churches.[1]

[1] See *Le Vray Pourtraict de la Ville de Beauvais* by Raymondus Rancurellus of 1574, published most recently in GEMOB, *Bulletin*, V, 1978, p. 5.

From whatever direction the traveler approached, he would descend to the city by a slope that varied from fairly steep (road from Amiens, to the north) to precipitous (from Gisors, to the southwest).[2] Rising out of this basin and towering above the rooftops of the surrounding houses would be seen the yellowish gray bulk of the cathedral. Beauvais, as a city site, is the antithesis of Laon. The multiple towers of Laon Cathedral effortlessly dominate the surrounding countryside for miles in every direction. The Gothic cathedral of Beauvais, on the other hand, heaves itself out of the basin in which it is situated thanks only to its prodigious height.

The cathedral was located in the episcopal *cité* (Fig. 2), the heart of Beauvais that had grown from the Gallo-Roman *castrum*. The domination of the clergy over the *cité* had been established already in the early Middle Ages. The *cité* walls enclosed a rectangular area with sides of roughly 260 by 370 meters.[3] Constructed of rubble, concrete, and bricks faced with small cubic stones (*pastoureaux*), probably around the third century A.D., the walls of the *cité* were known in the Middle Ages as the "Saracen Walls."[4] A seventeenth-century historian described the foundations of the walls as ten feet deep and ten feet wide.[5] The wall itself, eight feet thick and twenty-four feet high,[6] was punctuated with rectangular and circular towers and pierced by two main gateways, the Gloria Laus opening into the town and the Porte de Limaçon toward the exterior to the northwest. The road linking the two gates running in a direction roughly west-northwest to east-southeast divides the *cité* into two unequal parts.[7] The smaller part (northeast) was dominated by the cathedral church of Saint-Pierre (before 1225 this would have been the church now known as Notre-Dame-de-la-Basse-Œuvre), the collegiate church of Notre-Dame-de-Châtel, and the episcopal palace and the canons' houses. Whereas in many other French cathedral complexes the bishop's palace was located to the side (often south) of the choir, at Beauvais the palace was to the west of the cathedral, with its *corps de logis* founded against the Gallo-Roman wall. Writers have speculated that this site was acquired when Bishop Roger gained the country of Beauvais in the early eleventh century and that previously the bishop had been lodged in a palace to the south of the cathedral, but there is no firm evidence upon which to base this assertion. The bishop's palace was linked with the cathedral by a covered passage or gallery that ran at first floor level over the southern side of the cloister (immediately alongside the nave of the *Basse-Œuvre*) to enter the present transept at pavement level.[8] The higher ground to the east of the site may perhaps be explained through the dumping of debris from the foundations of earlier buildings. As the construction of the Gothic choir moved into the transept and nave, debris from the excavations was dumped in the western parts in an attempt to level the site.

The entire site on which the cathedral existed was thus free of the restrictions encountered by the bishops and chapters at, for example, Bourges, Troyes, or Le Mans, where new construction campaigns necessitated

[2] Loisel, *Mémoires des pays*, p. 60, noted this as one of the unusual features of Beauvais: *"que la ville soit bastie dedans un fons, et comme dans une prairie environnée de rivières. . . ."*

[3] Dr. Daniel, "De l'ancienne cité de Beauvais," *Mém. Soc. acad. Oise*, II, 1852, pp. 9–53; R. Lemaire, *Une Construction urbaine de défense au IIIe. siècle: Le Castrum de Bellovacis*, Centre Départementale de Documentation Pédagogique de l'Oise, Beauvais, n.d.

[4] Collection Bucquet-aux Cousteaux, Municipal Library, Beauvais, XXVI, p. 346 (hereafter cited as Bucquet-aux Cousteaux).

[5] Cited in Daniel, "De l'ancienne cité," p. 15.

[6] Lemaire (*Une Construction urbaine*) gives a thickness

of 2.60 m.

[7] The rue Saint-Pierre corresponded to the *decumanus* of the *castrum*. No *cardo* seems to have existed.

[8] The "cloister" is made up on the west side by the salle Saint-Pierre, a large chamber that embodies substantial amounts of eleventh-century masonry. To the east is the sixteenth-century chapter house, while to the south, alongside the *Basse-Œuvre*, is a gallery that is attributed to Bishop Pierre of Savoisy (1398–1412). Above this runs a first-story passageway (postmedieval), joining the transept at pavement level, reflecting the drop in the ground to the west. See Delettre, *Histoire du diocèse*, II, p. 528, and P. Bonnet-Laborderie, *Cathédrale Saint-Pierre, Beauvais*, GEMOB, Beauvais, 1978, pp. 37–39.

breaking through the Gallo-Roman walls, or at Amiens, where the bishop and chapter were unable to gain control over the area to the west of the cathedral and where another structure existed on the site (the church of Saint-Firmin), which would have to be moved to another location.[9] In the later Middle Ages the land around the cathedral choir was occupied by canons' houses, many of them built with their backs to the Gallo-Roman wall.

The *cité* was dominated in a physical sense by the cathedral of Saint-Pierre and in a jurisdictional sense by the cathedral clergy. The bishops were simultaneously counts of Beauvais and thus exercised considerable jurisdictional and economic powers not only over the county, but also over the *bourg* that had developed with the industrial and commercial growth of the eleventh and twelfth centuries.[10]

The relatively dense settlement of the rich farmland of the Beauvaisis, coupled with rapid commercial and industrial development of the area, had produced considerable wealth, and during the late eleventh and twelfth centuries much of this wealth was expended in the construction of lavish churches. These great churches embodied many of the important features characteristic of Early Gothic architecture, such as, for example, enhanced verticality in the central vessel expressed in the use of a galleried or four-story elevation, and the early use of rib vaults, which led to the coining of a new vocabulary of forms of articulation appropriate for use in rib-vaulted structures. One thinks particularly of the monastic church of Saint-Lucien, Beau-

vais, in which the steep three-storied galleried elevation of Jumièges was employed and where rib vaults were used at a very early date;[11] of the monastery church of Saint-Germer-de-Fly, with its early use of a rib-vaulted ambulatory and coherently expressed diagonal articulation of the supports;[12] and the collegiate and parish church of Saint-Vast and Saint-Etienne, Beauvais, another pioneering monument in the early use of rib vaults, with supports that express the new diagonality of the rib.[13]

Despite these exciting developments between the late eleventh and mid-twelfth centuries, the area had failed to participate in the structural revolution that is called High Gothic. The western bays of the nave of the church of Saint-Etienne, Beauvais, together with the nave high vaults, probably constructed after the fire of 1180, represent "High Gothic" architecture in Beauvais in the period just before the construction of the new cathedral. This was essentially a form of Romanesque with pointed arches and modernized profiles and sculptural forms.

Given the wealth and power of the bishop-counts of Beauvais and the importance of the area in mid-twelfth-century architecture, we might have expected to find some evidence of twelfth-century construction at the cathedral itself (Figs. 3, 4). The pre-Gothic cathedral, the oldest church in the *cité*, which was damaged in fires in the 1180s and in 1225, was progressively demolished to make way for the Gothic cathedral.[14] The nave of the old cathedral still exists in its three western bays, with

[9] At Beauvais, as far as we know, the only restrictions of site were the rue Saint-Pierre, the remains of the previous cathedral, and the great *beffroi*; see Abbé L. E. Deladreue, "Les Maisons canoniales du chapitre de Beauvais et leurs possesseurs," *Mém. Soc. acad. Oise*, VII, 1868, pp. 291–347.

[10] Fontaine, *Histoire politique*, I, pp. 72–118, 181–241, provides a description of medieval Beauvais. See also P. Goubert, *Cent mille provinciaux au XVIIe. siècle, Beauvais et le Beauvaisis de 1600 à 1730*, Paris, 1968, and R. Lemaire, *Beauvais hier et aujourd'hui*, Le Coteau, 1986.

[11] M. Aubert, "A propos de l'église abbatiale de Saint-Lucien de Beauvais," in *Gedenkenschrift Ernst Gall*, Munich, 1965, pp. 51–58; S. Gardner, "Notes on a View of Saint-Lucien at Beauvais," *Gaz. des Beaux-Arts*, XCVI, 1980, pp. 149–156; J. Henriet, "Saint-Lucien de Beauvais, mythe ou réalité?" *Bull. mon.*, CXLI, 1983, pp. 273–294.

[12] P. Héliot, "Remarques sur l'abbatiale de Saint-Germer et sur les blocs de façade du XIIe. siècle," *Bull. mon.*, CXIV, 1956, pp. 81–114; M. Pessin, "The Twelfth-Century Abbey Church of Saint-Germer-de-Fly and Its Position in the Development of First Gothic Architecture," *Gesta*, XVII, 1978, p. 71.

[13] Stanislas de Saint-Germain, *Notice historique et descriptive sur l'église Saint-Etienne de Beauvais*, Beauvais, 1843; V. Leblond, *L'Eglise Saint-Etienne de Beauvais*, Paris, 1929; A. Henwood-Reverdot, *L'Eglise Saint-Etienne de Beauvais*, GEMOB, Beauvais, 1982; J. D. McGee, "The 'Early Vaults' of Saint-Etienne at Beauvais," *J. Soc. Arch. Hist.*, XLV, 1986, pp. 20–32.

[14] Our understanding of the *Basse-Œuvre* is far from complete. Extensive excavations have been undertaken by E. Chami, who is preparing an authoritative new book on the subject. He has published periodic excavation reports in

another three bays of the south nave aisle. The half-demolished former cathedral has been known since the Middle Ages as the *Basse-Œuvre*, expressing the limited height of the structure as well as its situation somewhat lower than the Gothic choir. The nave, a wooden-roofed three-aisled basilica, originally extended nine bays. The cubic stones (*pastoureaux*) that were used to face the walls had been recovered from the Gallo-Roman wall. The similarity between the walls of the old cathedral and the city walls caused the antiquarians of Beauvais to consider this a pre-Christian temple. The pavement level has been raised considerably since the time of the original construction; instead of sixteen meters, as at present, the nave then rose about nineteen meters above pavement level. The six western bays had octagonal piers; these six bays were probably terminated to the east by a diaphram arch. The three eastern bays have a variety of pier types: cruciform and rectangular.

The footings of the two western piers of the crossing of the *Basse-Œuvre* have been uncovered. They are about two meters square and are placed just to the east and considerably to the north of the present western crossing piers of the Gothic cathedral. From the square crossing of the *Basse-Œuvre* was generated an aisleless transept, about forty-two meters in total length. The eastern wall of the transept and the eastern crossing piers of the *Basse-Œuvre* have not been found. They presumably ran along a line just to the west of the eastern piers of the Gothic transept.

No traces of the foundations of the pre-Gothic choir have ever been found, nor indeed is it likely that they will be, since the excavation in the thirteenth century of the foundations of the Gothic choir certainly led to their total destruction. It is probable that the old

choir was of considerable length, since it would have to provide seating for a sizable chapter. We can never be certain about the circumstances of the demolition of the old choir, yet it is important to speculate as to how this event may have affected the construction of the Gothic choir. The existence of a sequence of foundations of altars and chapels culminating in the consecration of the high altar in 1222 suggests most strongly that the choir of the old cathedral had been rebuilt in the wake of the fires in the 1180s (see Appendix A and Chapter III). If this were the case, then the choir would have been a tall, stone-vaulted structure that might have survived the fire of 1225, which burned the roof of the old transept and nave. Although no physical evidence survives to allow us to be certain, this might have provided the reason why the earliest work on the Gothic choir was concentrated upon the extremities of the transept arms and outer walls of the aisles, thus making it possible to leave the old choir intact for as long as possible (Figs. 21, 22).

The excavators of the *Base-Œuvre* (Fig. 4) have uncovered the foundations of a provisional choir in the form of a *chevet plat*, extending just to the east of the western crossing piers of the old cathedral. This provisional choir was constructed in the thirteenth century after the old choir had been demolished to make way for the new work. When it became apparent that the new work would not advance rapidly westward, making the total demolition of the *Basse-Œuvre* not necessary, it was decided to adapt the old, half-demolished structure for use as a parish church. This involved the construction of a modest choir and a new portal (Fig. 40) to provide access into the south nave aisle.[15]

In the angles between the west walls of the

Archéologie médiévale, I, 1971, pp. 277–280; III/IV, 1973/74, p. 403; VI, 1976, pp. 339–341; VII, 1977, pp. 259–261; and XI, 1981, p. 275. He is careful to remain unspecific about the date of the structure, commenting that it has generally been put in the second half of the tenth century. C. Heitz, *L'Architecture religieuse carolingienne*, Paris, 1980, pp. 197–199, dates the structure to the period of Bishop Herveus (d. 998). Bonnet-Laborderie, *Cathédrale Saint-Pierre*, p. 23, discusses the ambiguity of the various dedications associated with the pre-Gothic churches of the

episcopal group at Beauvais (Notre-Dame, Saint John, and Saint Peter). With the construction of the Gothic choir in the thirteenth century the term *Nouvel-Œuvre* was applied exclusively to this new work, which was known as Saint Peter's, while the Notre-Dame designation was applied to the remains of the old cathedral (the *Basse-Œuvre*), which became a parish church.

[15] The portal is very badly weathered. The tympanum is in the form of a quatrefoil surmounting two trefoiled arches. The small rosettes in the moldings around the arches

transept and the nave of the old cathedral existed ancillary buildings of considerable extent, dating from the same period as the main church. These chambers presumably served as sacristy, scriptorium, and the like.

Along the south side of the nave, in the late Middle Ages, were constructed the workshops and houses of the masons, carpenters, and other artisans involved in the construction of the transept of the cathedral. These workshops and houses were demolished and eventually buried under the debris of the Gothic construction as the new work moved westward.

To the west of the *Basse-Œuvre*, recent excavations have uncovered the remains of a Gallo-Roman hypocaust, and a little to the south of the west façade, an apsidal end and south transept of a small religious structure were found. One of the two reliquary boxes found in this building contained a coin of Bishop Herveus (died 998). While this coin provides confirmation of the documentary sources emphasizing the role of this bishop in the construction of the old cathedral, the main dating evidence for the structure is derived from the analysis of stratigraphy and ceramic fragments; a date in the second part of the tenth century or early in the eleventh century is indicated.

To the south of the choir of the old cathedral stood a freestanding bell tower constructed of ashlar masonry in its lower parts and wood in its upper parts. This tower is mentioned in the sixteenth-century documents relating to the start of work on the cathedral transept as well as in many other written sources, and it is depicted in numerous engravings and plans (Fig. 2). It was demolished around 1800. The use of ashlar masonry rather than the small cubic stones of the

Basse-Œuvre would suggest that the bell tower was later than this church. The primitive architectural forms of the tower lead one to believe that it must have been constructed at an early date. Such "primitive"-looking freestanding bell towers, were, however, constructed in the period up to and including the fourteenth century.[16] It seems possible that the bell tower at Beauvais belongs to the period immediately preceding the Gothic work after the destruction of the crossing tower of the *Basse-Œuvre*. The thirteenth-century transept arms embodied a provision for bell towers in their eastern angles. As it happened, however, these bell towers were never constructed, and the great crossing tower of the sixteenth century collapsed soon after it was completed. The old tower therefore served to hang the great bells of the cathedral and was also a prison.[17]

The foundations of the Gothic choir are imperfectly known. Some of the footings of the piers were excavated by the restorers of the cathedral in the nineteenth century. The restoration drawings left by the architects Vital and Sauvageot show foundations composed of large blocks of stone, descending like a staircase, so that the platform widens as it goes down. Sleeper walls are shown between the individual piers. The *expertise* carried out prior to the campaigns of construction of the sixteenth-century transept revealed that the foundations descended to a depth of about thirty feet. The author of a recent study has suggested that they rested upon a bed of rock (chalk, to be specific).[18]

The foundations of the sixteenth-century transept piers have been uncovered in the excavations of the *Basse-Œuvre*. These foundations are composed of large, rectangular blocks of stone, forming a platform for each

---

and the quatrefoil are comparable with the similar forms in the window frames of the radiating chapels of the choir. A date in the 1240s is proposed for these chapels.

[16] For example, the tower of the parish church of Saint-Jean-au-Marché in Troyes; see P. Piétresson de Saint-Aubin, "L'Eglise Saint-Jean-au-Marché à Troyes," *Bull. mon.*, LXXXIX, 1930, pp. 47–111.

[17] The defensive function of the tower is emphasized in the eighteenth-century plan of the *cité* in Bibl. Nat., Collection de Picardie, CLXII, fol. 24 *bis*. On fol. 27 the writer confirms the function of the tower as a *clocher*, or bell tower.

[18] J. Kerisel, "Old Structures in Relation to Soil Conditions," *Géotechnique*, XXV, 1975, pp. 449–451. An unpublished study has also suggested that the foundations stopped short of bedrock; see J. Delatouche, "La Cathédrale de Beauvais: L'Effondrement des voûtes, l'écroulement de la tour lanterne, les fondations." For the restoration work of Vital and Sauvageot, see Appendix B.

pier. The foundations in the transept widen as they descend and are linked by sleeper walls.

Abbé Marsaux left us a tantalizing glimpse of the choir foundations when he referred to the excavation completed by the local architect Frederick Beauvais. Marsaux claimed that Beauvais had found that certain piers were placed in such a way as to overhang their foundations. Unfortunately, he failed to define exactly which piers were involved, merely indicating that they were in the ambulatory (main hemicycle piers, or piers dividing the chapels?).[19]

The stone employed throughout the Gothic choir is a hard chalk, with sizable pieces of flint embedded therein. This material is even used for the slender shafts in the exterior upper choir. Several distinct types of chalk can be discerned, some slightly more yellow and hard, others with a whiter surface, more ravaged by the effects of weather. The written sources tell us of a quarry, the carrière Saint-Pierre, located between the villages of Bongenoult and Frocourt.[20] Deep earth workings and piles of debris are still visible in this location, about four kilometers to the southeast of Beauvais. Local tradition indicates that the main quarry was entirely subterranean, with a narrow entrance that has been blocked. A similar subterranean chalk quarry, once belonging to the church of Saint-Etienne, Beauvais, can still be visited about three kilometers to the south of the city, close to Saint-Martin-le-Nœud. A softer type of chalk, also derived from local sources, is found in the vault severies.

The Thirteenth-Century Choir: Plan

The parts of the Beauvais choir completed in the thirteenth century (figs. 5, 6) include the beginnings of a spacious aisled transept equipped with towers flanking the transept façades, a five-aisled choir of three bays, and an eastern hemicycle of seven segments, ringed by a single ambulatory of seven bays, and seven shallow five-sided radiating chapels.

The plan of the eastern aisles of the transept arms reveals the existence of an ambitious program. The transept extends a full bay beyond the five-aisled body of the choir, and the transept façades were to have been flanked by towers (never actually completed).[21] Thus, the Beauvais transept must be considered in relation to Chartres Cathedral, which embodies these same features, rather than the later plans of Reims or Amiens cathedrals, both of which have reduced transepts. It is clear that the aisled, towered transept was becoming obsolete by the 1220s. At Beauvais the plan allowed for great windows opening into the lower parts of the towers, flanked by flat-faced buttresses. Portals were not intended in the transept aisles. The inner corners of the transept towers (Fig. 12a) were to be supported by massive compound piers composed of cruciform bodies with the sides arranged in a series of steps, each one enclosing a shaft. Sixteen shafts are provided, four large ones for the inner orders of the four transverse arches, four smaller ones for the diagonal ribs, and eight smaller still for the outer orders of the main transverse arches. Not even in the heavy structure of Chartres Cathedral do we find tower-supporting piers of this mass in the transept arms.

The overall proportions of the transept (Fig. 8) may have been fixed with the help of a simple modular system where the module was derived from the thickness of the aisle wall (1.54 m, or 4 feet 9 inches in royal feet). Five such modules fit into the square base of the transept tower, four and a half into each of the double

[19] Abbé, L.-H. Marsaux, "Cathédrale [de Beauvais]," *Cong. arch.*, LXXII, 1905, pp. 4–15.

[20] A charter dated 1356 (Arch. Oise, G 813) refers to the "*quarrieres nommées les quarrieres Saint Pierre sceans au dessus de Bongenoul.*" Another charter, dated 1408, in the same dossier describes "*prés des villes et villages que l'en dit Bongenoul et Frocourt une carrière de pierre blanche bien ancienne.*" In the "*layette de la carrière*" in the inventory of the chapter archive many references are made to the "*carrière de Saint-Pierre*" and the "*voye de la carrière*" along which the stones were carted into town. A document dated 1248 confirmed that the Bongenoult quarry was already in use during the construction of the Gothic choir.

[21] On transept towers, see P. Héliot, "Sur les tours de transept dans l'architecture du moyen âge," *Revue archéologique*, 1965, I, pp. 169–200; II, pp. 57–95.

aisles, and ten units fit into the span of the central vessel. The total span of the transept is thus thirty-eight modules. It is also worth noting that the span of the tower bay (five modules) plus the outer aisle (four and a half modules) constitutes exactly one-quarter of the total north-south span of the transept ($9\frac{1}{2} \times 4 = 38$).

In the three straight bays of the Beauvais choir a wide central vessel (about 15.30 m in span) is flanked on each side by narrow double aisles. Both inner and outer aisles are made up of rectangular bays arranged with their long sides running in an east-west direction. Each of the aisles is about seven meters in width.

Three special features characterize the Beauvais plan in the straight bays of the choir (Fig. 8). First, the combination of an unusually wide central vessel with slender, widely spaced piers and narrow aisles produces a high degree of optical continuity between the space of the central vessel and that of the aisles. Second, it is noticeable that the east-west dimensions of the bays in the main arcade increase significantly toward the east end of the choir. The westernmost bay (5 6), which corresponds to the eastern aisle of the transept, spans about 7.80 m. This is already a very wide bay; the east-west spans of the Amiens nave are around 7.40 m. The second bay at Beauvais (6 7) increases significantly in size by about three royal feet to 8.74/78 m. Finally, the third bay opens wider still to 8.81 m in the south arcade and an astonishing 9.05 m in the north. This progressive widening is exactly the opposite of the arrangement at Amiens Cathedral, where the bay adjacent to the crossing is the widest, and the bay adjacent to the apse the smallest. A larger bay next to the apse is, however, found in Noyon and Le Mans cathedrals.[22] A narrower bay at the base of the apse can serve to reduce the abrupt transition from the slow rhythm of the straight bays of the choir to the staccato of the closely spaced piers of the apse. Viollet-le-Duc considered that the narrower bay adjacent to the crossing at Beauvais was intended as a support for an ambitious crossing tower.[23] Branner associated the wide third bay with the desire of his "master of Beauvais" to open up the aisles to the oblique gaze of the beholder in the central vessel.[24]

A closer study of the dimensions of the east-west span of bay 7 8 reveals that the bay was originally intended to have been somewhat narrower. The span of the exterior buttresses on the south side is only 8.72 m (less than the adjacent bay to the west, bay 6 7, which is about 8.76 m in the central vessel). The interior spans open progressively, as has been demonstrated, reaching as much as 9.17 m in the intermediary piers of the north aisle. The progressive opening in the east-west spans of bay 7 8 as we go from south to north indicates that the hemicycle system is not aligned with that of the straight bays (Fig. 10). In fact, the hemicycle has been swung in a clockwise direction in relation to the western part of the building. This rotation, which surely resulted from a mistake in the laying out of the lower parts of the building, caused the northern part of the radiating chapel system to move away from the northern part of the body of the church, with the gap becoming increasingly wide toward the northern periphery of the building. This is already visible in the extra-wide span employed in the arch between the intermediary aisle piers. The visual effect of the misalignment is even more striking from the exterior (Figs. 32, 33). The lower parts of the exterior buttress at B 8 are placed in accordance with the grid system of the western parts of the building. This buttress rises to form the upright for the flying buttress system supporting the base of the apse on the north side and therefore had to be aligned with the grid system of the hemicycle. The constructors realized that a misalignment existed when they reached the level of the crocket cornice

[22] C. Seymour, *Notre-Dame of Noyon in the Twelfth Century: A Study in the Early Development of Gothic Architecture*, New York, 1968. For Le Mans, see F. Salet, "La Cathédrale du Mans," *Cong. arch.*, CXIX, 1961, pp. 18–58.

[23] Viollet-le-Duc, *Dictionnaire*, IV, p. 175.

[24] Branner, "Maître de Beauvais," p. 80.

above the sacristy roof. At the level of this cornice the mass of the buttress is diminished on the west side, but not on the east. The effect of this is to shift the upright a little to the east. As the construction went upward, however, it was realized that this adjustment was inadequate, and finally the unit was abandoned altogether, terminated in a sloping roof in order to protect it from the rain, and a new upright was begun, pushed well to the east of the old one and placed partially over the staircase turret (Figs. 48, 61). These adjustments in the superstructure of the building reflect an error that had been made in the layout of the plan. Specifically, they resulted from the lack of alignment between the interior arches and piers on the north side with the lower parts of the exterior envelope. This lack of alignment resulted from the fact that the hemicycle system does not follow the same axis as that defined in the straight bays but is turned slightly to the right.

The isolation of these three special features of the Beauvais straight bays—widened central vessel, bays widening to the east, and the lack of alignment in the east end—allows us to define the characteristics that set Beauvais apart from contemporaneous cathedrals. The great width of the central vessel may, or may not, have been part of the original intent of the first master designer who initiated the plan. The twisted axis obviously resulted from a mistake and suggests the existence of two distinct building campaigns, one including the envelope of the straight bays and the other including the hemicycle system.[25]

The hemicycle (Figs. 6, 9) is a highly unified, and accurately laid out, composition designed around two great circles generated from a center point lying about 2.40 m east of the eastern transverse arch of the choir. On the outer cir-

cle (radius of about 14.5 m) lie the center points of the piers dividing the chapels of the ambulatory. The radiating lines forming the divisions between the seven segments meet at angles of about 28 degrees.[26]

It seems quite clear that the designer had intended to divide the circumference of the outer circle into thirteen equal segments. Thus, the crown of radiating chapels should be considered as expressing seven-thirteenths of a full circle.

The circumference of the inner circle gives the center points of the six piers of the hemicycle. The two piers at the base of the hemicycle do not lie upon this circumference, but belong to the rectilinear grid system of the choir straight bays. This accounts for the wider gaps between the piers at the base of the system (4.82 m center to center, as opposed to 3.75 m in the central part of the hemicycle).

A key factor determining the relationship between the radii of the inner and outer circles was the desire to have the span of the radiating chapels equal (more or less) the width of the inner aisle and ambulatory. The former spans are around 7.20 m and the latter 7.00 m. This consideration seems to have led the designer to choose a thirteen-sided figure rather than a simple duodecagon for the composition. The latter choice would have given chapels that would have been much too wide in relation to the aisles.

Opening from the ambulatory are seven five-sided chapels divided by wedge-shaped blocks of masonry. Although the spans of the arches forming the chapel mouths are regular, the sizes of the chapels are not. The two chapels at the base of the system are formed where the radii of the hemicycle meet the rectilinear plan of the body of the choir and are therefore rather smaller than the others. The other five

---

[25] One supposes that a Gothic cathedral would be laid out with ropes pegged to the ground and a grid system whose rectilinear quality would be controlled through the use of Pythagorean triangles. Once work had actually begun, however, and the site had become muddy and punctuated by water-filled holes, some of the precision embodied in the initial vision of the plan might have been lost. In other words, irregularities and misalignment might easily have oc-

curred in a single, unified campaign of construction. It will be seen, however, that several other factors also suggest a break in the sequence of construction at the base of the hemicycle.

[26] See Murray, "Choir of the Church of Saint-Pierre"; N. L. Prak, "Measurements of Amiens Cathedral," *J. Soc. Arch. Hist.*, XXV, 1966, pp. 209–212.

chapels were intended to be the same size. In reality, however, some slight variations are noticeable in their width and depth. The largest chapel is that of Saint Vincent, immediately to the south of the axial chapel.

The plan of each radiating chapel results from the attempt to fit an octagonal form (eight segments of 45 degrees) between the radiating lines of the overall hemicycle composition. Thus, the side walls of each chapel are not parallel, as would be found in an octagon, but they open more widely to the depth of the chapel. The radii running to the angles of each chapel form angles of about 48 degrees at the center point, and the walls meet at angles of about 134 degrees. The dividing walls between the chapels, at their thinnest points, are about 0.80 m in thickness, increasing to 2.11 m toward the outside. The exterior walls are 0.75 m in thickness and have small buttresses (1.30 m in thickness) set against their angles.

The choice of a plan type for the hemicycle would certainly have taken place within the context of a discussion between the master masons and the clergy, since factors of a liturgical and iconographic nature were involved. The clergy would be interested in finding space for the key altars (some of which were already endowed) and in making reference to certain prestigious prototypes. In terms of the logistics of the design, the choice was limited to one of the several varieties of five-sided composition (5/8, 5/9, or 5/10), or seven-sided composition (7/12, 7/13, or 7/14). The 5/10 composition had been particularly popular in the previous generation (Notre-Dame of Paris, Bourges, and Reims, for example). This choice would have lent a much slower rhythm to the design, with the opportunity of disposing considerable masses of masonry at the main exterior buttresses. Given the broad bay system of the Beauvais choir, such a plan would have created a more harmonious ensemble than the actual seven-segment scheme, which produces a sharp change of mode from the wide spaces of the choice to the staccato of the east end.

In general terms, we are dealing with a double-aisled choir terminated in a hemicycle ringed by a single ambulatory. Thus, the radiating chapels occupy the space that might have constituted the outer ambulatory (as at Notre-Dame of Paris, Chartres, and Bourges). In this way, the designer has produced a building that would be more economical to build and avoided the problems caused by the progressively wider spans created by a double ambulatory scheme. The reduction of a double aisle to a single ambulatory had already been embodied in the choir of Reims Cathedral, but here the use of a five-segment hemicycle produced very spacious chapels that are allowed to project to a considerable depth. At Beauvais, on the other hand, the use of a rather narrow ambulatory ringed by very shallow chapels pulls the periphery of the building toward the center. The beholder in the central vessel is able to see through the diaphanous screen of the hemicycle piers into the crown of chapels, each one made up of two walls bearing delicate tracery patterns and three windows. The ultimate prototype for such a composition is obviously Suger's Saint-Denis, but much closer in time and geographical location is the choir of Soissons Cathedral. The five shallow chapels of Soissons were transformed into a seven-segment composition in the Cistercian churches at Longpont (Fig. 161) and Royaumont (Fig. 171), which provide the immediate prototypes for the Beauvais scheme.

Thus, the pulling inward of exterior buttresses and chapels in the Beauvais hemicycle produces a composition that seems to be reduced or contracted—in sharp contrast to the more expansive western end of the choir with its generous aisled transept projecting a full square bay beyond the body of the choir, and its massive walls and heavy towers (the latter never actually built). The twisted axis of the hemicycle, as compared with the choir straight bays, suggests that the two parts may belong to two distinct campaigns. This hypothesis is confirmed by an analysis of the stylistic handwriting expressed in the details of articulation—piers, capitals, molding forms, and tracery.

The Thirteenth-Century Choir: Elevation

The study of the ground plan has revealed that the drive for spatial unity was a major preoccupation in the minds of the designers of Beauvais Cathedral. Nevertheless, it is obvious that the total spatial economy of the cathedral is far from possessing the grand unity of a structure such as the cathedral of Bourges (Figs. 158, 159). In the latter building, the same pyramidal spatial organization of the five-aisled superstructure (lower outer aisle, tall inner aisle, taller central vessel) prevails throughout, whereas at Beauvais the presence of a transept and the abrupt termination of the low outer aisle at the base of the hemicycle produce considerable diversity in the spatial economy of the building (Fig. 11). The designers of the Beauvais choir have created a unique spatial system by flanking the central vessel with two L-shaped corridors forming the tall inner aisle. The vertical shafts of the Ls are linked by the curving ambulatory, while the horizontal bases of the Ls are turned one away from the other to continue into the transept arms. The tall inner spaces of the central vessel and the inner aisle are surrounded by a series of separate cells of outer, lower space in the double-bay units of the outer aisles and in each of the seven radiating chapels.

In analyzing the structure of the elevation that produces this diversity of spatial effect, it would be correct to recognize not one type of elevation, but rather, three. The first of these elevational types is to be found in the transept arms, which are heavy structures with thick walls (about 1.80 m at the base) and massive tower-supporting interior compound piers (Figs. 76, 77, 82, 85, 86, 92, 94, 95). The square outermost bays of the eastern aisles of the transept arms ascend to a height of about 21 m (to the keystone), this steep space then being subdivided into three levels: a lower level corresponding to the windows placed in the outer walls, a middle "triforium" passage, and an upper rose window.[27] In the triforium, as well as at the level of the rose, interior and exterior passages run side-by-side within the thickness of the wall. At the middle level, the inner and outer passages are linked by means of small openings that form a premonition of the glazed triforium. In the exterior elevation at this point (Figs. 42, 44) we see a simple expression of the interior levels: window, passageway, and rose. Great flat-faced buttresses flank the outermost bay of the transept aisle. These buttresses would have continued up to form the angles of powerful towers.

The second type of elevational system is found in the choir straight bays (Figs. 18, 19), where there is a five-aisled basilica with low outer aisle, tall inner aisle, and steeply proportioned central vessel. The elevation of the central vessel is divided into three levels: a tall arcade opening widely onto the inner aisle, a glazed triforium, and a very tall clerestory level. Whereas the pyramidal section of Bourges Cathedral (Figs. 158, 159) is inscribed in an equilateral triangle with its base extending to the outer aisle walls and its apex at the keystone of the high vaults, the total section of the straight bays of Beauvais Cathedral (Fig. 18) is close to a square.[28] This reveals the relative steepness of the Beauvais elevation in comparison with Bourges. There are certain other ways in which the square was used in order to fix the proportions of the Beauvais elevation. It is striking that the height of the piers of the main arcade, up to the abacus, is about 15.40 m, and that the width of the main vessel is around 15.30 m. This creates a square, with its base line at floor level, placed between the axes of the main piers, with its sides formed by the piers themselves. The height of the triforium sill (22.71 m in the straight bays) is very close to the span of the central vessel added to the inner aisle (15.45 + 7 = 22.45), and a further such

---

[27] By definition, a triforium is a mural arcade in the wall of the central vessel occupying the space between the top of the arcade and the point where the lean-to roof of the aisle meets the central vessel. Thus, the passage in the Beauvais transept is not a real triforium, although it resembles one.

[28] The keystones of the great vaults are about 46.75 m above the pavement; the width of the choir (to the outer surfaces of the aisle walls) is 45.50 m.

square placed at the level of the triforium sill will give the height of the capitals of the high vaults. Finally, three such squares can be fitted between the pavement and the keystone of the high vaults. The inner aisles have exactly the same steep proportions as the central vessel. When the span is multiplied by three, the result gives the height of the keystone ($7 \times 3 = 21$; actual height is 21.28 m).

Of course, the existing upper choir does not necessarily reflect the intentions of the original builders, and there is a good chance that the choir was actually increased in height during construction, as will be demonstrated in Chapter v. As a result of a change of plan introduced around 1250, an extra five meters were added to the clerestory. The original scheme would have given a transverse section closer to an equilateral triangle, like Bourges.

This analysis of the existing section of the Beauvais choir in terms of square schematism allows us to compare the extreme verticality here with the more moderate proportions employed elsewhere. At Reims Cathedral, for example, the span of the central vessel, projected upward, will reach the crown of the arcade arch—in other words, the main piers at Reims are relatively much lower than those of Beauvais. Amiens Cathedral provides the only close comparison with Beauvais, with a height-to-width ratio of close to three to one. At Amiens the triforium sill marks the halfway point of the elevation, whereas at Beauvais the triforium sill is well below the middle point, thus giving a very tall clerestory. The Beauvais choir offers a marked contrast between the exaggerated verticality of the clerestory and the strong emphasis on horizontality in the lower structure. This is all the more interesting since in the generation after Chartres Cathedral, a structure where the height of the arcade equals the height of the clerestory, there was a general tendency to move toward a reduction in the relative height of the clerestory. Beauvais Cathedral should be considered together with the collegiate church of Saint-

Quentin in embodying such a steep upper superstructure.

A comparison with Amiens and Bourges cathedrals is most useful in allowing us to define the special characteristics of the proportions of the aisles. Thus, while the inner aisles at Beauvais and Bourges are similar in height, the outer aisle at Beauvais is much taller than its counterpart at Bourges. This is because the plan at Beauvais incorporates radiating chapels, and if the outer aisle were any lower, the proportions of these chapels would be impossibly stunted. At Amiens, on the other hand, the choir has double aisles of the same height, and the outer aisle here is obviously much taller than at Beauvais.

The combination of a low outer aisle with a very tall central vessel at Beauvais had important implications for the design of the buttressing system: a very considerable extent of the height of the outer upright of the flying buttress system was left exposed over the aisle roofs (Figs. 18, 32–39). This feature also can be understood as resulting from the choice of flyers, which have a rather shallow angle of inclination, and from the relatively wide central vessel placed inside narrow aisles. These characteristics combine to produce towering uprights that dominate the exterior and that lend the overall section of Beauvais Cathedral a distinctly square appearance. The sheer height of the uprights of the flying buttress system is obviously of considerable importance in view of the fact that the intermediary upright is placed in such a way that a part of its mass overhangs the inner aisle (the *porte-à-faux* defined by Viollet-le-Duc).[29] Similarly, the more massive outer upright overhangs the outer aisle (Fig. 18). Such overhang is fairly common in Gothic structures, and, in itself, need not be structurally dangerous. However, at Beauvais the shifting intentions of the builders have brought an increase in the load carried by the uprights (through the heightened clerestory) as well as a reduction of the mass of the aisle piers below.

[29] Viollet-le-Duc, *Dictionnaire*, i, p. 70.

It is particularly important to note that this eccentric placing of the intermediary flying buttress upright over the aisle piers of the Beauvais choir exerts a load on an area that, for other reasons, may be considered already structurally weak. Whereas in a building with two aisles each having the same height (for example, the choirs of Chartres, Reims, or Amiens cathedrals), the thrusts of the transverse arches of the vaults of the inner and outer aisles interact at the same level, at Beauvais the use of a tall inner aisle meant that the transverse arches of the outer aisle tend to bend the slender intermediary aisle piers toward the center of the building at a point where these piers are not supported by the arches and vaults of the inner aisle.[30]

The tendency of these piers to bend inward is well documented in the drawings and photographs left by the restorers of the building in the decades around 1900 (Fig. 23), when most of these piers were almost entirely rebuilt. Pier C 7 in the north aisle has been a particular problem, having been rebuilt once around 1300 and again around 1900. The greatest deformation seen anywhere in the horizontal courses of the choir is found in the triforium sill over this pier (Fig. 101). The sill droops downward over the pier and rises again on the other side, indicating that considerable settlement has taken place.

Thus, the very type of pyramidal section used at Beauvais incorporated inherent structural weaknesses, which were exacerbated by certain eccentric features peculiar to this particular building. Finally, it is worth noting that the combination of the narrow inner aisle with the flying buttress upright placed in a position of overhang over the inner aisles produces a flyer against the central vessel that is very short indeed, about 4.50 m, as opposed to more than 7.00 m at Amiens Cathedral.

Were these towering flying buttress uprights part of the original scheme at Beauvais? It will be demonstrated in Chapter v that a significant detail of the earliest upright to be constructed (B 6, on the north side; figs. 58, 59) suggests that they were originally intended to have been considerably lower. The original pair of flying buttresses, a lower one for the vaults and an upper one for the clerestory wall, spring from a relatively low level on this upright. As a result of a change of plan (probably introduced in the 1250s), the upper flyer was made into the unit supporting the vaults and a third unit was added to support the clerestory wall.

The third and last type of elevation found in the Beauvais choir is in the east end of the building, the hemicycle (Figs. 17, 20). Here the radiating chapels replace the outer aisle, and the outer upright of the flying buttress system sits on top of the wedge-shaped blocks of masonry between the chapels. Since these blocks of masonry have been pulled inward toward the central part of the building in relation to the exterior buttresses of the straight bays, the span between the outer upright and the central vessel is greatly diminished (Figs. 33–39). The result is a buttressing system that is even more steeply vertical than the already very steep elevation of the straight bays. Moreover, the outer upright seems to be pulled inward to such an extent that it almost touches the clerestory wall of the inner aisle. Miniscule flyers now link the outer and intermediary upright. Indeed, one wonders why the designer bothered with double flyers at all, since the total gap from outer upright to central vessel is now in the region of seven to eight meters, which could have been spanned with a single flyer.[31]

The reason for the use of the intermediary upright has been explained in terms of structural considerations: that it would diminish the gap so that the flyer would not be too long,

[30] The theory of bending under an eccentric load is clearly explained by R. Mark with K. D. Alexander and J. F. Abel, "The Structural Behaviour of Medieval Ribbed Vaulting," *J. Soc. Arch. Hist.*, XXXVI, 1977, pp. 241–251.

[31] A similar arrangement with double flyers over the double aisles of the choir and a single span over the ambulatory can be found at Troyes Cathedral.

and therefore too heavy in relation to the load supported in the central vessel.[32] Optical considerations were probably even more important than structural ones. A hemicycle system with flying buttresses having a single span combined with straight bays with double-span flyers would have produced a jarring effect in a building where uniformity of optical effect was obviously one of the major goals of the designers. When the elevations of the hemicycle and the straight bays are compared, the former gives the impression of being something of a compromise. This over-close spacing of outer and intermediary uprights is new; earlier Gothic structures provide little precedent. The Amiens choir, which employs a similar arrangement, is, in execution at least, roughly contemporaneous with the comparable work at Beauvais. At Amiens, however, the height of the upright is much less than at Beauvais.

The only existing discussion of the overhanging intermediary uprights of the flying buttresses of the Beauvais hemicycle has been based upon the theory of structural rationalism, suggesting that the intermediaries were intended as active agents against the outward thrust of the high vaults, transmitted by the flying buttresses.[33] In order for the intermediary uprights to have hinged inward in the way suggested, they would have had to possess a certain elasticity in the area of the base—a characteristic that is, of course, absent in masonry construction.

The odd spacing of these intermediaries might be explained more convincingly in light of certain unexpected problems encountered in the sequence of construction. It will be demonstrated that construction in the Beauvais choir moved from west to east, with the hemicycle the last part to be constructed. The extraordinarily steep arrangement of the hemicycle section is the result of two factors: the contracted or reduced nature of the hemicycle plan that has led to the buttress uprights being drawn inward toward the center, and an in-

crease in the height of the central vessel. It may have been originally intended to bridge the relatively narrow gap from outer upright to central vessel with single rank flyers. But the demonstration of this hypothesis must await a more careful exploration of the archaeological and stylistic evidence, presented in Chapter v.

Space

As one attempts to capture in words the overall impression of space and mass, light and line, color and texture that the choir of Beauvais Cathedral creates (Figs. 120–124), it is impossible to escape from a preoccupation with what might have been. Had the nave been completed, the beholder would have been able to add the necessary horizontal distance to appreciate this extreme verticality. The overall proportions of the Beauvais central vessel are very similar to those at Amiens. However, because the latter cathedral is complete, the general spatial effect seems more harmonious. Had the restorers of Beauvais Cathedral who were charged with the repair of the building after the collapse of 1284 not felt constrained to add the additional piers in the main arcade, the horizontal views penetrating the aisle would also counteract the impression of excessive verticality. Similarly, there is an obvious lack of balance in the lighting of the choir, since the repairs following the bombardments of 1940 have left many of the windows blocked, and a zone that was intended to be well lit (aisles and transept towers) is now somber.

Space, on the one hand, is the negative void left between three dimensions: height, width, and length. On the other hand, to the visitor of the great Gothic cathedral, space becomes a positive entity, defined by great expanses of translucent surface or diaphanous screen, made sculptural in the half-cylinder of the hemicycle, and made mysterious by glimpses

[32] J. Heyman, "Beauvais Cathedral," *Transactions of the Newcomen Society*, XL, 1967–1968, pp. 15–36.

[33] Viollet-le-Duc, *Dictionnaire*, IV, p. 180.

into the half-perceived realms of the peripheral aisles, ambulatory, and radiating chapels, and illuminated by light that is at once physical and metaphysical. Thus, space can be defined in a rational way, and it can be experienced.

In rational terms, space is often described as a dialectical process.[34] Thus, we may remark that a building has verticality in its piers, in its windows, in its total proportions. Then we go on to notice that if the building is vertical, it is also horizontal; the orthogonals created by the lines of the abaci, by the molding over the arcade, and by the sill of the clerestory windows produce a kind of mesh or grid with the verticals and provide points of reference that allow us to "read" the building. A similar dialectic is created in the opposition between unified space and a space that is conceived in terms of a number of watertight pockets that have little or no interaction. In most medieval buildings, the reality will generally lie somewhere between these two extremes. Jantzen's commentary on the "diaphanous" quality of the Gothic envelope is a very helpful one: we see the space of the central vessel as something that is unified in itself, but that communicates with the aisles, chapels, and galleries if the latter are present.[35]

In more irrational terms, space is something we experience rather than perceive. A particularly beautiful description of the space of Beauvais Cathedral as experience was composed by Gustave Desjardins, the mid-nineteenth-century archivist who wrote an important monograph on the cathedral.[36] He recounts the experience of sitting in the choir on a summer's evening and watching the shifting light define the interior space. As the sun's rays circle around to the south and west, the colors change, the interior masses slowly lose their strength, and one is left with four tiers of disembodied windows, until at last the patterns formed by the tracery and the colors of the stained glass finally disappear.

However, Desjardin's description would apply to almost any of the great Gothic cathedrals. Can we avoid resorting to such well-established formulas in our description of the space of the Gothic choir and refine our terms in such a way as to apply specifically to the genius of this particular work?

Much has been written on the excessive lightness (i.e., lack of mass) of this monument, the devaluation of the wall and the extraordinary spatial unity. There is some truth in all this, but it is necessary to repeat that the main arcade of the Beauvais choir is thicker than that of Reims or Chartres, the most massive cathedrals of High Gothic. It is clear that the designers' approach to mass evolved as the building went up. Whereas the builders of the 1260s used slender supports and thin walls (in the upper choir), the earliest work (east aisle of the transept) embodies massive outer walls close to two meters in thickness.

In disposing the interior spaces enclosed by these masses, the builders have designed a steeply vertical central vessel around a series of squares: squares exist in the central span as defined by the axes of the piers (span equals height of pier to abacus), in the height from the sill of the triforium to the high capital, and in the piling up of three similar squares to give the height of the keystone. Although the first (westernmost) arcade has a span of one-half the central vessel, as though a system of cubes was intended, in the second and third bays of the arcade this regularity is lost, as the bays become broader toward the east end of the building. It is tempting to suggest that the designers had a sytem of perspective-correction in mind—thus, the effect of foreshortening in the eastern bays is reduced on account of their wider spans.

Two spatial realms are created in the body of the choir, and the beholder (or the camera) finds it difficult to comprehend them both at the same time. The central vessel soars to a height of three times its span, the most ex-

[34] The famous description of Hagia Sophia by Procopius may be understood in such dialectical terms; see C. Mango, *Art of the Byzantine Empire, 312–1453,* Englewood Cliffs, 1972, pp. 72–78.

[35] H. Jantzen, *High Gothic,* New York, 1962.
[36] G. Desjardins, *Histoire de la cathédrale de Beauvais,* Beauvais, 1865, pp. 7–8.

treme elongation found in any High Gothic cathedral. The north-south span of the central vessel is also greater than that found at Amiens and Reims cathedrals, placing emphasis upon the central space. The impression of vertiginous height is enhanced by the vertical tracery cage that links the glazed triforium and the clerestory into a single zone.[37] In the original choir this glass box was vaulted in three broad quadripartite bays. The effect of such expansive spatial canopies hovering over this tall tracery box must have been rather startling, and one is tempted to resort to formulas such as those created by Procopius to describe Hagia Sophia in order to convey an impression of these three broad vaults seeming to hover atop a flood of light, rather than resting upon anything resembling solid masonry.[38]

The second spatial realm is in the lower building, where the wide arcade openings allow us to see a series of diaphragms (arcade and chapel openings) that open outward in a descending order of peripheral spaces. This expansive spatial zone is perceived as a contrast to the verticality of the central vessel. The clerestory windows of the inner aisle, wide and stubby, set up a rather slow rhythm around the base of the building. This horizontal accent is emphasized by the band triforium of the inner aisle, also glazed. The combination of widely spaced arcade, narrow inner aisle and ambulatory, together with the very shallow projection of the radiating chapels helps to keep the peripheral spaces well within the optical range of the viewer in the central vessel. At Bourges Cathedral the use of a similar five-aisled pyramidal section leads to an intriguing ambiguity of an intellectual kind—should we read the elevation as composed of three or five stories? At Beauvais this ambiguity does not exist. The great height and width of the central vessel tend to entrap the visitor's attention. If the visitor goes on to consider the peripheral spaces, he will probably

be struck by the contrast between the two spatial realms, and he will find it difficult to consider them as part of the same spatial economy.

There is another dimension to the interior space of Beauvais Cathedral that has failed to receive adquate attention from art historians and visitors: the aisled transept (Figs. 75–77, 120, 121). Cutting across the tiered volumes of the low outer aisle, the steep inner aisle, and the towering central vessel, the transept allows the beholder to gain a direct experience of the different kinds of space. From a position to the west of the crossing the beholder sees four different worlds on each side. First one sees the base of a tower, appropriately massive and crowned with small rose windows. This expresses the cathedral as it presented itself to the exterior. Next, the beholder looks into the lower outer aisle. This view is cut off after only two bays by a blind wall decorated with tracery. The third world of Beauvais Cathedral is the inner aisle, elongated and graceful, turning away into the ambulatory and offering glimpses of the faceted chapels of the hemicycle. Finally, in the central vessel one experiences the same overall proportions as in the inner aisle. The beholder accustomed to the lower spaces of the aisles looks into the towering space of the central vessel with feelings of astonishment. And then, through the broad arcade on the far side, the beholder sees the same elements repeated in descending order. At Bourges Cathedral the absence of a transept causes the beholder to feel somewhat trapped in the aisles (especially the outer aisle), which assume the character of closed corridors.

A truly stunning effect of the edifice, as originally conceived, was the entrance through the transept portal, with the central vessel of the transept opening directly to the front, while to the side the visitor would see the brilliantly lit base of a tower (illuminated on three levels) and the central vessel, perceived diagonally

---

[37] Branner ("Maître de Beauvais") had reconstructed the original clerestory with windows of four lancets: however, the great spans of the openings, the evidence of the reused parts of tracery in the present clerestory, and the compari-

sons with Amiens choir all point to the existence of a six-unit window.

[38] Mango, *Art of the Byzantine Empire*, pp. 72–78.

through the widely spaced piers. The use of a very tall inner aisle is important in this respect, since it allows the gaze of the beholder in this transept arm to ascend to a point toward the top of the clerestory windows.

Art historians, preoccupied with the question as to whether Beauvais belongs to the "family of Chartres" or the "family of Bourges," have neglected this glorious transept. It is possible that the designers of Beauvais have looked beyond the perimeters of High Gothic and have found prototypes in the third abbey church at Cluny and in Notre-Dame of Paris.[39] Both these monuments embody pyramidal space intersected by a transept.

Many of the above observations remain "might-have-beens." Perhaps the very failings of the building have rendered it more approachable. Conceived as a new synthesis, it embodies an attempt to realize a sublime idea. It failed, and it is difficult to escape from the symbolism of this failure. We tend to perceive the faults of the building as somewhat reassuring signs that its builders were human and that the excellence of their techniques and the quality of their materials were limited.

Massing

The colossal yellowish gray silhouette of Beauvais Cathedral (Figs. 31–39) towers up out of the basin in which the city is located. The truncated quality of the building, lacking a nave, only serves to enhance its impressive verticality. A closer inspection reveals a choir in the form of a relatively short vessel crossed by a transept of monumental proportions. On the plan it is evident that the transept projects a full bay beyond the body of the choir—in fact, it seems even larger. This illusion results from the five-aisled arrangement of the choir, with its low outer aisle, taller inner aisle, and very steep central vessel. The massive bulk of the body of the transept thus projects out a

full three bays from the central body of the choir, and given the fact that the site would only allow for a relatively short nave, the building would have had a strongly cruciform quality. The mass of the transept was to have been accented by means of twin towers flanking the façades. The lower parts of two such towers were built to the east of the transept arms. The great height of the central vessel of the transept arms would cause the upper parts of these towers to be incredibly attenuated.

An obvious contrast exists between the expansive quality of the transept and the contraction of the east end of the choir where the radiating chapels are pulled well inside a half-circle whose center is at the middle of the hemicycle and whose diameter equals the width of the choir to the outer walls. This half-circle actually exists in the form of a stone plinth under the chapels, which prevents rainwater from running down the walls and buttresses directly into the foundations.[40] The circular sweep of the plinth establishes a horizontality that is reflected again in the dense arrangement of the shallow radiating chapels of equal projection, which form a crown of many facets, ringed by the emphatic moldings of the windowsills and buttress offsets. The same horizontal sweep is repeated in the smooth curve of the hemicycle wall, capped by a balustrade unbroken by pinnacles.

The tiered effect of the exterior—with the inner aisle and ambulatory appearing almost as a gallery, reminiscent somewhat of Noyon, Mantes, and Notre-Dame of Paris—is denied by the emphatic verticality of the uprights of the flying buttresses. This is surely the most extraordinary feature of the exterior massing of the Beauvais choir! More than ever before, a virtue has been made of the necessity of providing support for the arches and vaults of the central vessel. There is a certain symbolic quality to the fact that we glimpse the tiered body of the choir with its references to venerable prototypes, such as Cluny III or Notre-

---

[39] At Notre-Dame the gallery space behaves in the same way as the inner aisle at Beauvais Cathedral, turning ninety degrees into the eastern aisle of the gallery and forming an

L-shaped corridor; see the suggestive drawing in Bony, *French Gothic Architecture*, Fig. 133.

[40] In its present form this plinth is restored.

Dame of Paris, only through this jungle of towering vertical members, which superimpose an emphatic square over the triangle of the pyramidal elevation.

It has been demonstrated earlier that the great height of the outer uprights of the flying buttresses was the result of three factors: the very tall central vessel, the use of flyers with a relatively shallow pitch, and the use of narrow side aisles. The articulation of the lower parts of the buttresses is achieved by means of a rapid series of offsets whose main function is a visual rather than a structural one—in other words, to establish a series of horizontal references swathing the lower part of the building. The arrangement lends to the buttresses a strong similarity to their counterparts in the Amiens choir (Fig. 147) and in the Sainte-Chapelle, Paris (Fig. 168). Similar horizontal emphasis results from the band of stumpy lancet windows opening into the ambulatory and inner aisle. In the towering upper part of the uprights a different arrangement is adopted, and the sheer flanks of the uprights are articulated by means of delicate shafts and gabled aediculae. These cagelike skins of shafts and arches disguise the bulk of the upper buttresses and echo the openwork tabernacles that existed at the main supports.[41] The mass of the piers has been greatly reduced, and the upper wall has been made incredibly thin. When the reduction of mass in the supports and upper wall of the central vessel is considered in relation to the extreme elongation of the bays of the choir, the audacity of the designers seems quite astonishing. The development of Gothic architecture is sometimes seen as the transferring of the elements of support from the lower parts of the building to the upper parts.[42] At Beauvais the muscles of the support system have also been pushed outward and are disposed around the outer periphery in the form of the massive outer uprights that stand as guardians of the fragile stone-and-glass superstructure of the central vessel.

[41] These main supports have since been rebuilt and are now solid.

[42] Bony, *French Gothic Architecture*, p. 216.

CHAPTER II

Kings and Bishops, Chapter and Commune: The Historical Context

The flowering of Gothic architecture and the construction of the great French Gothic cathedrals is both an artistic and a historical phenomenon. A cathedral is an event as well as a monument, and an understanding of the circumstances of the construction can add an extra dimension to the interpretation of the physical forms of the monument.

The construction of Beauvais Cathedral as a historical process involved the agency of four overlapping institutions: the monarchy, the bishops, the chapter, and the commune. The relative power of each of these four institutions was in the process of change, and these adjustments were liable to produce interludes of violent conflict. The start of work on the Gothic choir in 1225 was made possible through a particular set of circumstances that was transformed within some seven years of the laying of the first stone. A violent urban

uprising in 1232–1233, and the subsequent interdicts and confiscation of episcopal revenues, brought great changes to the political balance of power in Beauvais as well as to the architectural forms of the nascent cathedral. Conversely, the construction of the cathedral involved colossal expenses, and the raising of the necessary cash created new tensions in the relationship between the clergy and the *communiers* of Beauvais, tensions that were expressed in civic uprising and social change. Major building projects and social and economic change are bound together in a dynamic relationship that has long been recognized by the historian, but has been somewhat neglected by the art historian.[1]

The existing secondary sources on Gothic architecture tend to overemphasize the role of the Capetian monarchy and the bourgeois class at the expense of the clergy and the rural population. For Viollet-le-Duc, Gothic archi-

[1] Ada Levett has provided a useful discussion of the impact of the construction of the nave of Winchester Cathedral on the organization of the estates of the see of Winchester in *The Black Death on the Estates of the See of Winchester*, Oxford Studies in Social and Legal History, v, Oxford, 1916. An example of a study of the same problem,

seen through the eyes of the art historian, can be found in R. Branner, "Historical Aspects of the Reconstruction of Reims Cathedral, 1210–1241," *Speculum*, XXXVI, 1961, pp. 23–37. See also M. Warnke, *Bau und Überbau: Soziologie der Mittelalterlichen Architektur nach dem Schriftquellen*, Frankfurt am Main, 1976.

tecture was the expression of the new secular spirit. Arnold Hauser saw something essentially bourgeois in the forms of Gothic, and Henry Kraus has pointed to the connection between the participation of the bourgeois in any given construction project and the successful completion of that project.[2] In the case of Beauvais Cathedral, Lopez has postulated that a dynamic connection existed between the construction of the cathedral and the economic life of the city.[3] He saw the construction of the cathedral as a nonproductive effort (unlike bridge building) that crippled the economic vitality of the city.

In the absence of adequate documentation, it is easy to become too preoccupied with the "forces" that seem to underlie social, economic, and political change and to adopt an essentially deterministic attitude toward historical causation. Similarly, with our twentieth-century interest in trade and technology, it is easy to forget the contribution of the rural population to cathedral construction. A recent study of the country around Chartres has suggested that a major part of the revenue for cathedral construction was derived from the clergy's rural holdings.[4]

A balanced interpretation of the construction of Beauvais Cathedral should avoid any such preoccupation with the forces behind historical developments or with the rise of the middle class. What should be allowed is due recognition to the accidental: the peculiar circumstances of Beauvais in the early thirteenth century, the force of personalities and artistic visions, and the intervention of the unexpected event that can alter what would otherwise have been seen as the "course of history."[5]

Whether a cathedral project thrived or failed depended very much upon the peculiar balance of power in the city where the project was undertaken. Thus, in Troyes, for example, the bishop and chapter were relatively poorly endowed in holdings within the city and did not gain directly from the dramatic expansion of commerce and industry that took place in the twelfth century.[6] It is no surprise to find that the cathedral, although built on a grand scale, shows signs of cost cutting and that it still remained unfinished at the end of the thirteenth century. In Beauvais, however, the bishop was simultaneously a peer of the realm and count, with considerable powers over the developing industrial and commercial *bourg*, and there is every reason to believe that the fabric fund of the cathedral was enriched directly from these sources. The bishop's status is reflected in the protocol of the ceremony marking his entrance into the city. At Troyes he was forced to give up his horse to the abbess and nuns of the powerful house of Notre-Dame-aux-Nonnains. At Beauvais, on the other hand, the ceremony provided symbolic expression of the bishop's status as lord of the entire city. Thus, he received the pledge of unqualified loyalty of the bourgeois of the city, saving only their loyalty to the king.[7]

Kings

The fact that the period of the construction of High Gothic cathedrals coincided with the dramatic augmentation of the territory under the direct control of the Capetian monarchs has led some historians to suppose that a di-

[2] E. Viollet-le-Duc, *Entretiens sur l'architecture*, 2 vols., Paris, 1863–1872, esp. I, pp. 275–277; A. Hauser, *Social History of Art*, New York, 1951, I, pp. 232–265; H. Kraus, *Gold Was the Mortar: The Economics of Cathedral Building*, London, 1979.

[3] R. S. Lopez, "Economie et architecture médiévales: Cela aurait-il tué ceci?" *Annales. Economies-Sociétés-Civilizations*, VIII, 1952, pp. 433–438.

[4] A. Chédeville, *Chartres et ses campagnes (XIe.–XIIe. siècles)*, Paris, 1973.

[5] That the seemingly inevitable course of history can be turned aside by an accident has been recognized by J. Gillingham, "The Unromantic Death of Richard I," *Speculum*,

LIV, 1979, pp. 18–41. The importance of the events of these years in determining the political geography of Europe has been emphasized by Y. Rénouard, "1212–1216, comment les traits durables de l'Europe occidentale moderne se sont définis au début du XIIIe. siècle," *Etudes d'histoire médiévale*, Paris, 1968, pp. 77–91.

[6] M. Bur, *La Formation du comté de Champagne: v.950–v.1150*, Nancy, 1977. For an excellent general study of the different circumstances of cathedral construction, see A. Mussat, "Les Cathédrales dans leurs cités," *Revue de l'art*, LV, 1982, pp. 9–22.

[7] Loisel, *Mémoires des pays*, pp. 127–129.

rect connection might exist between the two phenomena.[8] Kings Louis VI and Louis VII had both enjoyed close relations with Abbot Suger and the monastery of Saint-Denis, the burial place of many of their royal predecessors, and it has been easy to assume that the reconstruction of the monastery church under Abbot Suger was the expression of resurgent royal power.[9] However, in the mid-twelfth century the Capetian kings were still struggling to assert their authority over their own domaine, and the reality of centralized monarchical authority was still more than half a century away. Gothic Saint-Denis was a visionary structure: a jump forward that paradoxically embodied an attempt to revive the glories of the Early Christian and Carolingian past. The abbots and bishops who rebuilt their churches in the second half of the twelfth century in the aftermath of Saint-Denis were not expressing a vision of a lost past, but rather the very real power and wealth that they enjoyed in the form of agrarian and urban rights and possessions. Gothic architecture was not primarily the expression of royal power or the rise of the bourgeois, but was the affair of the higher clergy. Relations between members of the higher clergy and the monarchy were not static. Louis VII, aware of his weakness in the face of Henry II of England, worked carefully to cement his alliance with the higher clergy and generally avoided major confrontations.[10] However, the situation changed radically with the growth of the real power of the monarch in the reigns of Kings Philip Augustus, Louis VIII, and Louis IX.

The events of the years around 1200 brought a series of dramatic changes in the map of northern France.[11] In the twelfth century the ecclesiastical enclave controlled by the bishops of Beauvais constituted a strategically important buffer zone between the royal domain and the potentially hostile county of

Flanders and duchy of Normandy to the north. The river Epte and the *vidame* of Gerberoy provided the bastion against incursions from the Anglo-Normans. French kings were accustomed to rely upon the bishop-counts of Beauvais for support. Bishop Henry of France (1148/49–1162) was the son of Louis VI and brother of Louis VII, and Bishop Philip of Dreux, the cousin of King Philip Augustus, was the very epitome of the loyal bishop-warrior.[12]

There is every reason to believe that King Philip Augustus was acutely aware of the strategic and economic importance of the lands immediately to the north of the royal domain. The marriage of the young king to Isabella, daughter of Baldwin V, count of Hainault, and niece of Philip of Alsace, count of Flanders, announces the importance of the lands to the northeast of the royal domain. Through this marriage, Philip Augustus was able to gain control of considerable lands immediately adjacent to the Beauvaisis.[13]

The conquest of Normandy after 1204 and the defeat of the Flemish-imperial alliance at the Battle of Bouvines in 1214 transformed the Beauvaisis from a key buffer zone to a peaceful enclave. This state of peaceful prosperity, which remained basically undisturbed until the onset of the Hundred Years' War more than a century later, provided the vital prerequisite for the enormous effort involved in the construction of the cathedral. Whereas Bishop Philip of Dreux (1175–1217) had been forced to spend a considerable part of his episcopal revenues in the military service of his monarch, Bishop Miles of Nanteuil (1217–1234) spent his surplus income (and, indeed, more than the surplus) in the construction of the Gothic cathedral. In this sense, the construction project can be linked with the creation of a unified territorial block under the Capetian monarchs.

[8] G. Duby, *Le Temps des cathédrales*, Geneva, 1976.

[9] For Saint-Denis, see E. Panofsky, *Abbot Suger on the Abbey Church of Saint-Denis and Its Art Treasures*, Princeton, 1979.

[10] M. Pacaut, *Louis VII et les élections épiscopales dans le royaume de France*, Paris, 1957; idem, *Louis VII et son royaume*, Paris, 1964.

[11] Most recently, see E. Hallam, *Capetian France, 987–*

1328, London, 1980. See also R. Fawtier, *The Capetian Kings of France*, London, 1960; and M. Bloch, *La France sous les derniers Capétiens, 1223–1328*, Paris, 1958.

[12] H. Géraud, "Le Comte-évêque," *Bibl. Ecole Chartes*, 1st ser., v, 1843–1844, pp. 8–36.

[13] Hallam, *Capetian France*, pp. 127–128. Philip gained Artois, his wife's dowry, and also parts of the Vermandois, the city and county of Amiens, and sixty-five castles.

In another sense, however, the expansion of the monarchy imposed new limits upon the power and wealth of the clergy. Already during the episcopate of Philip of Dreux, considerable inroads had been made by King Philip Augustus, and under Bishop Miles of Nanteuil, King Louis IX was able to intervene in a matter that involved the bishop-count's powers of jurisdiction over his own city.

The independence of the Beauvaisis from the Ile-de-France was expressed in a variety of ways, including the use of a system of weights and measures and monetary units that differed from the equivalent units in the Ile-de-France. The expansion of royal power under Philip Augustus, however, led to the imposition of the royal monetary system in Beauvais. Until the early decades of the thirteenth century the bishop-counts of Beauvais had minted their own coins, and the episcopal sou was worth somewhat more than the royal sou. In 1214, however, King Philip Augustus demanded that the bishop and chapter should accept the use of the royal coins at the same value as the episcopal coinage, thus forcing the devaluation of the local currency.[14] The chapter resisted this order, but Bishop Philip of Dreux acquiesced and even assisted the king with the confiscation of property belonging to the recalcitrant chapter. He changed his mind later and attempted to reverse the decision, but Philip Augustus succeeded in his attempts to secure the validity of the royal coinage and to put an end to the power of the bishop-counts to mint their own coins. Local units of measurement were still in use in Beauvais in the late Middle Ages, although it is significant to note that the cathedral seems to have been laid out by master masons who used the royal foot.[15]

In other respects the king and bishop generally moved in harmony in the period immediately preceding the construction of the Gothic cathedral. However, the death of King Philip Augustus in 1223 and his cousin, Bishop Philip of Dreux, in 1217 marked the end of a period of peaceful relations between king and bishop. Bishop Miles of Nanteuil was absent on crusade between 1217 and 1220. He seems to have enjoyed good relations with King Louis VIII (1223–1226), with whom he campaigned in the Albigensian crusade of 1226. Bishop Miles was present at the premature death of the monarch at Montpensier on November 8, 1226. Together with the archbishop of Sens and the bishop of Chartres, Miles promised obedience and loyalty to Louis VIII's young son (then only twelve years old) and support for the regency of Blanche of Castile, the dying king's Spanish wife.[16]

Several of the chroniclers of the reign of Louis IX describe the acute difficulties caused by the opposition of certain powerful barons to the regency of Blanche of Castile.[17] An important group of opponents was based in the north, with strong connections with the area around Beauvais. The count of Boulogne, Philip Hurepel, son of Philip Augustus, maintained an independently ambiguous position of hostility alternating with support. The powerful house of Dreux, which had supplied two bishops to the seat of Beauvais (Henry of France and Philip of Dreux), was represented by count Robert Gateblé of Dreux and his three brothers, John of Braine, count of Mâcon; Henry of Braine, treasurer of the Beauvais chapter and later archbishop of Reims; and Peter "Mauclerk," count of Brittany. The house of Dreux, descended from Louis VI, nursed certain pretensions to the French throne. Whereas Robert was ambivalent in his attitudes (he supported Blanche for a while), Peter Mauclerk constituted a real threat. In

---

[14] Labande, *Histoire de Beauvais*, p. 277.

[15] The compound piers in the transept have a core made up of a series of steps, each measuring one royal foot.

[16] Delettre, *Histoire du diocèse*, II, p. 249.

[17] William of Nangis, *Gesta Sanctae Memoriae Ludovici, Recueil des historiens*, XX, Paris, 1840, pp. 309–465; John of Joinville, *Histoire de Saint Louis, Recueil des his-*

toriens, XX, Paris, 1840, pp. 190–304; Matthew Paris, *Chronica Majora, Rolls Series (Rerum Britannicarum Medii Aevi Scriptures)*, LVII, III, ed. H. R. Luard, London, 1876, p. 118; M. W. Labarge, *Saint Louis: The Life of Louis IX of France*, London, 1968, p. 34; Le Nain de Tillemont, *Vie de Saint Louis, roi de France*, ed. J. de Gaulle, 6 vols., Paris, 1847–1851, esp. II, pp. 31–49.

the south the main danger came from the duke of Guienne, Henry III, king of England, and his allies such as Hugh of Lusignan, count of La Marche. Moreover, in the earliest years of Louis's reign, the count of Champagne, Theobald, joined Peter Mauclerk and Hugh of Lusignan in opposition to Blanche of Castile.

Helped by Robert, count of Dreux, and Cardinal Romanus of Saint Angelo, the papal legate, Blanche was able to raise an armed force and march on Tours and Chinon (1226–1227). The count of Champagne quickly withdrew his support from the rebels, and in 1227 Hugh of Lusignan and Peter Mauclerk made their submission.

The barons' movement in France, like its subsequent counterpart in England, was characterized by a considerable degree of political unity among the barons (a "parlement" was held at Corbeil, and joint military action was taken against the count of Champagne), and also by an intense jealousy of any "outsider" who might attempt to control the monarch. Blanche of Castile, a Spaniard and a woman, was clearly considered as such, and an attempt was made by the barons to gain possession of the person of the king.[18] When this failed, certain magnates resorted to efforts to undermine the reputation of the regent; she was accused of having sexual relations both with Theobald of Champagne and with the papal legate.[19]

Interestingly, while no source gives the name of Miles, bishop of Beauvais, either in connection with those who lent their military support to Blanche of Castile, or with those who opposed her, his name is mentioned as one of those who attempted to challenge the sovereignty of the king over the ecclesiastical magnates (Miles claimed to owe allegiance only to the patron of his diocese, Saint Peter) and as one of those propagating the rumor that Blanche was with child by the papal legate.[20] According to the anonymous Chronicle of Reims, Blanche went to considerable lengths to disprove this allegation, appearing one day in her council in a robe that she cast off to show her flat silhouette as proof that she was not pregnant. The chronicler suggested that the regent formed a strong dislike for the proud bishop, and, as will be seen later, the moment soon arrived when she was able to take her revenge.

Thus, hatred seems to have developed between the powerful regent and the bishop of Beauvais on a personal level. A broader issue also troubled relations between the monarchy and certain ecclesiastics in the opening years of the reign of Louis IX: the redefinition of the relationship between *sacerdotium* and *regnum* implicit in the policies and writings of Pope Innocent III and in the fourth Lateran Council.[21] Ecclesiastics were led to the use of powerful spiritual weapons (excommunica-

[18] William of Nagis, *Gesta*, p. 315. The barons attempted to seize the young Louis at Montlhéry, near Paris. The king was rescued by an apparently spontaneous countermove by the population of the capital city.

[19] Matthew Paris, *Chronica Majora*, p. 119. Paris refers to a "*rumor irrecitabilis ac sinister: scilicet, quod dominus legatus secus quam deceret se habebat adversus dominam Blancam.*" Ibid., p. 196: "*Indignabantur enim talem habere dominam, quae, ut dicebatur, tam dicti comitis quam legati Romani semine polluta, metas transgressa fuerat pudicitiae vidualis.*"

[20] *Fragment d'une chronique anonyme dite Chronique de Reims, Recueil des historiens*, XXII, Paris, 1865, p. 304: "*Or vous redirons de l'esleut de Biauvais, auquel li apostoles avoit bailliet à tenir les vaux d'Alisse* [this refers to the tenure of the duchy of Spoleto and the March of Ancona] *qui s'en revint en France par Canteleu. Et i estoit adont li cadonnaus, et preéchoit des crois. Et li évesques preéchoit d'autre cose; quar il preéchoit et pourcachoit que nus des archevesques ne des évesques dou roiaume ne respondist*

par devant le roy. Et en tenoient souvent lor parlement à Saint Quentin en Vermandois; et fu au tans l'archevesque Henri de Braine, qui bien s'i acordoit, et moult des autres évesques aveuc lui. Et avint que la roine le sot par aucun des évesques qui ne se voloient mie accorder. Et enquore fist li esleus de Biauvais pis assés; quar il mist sus la roine que elle estoit toute grosse du cardonnal Roumain: dont il se mentoit. Mais la roine n'en faisoit nulle semblance, anchois le couvroit en son cuer, et pensoit que elle li mèteroit bien en lieu et en tans."

[21] B. Tierney, *The Crisis of Church and State, 1050–1300*, Englewood Cliffs, 1964; Labarge, *Saint Louis*, p. 27; G. J. Campbell, "The Attitude of the Monarchy Towards the Use of Ecclesiastical Censures in the Reign of Saint Louis," *Speculum*, XXXV, 1960, pp. 535–555; O. Pontal, "Le Différend entre Louis IX et les évêques de Beauvais," *Bibl. Ecole Chartes*, CXXIII, 1965, pp. 5–34; Chanoine Rome, "Henri II de Braisne, archévêque de Reims (1227–40), Blanche de Castille et Saint Louis," *Trav. Acad. nat. Reims*, CLIV, 1941–1946, pp. 71–92.

tion and interdict) as retaliation against injuries inflicted by the secular arm. Both sides accused the other of attempting to expand its judicial rights. Two important cases of the use of interdicts involved the archbishop of Rouen and Bishop Miles of Beauvais. In the former case, excommunication was met by the seizure of temporalities and a deadlock that lasted seven years. A consideration of the latter case necessitates a review of the special status of the bishop-counts of Beauvais.

Robert Fawtier has written: "The hour that struck the death of Louis VIII [in 1226] was arguably the most critical in the history of the Capetian family. . . . For in 1226 there arose the most redoutable coalition of great barons which the House of Capet had ever had to face."[22] Even more dangerous than the ill-coordinated efforts of vacillating barons were the implications of the new definition of the superiority of the spiritual power over the temporal, as propagated by Pope Innocent III. The Gothic choir of Beauvais Cathedral was begun in 1225 at the initiative of a bishop considered by Blanche of Castile to be among the disaffected magnates—one who claimed independence from the monarch as far as his temporal domain was concerned. The cathedral expresses the economic surplus possible in the rich lands to the north of Paris, now securely surrounded by Capetian-controlled territories. It also expresses the triumph of the church (this is the church of Saint Peter) and the proud independence of a rebel peer of the realm. Whereas it had suited Philip Augustus to maintain the bishop-count of Beauvais in a state of powerful independence, Louis IX and Blanche of Castile, for personal as well as political reasons, showed themselves much less ready to tolerate such independence.

Bishops and Diocese

The territorial definition of the diocese of Beauvais owes its origin to the divisions of Gaul under the Roman Republic and Empire into *cités, pagi,* and *vici.*[23] It has been suggested that Beauvais developed from two distinct centers, Bratuspantium, the regional center of the Bellovaqui, situated in the marshy area at the confluence of the rivers Thérain and Avelon, and Caesaromagus, the Roman settlement on the higher ground forming the slopes of Mont Capron.[24] The Germanic invasions of the third century imposed the necessity of a reliable system of defense, which was afforded by the canalization of the waters of the Thérain to provide ditches or moats for a new city wall, probably constructed in the course of the third century. This *castrum,* subsequently dominated by the bishops of Beauvais, was to form the medieval *cité* (Fig. 2).

The diocese under the control of this center formed a roughly triangular shape, whose northern boundary ran between the sources of the Matz, the Aronde and the Bréche, and adjoined with the diocese of Amiens. The southeast side corresponds roughly with the line of the river Oise, but it crossed the river near Pont-Sainte-Maxence to englobe numerous parishes on the far side of the river, including that of Royaumont. At its southern point (the apex of the triangle) the diocese included Isle-Adam, adjoining the diocese of Paris. The boundary then ran along a line corresponding roughly to the escarpment that divides the Beauvaisis from the Vexin. Finally, in the upper part of the western side of the diocese, the boundary runs along the river Epte. The diocese of Beauvais adjoins the diocese of Rouen along this western side. It forms a geographical unity based on the middle waters of the river Oise and six of its tributaries, of which the river Thérain was the most important. This is chalk country. The northern part borders on the plateau known as the plain of Picardy, while the southern part is deeply grooved with valleys cut out by the tributaries of the Oise. The underlying chalk is covered to a greater or lesser extent by alluvial deposits of some fertility, and the proportion of the

---

[22] Fawtier, *The Capetian Kings,* pp. 27–28.
[23] Launay, Fauqueux, and Launay, *Essai d'histoire régionale,* pp. 19–44; Loisel, *Mémoires des pays,* pp. 14–20; Louvet, *Histoire et antiquitez,* I, pp. 31–35; Delettre, *His-toire du diocèse,* I, pp. 9–15; *Dictionnaire d'histoire et de géographie ecclésiastique,* VII, Paris, 1934, pp. 255–302.
[24] Lemaire, *Une Construction urbaine,* p. 2.

land constituting rich farmland is considerable. Anthoine Loisel, writing in the seventeenth century, described the land in glowing colors, as being very rich, and most productive in wheat, fruit, forests, and meadows with excellent flocks of sheep, "and generally all kinds of wealth that could be desired to support human life."[25] In the Middle Ages the hills immediately around Beauvais were covered by rich vineyards. The productive nature of the soil encouraged fairly dense settlement, which was increased by the development of Beauvais as a commercial and industrial center.

The arrival of Christianity in the Beauvaisis is shrouded with legend. It is said that the evangelist Lucien, a simple priest, in the third century came directly from Rome and became the first bishop of Beauvais.[26] He and his companions Maxien and Julien fell victim to the persecution of the prefect Rictius Varus. They were said to have been decapitated on the right bank of the river Thérain above Beauvais. The body of Lucien was then translated to the site to the northwest of the city where the great Benedictine abbey of Saint-Lucien was later constructed in his honor.

The county of Beauvais was first designated as such in the early ninth century.[27] Very little information survives concerning the early counts. In the mid-ninth century the city was devastated by the Normans. As a result of this attack the old walls were rebuilt, and the city was spared further destruction in the Norman incursions of the late ninth and early tenth centuries.

Nothing is known of the cathedral church during the first centuries of Christianity in the Beauvaisis, and very little is known about the bishops. Even the various lists of bishops' names differ considerably one from another.[28] The first documentary sources relating to a building that was presumably the cathedral of Beauvais are connected with the name of Bishop Hervé, or Herveus.[29] This bishop (died 998) was said to have given two mills and twelve houses so that the revenues that accrued might be applied toward the construction of a new church of Saint-Peter.

At the beginning of the eleventh century Eudes II, count of Champagne, was also count of Beauvais.[30] However, the power of the counts in the city of Beauvais had been steadily undermined by the growing domination of the bishops. Already, before 1015, Eudes had given over to the bishop a part of his domains and his revenues in the suburb and in the surrounding area. Then in 1015 Eudes ceded to Bishop Roger most of the possessions, rights, and revenues that he still held in the county of Beauvais. Thus, the bishops became direct vassals of the kings of France and in the course of the eleventh and twelfth centuries peers of the realm. Roger made over his lands at Ailly (in Normandy) and Monchi-la-Gache (Vermandois) to the chapter. Loisel, writing in the early seventeenth century, remarked that the chapter continued to enjoy these lands, just as the bishops of Beauvais continued to enjoy the county.[31]

Roger was also responsible for the installation of Francon as *vidame* and commander of

---

[25] Loisel, *Mémoires des pays*, p. 21; for the geography of the diocese, see pp. 15–20.

[26] Delettre, *Histoire du diocèse*, I, pp. 29–40, 111–123; Loisel, *Mémoires des pays*, pp. 70–79; Louvet, *Histoire et antiquitez*, II, pp. 130–131.

[27] Vercauteren, *Etude sur les civitates*, pp. 264–287, esp. p. 270.

[28] Delettre, *Histoire du diocèse*, passim; Loisel, *Mémoires des pays*, pp. 64–129; Louvet, *Histoire et antiquitez*, II, pp. 128–130; idem, *L'Histoire de la ville*, pp. 153–157.

[29] See the above mentioned sources, and also V. Leblond, "L'Eglise de la Basse-Œuvre et la cathédrale Saint-Pierre de Beauvais, leur date de construction," *Mém. Soc. acad. Oise*, XXV, 1925, pp. 139–143. Two texts are cited to demonstrate that Bishop Herveus initiated campaigns of construction. A charter of Bishop Drogo (ca. 1040) refers to "*Decessor noster bone memoria Herveus episcopus hec molendina*

construxit sua tali intentione devulgata ut in edificatione templi novi, quod tum edificabat, ea sancto Petro offerret atque donaret," and the necrology of the cathedral recorded: "*VI idus aprilis, obiit Herveus episcopus, qui dedit Sancto Petro mansos duodecim in suburbio et duo molendina ad constructionem novi operis*" (Louvet, *Histoire et antiquitez*, II, p. 175). Leblond favored a mid-tenth-century date for the start of construction on the *Basse-Œuvre*, arguing that Bishop Herveus merely continued a construction project that had already been begun. On the basis of certain eighteenth-century sources (now lost) he attributed the start of work to Bishop Hugh (in 949). See also V. Leblond, *La Cathédrale de Beauvais*, Paris, 1956, p. 9.

[30] Vercauteren, *Etude sur les civitates*, p. 277; Labande, *Histoire de Beauvais*, pp. 25–33.

[31] Loisel, *Mémoires des pays*, pp. 89–90.

the château of Gerberoy, the front line of defense of the Beauvaisis against Norman attack. He is said to have continued the work of construction on the new cathedral. On his death in 1022 or 1024, he was buried in the choir of this new cathedral. He left his missals, pontificals, and certain items of his treasure to the church.[32]

Roger's successor, Guerin (1022–1033) donated the altar of Saint Stephen to the cathedral. The construction work, according to the antiquarians of Beauvais, was substantially complete by the episcopate of Drogon (1033–1058).[33]

The twelfth century saw a spate of religious foundations: both the reestablishment of old communities and new foundations. Bishop Drogon (1033–1058) founded the abbeys of Saint-Paul and Saint-Symphorien (immediately to the south of Beauvais), reestablished Breteuil and Saint-Germer-de-Fly, and endowed the collegiate churches of Saint-Barthélemy and Saint-Laurent. His successor, Guilbert (1059–1063), was also generous in his foundations, and the movement continued into the episcopate of Guy (1063–1084), who founded the abbey of Saint-Quentin (close to Saint-Lucien to the northwest of the city) and endowed it with many of his churches, including the church of the episcopal town Bresles. Guy was also instrumental in the creation in 1072 of the chapter of Saint-Vast, which was given the church of Saint-Etienne in the city of Beauvais. Partly as a result of these alienations of episcopal lands and jurisdictions, Guy incurred hostility mainly from his chapter. In particular, the bishop was accused of dissipating the revenues and possessions of the diocese. This accusation reflected, in part, jealousy caused by the generosity that the bishop had shown to the abbey Saint-Quentin.

A full account of the bishops of the eleventh and twelfth centuries lies beyond the scope of this study. With the period of Bishops Henry of France, Bartholomew of Montcornet, and Philip of Dreux we reach the time immediately preceding the construction of the Gothic choir. Henry of France (1148/49–1162) personified both the chapter's desire to advance its interests through the appointment to the episcopate of well-connected candidates, and the influence of the reformed monastic orders. Bishop Henry, the son of King Louis VI and Adélaïde of Savoy, had held numerous ecclesiastic benefices, including prebends at Orléans and Tours and the office of treasurer at Beauvais. In 1146, however, he fell under the influence of Saint Bernard of Clairvaux. Henry gave up all of his benefices and remained with Saint Bernard for three years. When elected bishop of Beauvais, Henry at first refused to accept the office, but he was persuaded to change his mind, so we are told, through the insistence of Saint Bernard himself.

Soon after his appointment, the bishop quarreled with his brother, the king of France (Louis VII). The dispute ended only after Saint Bernard interceded for the bishop and after a visit to Rome. The quarrel did not, however, seem to have inflicted permanent damage upon relations between bishop and king. Soon afterward, Louis VII maintained the right of the bishop in a confrontation with the commune of Beauvais over jurisdictions in the city. In 1160 the bishop of Beauvais and his brother, Robert, count of Dreux, were involved with military operations against Henry II of England in Normandy. In 1162 Henry of France replaced Samson as archbishop of Reims.

Henry's successor at Beauvais, Bartholomew of Montcornet (1160/62–1174/75), also was of noble birth, and he had been treasurer of the chapter of Laon cathedral and archdeacon at Reims.[34] His name is associated with the foundation of new prebends for the collegiate church of Notre-Dame-du-Châtel, situated to the northwest of the cathedral. The choir of this church is said to have been completed in the time of this bishop.

Much of the career of Bishop Philip of

[32] Delettre, *Histoire du diocèse*, I, pp. 438–439.
[33] Ibid., pp. 453–471.
[34] Ibid., pp. 143–161. See also Louvet, *Histoire et anti-*

quitez, II, pp. 306–307; and *Gallia Christiana*, IX, Paris, 1751, col. 731.

Dreux (1175–1217) was inextricably connected with the activities of his cousin, King Philip Augustus.[35] The bishop-count of Beauvais was the nephew of Henry of France and son of Robert of France, count of Dreux, and Agnes, countess of Braine and Bar-sur-Seine. He was elected at the instigation of his uncle, Henry of France, former bishop of Beauvais. The bishop was able to use his family connections to some advantage—his cousin, the king, agreed to cede his *droit de gîte* in Beauvais in return for a fixed payment of one hundred pounds.

Fires are recorded in Beauvais in 1180 and 1188.[36] It is impossible to determine whether there were indeed two fires, or if a single incident changed into two as a result of a mistranscribed date. Serious fires also took place in 1188 in Amiens, Auxerre, Chartres, Provins, Tours, and Troyes, and there is some suspicion that these fires may have been caused not only by the drought but also by arson. Beauvais Cathedral was said to have been burned, together with several other churches in the city.

In the following year (1189) the bishop set out on crusade. A number of unflattering anecdotes have grouped themselves around the person of this bishop of Beauvais, as indeed was also the case with his successor, Miles of Nanteuil. Bishop Philip of Dreux was said to have accepted bribes from Saladin in order to delay the Christian attack on the city of Ptolemy, so that the siege machines might be burned.[37] After the departure of King Philip Augustus and the death of the Duke of Burgundy, the bishop-count of Beauvais assumed a position of preeminence among the crusaders. King Richard of England remained a little longer, but he later fell into captivity at the hands of the emperor, Henry VI. The bishop-count of Beauvais worked for the interests of his king in attempting to prolong the captivity of King Richard. Quite understandably, the English king developed a cordial hatred of the bishop-count. On Richard's release, the English resumed their offensive, Richard's brother John marching on Gerberoy, to the west of Beauvais, while his captains attacked Milly. An attempt on the part of the bishop-count to relieve the city was unsuccessful, and Philip of Dreux was captured and imprisoned, first at Rouen and then at Chinon. Historians record several versions of the story, recounting that the pope, when requested by the chapter of Beauvais Cathedral to intercede for the release of their bishop, responded to the message (which was accompanied with the blood-stained tunic of the bishop) with the retort that this could not be the tunic of his son and that the king (Richard) should follow his own wishes, since Philip of Dreux preferred the service of Mars to that of Jesus Christ.[38] The bishop-count remained *hors de combat* until 1200, when he was released on the payment of a considerable ransom, said to have been as much as ten thousand silver marks.

The capture of the bishop of Beauvais inaugurated an unfortunate period for the French, during which they suffered the humiliating defeat in 1194 at Fréteval in which the royal archives were lost. The construction of the seemingly impregnable Château Gaillard guarding the lower Seine and a new Anglo-Flemish alliance placed Philip Augustus in a critical situation, but the accidental death of King Richard during the siege of a château in the Limousin reversed what had seemed the inevitable tide of war, culminating in the English loss of Normandy.[39]

After the death of Archbishop William of Champagne in 1202, Philip of Dreux had been elected archbishop of Reims, but his election was annulled because of the objections made concerning his character by the archdeacon of Reims, Thibaud of Perche.

In 1210 Philip of Dreux campaigned in the Albigensian crusade led by Simon of Montfort. The bishop of Beauvais was accompanied by his brother and the bishop of

---

[35] Delettre, *Histoire du diocèse*, II, pp. 162–233; Louvet, *Histoire et antiquitez*, II, pp. 307–361; *Gallia Christiana*, IX, cols. 732–740.

[36] See Appendix A, item 1.

[37] Géraud, "Le Comte-évêque," p. 12.

[38] Louvet, *Histoire et antiquitez*, II, p. 316.

[39] Gillingham, "The Unromantic Death."

Chartres. We are told that the two bishops quit the crusade before their statutory forty days of service were up, "leaving the work of Christ prey to the greatest difficulties and perils."[40]

Philip of Dreux seems to have been somewhat preoccupied with warlike activities at the expense of his duties in upholding the power and prerogatives of his office. He made several concessions to the commune and to the king that were damaging to the interests of the clergy. In his early years as bishop, he had conceded to the elected council of the commune known as the *pairs* the right to elect one or two mayors from their own body.[41] This provided the commune with potential leadership and certainly enhanced its political power.

It has already been seen that Philip of Dreux failed to uphold the episcopal monopoly on the minting of coins—indeed, the use of episcopal coins diappeared after this period. Frustrated by their bishop's capitulation to the king, the chapter complained in the following terms:

> My Lord, you know perfectly well that a certain count freely gave the county of Beauvais to the church of Saint Peter. You and your predecessors have held it until now with such a franchise that the king of France did not have the right to publish his orders or prohibitions in Beauvais, and could neither seize nor arrest. However, you have encouraged the king, our seigneur, to seize and hold our rents, our houses, and other things, and you have allowed him to usurp episcopal rights, as a result of which your church is clearly disfranchised in several ways. We require you, then, to stave off, as is your duty, the secular arm and the royal power. We also require you, in the name of the cathedral, of the church of Saint-Lucien, of Saint-Quentin and the monastery of Beaupré, and of Froidmont, to restore the rents and houses that you have seized, both

on the part of the king and on your own part [and] to make full amends for the damages you have caused to churches, both by your deeds and by your defaults.[42]

It is the thesis of this chapter that the Gothic choir of Beauvais Cathedral should be seen as the swan song of the ecclesiatical aristocracy, enriched by increased revenues from their estates and urban holdings, but already undermined by the growing power of the monarch. The impassioned words of the chapter to the bishop who preceded the founder of the Gothic cathedral provide the most powerful evidence for this thesis.

In his last years the warrior bishop was involved in violent château warfare with his powerful neighbour, the countess of Clermont and her cousin, the count of Boulogne, Renaud of Dammartin. This hostility led the bishop-count of Beauvais to play a key role in the battle of Bouvines in 1214, in which Renaud fought for the enemies of the French king.[43] On the left flank of the French army at Bouvines, Philip of Dreux found himself matched with the count of Salisbury. The impetuous attack of the bishop-count unhorsed Salisbury and turned the battle in favor of the French. The *communiers* of Beauvais also played an important role in the victory. The bishop-count died three years after the battle of Bouvines.

The new bishop was Miles (Milo, or Milon) of Nanteuil, third son of Gaucher I of Châtillon, seigneur of Nanteuil, and Helvide, dame of Nanteuil.[44] On the death of Gaucher I of Châtillon (in 1188 or 1190), the eldest son, Gaucher II, became seigneur of Nanteuil. The second son, William, was seigneur of Autrèches, while the third son, Miles, was destined for the church, becoming a canon of the chapter of Reims Cathedral and after 1202 its provost. He tried, unsuccessfully, to purchase

---

[40] For the Crusade, see P. Belperron, *La Croisade contre les Albigeois et l'union du Languedoc à la France (1209–1249)*, Paris, 1945; J. Madaule, *The Albigensian Crusade*, London, 1967. For the role of Bishop Philip of Dreux, see E. Griffe, *Le Languedoc cathare au temps de la croisade (1209–1229)*, Paris, 1973, esp. p. 38.

[41] Delettre, *Histoire du diocese*, II, p. 166; Labande, *Histoire de Beauvais*, p. 64.

[42] Ibid., pp. 277–279.

[43] G. Duby, *Le Dimanche de Bouvines, 27 juillet, 1214*, Paris, 1973.

[44] For the genealogy of this family, see W. M. Newman, *Les Seigneurs de Nesle en Picardie (XIIe.–XIIIe. siècle). Leurs chartes et leur histoire: Etude sur la noblesse régionale ecclésiastique et laïque*, 2 vols., Philadelphia, 1971, esp. I, pp. 227–228, 247.

the office of archbishop for three thousand pounds.[45] Miles had two younger brothers (Guy and Andrew) and two sisters, of whom the elder (Agnes) married Nicholas II, seigneur of Bazoches. The brother of Nicholas II of Bazoches (Jacques, the fourth son) was treasurer of the chapter of Soissons Cathedral and in 1220 became the bishop of Soissons. Jacques of Bazoches was to be a close associate of Miles, bishop of Beauvais. A last aspect of the family worthy of mention is the background of Miles's aunt, Adele or Dreux, wife of Guy II, seigneur of Châtillon, for Adele was half-sister of the former bishop of Beauvais, Philip of Dreux. In dealing with the genealogy of bishops and chapters, we face an immensely complex, interrelated seigneurial mafia.

Some sources give the date 1217 for the election of Miles as bishop of Beauvais, and some give 1218.[46] Delettre records the form of the oath taken by Miles, "I promise to conserve in good faith the rights, privileges, and liberties together with the praiseworthy and established customs of the church of Beauvais, may God and the Holy Scriptures be my help."[47] He confirmed the privileges of the chapter, its rights of excommunication and the right to publish and execute its sentence on all canonical lands. In 1218 Miles founded the abbey of Penthemont to the southwest of Beauvais, a house of Cistercian nuns.[48] Accompanied by his brother, he then departed to participate in the fifth Crusade. Jacques of Bazoches, bishop of Soissons, administered the diocese during his absence.

The accounts of Miles's participation in the siege of Damietta are not particularly flattering to the bishop-elect. One source associates the failure of the crusaders to take the city with the name of Miles, who was said to have been as proud as Nebuchadnezzar.[49] He was captured soon afterward, to be released, for a considerable ransom, only in 1222. On his return from Egypt to France, he was consecrated, at his own request, as bishop of Beauvais by Pope Honorius III.

Miles was at the funeral at Saint-Denis of Philip Augustus (died July 14, 1223) and at the consecration of Louis VIII (August 6 or 8, 1223).[50] The bishop seems to have enjoyed good relations with King Louis VIII.

In 1225 the cathedral of Beauvais was badly damaged by fire. The bishop summoned a meeting of the chapter, promising to his canons to allocate one-tenth of his revenues to the purpose of reconstructing the cathedral over a ten-year period. A similar contribution of a tithe was promised by the chapter.[51]

We have no further information concerning the involvement of Miles with the construction of the Gothic choir of Beauvais Cathedral. In the following year, 1226, his name is associated with the introduction of Franciscans to Beauvais. Tensions quickly developed between members of the new orders and the established clergy, especially over the methods used by the mendicants to raise money for new buildings. They were accused of accepting money from usurers and of undermining the authority of the established clergy.[52]

In 1226 Miles left Beauvais to participate in the Albigensian crusade. King Louis VIII fell sick at Montpensier on his return from the seige of Avignon and called to him the archbishop of Sens and the bishops of Beauvais

[45] Ibid., p. 227.
[46] Pontal, "Le Différend," p. 7; Gallia Christiana, IX, col. 740; and Louvet, Histoire et antiquitez, II, p. 361, give the year 1217. Labande, Histoire de Beauvais, p. 69, specifies December 19 of that year. Newman, Les Seigneurs, I, p. 227, gives 1218.
[47] Delettre, Histoire du diocèse, II, p. 235. The author affirmed that while this was certainly not the first time the oath had been used, this occasion provides us with the first written formula.
[48] Ibid., p. 237.
[49] La Chronique de Rains, publiée sur le manuscript unique de la Bibliothèque du Roi par Louis Paris, Paris, 1851, pp. 92–98: "Comment les Sarrasins orent victoire par

le vesque de Biauvais. . . . ils avoient illuec demouret plus de 2 ans et i avoient soufiert caut et froit et grandes mesaises eut. Et i avoient despendu de leur: et estoient sur le point de prendre la cité: ne ja ne s'i accorderoient. Et à la vérité dire, cil estoient pris par lor orguel et par l'esliut de Biauvais qui plus avoit d'orguel en lui que n'ot Nabugodonosor qui par son orguel fu mues 7 ans en bieste."
[50] Delettre, Histoire du diocèse, II, pp. 241–242.
[51] Louvet, Histoire et antiquitez, II, pp. 363–365. See also Appendix A, item 4.
[52] Delettre, Histoire du diocèse, II, p. 248; G. Hermant, Histoire ecclésiastique et civile de Beauvais et du Beauvaisis, 5 vols., Bibl. Nat. MS fr. 8579–8583, esp. II, pp. 710–717.

and Chartres, asking them to promise obedience to his son Louis, then twelve years old, who was to be placed under the tutelage of his mother, Blanche of Castile, as regent.[53] Louis VIII died on November 8, 1226, and Louis IX was crowned by the bishop of Soissons, Jacques of Bazoches, since the metropolitan seat at Reims was vacant. Soon after, Henry of Braine, another member of the powerful house of Dreux, was elected archbishop of Reims.[54]

In addition to founding the abbey of Penthemont for Cistercian nuns, Bishop Miles of Nanteuil was involved with two other Cistercian houses of much greater importance. In October 1227 he was present (together with the bishop of Chartres, King Louis IX, and Blanche of Castile) at the consecration of the great Cistercian church of Longpont, near Soissons.[55] Jacques of Bazoches, bishop of Soissons, who had been an important patron of this church, carried out the consecration ceremony. In the Cistercian order the use of an ambulatory and continuous crown of radiating chapels had become acceptable by the last decade of the twelfth century. Longpont was the first Cistercian church to embody a plan that closely resembled the type used in secular cathedrals, with seven salient radiating chapels arranged around an ambulatory.[56]

In the following year Louis IX (perhaps at the instigation of Blanche of Castile) decided to found a new Cistercian house rather than the Victorine house stipulated in the testament of his father, Louis VIII. A site in the diocese of Beauvais (Cuimont, later known as Royaumont, near Beaumont) was chosen for the new foundation.[57] Miles of Nanteuil is said to have welcomed the decision and to have ceded

a piece of land that had belonged to the priory of Boran. Monks were installed at Royaumont in 1228, and the dedication of the church took place in 1236. There is no indication as to whether the church had already been begun in 1228, or what stage of completion had been reached by the consecration date. Architecturally, the Royaumont plan was a copy, with some adaptations, of the choir of Longpont.

Thus, Miles of Nanteuil seems to have followed the typical pattern of the bishops of Beauvais: generous patron of religious communities in general and Cistercians in particular, and warrior in the cause of the king of France and the Catholic church. Whereas his predecessor, Philip of Dreux, must have devoted a large proportion of his surplus wealth to warlike activities, the new era of peace in the Beauvaisis allowed Miles to spend heavily on the construction of the new cathedral. Although he undoubtedly was a very wealthy prelate, enjoying both the revenues of the diocese and county of Beauvais, the financial burden of his various undertakings proved to be too great for him. The chronicler Alberic of Trois-Fontaines tells us that overwhelmed with debts, the bishop approached the pope for assistance, and that he was given the duchy of Spoleto and the march of Ancona so that he could supplement his income and also so that he could help the pope against the emperor.[58] The undertaking led only to further financial losses, however, since on his return from Italy in 1230 Miles's party was ambushed, and his baggage was stolen.

It was after his return from Italy that Miles is said to have propagated the seditious theory that ecclesiastics did not owe allegiance to the

[53] Delettre, *Histoire du diocèse*, II, p. 249.

[54] Rome, "Henri II de Braisne."

[55] Delettre, *Histoire du diocèse*, II, pp. 250–252; E. Lefèvre-Pontalis, "Abbaye de Longpont," *Cong. arch.*, LXXVIII, 1911, part 1, pp. 410–427.

[56] C. Bruzelius, "Cistercian High Gothic: The Abbey Church of Longpont and the Architecture of the Cistercians in France in the Early Thirteenth Century," *Analecta Cisterciensia*, XXXV, 1–2, 1979.

[57] H. Gouïn, *L'abbaye de Royaumont*, Paris, 1932; P. Lauer, "L'Abbaye de Royaumont," *Bull. mon.*, LXXII,

1908, pp. 215–268.

[58] Le Nain de Tillemont, *Vie de Saint Louis*, pp. 172–173; *Gallia Christiana*, IX, col. 741; Alberic of Trois-Fontaines, *Chronicle, Recueil des historiens*, XXI, Paris, 1855, pp. 595–630, esp. p. 604: "*Milo, Belvacensis episcopus, innumeris obligatus debitis, ad papam abiit, qui constituit eum dominum ducatus Spoleti et Marchiae quae dicitur Garneri; et totam terram illam per triennium fere potenter obtinuit. In reditu vero, tetenderent ei insidias vicini Lombardi, ita quod plus ibi perdidit quam lucratus sit.*"

king of France and that Blanche of Castile was bearing the child of the papal legate. The Chronicle of Reims relates that the bishop's harsh treatment of the bourgeois of the city of Beauvais provided the ideal pretext for royal intervention in the affairs of that city.[59] William of Nangis suggested that the insurrection of 1232/33 in the city was the result of friction between the more powerful groupings among the bourgeois (the *majores*, primarily money changers) and the *populares*, made up of the other twenty-one professions in the city.[60] The bishop was accused of favoring the latter at the expense of the former. The struggle came to a head as a result of the lack of precision in the procedures followed for the election of the mayor of the commune. As a result of an undecided election and the absence of the bishop from the city, the king intervened and appointed as mayor a bourgeois from Senlis, Robert of Murat.

The inhabitants of Beauvais, furious to see a "foreigner" appointed as mayor, rose against Murat, attacking and burning the house in which he had taken refuge. Twenty people were killed and thirty more were injured in the ensuing fracas. Murat sent a courier to the king at Beaumont, and news also reached the bishop who was already on his way from his palace at Bresles to Beauvais. Eighty of those involved in the riot appealed to the bishop for clemency, claiming that they

had merely been attempting to uphold the rights of the commune. Louis IX came first to Bresles and then insisted on going on to Beauvais to render justice, despite Miles's representation of the right of the bishop-count of Beauvais to high, middle, and low justice in his city. The young king, accompanied by Blanche of Castile, went on to Beauvais, summoned those suspected of guilt, and banished those judged guilty. Fifteen houses were demolished as punishment for the leaders. Finally, the king demanded eight hundred pounds as his *droit de gîte* for the five days he had spent at Bresle and Beauvais. Bishop Philip of Dreux had been allowed to commute this feudal imposition for a payment of only one hundred pounds, and Miles of Nanteuil asked for a delay so that he could discuss the matter with his chapter. Taking this request as a refusal, the king seized the bishop's palace in Beauvais and left Simon of Poissy and several other knights to guard the bishop's palace after his own departure. The latter were given three warnings on consecutive days and then excommunicated. The king seized the temporalities of the bishop, and the contents of the palace (wine and furniture) were sold.

It is difficult to escape the conclusion that Louis and Blanche of Castile, in addition to their desire to consolidate royal authority, were also motivated by the desire to punish the bishop of Beauvais. This punishment

---

[59] *Chronique de Reims, Recueil des historiens*, XXII, pp. 304–305.

[60] Confusion between Old Style and New Style has produced an ambiguous date: 1232/33; see William of Nangis, *Chronicon, Recueil des historiens*, XX, Paris, 1840, p. 547: "*Apud Belvacum urbem Galliae facta est dissensio inter majores et minores villae burgenses, unde pluribus ex majoribus occisis, multi de minoribus capti per diversa loca regni Franciae sunt carceribus mancipati. Et quia Ludovicus sanctus rex manum ultricem apposuerat tamquam superior, Milo, ejusdem civitatis episcopus et comes, episcopatum supposuit interdicto.*" It seems that the alien mayor was supported by the *majores*, but that Miles of Nanteuil favored the popular party; see Vincent of Beauvais, *Speculum Historiale*, XXX, p. 137, reprint, Graz, 1965: "*Namque Milo, eiusdem urbis episcopus, tanquam faveret minoribus, in hoc facto suspectus habebatur.*" See also Louvet, *Histoire et antiquitez*, II, p. 366: "*Durant son regne en l'an 1232 s'estant meuë dispute et contention entre les Changeurs et le menu peuple de la ville de Beauvais, pour l'eslection d'un Maire, le Roy S. Louys en auroit fait un de la ville de Senlis,*

nommé Robert de Moret ou des Mureaux. Ce qui ne fut pont agreable a l'Evesque de Beauvais d'autant qu'il disoit que par l'establissement et creation du Maire de la ville de Beauvais on devoit eslire treize Pairs, dont deux luy devoient estre presentés pour faire chois de celuy qui seroit Maire. . . . Et de fait le Lundy devant la Feste de la Purification de la Vierge, la sedition fut si grande, que les Maire, Pairs et Eschevins furent assaillis et constraints d'eux retirer et sauver en la maison d'un armurier, où la population les assiegea, tellement qu'ayant mis la feu en la maison prochaine, elle les contraignit de venir en sa misericorde, apres en avoir tué vingt personnes et blessé trente." For a general account of the beginning of the struggle and the subsequent councils and interdicts, see Pontal, "Le Différend." Pontal emphasized the very serious nature of the affair, claiming that it signaled the termination of the theocratic doctrines of Gregory VII and Innocent III. Pope Gregory IX wrote of the struggle: "*Graviter in lesione Belvacensis ecclesia, tota Gallicana, immo universalis Ecclesia ledebatur*" (Pontal, p. 5).

might be explained both in light of Miles's claim to owe allegiance only to Saint Peter (not to the king) and also the scandalous rumors that he is said to have propagated about the relationship between Blanche and the papal legate.

Miles appealed to his metropolitan, Henry of Braine, archbishop of Reims. The former treasurer of Beauvais and member of the house of Dreux was sympathetic to the bishop, and there followed a series of ecclesiastical councils intended to represent the case to the king, threatening interdict if he failed to restore the confiscated rights and temporalities of the bishop of Beauvais. The archbishop convoked a council at Noyon on February 20, 1233. Present at the council were the archbishop and the bishops of Beauvais, Soissons, Laon, Châlons, Cambrai, Arras, Amiens, Senlis, and Thérouanne. Miles of Nanteuil recounted the actions of the king at Beauvais, representing the written evidence from the episcopate of Henry of France that justice in the city of Beauvais was entirely in the hands of the bishop. The council appointed three commissioners to present the plaint of the bishop to the king. On March 13, 1233, a second council met at Laon to hear the report of the commissioners, which was entirely favorable to the case of the bishop of Beauvais. It was decided that if the king failed to respond favorably the entire province of Reims would be placed under interdict. At the council of Senlis (Ascension 1233) the ecclesiastics were informed that the king remained intractable. He even refused to see the archbishop of

Reims in person. At Saint-Quentin in September 1233 it was decided that the interdict of the province would commence in the second week of November. The interdict was duly imposed, but the bishop of Noyon and the chapter of Senlis refused to observe it. The king, who was clearly trying to undermine the unity of the ecclesiastics, announced that the bishop held "*en baronnie et foi d'hommage,*" everything that he (the bishop) possessed in Beauvais, and that the full severity of the *droit de gîte* had been imposed because the bishop was suspected of sedition.[61] The movement against the bishop of Beauvais gathered strength among the ecclesiastics, the dean of the Amiens chapter, Simon d'Arcy, expressing the view that he could not uphold the interdict because he had not been at the synod of Saint-Quentin. The interdict on the province was raised on the Sunday before Christmas of 1233. Miles, on hearing of the raising of the interdict, placed his church under the protection of the Holy See. On the request of Pope Gregory IX, Miles raised the interdict on his own diocese in July 1234 and set out for consultations in Rome. He died on the road south on September 6, 1234.[62]

The unrest spread to the city of Reims. The archbishop was unpopular with the bourgeois because of his demand for one-tenth part of a loan that had recently been made by the commune of Reims to the city of Auxerre.[63] The bourgeois of Reims rioted, attacking the archbishop's fortified house at the Porte de Mars and erecting barricades. On November 9 the chapter was forced to flee, remaining in exile

---

[61] Pontal, "Le Différend," p. 16.

[62] Ibid., p. 19; and Alberic of Trois-Fontaines, *Chronicle, Recueil des historiens*, XXI, p. 614: "*Milo, Belvacensis episcopus, apud Camerinam civitatem Italiae moritur; post quem Gaufridus in episcopum eligitur.*" See also Guillelmus de Nangiaco, in *Recueil des historiens des Gaules et de la France*, XX, ed. J. Naudet and P.C.F. Daunou, Paris, 1840, p. 547: "*Et quia Ludovicus sanctus rex manum ultricem apposuerat tamquam superior, Milo, ejusdem civitatis episcopus et comes, episcopatum supposuit interdicto: sed dum Roman pro hac re proficisceretur, in itinere obiit: cujus successor Gaufridus eidem causae insistens, dies paucos et aflictione plenos in episcopatu peregit.*" Concerning the death and testament of Bishop Miles, P. Louvet wrote (*Histoire et antiquitez*, II, p. 377): "*Les Historiens de la France nous laissent par escrit que cet Evesque ayant mis l'interdit en son*

Diocese plustot par despit du Roy, que meu d'autre zele et craignant son courroux, il s'achemina à Rome en l'an 1234 où il mourut sans rien effectuer de son entreprise. Les obituaires de ce temps sous le sixiesme de Septembre portent que 'Obijt bonae memoriae Milo Episcopus qui dedit S. Petro praeposituras terrae Capituli videlicet redditus praepositurarum et totius terrae iustitiam, dedit executionem sententiaram suarum ab illis latarum in malefactores suos, dedit totam decimam quam habet Capitulum apud Morangle, dedit tunicam dalmaticam, casulas rubeas, tunicam rubeam de opere Sarracenorum, cappam rubeam et brodatam ad equos volantes, et plura alia ornamenta. Item, sanctuaria, Caput B. Mathei Apostoli et Evangelistae, virgam Aaron, turribulum argenteum.'"

[63] Pontal, "Le Différend," p. 19; Branner, "Historical Aspects."

until 1236. Similarly at Soissons the temporalities of the chapter were seized. Such attacks tended to force the cathedral chapters to move more closely into accord with the bishops in the general struggle.

The new bishop of Beauvais, Godfrey (or Geoffrey) of Clermont (also called "of Nesle"), had been dean of the Beauvais chapter and a strong supporter of Miles. Louvet reported that he was consecrated on Christmas Day 1234 in the presence of the bishop of Soissons and the abbots of Saint-Lucien and Saint-Quentin—a rather limited audience.[64] He further reported that during his episcopate there was a certain Eudes who took the quality of bishop of Beauvais, but we are not informed whether Eudes was an antibishop or a coadjutor. In June 1235, with the full support of his chapter, Godfrey reimposed the interdict on the diocese of Beauvais and then left for Rome. The archbishop of Reims continued the struggle against the king, placing the whole province under interdict once again in November 1235. The struggle in the city of Reims was terminated by early 1236, but the Beauvais affair dragged on. Bishop Godfrey returned to his diocese with Pope Gregory's support. He died in August 1236 without having raised the interdict. The see of Beauvais, having become vacant, fell as regalia into the hands of the king.

Pope Gregory IX, embroiled in difficulties with the emperor, adopted a conciliatory attitude to Louis IX, enjoining the bishops to exercise more restraint in their use of interdicts and excommunications.[65] The king then authorized a new election, and in May 1238 the pope instructed the chapter to lift the interdict on the diocese. The new bishop, Robert of Cressonsac or Cressonessart, former dean of the chapter, was elected in June 1238.[66] He conceded to the king the *droit de gîte* at one hundred pounds per annum, regardless of whether the king came to Beauvais or not, and a further one hundred pounds if he did come. The bishop's temporalities were restored, and they seem to have been enjoyed by the king between 1232 and 1238.[67] In future disputes between the commune, bishop-count, and chapter of Beauvais, the king's intervention was generally solicited.[68] In 1248 the bishop left with Louis IX to participate in the Crusade. He died on the island of Cyprus.

Bishop William of Grez (1249–1267), unlike his predecessors, was a learned man, a doctor of the university of Paris. He seems to have lent his support to the illustrious and litigious canon of the Beauvais chapter, William of Saint-Amour.[69] Born in 1202 of modest parentage in Saint-Amour (Franche-Comté), William became a canon of the Beauvais chapter in 1238. In the 1250s he played a memorable role in the struggle between the secular orders and the Franciscans and Dominicans over the right of the mendicants to teach at the university. In his major work, *Tractatus de periculis novissimorum temporum*, William of Saint-Amour identified the members of the mendicant orders as the false prophets sent to prepare the way of the Antichrist and the end of all time. William's case expressed the deep fear and suspicion of the secular clergy directed toward the mendicants who threatened the established *ordo ecclesiasticus* where spiritual authority was founded upon temporal possessions. William's writings also expressed a desire to preserve the power of the bishop and local synod in the

---

[64] Louvet, *Histoire et antiquitez*, II, p. 377.

[65] Pontal, "Le Différend," p. 30.

[66] Ibid., p. 31. Delettre, *Histoire du diocése*, II, p. 284, gave the date 1237 for Robert's accession. Newman, on the other hand, has Robert elected in August or September 1239 (*Les Seigneurs*, I, p. 247).

[67] See Appendix A, item 6.

[68] Pontal, "Le Différend," p. 33.

[69] Delettre, *Histoire du diocèse*, II, pp. 309–327; Louvet, *Histoire et antiquitez*, II, pp. 430–431; G. Hermant, *Histoire ecclésiastique*, II, pp. 770–799; article in *Dictionnaire de la spiritualité*, VI, Paris, 1967, pp. 1237–1242; D. L. Douie, *The Conflict between the Seculars and the Mendicants at the University of Paris in the Thirteenth Century*, London, 1954; M. Perrod, "Etude sur la vie et sur les œuvres de Guillaume de Saint Amour, docteur en théologie de l'Université de Paris et chanoine de Beauvais et de Mâcon (1202–1272)," *Mémoires de la Société d'émulation du Jura*, ser. 7, II, 1902, pp. 61–252; E. Aegerter, "L'Affaire du De Periculis Novissimorum Temporum," *Revue de l'histoire des religions*, CXII, 1935, pp. 242–272; M.-M. Dufeil, *Guillaume de Saint Amour et le polemique universitaire parisienne*, Paris, 1972.

face of papal incursions. It seems most significant that this canon of the Beauvais chapter was locked in controversy with the greatest leaders of the new orders, Saint Bonaventure and Saint Thomas Aquinas, at precisely the moment when the Beauvais upper choir was under construction. The architectural experience of the Beauvais choir has sometimes been compared with the ecstacy reached through the intellectual exercises prescribed by Saint Bonaventure. However, the realization of this sublime image of the Heavenly Jerusalem at Beauvais was only possible thanks to the enormous temporal resources of the bishop-count and the chapter—temporal resources renounced by the mendicants.

The leaders of the diocese of Beauvais seemed condemned to fight losing battles: Miles of Nanteuil against the growing power of the monarch and his ability to intervene in the affairs of the city, and William of Saint-Amour against the most powerful theologians of his day, Saint Thomas Aquinas and Saint Bonaventure, who enjoyed the support of the king himself. Beauvais Cathedral is the physical expression of the swan song of ecclesiastical aristocracy. It is particularly interesting to find William of Saint-Amour evoking an image of the bishop whose task it was to do battle with the dangers of the present time, mounting his high tower in order to survey the surrounding countryside for impending dangers. Despite the enthusiastic support of the secular doctors of the university as well as of many bishops, William of Saint-Amour was condemned by Pope Alexander IV and died in his native village in 1272.

About Bishop William of Grez himself we know little. Godefroy Hermant tells us that he had the great chapel of the episcopal palace rebuilt and equipped with stained glass and painting similiar to that of the Sainte-Chapelle.[70] This fact, coupled with his generosity toward the fabric, suggests that he was a "building bishop" and that he might have taken an interest in the construction of the upper choir.

At Beauvais the tenure of an enthusiastic building bishop tended to coincide with episodes of acute urban unrest. This is true of Miles of Nanteuil, William of Grez, and Simon of Clermont. Under William of Grez, renewed conflict with the commune resulted from the attempt on the part of the bishop to enforce the royal statutes against usury; one wonders whether this policy was not also intended to undermine some of the wealthy patrons of the mendicant orders in Beauvais. Members of the commune expelled the episcopal sergeants, and the bishop responded with an interdict. The Paris parlement pronounced in favor of the bishop, requiring members of the commune to make amends for the damage they had caused. Several other issues also brought acute tension between bishop and commune—issues that generally resulted from the bishop's desire to continue to maintain episcopal jurisdiction at all levels in Beauvais, and the realization on the part of members of the commune that it might be to their advantage to appeal to royal arbitration.

It will be suggested that this bishop directed the considerable resources of the diocese and county toward the construction of the upper choir, which surpassed all others in scale and delicacy of construction. It is thus of considerable interest to find him involved in the consecration of the new chapel at the nearby monastery of Saint-Germer-de-Fly in 1259—a chapel with obvious stylistic connections with the work of Pierre of Montreuil and the upper choir of Beauvais Cathedral. Bishop William also consecrated a new *châsse* for the remains of Saint Lucien; the shrine was said to be in the form of a tall church supported by flying buttresses. Around the apse of the model church were images of the twelve apostles and an image of Saint Lucien himself. In the upper choir of Beauvais Cathedral (around the hemicycle) niches sheltered monumental statutes, including an image of the sainted patron of the diocese, Lucien. The inauguration of the new *châsse* took place at Easter 1261.

William of Grez died in 1267, leaving a considerable sum of money for the fabric of the cathedral. He seems to have been the first

---

[70] Hermant, *Histoire ecclésiastique*, II, pp. 754–755.

bishop to have been buried in the chapel of the Virgin, the axial chapel of the Gothic cathedral. His epitaph records that he completed a great part of the construction of the church.

During the episcopate of Renaud of Nanteuil (1267–1283) the new choir was inaugurated; the first mass was held on the eve of All Saints 1272. In 1274 the bishop again clashed with the commune.[71]

In general terms, the temporal domain and power of the bishops of Beauvais increased sharply with the episcopate of Bishop Roger, then diminished, partly because of the numerous alienations of rights and holdings to religious communities (including the chapter of Saint Peter) in and around Beauvais, but more particularly because of the growth of the power of the commune and of the monarchy. Louis VII had confirmed that his brother Henry of France enjoyed all rights of justice in Beauvais. The affair of 1232–1238 showed that this was no longer the case. More will be said of the precise way in which the bishop's powers were diminished when we come to review the development of the commune. This institution held certain ill-defined rights of "low justice" in Beauvais. The very lack of definition of procedures was itself a source of weakness for the bishops of Beauvais since the only arbitrator between the bishop and the commune was the king of France. By the first half of the thirteenth century the king was no longer a distant suzerain but was a very real sovereign with some direct powers of control over the city. The struggle of 1232–1238 was instrumental in this transformation.

The Chapter

In the period under consideration the chapter of Saint Peter[72] consisted of a group of between forty and fifty canons including dignitaries living a life that could not be called "regular"; in other words, they did not share a common table or dormitory, but resided in their own houses to the east and to the south of the cathedral. The basis of a canon's income was a prebend, derived from the land held by the chapter and generally paid in kind. Definitions of the number of prebends, half-prebends, and dignitaries vary according to the date of the source consulted. In 1267 there were at least thirty-nine canons, including eight dignitaries. Loisel, however, writing in the eighteenth century, described six dignitaries (dean, chanter, underchanter, archdeacon of Beauvais, archdeacon of Beauvaisis, and treasurer), forty-two canons (including the chancellor and penitencier), six half-prebends, four *marguilliers*, and an unidentified number of vicars, chaplains, and choir boys.[73]

The temporal domain of the chapter comprised outright possessions of farms or granges, rents, tolls, rights of justice, and other rights held on a mass of lands concentrated mainly on the right bank of the river Oise, spread over an area corresponding roughly to the modern department of Oise.[74] By far the most important holdings of the chapter were within a circle drawn around Beauvais, having a radius of about fifteen kilometers. In addition to the mass of holdings in this area, important groups of holdings also existed on the plateau of Thelle between the Thelle and Thérain, and in the north of the diocese on the Picard plain.

Revenues from these possessions were not channeled into a central fund and then allocated as stipends and operating expense budgets, but rather were organized in nine regional groups, each one providing a certain number of prebends varying from four to nine.

The canon's income was made up from the *gros fruits* of the prebend, six daily loaves of chapter bread, and cash distributions that were made at various offices. The *gros fruits*, generally paid in kind, were worth sixteen

[71] Delettre, *Histoire du diocèse*, II, pp. 328–350.

[72] For the chapter, see esp. Labande, *Histoire de Beauvais*, pp. 182–200; Loisel, *Mémoires des pays*, p. 45; Louvet, *Histoire et antiquitez*, I, pp. 31–47; Newman, *Les Seigneurs*, I, pp. 231–238; and Arch. Oise, G 2353, a *Pouillé* of 1405.

[73] Loisel, *Mémoires des pays*, p. 45. Louvet, *Histoire et antiquitez*, I, p. 47, lists thirty-six chaplains. He does not include the chaplains of the chapel of Notre-Dame.

[74] B. Guenée, "Le Temporel du chapitre cathédrale de Beauvais à l'époque de la guerre de cent ans (1333–1444)," Diplôme d'études supérieures d'histoire, n.d.

muids of grain according to the local measure. It has been calculated that the value of a prebend plus distributions that a canon might expect to receive would have been worth about one hundred and sixty pounds *parisis* in the fourteenth century. The distribution made in cash at matins, vespers, and other offices, during Sunday processions, feast days, anniversary services, and so on provided almost half of this income.[75] Thus a period of interdict, when all divine services ceased, must have imposed special financial problems.

In the fourteenth century, forty-six prebends and eight half-prebends existed. An ordinary canon would hold a single prebend, as did five of the dignitaries. The dean, however, held two such prebends, and the chapter and underchanter each held one and a half prebends. In addition to their prebends, the dignitaries of the chapter disposed of their own special temporalities; that of the dean brought him an additional five hundred and sixty pounds per annum in 1320, and that of the treasurer about eight hundred pounds.[76]

The widespread extent of the domains of the chapter and the fact that a considerable proportion of the canon's revenue was paid in kind rather than cash shielded them from the effects of devastation during war and also from the effects of inflation. Such benefices, especially those of the dignitaries, would obviously have been considered as highly desirable.

Studies of the genealogy of the great local families and their relationship with the cathedral chapters have revealed the existence of a kind of interknit "seigneurial mafia."[77] Perhaps the most spectacular case involves the family of the seigneurs of Bazoches. In the first half of the thirteenth century, in one generation, the three eldest members were secular seigneurs, but the six youngest were all high-ranking ecclesiastics in the chapter of the ca-

thedral of Soissons and the convent of Notre-Dame.[78] Despite attempts on the part of the bishop, king, and pope to infiltrate or control the chapter in this period, it remained predominantly under the influence of the powerful local families that provided its members. Since in this period the choice of bishop was made by the chapter through free elections, the bishops tended to share the same local seigneurial background. This pattern was to change radically in the later Middle Ages, when the power of the pope or of the king to appoint a bishop led to the selection of men without local ties, generally for reasons of political patronage, and who were frequently absentee officeholders. It seems obvious that such a bishop or canon would have regarded his temporalities in terms of pure profit and would have had little interest in investing a substantial part in the fabric of the cathedral. At Beauvais in the thirteenth century local families such as those of Nanteuil-le-Hardouin, the Auneuil, and the Cressonsac dominated the chapter and the episcopate, and they expressed their local pride in terms of the construction of the new cathedral.

The dignitaries of the chapter, with the exception of the elected dean, were at the disposition of the bishop. The dean controlled matters of discipline within the chapter. Each archdeacon had a geographical area for which he was responsible, and he exercised rights of visitation over the rural deans and the parish priests in their defined areas. The treasurer, the best-paid officer, administered the temporalities of the chapter, sometimes with the aid of lay provosts.

The chapter had a general responsibility for the fabric of the cathedral—the term "fabric" being understood to include maintenance of the cathedral buildings, furniture, liturgical equipment such as vestments and altars, as well as new building. From fourteenth-cen-

---

[75] This is confirmed both by the calculations of Guenée ("Temporel du chapitre") and the statement of Louvet (*Histoire et antiquitez*, I, p. 160): "*l'on peut cognoistre qu'aiant esté ordonné par lesdicts Arrests que la moitié du revenu de l'Eglise de S. Pierre de Beauvais seroit employée en distributions, desquelles les absens seroient privés.*"

[76] That the Beauvais chapter was relatively well endowed

may be demonstrated by means of a comparison with the chapter of Troyes Cathedral. In the fourteenth century a canon at Troyes would have received about sixty-five pounds, almost exactly the same sum as the salary of the master mason; see Murray, *Building Troyes Cathedral*.

[77] Newman, *Les Seigneurs*, I, pp. 1–12.

[78] Ibid., p. 125.

tury evidence, it has been established that the temporalities of the fabric were clearly distinguished from the other temporalities of the chapter.[79] Among the properties assigned to the fabric were included a farm at Saint-Germer, some land at Litz, a quarry, a rent of twenty pounds, and several other *cens*, or rents. In the fourteenth century this brought a total revenue of about fifty pounds per annum. Several other supplementary sources existed. On the appointment of a new canon, a sum of ten pounds was paid into the fabric.[80] Sales of candles were made for the profit of the fabric. Profits from burials went to the same fund, as did the profits of amends imposed upon delinquent members of the chapter.[81] The most important source was provided by the allocation of a proportion of the annates of all newly appointed priests in the diocese. Finally, the contributions of the faithful of the diocese should not be underestimated, for a total of about five hundred pounds resulted from these combined sources. Such an annual income would have been adequate for maintenance, but when major new work was undertaken, special measures would obviously become necessary (see the charter of Bishop Miles, Appendix A).

In general, the power of the chapter underwent a steady increase through the Middle Ages. Unlike the bishops, the chapter refrained from alienating lands and jurisdictions for the foundation of new religious communities; its possessions would thus continue to grow. From the twelfth century, the chapter exercised jurisdiction over its own members and dependents within a defined geographical area. Bishop Ansel was responsible for a dramatic increase in the power of the chapter. On February 15, 1100, he gave the canons rights of justice over their mills in and around Beauvais, the power to make public proclamations (*bans*), the right to hear certain cases of lar-

ceny, and the right of excommunication, even over the bishop's own sergeants.[82] King Louis VI confirmed and augmented the rights of the chapter. By the twelfth century, we find the chapter virtually independent of the bishop and able to deal with him almost as an equal. In 1212 Bishop Philip of Dreux excommunicated a canon called Lancelin, but on the vehement protests of the chapter, the bishop weakly claimed that he had only acted in this way because he had thought that Lancelin belonged not to the cathedral chapter, but to the collegiate church of Notre-Dame-du-Châtel, and that he did not intend to usurp any new rights.[83] In 1301 Bishop Simon of Nesle was unable to force the illegal holder of the office of underchanter to renounce that position.[84] The canons' justice extended over the cathedral, the place Saint-Pierre to the south of the cathedral, and their own houses. Cases of justice involving their own members were heard by full meetings of the chapter. In its rights of excommunication and interdict, the chapter was even more powerful than the bishop, who, each time he used that weapon, had to make a declaration that no prejudice was intended to the privileges of the chapter.

With the increased power of the chapter came an increased involvement in the construction of the cathedral. Whereas the charter of Bishop Miles of 1225 reveals that the initiative for the Gothic campaigns of construction came from the bishop, and the canons were constrained to follow that initiative, the Late Gothic campaigns of construction were initiated primarily by the chapter.[85]

The Commune

Whereas the king might contribute directly to church building (for example at Royaumont), and the bishop and chapter might

---

[79] Guenée, "*Temporel du chapitre,*" pp. 80–81.

[80] This payment of ten pounds for the cope of a newly appointed canon goes back at least to 1385; see Bucquet-aux Cousteaux, XXVII, p. 146.

[81] As confirmed by many entries in the records of the deliberations of the chapter, for example as given in 1413 by the copyist of Bucquet-aux Cousteaux, XXVI, p. 162: "*Lau-*

rent Bacon chapellain amendé de 2 blans a Paris au procureur de la fabrique pour avoir manqué deux fois a sonner la messe."

[82] Labande, *Histoire de Beauvais*, p. 186.

[83] Louvet, *Histoire et antiquitez*, I, pp. 280–281.

[84] Ibid., p. 281.

[85] See Chapter VII.

channel their revenues directly into the fabric and determine some aspects relating to the shape of the new building, the role of the commune is a more indirect, or even negative one.[86] Examples can be found of the artistic patronage of the various guilds of a cathedral city (for example in the stained-glass windows of Chartres), but it was also fairly common to find a direct clash between the bishop and chapter on the one hand, and the commune on the other.

The origins of the medieval commune are to be found mainly in the associations formed by commercial interests, manufacturing groups, and religious confraternities. The first group is of particular importance since its interest in communications and trading over a wide geographical area tended to bring it into conflict with established landed seigneurs, each with a particular local bailiwick to defend. Associations were therefore formed and royal confirmations procured in order to ensure protection and freedom of movement for persons and goods. Similarly, groups of city dwellers involved in such industries as textiles or leather production would seek to gain control over the organizations of their own industry (for the regulation of quality standards, etc.) and to develop their own budgetary planning. Hence the interest in freedom from the power of the local seigneur to impose arbitrary taxation. Some cases can be found where a religious confraternity formed the kernel of the incipient commune: for example, the confraternity of the Assumption of the Virgin at Mantes, which met in the church of Notre-Dame.[87]

The most essential element of the constitution of a commune was the oath, generally administered under appropriately solemn conditions. Members of the commune would bind themselves to render mutual service in case of need, to remain loyal to the commune, and to refrain from aiding in any way the enemies of the commune. Other essential elements of the constitution of a commune would generally include control over taxation (with incidence determined by the commune), some control over the organization of local industries, and some rights of low justice.

The origins of the commune in Beauvais are obscure. It seems probable, however, that such an organization existed by the end of the eleventh century. The original charter of foundation no longer exists, and the earliest evidence concerning the commune of Beauvais is provided by a legal case arising from the chapter's complaint that bridges and obstructions erected in the river by the cloth dyers were preventing the flow of water necessary for the operation of mills.[88] The two parties are designated *canonici* on the one hand and *burgenses* on the other; some association on the part of the latter is therefore recognized. The judgment pronounced in the presence of Bishop Ansel recognized that a previous bishop had allowed such obstructions to be placed, and that the present bishop would maintain the established rights of the *burgenses* to place such obstructions. Labande suggested that the initial development of the commune was sponsored by the bishops themselves (especially Bishops Guy and Foulques in the mid-eleventh century) who hoped to conjure up an ally against the pretensions of their chapter.[89] The period of difficulties over the episcopal election (1101–1104) certainly provided a power vacuum conducive to the growth of the commune. Louis VI, the "*père des communes*," supported the infant institution in certain respects. The same king was the first to grant confirmation of the charter of the commune.

The content of the charter is known only through the form of the confirmation granted by Louis VI (1144) and Philip Augustus (1182).[90] In the preamble it is defined that the

---

[86] For discussions of the commune, see Labande, *Histoire de Beauvais*, passim; Loisel, *Mémoires des pays*, pp. 161–185; A Luchaire, *Les Communes françaises à l'époque des capétiens directs*, Paris, 1890; E. Morel, "Le Mouvement communal au xiie. siècle dans le Beauvais et aux environs," *Mém. Soc. acad. Oise*, XVII, 1899, pp. 481–499; C. Petit-Dutaillis, *Les Communes françaises: caractères et évolution des origines, au XVIIIe. siècle*, Paris, 1947.

[87] Luchaire, *Les Communes*, p. 34.
[88] Labande, *Histoire de Beauvais*, p. 55.
[89] Ibid., p. 56.
[90] Ibid., pp. 267–271.

inhabitants of Beauvais had been given their commune by King Louis VI.[91]

Our interests here lie not with the general development of the commune, but more specifically in the economic and organizational aspects of the construction of the cathedral. It is clear that with the development of the commune, the bishop lost some of his rights to "low" and "middle" justice within the city and suburb of Beauvais. Such a loss undoubtedly would have had financial implications. This, in itself, was hardly criticial, for the temporalities of the bishop-count outside of Beauvais, as well as within, remained substantial. The real significance of the commune as far as the judicial rights of the bishop were concerned was not the ill-defined clauses of the charter of confirmation, but the presence of the king as potential guarantor of these clauses, to be appealed to in cases of doubt. The king might uphold the bishop's claim to all justice in Beauvais (as did Louis VII in 1151), but the door was left open for royal intervention in the affairs of the city. This process was accelerated in the thirteenth century by the failure of Bishops Miles of Nanteuil and Geoffrey of Clermont to maintain their case against the king, and later by the economic and military pressures of the Hundred Years' War.

If the existence of the commune clearly led to a loss of judicial rights (and thus revenues) for the bishop, the purely financial implications of the situation are harder to assess. The commune involved a kind of feudal mutation; instead of fealty to a seigneur, the *communier* now swore allegiance to the commune. He exchanged the burdens of arbitrary *tailles* and the imposition of *mortmain* for other burdens: a communal *taille*, special taxes imposed by the king, military service, guard of gates and fortifications, and obedience to the mayor and peers. The point of the greatest interest for the construction of the cathedral is the question of the extent to which the bishop was able to command from the commune the payment of substantial taxes paid in cash. The only evidence that exists to provide an answer to this question is the 1260 account of the commune.[92] No payment of any annual tax to the bishop is recorded, although a payment to the bishop of four hundred pounds is recorded "because of the peace made by Peter of Fontaines and Jacques of Arras."[93] Payments to the king, on the other hand, were heavy.

It seems probable that any financial losses

[91] The following represents a summary of the main items in the charter. All men dwelling both *in civitatis* (i.e., the Gallo-Roman *castrum*) and *in suburbio* were required to swear allegiance to the commune. They were to render mutual assistance. The peers (*pares*, French *pairs*) of the commune would render justice in respect to injuries committed against *communiers* if they were not satisfied that the guilty party had made sufficient amends. If a visiting merchant were robbed in the city of Beauvais, and if plaint were made to the peers of the commune, and if the suspected robber were taken in Beauvais, the case would be heard by the peers. Only the king himself or his *dapifer* could hear a case in Beauvais involving a crime against a *communier*. If a man brought by the bishop into the city were to commit a crime against a *communier*, such a case should be heard by a tribunal of peers. The number of *juniores* in each mill was fixed at two, and cases involving differences were referred to the tribunal of peers. The bishop's right to take horses from the commune was fixed at three if the bishop were going to attend one of the communal courts or to participate in military activities and one if the bishop wanted to send fish to the king. No *communier* was to help or communicate with the enemy of the commune in time of war. The height at which cloths were suspended during manufacture was fixed. The peers were required to swear that they would not unfairly help their friends, not injure their enemies by spite, and finally the judgment of the peers was confirmed. It is noticeable that in the later confirmation of the communal charter granted by Philip Augustus (1182) the existence of a mayor is defined, in addition to the peers. A clause of this charter confirmed that thirteen peers were to be elected, from whom would be chosen either one or two mayors. This concession must have been made by Philip of Dreux, during whose episcopate, as we have seen, substantial concessions were also made to the king.

[92] C. Dufour, "Situation financière des villes de Picardie sous Saint Louis," *Mém. Soc. ant. Pic.*, xv, 1858, pp. 583–681; Labande, *Histoire de Beauvais*, pp. 286–288. The commune's receipts came from the *droit de chausée* paid at the gates of the city, from *aumones* (alms), amends, the sale of rents, and the *taille*. The total receipt was 7,784 pounds 6 sous 4 deniers, of which 5,204 pounds came from the *taille*. Money was also raised by loans; thus, in the 1260 account 1,419 pounds 11 sous was paid as usury. Expenses included maintenance of streets and fortifications, officers' wages, feudal aids, gifts to the king and his officers' expenses incurred in the service of the commune, expenses involved in legal cases and the chancellory, rents, interest, and petty expenses. Payments to the king were among the heaviest burdens; in the 1260 account, where the total expense amounts to 3,049 pounds 6 sous 2 deniers more than half this sum (1,750 pounds) was involved in a payment to the king "pour le pes d'Engleterre."

[93] Labande, *Histoire de Beauvais*, p. 286.

incurred by the bishop in terms of his diminished role in the judicial matters of the city would have been more than compensated for by the greatly increased volume of commerce and industrial effort that would accompany the growth of the commune. The textile industry, long established in Beauvais, underwent a dramatic expansion at the end of the twelfth century. Bishop Bartholomew of Montcornet was particularly active in promoting the development of this industry. He not only constructed new fulling mills himself, but also allowed the abbey of Saint-Quentin to build thirty mills in the space of five years. All the mills had, in principle, belonged to the bishop, but by the end of the twelfth century most of them had been ceded to the chapter. The bishop enjoyed important rights over the sale of cloths. He owned the cloth hall in Beauvais, and goods could be displayed there only after the payment of a certain sum to the bishop. Similarly, the bishop held very important rights on the movement of wine in and out of the city. The same applied to the distribution of fish and to the production and distribution of bread in the city. It was probably because of the overzealous imposition of these taxes of an "indirect" nature that the bourgeois of Beauvais were led to complain that the bishop was encumbering them wrongly and without reason ("*les escumenioit à tort et à mauvaise cause*").[94] The bishop's need for cash revenues in order to pay the workshop of the new cathedral no doubt led him to attempt to tap the growing wealth that trade, industry, and increased population had brought to the city of Beauvais. It is impossible to estimate the extent to which episcopal revenues were augmented by this urban growth, since already by the early thirteenth century large portions of the episcopal income from the city had been granted in fiefs to certain clients of the bishops, the *franc-hommes*, who, in return for their incomes, owed certain duties, often of a highly ephemeral nature, and who owed court to the bishop's tribunal.[95]

Luchaire has suggested that certain communes, forgetting their differences with bishop and chapter, might adopt the cathedral as the symbol of their civic pride and identity, borrowing the cathedral bell tower as their *beffroi*, used to summon *communiers* and peers to important events.[96] At Beauvais, the parish and collegiate church of Saint-Etienne and Saint-Vast was the church adopted by the commune. Loisel recounts that on July 31 the commune would assemble in the cemetary to the sound of the bells of the church for the business of electing a new mayor.[97] The outgoing mayor would climb into an elevated podium against the north transept of the church to make his adieu. On the following morning, after a mass at the church, the *communiers* would procede to the town hall where the election would take place. Thus, the bell tower of the church of Saint-Etienne provided the symbol for the pride of the commune of Beauvais. The cathedral of Saint-Pierre, for the inhabitants of Beauvais, would express the temporal and spiritual authority of the bishop and chapter, whose interests sometimes were in conflict with those of the commune.

The direct involvement of the commune in the construction of the cathedral was probably slight. The master masons themselves probably formed no part of the *corps de métiers*, since the peripatetic nature of their work allowed masons to escape from the regulations imposed upon other such professional groups. Because of the highly specialized nature of the work, it is unlikely that upper-echelon masons would be recruited from the city; a master mason in a cathedral shop would almost certainly have worked in a similar workshop in another city. The lower ranks of the workshop might have been filled with local men, however, and the presence of a large, cash-paid workshop in the city would have provided various kinds of stimulus to the economic life of the city. Similarly, the need for cash with which to pay the workshop would have affected the attitude of the clergy toward

94 *Chronique de Reims, Recueil des historiens*, XXII, p. 305.
95 Labande, *Histoire de Beauvais*, pp. 142–165.

96 Luchaire, *Les Communes*, p. 106.
97 Loisel, *Mémoires des pays*, pp. 175–178.

the collection of tolls and other dues, and to the possible commutation of dues that had hitherto been paid in kind.

The general relationship between cathedral construction and the economic welfare of the medieval city has been discussed recently by Henry Kraus and André Mussat.[98] Both authors reach the well-founded conclusion that the success or failure of a particular project depended upon the balance of power prevailing at the time of construction, and both authors provide several useful illustrations of the dynamic relationship between cathedral construction and the attendant historical circumstances. The commune constituted a particularly volatile element in the balance of power since the bishop would be liable to regard his rights to indirect taxation over the commune as a source of funds for cathedral building. There is every reason to believe that construction costs were often much higher than anticipated, leading the clergy to increase taxation, which produced urban unrest. Such tensions accompanied the construction of the cathedrals of Noyon, Laon, and Reims. It will be seen that certain peculiarities in the form of the choir of Beauvais Cathedral can be interpreted only in light of an interrupted sequence of building occasioned by the riots and interdicts of the 1230s.

What of the economic impact of the construction upon the life of the commune? Only one attempt has ever been made to address this problem in connection with the construction of the choir of Beauvais Cathedral. R. S. Lopez in a provocative essay on the economics of cathedral construction published in 1952 noted:

> Beauvais, at the beginning of the thirteenth century, was able to pay the king the most important contribution of any town, save only that of Amiens. In 1248, again, Beauvais could make available a considerable sum for the crusade in Egypt. . . . But the fortune of Beauvais was completely surpassed by that of other towns that

had not started out so strongly. Should we remind ourselves of the gigantic efforts made by Beauvais to erect one of the most beautiful cathedrals in the world?[99]

Lopez has subsequently elaborated his case. In 1962 he wrote: "If we judge from its finances, Beauvais was then, and remained until the middle of the century, the first city of the royal domain after Paris. In 1259–60 the commune paid to Louis IX a *taille* of 3,500 pounds in two payments (Amiens, the second in importance, paying 1,237) and was preparing to pay off a public debt of 6,129 pounds."[100] But, noted Lopez, this early promise was not fulfilled in the economic development of the city in the later part of the century. Italian cities, although often richer than Beauvais, made no effort to construct on this kind of scale, and Lopez again pointed to the probable connection between the decline of Beauvais and an essentially nonproductive economic effort— cathedral building: "Speaking economically, it would have been much wiser to wait for [a period of] abundance to invest in the domain of art."[101] A thought all too familiar to benighted arts administrators!

Given the paucity of documentation and the ambiguity of some of the sources that do survive, it is difficult to be certain as to the causes that lay behind the relative decline of the city of Beauvais in the later Middle Ages or to pinpoint the date when this decline began. However, the alarming implications of the Lopez thesis as far as the relationship between society and the arts is concerned make it essential to point to three obvious shortcomings. First, and most important, Lopez is mistaken in his dating of the construction of the choir of Beauvais Cathedral, placing the start of work only in 1247, when in reality construction had already been under way since 1225. By arguing that the city was still in excellent economic health in 1259, Lopez provided a demonstration of the case counter to the one he was at-

---

[98] Mussat, "Les Cathédrales dans leurs cités"; Kraus, *Gold Was the Mortar*.

[99] Lopez, "Economie et architecture médiévales," p. 433.

[100] R. S. Lopez, *La Naissance de l'Europe*, Paris, 1962,

p. 221; see also idem, *The Commercial Revolution of the Middle Ages, 950–1350*, Englewood Cliffs, 1971.

[101] Lopez, *La Naissance de l'Europe*, p. 221.

tempting to prove, since the Gothic choir, under construction for some thirty-five years,
was substantially complete then. A second
proviso to the Lopez thesis concerns the use of
sporadic payments to the king as a measure of
the relative economic power of various communes. Unless there is a continuous sequence
of figures that have been computed in the
same way, it is difficult to make valid comparisons. Many years ago it was pointed out that
the payments made by Picard communes in
the royal aid of 1248 revealed the relative
prosperity of this area. Laon, for example,
paid 3,000 pounds while Beauvais paid
3,400.[102] By 1248 the cathedral at Beauvais
had already been under construction for
twenty-three years. The communal accounts
of 1260 were occasioned by an ordinance
passed by King Louis IX in 1256, after his unsuccessful crusade. The Beauvais account is a
complex piece of juggling of expenses and receipts, which seems to attest to the continuing
economic health of the city. A surplus was
shown in the current year's budget, but an
overall indebtedness of 6,131 pounds was anticipated for the end of the year because of
three factors: the debt inherited at the beginning of the year (4,240 pounds), a shortfall
anticipated in the new *taille*, and a sum of
1,750 pounds owing to the king. Now, although the accountant announced that this
sum had not been mentioned before, it is intriguing to find an identical sum registered as
an expense "for the peace with England." Is it
possible that the accountant had entered the
same sum twice in order to increase the anticipated debt, hoping thus to reduce future tax
indemnity? It certainly seems unlikely that the
total value of the commune of Beauvais would
be assessed at more than twice the value of the
Amiens commune. The account provides a
striking confirmation of the fact that the
greatest burden upon the communal budget
was not the bishop and chapter, but rather the
king. We are dealing with a kind of "new fed-
eralism" where the power of the local mag-

nate to tax and dispose of patronage was
being increasingly reduced through the
growth of "big government."

A third proviso to the Lopez thesis involves
the argument made so convincingly for
Chartres by André Chédeville—that the income of a bishop and chapter was drawn extensively from agrarian holdings, as well as
from the city.[103] Thus, the construction of a
cathedral can be seen as a transfer of resources
from the countryside to the town, which
would be enriched through the presence of a
large cash-paid workshop.

Despite these reservations about the Lopez
thesis, it is, nevertheless, quite clear that the
construction of the cathedral might bring negative effects of an indirect nature. The periodic riots in Beauvais, caused partly through
episcopal taxation, provided an opportunity
for royal intervention and "arbitration." Such
arbitration did not come cheaply and might
have led to the confiscation of episcopal revenues or to the imposition of massive fines
upon the commune. It is obviously most significant that the most extreme tension coincided with periods of intense construction on
the cathedral: the 1230s, 1260s, and after
1300.

Conclusion

The construction of the choir of Beauvais
Cathedral was primarily the affair of the
clergy and the masons. It also involved a dialogue with the Capetian monarchy and with
the commune, an institution expressing the
identity of the commercial and industrial
bourg and suburbs of Beauvais. The growing
power of the monarch was important in providing a secure political and economic base
conducive to cathedral building. Beyond this,
a symbolic link between Gothic and the monarchy existed through the personal connections between Kings Louis VI and VII and the
monastery of Saint-Denis. The reconstruction

[102] Dufour, "Situation financière des villes de Picardie,"
p. 586.

[103] Chédeville, *Chartres et ses campagnes*, p. 521.

of the monastery church of Saint-Denis in the mid-twelfth century had been financed through the increased profitability of reorganized agrarian estates, revenues derived from the growing commercial and industrial activities of the area, and voluntary contributions. In the aftermath of Saint-Denis, ecclesiastical magnates and their chapters sought to tap the same sources of wealth to create their own great monuments. Early and High Gothic architecture is essentially the expression of the power of the church—power that had existed since the early Middle Ages, but that was now made material thanks to the increased profitability of agriculture, the sharp rise in the price of grain, and the ability of bishops and abbots to tap the burgeoning wealth of their cities. Beauvais provides a classic case where the combination of ecclesiastical and secular power coupled with the importance of the city as a center of textile production produced very considerable revenues for the clergy. The colossal bulk of the Gothic choir is, above all, the swan song of the power of the church and the wealth of the bishop-counts.

We have reviewed the role of kings and bishops, chapter, and commune in the construction of the Gothic choir, but it would be inappropriate to close this chapter without naming a fifth and most powerful personage behind the great enterprise—namely, Saint Peter himself. The founding bishop, Miles of Nanteuil, maintained very close links with the papacy. He asked to be consecrated by the pope himself (Honorius III); when overwhelmed with debts he had recourse to papal assistance; and he met his end in a futile appeal to Pope Gregory IX in 1234. We should not underestimate the impact that the theories of Pope Innocent III and the enactments of the fourth Lateran Council might have had upon churchmen such as Bishop Miles.[104] Melchisidek was a favorite prototype of Innocent III, and the king of Salem who was also a priest of God may also have been a figure of interest to the bishop-count. Innocent III also justified his theories concerning the supremacy of *sacerdotium* over *regnum* through references to Christ's charge to Saint Peter (Matthew 16:18: "thou art Peter and upon this rock. . . ."), words that obviously would have been of special significance to the bishop of Saint-Pierre of Beauvais. "By Saint Peter," Bishop Miles is reported to have exclaimed to Blanche of Castile and the barons, "everyone here should know that I have no *seigneur* in the world other than the Apostle, in whose protection I am: I do not answer to any other *seigneur*."[105] The bishop of Beauvais was not alone in challenging the supremacy of the king. The bishop of Tours is also named in the great council of the secular magnates that took place at Saint-Denis in 1235.

In speaking of a "court style" of Gothic architecture of the 1240s, we have been curiously unaware of the fact that the 1230s and 1240s saw a real crisis in the relations between *regnum* and *sacerdotium* in France—a crisis that led to the expression of violently anticlerical sentiments on the part of the secular magnates and councillors who were closest to Louis IX. This anticlericalism was directed particularly at the alleged attempt of the clergy to expand their jurisdictional rights. Such disputes of rights to justice and the power of the bishop to levy taxation lay behind the great urban uprising of 1232–1233. Oppressed by the cost of his great construction project, Bishop Miles of Nanteuil, essentially bankrupt within five years of the start of work, was attempting to insist on the full range of tolls and taxes due to him from the bourgeois. In particular, he tended to lean on the wealthier elements of the population, including the money changers. A chain reaction ensued—almost like the sequential failure of a Gothic structure, with one event triggering the next. Oppressive taxation coupled with the confusing system for the election of the mayors led to royal intervention and the imposition of a foreign mayor. This led to urban rioting, which led to renewed royal intervention.

---

[104] K. Pennington, "Pope Innocent III's Views on Church and State: A Gloss to 'Per Venerabilem,' " *Law, Church, and Society: Essays in Honor of Stephan Kuttner*, ed. K. Pennington and R. Somerville, Philadelphia, 1977.

[105] *Chronique de Reims, Recueil des historiens*, XXII, p. 305.

The protest of the bishop was met with retaliation on the part of the king, which provoked excommunication of the king's agents, finally leading to the confiscation of the bishop's revenues. The construction of the cathedral was almost certainly brought to a temporary halt.

Behind these events lay both the apparently predetermined and the accidental. The appearance of inevitability is inherent in the chain reaction described above; the accidental element in the scenario was, above all, the clash of personalities between the proud bishop and the young king steered by his powerful mother.

CHAPTER III

Toward a Chronology for the Construction of the Gothic Choir

One of the most important components of a new monograph on a great medieval cathedral is the correlation of evidence derived from an analysis of the building with evidence from the study of its temporal framework in order to document the chronology of construction. Unfortunately, the preparation of such a chronology can become an end in itself, and it is important to remind ourselves that our task is essentially a means to the end of understanding the monument as a complex stratigraphy of artistic intentions within the changing temporal context.

While disagreements may continue over the definition of the successive campaigns of construction at the cathedrals of Chartres, Reims, and Amiens, the starting date for each of these monuments is well established. No such agreement has existed about the starting date for the Gothic choir of Beauvais Cathedral. Until the 1830s the choir was thought to have been a work of the late tenth century, begun under Bishop Herveus. By the mid-nineteenth century it was generally recognized that this was a work of the thirteenth century, but con-fusion over three alternative options for the start of construction (1180, 1225, 1247) has persisted down to our own days. Further confusion exists over the collapse that took place in 1284, with some sources referring to two collapses.

Existing Theories

It is necessary first to undertake a review of existing theories about the chronology of construction before attempting to establish a framework for a new understanding of this chronology. There is good reason for the confusion over two of the possible starting dates, 1225 and 1247. Although the Gothic choir was, indeed, begun in 1225, the parts of the monument that we most admire (radiating chapels, ambulatory, and central vessel) belong to the years after 1240.

The seventeenth century saw the start of serious efforts to compile histories of the diocese, city, and cathedral of Beauvais. This was a period of revulsion of taste against Gothic, and although the construction and collapse of the transept crossing tower of the cathedral were still within living memory in the first decades of the seventeenth century, writers of this period were not, for obvious reasons, equipped to deal with the problem of relating the written texts with distinguishable style phases in the building itself.[1] In addition to their ignorance concerning Gothic architecture, the early historians of the cathedral faced two further problems. Bishop Roger of Champagne, the bishop who had united the county and diocese of Beauvais, occupied a position of prime importance in the annals of Beauvais. His tomb, under a Gothic canopy, existed to the north side of the apse of the cathedral, close to the tomb of Miles of Nanteuil. It is not surprising to find that a powerful local tradition developed that Roger and his predecessor, Herveus, had been the founders of the present Gothic choir. This tradition was propagated, to some extent, by the efforts of the late medieval bishops of Beauvais to stamp out the memory of the contribution of the actual founding bishop, Miles of Nanteuil, who had committed a substantial proportion of his annual revenue to the fabric. Later bishops, however, claimed that although Herveus had given two mills to provide an annual rent for the fabric, it had never been customary for the bishop to contract to contribute a fixed annual payment.[2] The precedent of Bishop Miles was better forgotten. It was quite natural that historians should associate the existing cathedral with the generosity of Bishop Herveus and the achievement of Bishop Roger. Thus, Anthoine Loisel considered that the cathedral of Saint-Pierre had been founded in 991.[3] Similarly, Etienne de Nully wrote, "The church, based on the design of that of Cologne, was founded by Bishop Herveus in the year 1000."[4]

The work of Pierre Louvet, the remarkable seventeenth-century historian of Beauvais,

provided the basis for the understanding of the chronology of the cathedral for a century or more. He distinguished between the *Basse-Œuvre* (the nave) and the *Haut-Œuvre* (the new choir), writing, "It is certain that at the time when the walls of the city or citadel of Beauvais were constructed, the temple (after the end of the pagan era dedicated to the Virgin and Saint-Pierre) was constructed, since the form of the walls is quite similar, and because over the west portal [of the *Basse-Œuvre*] we can still see and distinguish some of the idols adored by the pagans."[5] In 997, Louvet continued, the new choir was begun by Bishop Herveus. This was substantially the choir existing at present: "This building, before it had been constructed and reduced [*reduit*] to the admirable form in which we see it at present, had suffered several major accidents. In the year 1225, at the hour of curfew, there came a great ruin to the vaults and to the great pillars of the choir. The result of this was that the chapter was unable to begin to celebrate divine service in the building until the Monday before All Saints, 1272."[6] Here we see the beginnings of an attempt to reconcile the local tradition of the tenth-century date for the Gothic choir with the surviving documents. Louvet was familiar with the 1225 charter of Miles of Nanteuil (he later published it in full) and with the texts recording 1272 as the date of the entry into the choir and relating to a great collapse (which actually occurred in 1284). In order to retain Bishops Herveus and Roger as the founders of the existing choir, Louvet had the collapse take place in 1225 and the work defined in the charter of Bishop Miles devoted to the repair and reconstruction of the damaged cathedral. In this way, Louvet was responsible for starting the legend of two collapses, one in 1225 and the other in 1284.

Denis Simon, writing in 1704, repeated the

---

[1] For accounts of the work of the historians of the city of Beauvais, see Leblond, *Inventaire-sommaire*, Introduction; and Dupont-White, "Les Antiquaires de Beauvais," *Mém. Soc. acad. Oise*, I, 1847, pp. 1–53.

[2] Arch. Oise, G 2353, *Pouillé* of the diocese of Beauvais, 21 vo.–26 vo.

[3] Loisel, *Mémoires des pays*.

[4] Etienne de Nully, "Notice de la cathédrale en 1685 par Etienne de Nully, chanoine de Beauvais," in Desjardins, *Histoire*, pp. 229–233.

[5] Louvet, *L'Histoire de la ville*, pp. 367–370.

[6] Ibid.

same basic story, with some variations.[7] He accepted the dating of the *Basse-Œuvre* to the period of Nero, when, he believed, the city walls had been built. The choir, Simon said, had been begun in 997. This choir was damaged in the fire of 1225, when the roof and vaults were burned and the pillars ruined, so that no services were held until 1227. This last date is obviously a mistranscribed rendering of 1272.

The various antiquarians whose notes and copies form the Bucquet-aux Cousteaux Collection are heavily dependent upon Louvet.[8] In Volume XXIII of this collection are several different accounts of the construction. One such account again refers to the two mills given by Bishop Herveus to Saint-Pierre for the construction of the new church. The writer notes that the *Pouillé* (survey of temporal possessions) of the church places the start of the new construction in the year 1000 and that Bishop William of Grez (died 1267) finished the work. The start of the divine service in the new church is placed in 1272. Thus, we are still dealing with writers who believed that the actual Gothic choir was a work of the tenth and eleventh centuries.

A second summary in the same Bucquet-aux Cousteaux Collection adds some extra dates. Referring to Louvet and the *Pouillé* of Saint-Pierre, the writer dates the church to the time of Bishops Herveus and Roger (990s–early 1000s). This church was burned in May 1180 (reference to Louvet), the master altar was consecrated in 1222, and the church was burned again in 1225, "which made a great ruin in the vaults and pillars of the choir." The divine service was begun in 1272 (reference to the *tablet* of the choir), and in 1284 the high vaults fell.

A third chronology in the same volume of the Bucquet-aux Cousteaux Collection has the choir finished by Bishop William of Grez, noting (incorrectly) that this prelate was buried in 1247. This account may have provided the

source for the date 1247, which finds its way into many of the later histories of the cathedral.

In a further lengthy "Memoire touchant l'Eglise cathédrale de St Pierre de Beauvais" in the Bucquet-aux Cousteaux Collection, Volume XXIII, the legend of the eleventh-century date for the existing choir was elaborated. The nave of the *Basse-Œuvre* was dated to the pre-Christian era. The eleventh-century masons of the choir, the source tells us, had not been subject to "the more exact rules of architecture" but instead had followed a Gothic design ("*un dessein gothique*"), building a church so tall, so delicate, and so beautiful that it became one of the principal ornaments of the kingdom, and was considered an architectural masterpiece. The tops of the piers of the apse were decorated with statues of Saint Lucien and his companions. However, the writer continued, the construction of this masterpiece was not entirely accident free. The piers had been too widely spaced and the vaults collapsed. When the repairs were made after 1225 the canons thought that they could simply rebuild the existing structure with the addition of tie beams hooked to the big iron pegs still visible in many of the piers. With this makeshift repair completed, the canons began the celebration of the divine office in 1272. In 1274 the chapter decided to transfer the bodies of Bishops Roger (died 1022) and Philip of Dreux (died 1217) from the old church to tombs in the new choir. Bishop William of Grez (died 1267), however, was buried immediately in the Virgin chapel behind the choir of the *Haut-Œuvre*. Subsequent episcopal tombs were placed in the sanctuary of the choir. In 1284, according to our account, the vaults fell for a second time (the first time had been in 1225), obliging the chapter to take stringent measures for the security of the church: the doubling of the number of piers in the straight bays of the choir.

Some of the new elements that appear in

---

[7] Simon, *Supplément*, pp. 52–53.

[8] This is a series of ninety-five handwritten volumes of notes and copies of medieval texts made by eighteenth-century antiquarians. This vital collection survived the fire of 1940 and is kept in the municipal library of Beauvais; see Leblond, *Inventaire-sommaire*.

this "memoir" cause problems in its internal logic. Why, it might be asked, if the existing choir was the one built by Herveus and Roger, was it possible to translate the latter bishop into that choir only in 1274?

This contradiction was noticed by the unidentified author of yet another discussion of the history of the cathedral contained in the Bucquet-aux Cousteaux Collection (Volume XXIII). This writer refrained from any attempt to compile a synthesis, but instead posed three questions: when was the choir begun, was it undertaken by a king or a bishop, and when was it completed? The writer began by repeating the usual formula: the choir has been begun by Bishop Herveus and completed by William of Grez. He noted, however, that Philip of Dreux had been buried in 1217 in the old church, remarking, "now if the new choir had been complete then, he would have been placed immediately in the position where he was [in the Gothic choir] and no translation would have been necessary." A gloss in the margin of the manuscript at this point notes that the master altar was consecrated in 1222, and that the bodies of Roger and Philip of Dreux were deposited in the *Haut-Œuvre* under a stone canopy in 1289. Mentioning the 1225 charter of Bishop Miles, the writer noted that it was also true that there must have been a special reason after 1225 to delay the entry into the new choir until 1272.

The writer of the *Gallia Christiana* made no effort to make any sense of the relationship between the dates provided by the written sources and the form of the building, merely noting that the city had been burned in 1180 and that a second fire in 1225 reduced the basilica of Saint-Pierre to such a ruinous state that the divine office could not be celebrated until 1272.[9]

Even by the first decades of the nineteenth century, the work of construction of the Gothic choir has still not been completely separated from the work of construction of the *Basse-Œuvre*. Thus, A.P.M. Gilbert noted in 1829 that the first foundations of the former cathedral were laid around 991 by Bishop Herveus.[10] Bishop Roger then continued the work: "Eight pillars were erected to support the enclosing wall of the sanctuary and the apse, after which were added the great piers of each side, along two parallel lines, in order to complete the construction of the choir. The statues of the sainted patrons of the diocese were placed over the capitals of the pillars, and that of Saint Lucien was placed on the first pillar supporting one of the arches at the end of the sanctuary." These details concerning the "old choir" of Bishop Roger could only have been derived by Gilbert from the existing Gothic choir. Gilbert has the old church burned in the fires of 1180 and 1225 and reconstructed by Miles of Nanteuil "on a much vaster plan." He mentions two collapses, one in 1272 (this is clearly based upon a misreading of the sources) and a second one in 1284.

E. Woillez, in his *Description* of 1838, was the first to be able to distinguish between the Gothic choir and its predecessor, but he inadvertently added yet another element of confusion. According to Woillez, Herveus's basilica was destroyed in the fires of 1180 and 1225 and reconstructed by Miles of Nanteuil: "William of Grez, fifty-eighth bishop (1249–1267) had the choir of the church constructed in 1247; it was completed in 1272, and the mass was held on October 31 of the same year, but the vaults, despite the precautions that had been taken, collapsed in 1284, on November 29, because of the wide separation of the lateral walls, bringing down in their collapse several exterior and interior pillars."[11]

The date 1247 was to be repeated by sub-

[9] *Gallia Christiana*, IX, cols. 741–742.

[10] A.P.M. Gilbert, *Notice historique et descriptive de l'église cathédrale de Saint-Pierre de Beauvais*, Beauvais, 1829, pp. 7–12. Of course, the published sources represent only a partial statement on the eighteenth- and nineteenth-century understanding of the chronology. One of the anonymous eighteenth-century contributors to the collection known as the Collection de Picardie (Bibl. Nat.) challenged

Louvet and Simon in certain important respects, noting that the *Basse-Œuvre* had never been a pagan temple, that a new cathedral had been begun under Bishop Herveus, and that this church had burned in 1225 and had been replaced by Bishop Milon (Miles); see Bibl. Nat., Collection de Picardie, CLXII, fol. 29.

[11] E. Woillez, *Description de la cathédrale de Beauvais*, Beauvais, 1838, pp. 4–5.

sequent historians until our own days. A further legend launched by Woillez is still repeated locally: "The construction of this part of the edifice [the choir] has been attributed to Eudes of Montreuil, the architect of Saint Louis, but we have been unable to discover anything to make us adopt this opinion as certain."[12]

In the 1860s two important new studies on the cathedral were published, one from the point of view of the archivist, and the other from that of the architectural historian. Gustave Desjardins was archivist of the Archives Départementales de l'Oise. His *Histoire* (1865) provides a wealth of textual sources for the campaigns of construction on the cathedral between the fourteenth and sixteenth centuries, but for the thirteenth century he conservatively gives only the 1225 starting point and 1272 completion date, although he does note that Etienne de Nully and M. Graves were mistaken in their belief that Beauvais Cathedral was a copy of Cologne Cathedral and was begun only in 1248.[13]

If the archivist was unable to find any documentary milestones between 1225 and 1272 relating to the campaigns of construction on the choir, the architectural historian added his powerful voice to the chorus favoring a start of major campaigns in the 1240s. Eugène Viollet-le-Duc, the first writer to attempt an analysis of the monument from an architectural point of view, wrote: "We have seen that the choir of Amiens Cathedral must have been begun between 1235 and 1244; the Beauvais choir was founded in 1225. But we have to confess that we cannot see anything in the middle parts of the building [*dans les parties moyennes*] which could be before 1240. However, in 1272 the choir was complete, since at this time the collapsed vaults were already being repaired."[14]

The date in the 1240s, thus confirmed by Viollet-le-Duc, was to be repeated by the historians of Beauvais Cathedral for more than a century. Abbé L. Pihan lent further credence to the 1247 date: "This building was the victim of the fires of 1180 and 1225, and in two different campaigns [*à deux reprises différentes*] Bishop Miles of Nanteuil, with the help of his chapter, seems to have undertaken the construction of another cathedral. The apse and the choir, properly defined, begun in 1247, were finished by October 31, 1272. It has been supposed that the plan of the chevet was given by Eudes of Montreuil, Saint Louis's architect."[15]

Abbé Marsaux's account of the chronology of the choir suggests that he had consulted Woillez's *Description*.[16] After mentioning the fires of 1180 and 1225, he has Bishop Miles of Nanteuil decide upon the construction of a new cathedral ("*Milon de Nanteuil resolut de reédifier une autre cathédrale*"), but the foundation of the choir and the apse was laid only in 1247. Two collapses are mentioned by Abbé Marsaux, one on October 31 (no year given) and the other in 1284. Writing soon after the important campaigns of restoration undertaken by the architects Sauvageot, Vital, and Beauvais, Marsaux leaves us with a tantalizing glimpse of the results of the excavation completed by the last-named architect in the central vessel of the choir: "The architect Beauvais discovered that the width of the choir was increased at the moment when the [first] courses were rising above the ground. In fact, the original piers [*ses piles primitives*] are placed in a position of overhang [*en porte-à-faux*] of around 0.60 m over the foundations on the side of the ambulatory, which go down to a depth of 10.60 m."[17]

Dr. V. Leblond, in his *Petite Monographie* (1926), like Desjardins, provided his readers

[12] Ibid. For Eudes of Montreuil, see L. Grodecki, "Pierre, Eudes et Raoul de Montreuil à l'abbatiale de Saint-Denis," *Bull. mon.*, CXXII, 1964, pp. 269–274.

[13] Desjardins, *Histoire*.

[14] Viollet-le-Duc, *Dictionnaire*, II, p. 336. See also Vol. I, p. 239, where the Beauvais choir is dated 1240–1250.

[15] Abbé L. Pihan, *Beauvais, sa cathédrale, ses principaux monuments*, Beauvais, 1885, p. 10.

[16] Marsaux, "Cathédrale," pp. 4–15. Leopold-Henri

Marsaux was born in 1842, the son of a planter in the forest of Compiègne. The Grand Séminaire at Beauvais had an endowed chair for archaeology, which was occupied by notable local figures such as Barraud, Abbé Renet, and Gustave Desjardins. Thus, Marsaux developed an interest in local archaeology. See Abbé L. Pihan, "Notice sur M. le chanoine Marsaux," *Mém. Soc. acad. Oise*, XX, 1907, pp. 5–26.

[17] The drawings of the architect Vital do not confirm this

with a wealth of documentary evidence, especially relating to the Late Gothic campaigns.[18] He noted that the old church had been burned in the fires of 1180 and 1225, and that Miles of Nanteuil and his chapter had engaged one-tenth of their revenues to the task of reconstructing the cathedral. In 1247 the papal legate approved this decision. Leblond also noted the important patronage of Bishop William of Grez (died 1267), whose epitaph recorded that he had founded four chapels and had given six thousand pounds to the fabric and a great bell. Leblond noted that this bishop was buried in the axial chapel dedicated to the Virgin Mary. By 1272, according to Leblond, "the apse and a part of the choir [which part?] were finished."[19]

Robert Branner's 1962 article on the *maître de Beauvais* provides the only recent analysis of the chronology of the choir.[20] His contributions to our understanding of the problem lie mainly in his apt description of the spatial qualities of the choir and in his emphasis upon the 1225 charter of Miles of Nanteuil as the starting point of campaigns of construction. He dismissed the 1247 date, which had been repeated by so many earlier writers, as based upon a misunderstanding. He repeated the details of the patronage of Bishop William of Grez as already defined by Leblond and the *Gallia Christiana*.

As discussed earlier, Branner proposed three main phases of construction, with the east end of the choir (the radiating chapels) completed after 1225, the west end of the choir and eastern aisle of the transept around 1245–1250, and the upper parts in the 1260s. Branner surprised himself with the extraordinary precocity of his *maître de Beauvais* at

work in the ambulatory and radiating chapels in the 1220s, and he was surprised once again at the *retardataire* appearance of the second campaign. Had he followed his instincts, he might have proposed a west-to-east chronology and avoided the necessity for surprise. Francis Salet expressed reservations about Branner's chronology, but despite this, most art historians have continued to adhere to the theory of an east-to-west construction sequence.[21]

Philippe Bonnet-Laborderie, in his recent book *Cathédrale Saint-Pierre*, chose to emphasize the stylistic homogeneity of the lower choir.[22] He believed that the old cathedral, finished at the end of the tenth century, was replaced by the Gothic choir, begun in 1225, without any intermediary construction. Yet he also maintained that the existing sacristy/treasury complex survives from some earlier cathedral. He suggested that the radiating chapels were built in the first years of construction, yet he also recognized the archaic quality of the transept towers.

The west-to-east chronology for the lower choir proposed by the present author in 1980 and confirmed in these pages has also been advocated by Kimpel and Suckale in their recent book, *Die gotische Architektur in Frankreich* (1985).[23] They seem to have been unaware of the 1980 article.

The Establishment of a New Chronology: Texts

The establishment of a more precise chronology for the construction of the Gothic choir is only possible through a reevaluation

---

porte-à-faux in the original piers of the Beauvais choir. On the other hand, the added (fourteenth-century) piers certainly did overhang their foundations; see Archives Départementales de l'Aube, Troyes, Fonds Vital, No. 328. Moreover, some sections show the ambulatory piers (between the chapels) overhanging their foundations. About the architect Frederic Beauvais we know little; he is listed as a member of the local archaeological society early in this century.

[18] Leblond, *La Cathédrale de Beauvais*.
[19] Ibid., p. 11.
[20] Branner, "Maître de Beauvais," pp. 78–92.
[21] Salet, review of Branner's "Maître de Beauvais." Salet

saw no basis for Branner's chronology or for his interpretation of the master of Beauvais as a revolutionary in reaction against the "academic" qualities of Amiens cathedral. Branner's chronology was accepted by L. Grodecki, *Gothic Architecture*, New York, 1977; by Bony, *French Gothic Architecture*; and most recently by R. Mark, *Experiments in Gothic Structure*, Cambridge, 1982.
[22] P. Bonnet-Laborderie, *Cathédrale Saint-Pierre*, pp. 25, 111, 175. See review by F. Salet, *Bull. mon.*, CXXXVIII, 1980, pp. 351–353.
[23] D. Kimpel and R. Suckale, *Die gotische Architektur in Frankreich 1130–1270*, Munich, 1985. The two most re-

of the primary written sources coupled with an intense analysis of the fabric of the cathedral.

A survey of the written evidence reveals the existence of some eleven sources or groups of sources that can help fix the chronology. These sources, together with brief commentaries, have been transcribed in Appendix A. It can be learned from these sources that fire(s) took place in 1180 and/or 1188 in which the old cathedral was damaged. The ensuing sequence of foundations and endowments (Fig. 7) culminating in the consecration of the high altar in 1222 suggests that the choir of the old cathedral was rebuilt in the decades after 1180 and was probably finished before 1217, since no donations to the fabric are recorded in the will of the late bishop, Philip of Dreux. The rebuilt choir would presumably have been a stone-vaulted structure and might have survived the worst effects of the fire of 1225. It has sometimes been suggested that some of this hypothetical structure of the 1180s–1200s is embodied in the existing choir—a possibility that recommends itself because of the archaic appearance of the sacristy/treasury chambers and the bases of the piers attached to the transept walls. However, it will be seen that these parts of the building are integrated in a stylistic and archaeological sense with the rest of the choir, and it is likely that the present structure in its entirety dates from after 1225. In that year Bishop Miles of Nanteuil established a lavishly endowed fabric fund for the reconstruction of the cathedral. Three years after the fire, in 1228, a charter makes reference to the high altar that was still in use—this might have been the altar in the old choir or the one in the provisional choir known to have been constructed between the western piers of the crossing of the old *Basse-Œuvre*. In 1233, some seven to eight years after the start of work, the financial arrangements defined in the foundation charter were adversely affected by the struggle between the bishops of Beauvais, Miles of Nanteuil and Godfrey of Clermont, and the king of France.

Thus, we are led to expect a well-financed and rapid start after 1225 followed by a sharp deceleration or even a temporary halt after 1233. We would expect a second campaign after the accession of Bishop Robert of Cressonsac, extending from the late 1230s into the 1240s. The evidence of the foundations of the altars suggests that the radiating chapels were only being put to use in the period between the late 1230s and the 1250s. Ultimately, however, our interpretation of the chronology of construction of the choir of Beauvais Cathedral must depend upon an analysis of the building itself.

Chronology: "Campaigns" of Construction

The disagreements that have existed over the chronology of construction of High Gothic cathedrals such as those of Chartres, Reims, and Amiens indicate that despite generations of study, simple answers have not been forthcoming. We should therefore be provoked not only to undertake a renewed inspection of the fabric of these buildings, but also (and more important) to review the expectations and presuppositions that we entertain about "campaigns" of construction.

We tend to approach the study of the great Gothic cathedral with the implicit belief that it was constructed in a series of readily discernible campaigns. These campaigns are assumed to reflect several factors: the economic situation where funds would be adequate only for a limited spell of concentrated building, the artistic situation where constantly changing taste led to periodic revisions of a stylistic and structural nature, and the human factor resulting from the limited life spans of any given master mason or administrator of the fabric. We define a "campaign" as a unified phase of construction within a certain time span following a recognizable plan, and we seek for the evidence for such a campaign in the isolation of a harmonious set of forms ex-

cent studies accept the west-to-east chronology, see J. Thiebaut, *Les cathédrales gothiques en Picardie*, Amiens, 1987 and M. Bideault and C. Lautier, *Ile-de-France gothique, I,*

Les églises de la vallée de l'Oise et du Beauvaisis, Paris, 1987.

isting in a given area of the building that can be defined between clear sutures in the masonry indicating where one group of masons has left off and another has started work. In fact, however, things were not necessarily so simple. Thus, if a section of wall were to be left unfinished, the masons would take care to leave *pierres d'attente* (waiting stones) tongued ready to receive the stones of the next phase of construction. The masons from the next phase might use stones cut to the same dimensions from the same quarry, and seven hundred years of weathering will obviously obliterate slight differences in the stone surfaces that might result from the fact that they were cut at points of time separated by five or ten years. If the junction between the old and new work threatened to be particularly messy, masons might even demolish existing work in order to effect an orderly transition. To make matters worse, nineteenth-century restorers had a habit of concentrating their efforts on tidying up such messy junctions with new facings. At Beauvais, despite the striking changes in the stylistic vocabulary in the west and east ends of the lower choir, few obvious sutures can be found in the regularity of the horizontal courses.

If the archaeological evidence is often ambiguous, so too is the evidence of style. Above all, we should challenge the assumption that a particular master mason would necessarily use the same forms over a prolonged period of time. On the contrary, it is reasonable to assume that if a campaign extended over many years, the master mason might be inclined to experiment with different forms and even (at the instigation of the patron or under the influence of continuously changing taste) make certain changes in the overall plan. The Beauvais choir was a structure of unprecedented type, and as work progressed new problems were encountered that might lead a mason to reach toward new solutions. Indeed, the building bears witness to a restless striving toward new forms.

It is particularly important to note that a certain overlapping might take place between a campaign that has been isolated on the basis of style and a campaign recognized through breaks in the regularity of stone coursing. This is because the forms used in the earlier work will have a way of imposing themselves on the later designers for mechanical as well as artistic reasons. Thus, in vaulting the western bays of the nave aisles of Troyes Cathedral, for example, Anthoine Colas in the 1460s was forced to respect the existing rib and arch springers dating from around 1300. He was thus unable to impose his own forms until one bay later.[24] Thus, the power of forms had a way of transcending the mechanical divisions between campaigns.

A final caveat involves our expectations as to what exactly a masons' workshop might be. Was there a highly centralized system of direction with the master contractor determining every aspect of design? Did the workshop operate as a unified group involving arrivals and departures of teams numbering in the scores or hundreds? While we can never achieve any degree of certainty, owing to the lack of documentation for thirteenth-century construction, it seems possible that a High Gothic workshop might resemble its Late Gothic counterpart in embodying a high degree of flexibility. Thus, given the large pool of semi-skilled labor in a city like Beauvais, it is likely that while the master mason might be someone with cathedral-building experience from one of the many ecclesiastical workshops of northern France, his assistants might include local masons who would remain in Beauvais in the case that the master mason might leave to seek work elsewhere.

Chronology: The Evidence of Style

Given the fact that the study of the stylistic characteristics of the choir of Beauvais Cathedral can allow us to recognize certain zones that embody a clearly defined stylistic handwriting, and that comparisons with other monuments can allow us to fix this handwriting in its temporal context, it seems best now

[24] Murray, *Building Troyes Cathedral.*

to embark on a more intense exploration of the stylistic elements of the choir.

An analysis of the lower parts of the choir reveals the existence of two distinct types of stylistic handwriting: one in the eastern aisles of the transept and exterior walls of the choir straight bays, and the second in the hemicycle and the piers of the main arcade. The former handwriting (Figs. 85–88, 92–95) is one of mass and mural plasticity, reminiscent, in very general terms, of the architecture of Chartres, Reims, and Laon cathedrals. The walls and arches are thick, the compound and attached piers (Fig. 12a) are made up of a series of rectangular steps with attached shafts, and the freestanding piers (Fig. 12c) are *piliers cantonnés* of a type identical to those in the Amiens nave dated in the 1220s (Fig. 144). The latter are somewhat too small for the size of the arches dictated by the design of the compound piers. It is possible, therefore, that the Beauvais workshop became subject to strong influences from Amiens a short time after the inception of the work. The capital sculpture and transverse arch and diagonal rib profiles are also similar to the forms of the Amiens nave. A type of window frame molding with an undulating profile (Beauvais, south transept façade; Fig. 44) can be understood in terms of links with the same source (Amiens, north transept). The base moldings of the Beauvais transept (Fig. 14) are bulbous, with a heavily projecting lower torus, similar to the profiles of the Amiens nave (Fig. 145).

The handwriting found in the Beauvais hemicycle (Figs. 115, 116) is one of slender supports, thin walls, sharp profiles, and optical illusion. These more sophisticated forms can be found in the radiating chapels, the ambulatory, and the hemicycle, as well as the piers of the main arcade (Fig. 12b), with their playful adaptation of the basic *pilier cantonné* design. The changing forms of the base profiles (Fig. 14) as well as the evolution of the sculpture of the capitals in the main arcade suggest that it was laid out in a west-east sequence, since the western piers have bulbous moldings, whereas at the east end, adjacent to the hemicycle, the projection of the lower torus becomes less, placing the design in closer proximity to the moldings of the hemicycle and ambulatory. The fact that the hemicycle is misaligned with the main body of the choir (Fig. 10) reinforces the impression that the two parts of the building were laid out as different campaigns.

The two different architectural modes meet in the choir aisles (Figs. 98–114). The lower walls of the outer aisle have plinths and piers of the transept type, yet at the level of the capitals and vaults the beaked type of abacus and capital and the sharp transverse arch profile resemble the forms of the radiating chapels and ambulatory. Thus, the internal logic of the building would suggest that work on the transept preceded that on the hemicycle. This is confirmed by the evidence afforded by comparisons with contemporary buildings. Whereas the transept is similar in overall plan to that of Chartres Cathedral, and many of the details match those of the Amiens nave, the forms of the hemicycle (beak capitals, slender detached shafts, and shallow molding profiles) are more comparable with the Amiens choir (Fig. 148) and the Sainte-Chapelle and the work of Pierre of Montreuil (Figs. 165, 169, 170), suggesting a date in the 1240s. It is true that there is a certain *retardataire* element in the chapels in the simple forms of the window tracery (Figs. 56, 57), but the same forms are present in the transept (Figs. 43, 45), and the continued use of the double-lancet window with oculus is also a feature of Reims Cathedral.

The sacristy/treasury chambers (Figs 47, 48) also fit into the same framework and were constructed from west to east. It is evident that the lower eastern chamber (Fig. 119), with its oddly-slanting exterior wall, different molding types, and well-developed star-shaped abaci, does not go with the western two-story construction. The western part (two stories) was built at the same time as the north transept. Only later was a third story added over the western chambers, and an additional room was built to the east.

The new evidence provided by the endowment of the chaplaincies of the altars of Saint Denis and the Madeleine (1238 and 1256; Fig. 7) as well as the knowledge that the axial chapel of the Virgin was endowed by the bishops Robert of Cressonac and William of Grez (the latter the first bishop to be buried in the chapel, in 1267) provides confirmation for the hypothesis that the radiating chapels of the hemicycle were put to use only in the late 1230s, the 1240s, and 1250s.

The same conclusion was reached independently by Michael Cothren, who has recently completed a study of the stained glass of the radiating chapels.[25]

The episode of the struggle of 1232–1239 provides further evidence, though of a circumstantial nature, to support the hypothesis of a west-to-east sequence. It would be difficult to imagine a start on such a lavish and expensive undertaking as the Beauvais transept, with its massive towers, directly after the financial crisis provoked by the confiscation of episcopal revenues. On the other hand, the hemicycle is very much "reduced Gothic," with no dado in the chapels, tracery that was simple and cheap to produce, and a reduction both in mass and adornment.

Conclusion

On the basis of the evidence summarized above, we may consider the construction of the lower choir of Beauvais Cathedral as falling into two main phases (Figs. 21, 22). The first began in 1225 and included the eastern aisles of the transept arms and the outer walls of the choir aisles, and the second phase ran from the late 1230s to the 1240s and included the radiating chapels and main arcade up to the triforium sill.[26] A third phase (1250s–1260s) gives us the upper choir from the triforium sill to the high vaults. The name of the appropriate bishop may be applied to designate each of these phases: thus, we will discuss the cathedral of Bishop Miles of Nanteuil, of Robert of Cressonsac, and William of Grez. The first phase is particularly complex, since it seems that soon after the start of work on the outer aisles of the choir and the eastern aisles of the transept, the workshop came under intense influence from Amiens—only thus can we explain the appearance of the characteristic *piliers cantonnés* on the east sides of the transept arms. Separated by the bulk of the old fire-damaged cathedral, two crews worked on the two flanks of the new choir. The crew on the south side tended to adopt more progressive forms than its counterpart on the north. The demolition of the old choir in the 1230s and 1240s allowed for the completion of the main arcade and the hemicycle and radiating chapels. A provisional roof at the level of the triforium still covered the choir until the last phase of completion in the 1250s and 1260s.

---

[25] M. W. Cothren, "The Thirteenth-Century Glazing of the Choir of the Cathedral of Beauvais," Ph.D. diss., Columbia University, 1980.

[26] The stylistic unity of the transept tower bays (extremity of each eastern transept aisle) suggests that each of these bays was brought to the height of the vault relatively quickly (by 1232), as reconstructed in our axonometric drawings. However, it is also possible that work on the upper tower bays was delayed until our second phase (1240s) and that an archaic style was employed.

CHAPTER IV

The Cathedral of Bishop
Miles of Nanteuil: An Ambitious
High Gothic Synthesis

Miles of Nanteuil had been bishop-count of Beauvais for seven to eight years when his cathedral was burned in the great fire of 1225. The charter issued by the bishop-count in that year (Appendix A) makes it quite clear that he provided both the initiative for the rebuilding of the cathedral and a major part of the funds for the fabric. The term "the cathedral of Bishop Miles of Nanteuil" is intended to convey this fact, as well as to provide a useful label for the construction that took place immediately after 1225. It has been seen that Miles belonged to a line of powerful bishop-counts who had presided over the see since the eleventh century. The struggle with the king that began in 1232 ended his episcopacy and sharply reduced the independence of the bishop-counts. This struggle may be seen, to some extent, as the personal vendetta of the regent, Blanche of Castile, against the proud bishop. On the other hand, the struggle also reflected the general intensification of control on the part of the Capetian monarchs, noticeable already in the reign of Philip Augustus. We may remember that Bishop Philip of Dreux had been re-

proached by his chapter in 1214 for conceding too much to this monarch. King Louis IX's demand in 1232 for his *droit de gîte* had the bishop over a barrel. If he conceded, he could expect little sympathy from his chapter, since he had given up episcopal privileges that he had sworn to defend. If he refused, then he could expect retaliation from the king. A third dimension of the struggle of the 1230s was the economic one: driven by a need to raise cash for his ambitious new architectural project, Bishop Miles was leaning heavily upon the bourgeois of Beauvais. Thus, we are told that Miles was in financial distress within five years of the beginnings of construction on his new cathedral, and that his excessive exactions were an additional factor behind the uprising of 1232.

These considerations enable us to gain a deeper understanding of the historical significance of the cathedral of Bishop Miles. It was an expensive project funded partly through the bishop-count's ability to tax the bourgeois of Beauvais, and it expressed the powerful independence of the bishop-counts and their chapter. It was begun in 1225 but left unfinished with the confiscation of episcopal temporalities in 1232. How much was built in this seven-year period?

It has been seen that there is a vocabulary of more massive, distinctly more archaic forms in the western part of the outer choir, from the transept towers to the base of the hemicycle. On the other hand, a very different vocabulary is found in the radiating chapels and main vessel. That the transept mode preceded that of the radiating chapels is demonstrated by the nature of their junction in the choir aisles—the former exists at a lower level in the building. We therefore designate this older part of the choir "the cathedral of Bishop Miles," in other words, the work begun in 1225 (Figs. 21a, 22a). This early work probably extended up to the vaults in the terminal bays of the transept arms, since the arches and ribs fit very comfortably with the shafts, capitals, and abaci that support them. The keystones in these tower bays are also of a simpler type than those in the adjacent bays of the transept (Figs. 85–88, 92–95) or in the choir aisle. The tracery patterns of the small roses in the terminal bays of the transept aisles fit into the context of the 1220s–1230s (Notre-Dame of Paris, west façade), and it is unlikely that this tracery would have been installed before the construction of the vaults. On the other hand, in the adjacent middle bays in the transept arms, the termination of the first campaign saw masonry brought up only to the level of the triforium sill, since beaked capitals and sharp profiles for the transverse arches are used about that point (Figs. 89, 96).

In the aisles of the choir straight bays, the early work extends as far as division 8 and as high as a point below the level of the capitals of the vaults of the outer aisle (Fig. 55). The evidence for this lies in the discovery of a single axis between divisions 5 and 8 coupled with the existence, at G 8, on the south side, of a base resembling those in the transept (Fig. 114).[1] In the north aisle (Figs. 100–104) a

change in the masonry (height of the courses reduced) is visible three courses below capital level in bay B 6 7. The outer wall was brought up to the level of the windowsill at a very early stage; this is evident since a windowsill was placed in B 6 7. It must have been realized very soon afterward that a window here was impossible owing to the double-level sacristy/treasury, and the wall was continued upward on the same plane, leaving the sill in place.

In the adjacent bay (B 7 8) a "window" was also begun (Fig. 106). Here a double-story sacristy was never planned, and the window jambs were carried on upward with the intention of glazing the topmost part, above the level of the sacristy roof. The bases for the jambs and the central mullion of this "window" (most of which are nineteenth century) are coursed in with the screen wall that constitutes the "window," and no irregularity can be detected. The stylistic vocabulary changes sharply as we go from the exterior wall of the outer aisle at B 7 8 to the wall forming the northern base of the crown of radiating chapels (Figs. 98, 99, 104). The break must come just to the left (west) of the bundle of shafts in the angle between the wall of the aisle and the wall joining at ninety degrees to form the base of the crown of radiating chapels.

In the envelope of the south aisles the forms of the first phase of work continue east as far as division 8. They are visible in the surviving bases attached to the interior surface of the envelope at G 7 and G 8 (Figs. 109, 114). On the other hand, the jambs and mullions of the chapel windows at G 6 7 and G 7 8 (Fig. 111) are rather more sophisticated, with multiple shafts for the window tracery. The undulating moldings used in the jambs of these windows relate the work to that found in the transept arms. It might be suggested that this is evidence for the existence of a more progressive team at work on this, the south side, which was more visible from the Rue Saint-Pierre. The exterior enclosing arch of chapel G 7 8 (Fig. 53), with its little rosettes set in the mold-

---

[1] The equivalent base on the north side at B 8 was restored in the nineteenth century.

ings, closely resembles the forms of the radiating chapels. The wall forming the termination of the outer aisle and the southern base of the crown of radiating chapels (Figs. 112, 113) clearly displays the more fully developed stylistic vocabulary of the radiating chapels. The suture runs just to the right (west) of the bundle of shafts in the angle between the outer wall and the chapel wall at G 8.[2]

The lower parts of the great buttresses at division 8 were laid out in conjunction with the earliest work, 1225–1232. The buttresses on both sides of the choir at this point are aligned with the grid system of the body of the choir and the transept, and their details are similar to those found in the buttresses at the western end of the choir. On the south side (Fig. 54) the lowest part of the staircase turret attached to the east of this buttress extends much farther to the east then is necessary. The redundant thickness is reduced by means of a heavy molding at the level of the sill of the chapel window. This projecting block of redundant masonry, entirely refaced in the nineteenth century, may be the remains of some earlier scheme for the base of the hemicycle. To what height was this buttress brought during the first phase of construction? Although the stones of the exterior surfaces of the buttress show little obvious sign of change, several bits of evidence suggest a height about halfway up the jambs of the chapel windows. The buttress encloses a staircase turret, and a change occurs in the dimensions of the treads of the stairs at this level, where the width increases from about 0.32 m (one foot) to about 0.36 m. If we assume that this marks the height of the earliest work, included will be the lowest staircase turret window (Figs. 54, 55), which is quite different from the windows in the upper parts of the turret. The lowest window is larger in both width and height; it is very well coordinated with the flow of the spiral staircase (unlike the upper windows), and it bears a close resemblance to its counterparts at Amiens Cathedral. The other four windows

above this level are much smaller, eccentrically placed, and poorly coordinated with the stairs.

As the staircase was continued upward beyond this height, an opening was made into the interior of the cathedral through the wall at the southern base of the crown of radiating chapels. This wall belongs to the second phase of construction. A wooden door closes the turret at a height just about this level. A final note suggesting that the lower parts of this buttress were begun before the radiating chapels: inspection of the exterior surfaces to the east of the buttress and turret reveals a most awkward transition from the lower parts of the turret to the first radiating chapel—although the surfaces here have been almost entirely refaced in the nineteenth century.

In the equivalent staircase turret on the north side attached to buttress B 8 (Fig. 49) similar changes can be detected in the dimensions of the stair treads and the forms of the windows, suggesting that early work (1225–1232) went up to about the same height. As on the south side, the top of this early work is marked by the presence of a door inside the staircase. The lowest part of the buttress and turret join the first chapel with considerable irregularity, contrasting sharply with the effortless transition at the equivalent spot at Amiens Cathedral.

We have surveyed the perimeters of the first campaign, the cathedral of Bishop Miles, which included the east side of the transept arms, the outer walls of the choir, and the western chamber of the sacristy/treasury complex. Each of these areas should be examined in more detail both in order to justify the chronology that has been proposed, as well as to define the genius of the designers.

The Thirteenth-Century Transept

The thirteenth-century transept of Beauvais Cathedral (Figs. 75–77, 120, 121) has gener-

[2] I had originally believed that the break was a little farther to the east. I am grateful to John James who brought the suture to my attention.

ally failed to attract the attention of visitors or scholars. The transept central vessel and western aisle, brilliantly lit and spacious, are the dazzling work of the Late Gothic architect, Martin Chambiges. The thirteenth-century eastern aisle, on the other hand, is dark and heavily encumbered with furniture.[3] In each transept arm three tall arches open into the eastern aisle. On the north side, the innermost arch and the crossing pier were rebuilt after the collapse of the crossing tower in 1573. On the south side, however, all three arches are original. The two outer arches (F G H 5) are rounded in form; they were designed with the compasses set at a relatively short radius. The geometry of the inner arch (E F 5) is quite different; the radius of the compasses was increased and a much more vertical kind of arch results. The transverse arches of the inner choir aisle echo this steeper form.

In the transept arm the two outer arches of the main arcade, with their rounder forms, belong to the cathedral of Bishop Miles of Nanteuil; the inner arch adjacent to the crossing was completed at a later date. All three arches have a double order: an inner square order flanked by rounded roll moldings, and an outer order with its angles also softened by rolls (Fig. 13). This type of profile is very common in Gothic architecture and is found in Amiens and Chartres cathedrals, Notre-Dame in Paris, and many other churches of the twelfth and thirteenth centuries. The soaring three-bay arcade opens into the eastern aisle of the transept, forming the base of an L-shaped corridor of space, which turns at ninety degrees to continue directly into the tall inner aisle flanking the central vessel of the choir (Figs. 120, 121). Each of the three bays of the eastern transept aisle has its own different kind of elevation.

The bays at the extremities of each transept arm (Figs. 85–88, 92–95) were intended to form the lowest parts of towers (never built), and they have an appropriately massive structure. The towers were to rest upon the two ex-

terior walls, which have great thickness (ca. 1.80 m at the lowest level), while the inner sides of the towers were supported by massive transverse arches (ca. 1.34 m in thickness) which are received by great compound piers, at B 5 and G 5 (Figs. 12a, 83). The interior elevation of each tower bay is organized in three stories: a great window, a passage composed of six trilobed arches arranged in a band, and rose windows opening both toward the exteriors of the façades and toward the east. The exterior walls are characterized, above all, by their appearance of heavy plasticity. The enclosing arches of the lower windows are very deep; the depth of the middle passage is emphasized through the existence of openings (now blocked) giving on to the parallel exterior passages, and the roses are enframed by rounded arches of such projection that they resemble little barrel vaults.

The transverse arches defining the inner sides of the terminal bays of the transept aisles have a double-order profile just like that of the main arcade. If the overall profile formed by these arches may be understood in terms of a square, the shape formed by the diagonal ribs of the tower bays is distinctly triangular (Fig. 13). Here an almond-shaped central order with its sharp edge pointing downward is set upon a flat-surfaced strip flanked by rolls. The pierced keystones of both the tower-supporting bays in the transepts are formed of undecorated Os.

The vocabulary of forms found in the supporting elements is very regular. Square-set capitals with heavily projecting abaci are used for the main, central orders of the transverse arches, while the outer orders of the main arches and the diagonal ribs are received on smaller capitals. When grouped together, the abaci of these three different types of capital form a regular series of right-angled steps.

Each capital is defined by a very heavy upper square abacus and a rounded lower neck. The designer has preserved a proportional distinction between the major and minor capi-

---

[3] The north transept is dominated by the enormous astrological clock constructed in the 1860s by M. Verité. The south transept was occupied by an organ tribune. Heavily damaged in World War II, this tribune has been recently removed.

tals: the former are considerably taller than the latter. The transition from the circular neck to the widely projecting square abacus is effected by means of a bell-shaped core, which flares outward toward the top, with a sharply defined upper rim. In one of the capitals (B 5), this bell-shaped core dominates the whole composition, and in all of the others, it constitutes the prime organizing element. Around this core are arranged crockets: blades of stylized foliage, starting as a broad leaf at the base, and diminishing in thickness as they curve outward toward the top, where they are terminated in a budlike knob. In most of the capitals of the small type, the crockets are merely applied to the corners, so that the knob provides a bracket for the projecting angle of the abacus. One of the larger capitals (B 5) also shares this simple arrangement. Most of the larger capitals, however, have additional shorter crockets in the interstices. The stark simplicity of the crockets, the bell-shaped core, and the heavily projecting square abaci lend to these capitals a strong resemblance to their counterparts in the nave aisles of Amiens Cathedral (1220s).[4]

Considerable variety is apparent in the details of the crockets at Beauvais, especially in the ridges and furrows that form their central "spine." The central crocket on capital A 5 (outer wall of the north transept) has five ridges; at E 5 we find crockets with four ridges, while elsewhere the use of two ridges predominates. One capital does not conform in any way to these specifications, lacking the central bell-shaped core as well as the surrounding crockets. At B 6 (Fig. 87), to the east of the north transept arm, we find fleshy leaves, with their stems forming the angles of the capital and their rounded lobelike crinkled edges rising to touch the angles of the abacus. Clearly an experiment in the Beauvais Cathedral workshop, this formula was never repeated. The presence of this exotic experimental type, as well as the very simple capital at B 5, may indicate that this level of the northern

transept arm was constructed a little earlier than the southern arm.

Progressing downward from the arches, ribs, and capitals, we come to the supporting piers and applied shafts. The freestanding piers at B 5 and G 5 (Fig. 12a) have sixteen shafts: four for the major transverse arches, eight more for the outer orders of these arches (two per arch), and four for the diagonals. The major shafts are placed on the four main axes of the pier (north, south, east, and west), and the minor ones are set in the angles formed by the series of square steps. It is interesting to note that each of these steps making up the body of the pier corresponds exactly to a royal foot of 0.325 m. Each of the sixteen shafts is terminated at its base by an attic molding of the water-holding type (Fig. 83). Unlike the western transept crossing piers at Amiens Cathedral, the piers at Beauvais lack base moldings for the right-angled corners protruding between each of the sixteen shafts. Each of these shafts has a small plinth, and all of these plinths sit on top of an eight-sided raft, which has a champfered edge. The pier plinths are somewhat ungainly in their general appearance, which is a result, mainly, of the rather loose relationship between the individual plinths for the shafts and the octagonal raft on which they sit. The crossing piers at Amiens show a much tighter control of the design process. The Beauvais piers resemble the tower-supporting piers in the main arcade of the choir of the church of Saint-Leu-d'Esserent (Fig. 174).[5]

Such are the free standing piers in the tower bays at the extremities of the transept arms. Attached to the exterior walls in this part of the building are various parts of the same vocabulary of forms, with the same arrangement of shafts placed in stepped angles and the same type of plinth. The series of right-angled corners and the substantial shafts run directly from the supporting members into the window jambs, lending to the latter a distinctly massive "structural" appearance.

[4] For the chronology of Amiens Cathedral, see A. Erlande-Brandenburg, "La Façade de la cathédrale d'Amiens," *Bull. mon.*, CXXXV, 1977, pp. 253–293.

[5] For Saint-Leu-d'Esserent, see E. Müller, *Le Prieuré de Saint-Leu-d'Esserent*, Pontoise, 1901; and A. Fossard, *Le Prieuré de Saint-Leu-d'Esserent*, Paris, 1934.

The tracery of the lower windows of the towers is composed of an eight-foiled oculus whose rim is held by (and merges into) the molding of the inner order of the window frame. Two pointed, uncusped lancets occupy the lower part of the window; their heads merge with the rim of the upper oculus. The central mullions have a cylindrical shaft in front, with a champfered edge in the rear, toward the glass surface. The capitals of the two window-enclosing arches have bold, square abaci, whereas the capital of the central mullion has a rounded abacus. Such windows exist to the north of the north transept (in the façade) and in the façade of the south transept. The eastern bay of the north transept remains blind, owing to the existence of the sacristy, and the eastern window of the south transept is a replacement unit dating from the Late Gothic period.

Three of the four roses in the upper parts of the transept tower bays are original, that to the east side of the north transept being a sixteenth-century restoration. The thirteenth-century roses have twelve petals defined by spokes that have the form of a double-cylinder, grasping the glass between the two rounded sticks. The spokes have rather heavy bases and capitals. The heads of the petals are formed by interlocking round arches (north side of the north transept), trilobed round arches (east side of the south transept), or trefoils that sit directly on top of the spokes (south side of the south transept).

Delicate trilobed arches enliven the six openings of the middle "triforium" level.[6] Each arch is formed of two pieces of stone, joined at the crown. They are supported on top of rather mechanical-looking crocket capitals borne by little columns sitting on top of bulbous bases. The outermost unit on each side of the group of six openings is partially blocked by solid wall. A somewhat awkward appearance results, but the arrangement was necessitated by structural considerations: the preservation of a sufficient mass of masonry at the points of support.

It is possible to determine one aspect of the builders' intention regarding the central segment of the interior walls of the transept façade. Attached to the capital of the main arcade of the south transept (Fig. 93), at the point where it meets the interior of the façade, there still survives a fragment of a small trilobed arch. Thus, the middle "triforium" level of the inner façade was to have continued as a horizontal band in much the same way as in the transepts at Chartres Cathedral. A similar band of trilobed arches runs across the west façade of Notre-Dame of Paris.

On the exterior façades of the transepts, the same horizontal band of trilobed arches would also have continued across the three segments: eastern aisle, central vessel, and western aisle. The gable of the central portal, had such a gable been intended, would have projected in front of this horizontal band.

The same three levels (window, "triforium," rose) are directly translated on the exterior. On the transept façades (Figs. 42–45) these three horizontal zones are framed by emphatic vertical divisions: flat-surfaced buttresses, which would have formed the angles of towers. The western buttress on each side houses a staircase turret. This staircase was partially accommodated in a square block projecting to the east of the main buttress impinging in an uncomfortable way into the space of the adjacent window. The east side of the tower is supported by an L-shaped element formed by two buttresses meeting at ninety degrees. The mass of the buttresses (both east and west) is reduced by means of heavy moldings at the level of the windowsill and at the base of the horizontal "triforium" passage. These two cornices determine the main horizontal divisions of the lower choir. The upper one, decorated with crockets, carries great gargoyles placed at the center point of the front surfaces of the buttresses. Two further

---

[6] The passage in the Beauvais transept is thus not a true triforium, since no aisle is present.

offsets (*glacis*) are applied to the front surface of the buttress between the lower sill and the upper crocket cornice. The rhythm thus created was one that would be carried all the way round the Gothic choir.

On the south transept (Fig. 44) the original buttress to the left (west) of the tower bay was partially demolished in the sixteenth century, and a highly decorated polygonal staircase turret has been constructed (see Chapter VII). The interior staircase was rebuilt at the same time. The equivalent buttress on the north side is original. A careful comparison of the lower windows of the north and south transept towers (Figs. 15, 43, 45) suggests that the unit on the north side is the older of the two. The outer order of the window frame on the north side is a roll molding received on a generously sized square capital. The capital has simple, spikey crocket blades at its corner angles. It is supported by a massive shaft resting on a plinth that sits on the windowsill. To the inside of the large outer shaft of the window frame a right-angled corner projects—this seems somewhat redundant, since its surfaces do not reflect any of the planes of the walls. An undulating molding formed of a central concavity flanked by two rounded rims then effects the transition into a slender cylindrical shaft for the outer order of the tracery. The capitals of the tracery are circular. In the equivalent window frame in the south transept façade, however, the redundant right-angled corner is omitted, and the crocket capital of the enclosing arch bears an additional spike. The outermost order of the southern window frame projects beyond the surface of the wall, forming a kind of hood molding, penetrating into the crocket band above. The surface of the wall above the window is thus cantilevered out beyond the lower surface, providing more space for the parallel passageways. It is hard to avoid the conclusion that the southern window exhibits the more fully developed forms. This projecting molding is a

feature of the windows of the nave and transept of Amiens Cathedral, and its appearance at Beauvais is in accord with other Amiénois features that appear after the start of work in the interior of the transept arms. A mural strip (not present in the north transept window) now divides the window from the flanking buttress.

The treatment of the middle passage level is very similar on each side: six small arches with trilobed tops, supported by cylindrical columns with four-crocketed capitals.

The rose of the north façade (Fig. 42), with its tracery composed of strangely archaic looking intersecting round arches, is tightly framed by an undulating molding of considerable projection. On the south side (Fig. 44) a completely different arrangement is found; the same kind of molding is used, but it forms a square frame leaving spandrels that are decorated with trefoils echoing the arrangement of the central rose of the west façade of Notre-Dame in Paris.[7] Also reminiscent of Notre-Dame is the tracery of the roses on this side: facing east a rose with trilobed arches, and facing south a rose with trefoils placed over trilobed arches. These patterns would be very much at home in the early 1230s, the trefoil over trilobed arches being used in the gallery of Notre-Dame in Paris and in the triforium of Troyes Cathedral and the abbey church at Saint-Denis.[8]

On the north side, the eastern face of the transept arm is concealed by the adjacent sacristy and treasury chambers, which were built simultaneously with the transept. The three-story elevation of the south transept tower turns the corner into the eastern wall of the transept arm (Fig. 46). Here the elevation is similar to that of the façade, but the exterior wall, above the level of the windowsill, has been thickened somewhat. This thickening is reflected in the fact that the wall enframing the window impinges further on to the sloping surface of the windowsill. This extra thickness

---

[7] For Notre-Dame of Paris, see M. Aubert, *Notre-Dame de Paris, sa place dans l'histoire de l'architecture du XIIe. au XIVe. siècle*, Paris, 1920.

[8] R. Branner, *Saint Louis and the Court Style in Gothic Architecture*, London, 1965, Figs. 33, 37, 43.

is disguised through the use of a generous-sized molding composed of two rounded rolls separated by a smoothly curved concavity. The molding is terminated at the bottom by a curving spur. Such an arrangement can also be found on the north transept of Amiens Cathedral. The extra thickness was not added after the construction of the windows; it represents a change effected at a point between the initial planning stage and the actual construction. Because of the presence of the extra wall thickness, the massive shaft supporting the window frame has been omitted, and we go directly from the undulating molding to the fine shaft for the outer order of tracery. The mullions of the tracery and the pattern in the upper part of the windows are post-1284 collapse. Similar thickening is applied to the wall of the adjacent chapel in the body of the choir. There is every reason to suppose that the choir chapel was constructed simultaneously with the transept.

Thus, it has been seen that each of the bays forming the bases of the towers intended for the eastern aisles of the transept is a stylistic unity, the north side seeming a little older than the south. This is not to say that one was constructed after the other. It is far more probable that in order to achieve a rapid pace of construction in the seven years from 1225 to 1232, two teams worked separately on the two sides of the building, with the northern team slightly in advance of the southern. Since the northern transept arm was contiguous with the sacristy/treasury complex, and since the treasury was needed for the considerable sums of cash for paying the workers, the decision to push on with the north side was an entirely logical one.

The comparison between the two transept arms also reveals the tendency of the southern team to thicken the exterior walls. This was partly to gain extra width for the double passageways, but it also reflects the growing awareness of structural problems that had not

been fully anticipated at the start of work. The angle between the east wall of the south transept and the exterior wall of the south choir aisle had to support a massive pillar for the flying buttress system. This pillar would have to overhang the generous-sized windows below. It was for this reason that the walls were thickened. Despite the extra thickness, the window frame of the southern chapel at G 6 7 (Figs. 37, 50) has failed, and an extra mass of masonry was added on the west side of the window.

Returning to the interior of the transept, when the middle bays of the eastern transept aisles (B C 5 6, F G 5 6; Figs. 76, 77, 89, 96) are compared with the terminal bays just examined, four differences are discernible. First, the lowest level of the elevation (toward the east) now opens into the low outer aisle of the five-aisled body of the choir. The arch has two orders with flat surfaces and angles softened by rolls, just like the main arcade of the transept. Second, the supporting elements are no longer compound piers, as before (in the extremities of the transept arms), but are now *piliers cantonnés* (Fig. 12c) with a main body in the form of a cylinder about 1.38 m in diameter, and four smaller shafts about 0.50 m in diameter.[9] The planning and dimensions of these *piliers cantonnés* are identical to the comparable units in the nave of Amiens Cathedral of the 1220s (Fig. 144); it is evident that the piers of Beauvais are direct copies. This observation is of considerable importance since it provides a firm indication for the dating of the Beauvais transept. Equally important is the presence of a strangely archaic feature in the base moldings of the *piliers cantonnés* in the Beauvais transept (Fig. 84)—a string of diamonds around the groove of the molding.[10] This feature is a reference back to the dogtooth patterns favored by Romanesque designers.

The *piliers cantonnés* at Beauvais are mismatched in size in relation to the compound

---

[9] For a discussion of the use of this type of pier, see D. Kimpel, "Le Développement de la taille en série dans l'architecture médiévale et son rôle dans l'histoire écono-

mique," *Bull. mon.*, CXXXV, 1977, pp. 195–222.

[10] The diamond points are found in the bases of piers C 5, C 6, and F 5 (not F 6).

piers. The stepped body of the compound piers determines the thickness of the transverse arch, which is about 1.34 m. This is rather thicker than the transverse arches of the main arcade in the cathedrals of Chartres, Reims, or Amiens, and it is too thick for the diameter of the cylindrical body of the *pilier cantonné* that receives the arches. At C 5 and F 5 in the main arcade of the transept (Figs. 76, 77, 82), the outer order of the arch finds no resting place on the abaci of the slender piers, and it has been necessary to add small projecting corbels (hereafter termed "angle corbels"), which receive the outer order of the arch. The capitals are organized in two zones: square capitals that receive the inner orders of the main arcade, which resemble the forms already described, and the main capital of the cylindrical body of the pier itself. The main capital has two ranks of crockets and a level of small leaves arranged just above the necking. One of the major crockets from the body of the capital provides the bracket necessary to support the projection of the angle corbel incorporated into the main abacus.

The third main modification in the middle bays of the eastern transept arms (Figs. 82, 89, 96) is the use of a pointed window rather than a rose in the uppermost level of the elevation. The window is formed of an oculus cusped in nine petals whose rim merges with the pointed enclosing arch of the window. Below the oculus are two pointed arches (like the heads of lancets without the vertical body). The central mullion of this composition is linked with the central shaft of the six-bay triforium, which is composed of trilobed arches. Thus, the tracery of the window is on the same plane as the arches of the band triforium, which leads to a considerable loss of the mural plasticity inherent in the tower bays of the transept.

Certain aspects of the arrangement of this upper window strike one as tentative and not fully successful. The upper windows are rather stubby and seem somewhat "squashed in" beneath the vaults. Such an observation is, of course, somewhat subjective; we may "feel" uncomfortable with the stubby nature of these windows in relation to the soaring verticality found elsewhere in the building. Further details confirm the suspicion that the design problems in this bay have not been fully resolved. The linkage between the window and the triforium involves not only the central mullion, but also the flanking shafts that receive the window-enclosing arch. To the left of bay B C 5 in the north transept (Fig. 89), this shaft is squeezed uncomfortably into the meager space between the shaft for the diagonal rib and the first colonnette for the triforium. To the left of the shaft is a small strip of masonry, which is discontinued after two courses (Fig. 87). This small detail is of enormous significance in our interpretation of the chronology of Beauvais Cathedral, since it indicates that a start had been made on a second bay, just like the tower bay, but that this work had been interrupted. Had it been continued, it would have provided a narrow framing device for the triforium just as exists in the transept tower bays. This provides confirmation that work had begun in the transept terminal bays and was advancing toward the center of the building. It is quite possible that the original intention was to complete all of the windows of the inner aisle in the same fashion as the transept terminals: in other words, with a deeply recessed rose.[11] This intention was never realized, however, since the first campaign (the cathedral of Miles of Nanteuil) was interrupted at the level of the triforium in the middle bay of each transept arm. In the same bay in the south transept arm, careful inspection reveals the presence of a similar narrow framing strip on the right (south) side of the triforium, indicating that the bay was also begun at the same time as the tower bay but also was left incomplete.

It will be seen that the equivalent units in the eastern part of the building (triforium of the ambulatory; Figs. 115, 116) are characterized by a quite mechanical kind of perfection.

---

[11] Such roses are used in the galleries of several churches, including Mantes and the choir of Saint-Etienne at Caen. It is not certain whether they were used in the gallery of Notre-Dame of Paris.

No hesitations or experiments here! It would be quite inconceivable to find that having achieved this degree of accomplishment in the ambulatory and choir aisles, the workshop would then begin an uncomfortable series of experiments in the transepts. In other words, the evidence suggests that the windows and triforium of the inner aisles were begun in the ends of the transept and that work proceeded to the center of the building and then to the east.

The hypothesis that work began in the terminal bays of the eastern aisles of the transept arms is confirmed by a study of the way in which these bays have been pegged by means of ties to prevent the piers from being pushed outward by the weight and thrust of the transverse arches and vaults. Such pegging was standard practice in the process of cathedral construction. Obviously, once an arcade is complete, each pier will be subject to thrust from the arches on either side, but in the process of building such an arcade, the most recently constructed pier would be subject to thrust from one side only and would therefore be tied to the previous pier. The terminal bays in the transept arms (Figs. 85, 88) were heavily tied with wooden beams (all of which have been removed except one in the north transept) as well as with iron rods attached to iron eyes sunk into the masonry. The arches adjacent to the crossing piers are not tied (Figs. 75–77). The extensive use of tie beams in the terminal bays of the transept was necessary in a situation where these bays were brought up to their full height and vaulted but were not yet receiving support from the adjacent bays.

The last important feature of the middle bays of the transept aisle (Fig. 88) is the use of a transverse arch profile that has been very much reduced in thickness. Such a narrow transverse arch (Fig. 13) with a profile in the form of an almond shape flanked by squarish shoulders and two rolls defines the inner sides of the middle bays of the transept arms (at C 5 6 and F 5 6). This type of sharpened transverse arch may be associated with the second phase of construction of the choir in the 1240s. Since a square capital with its broad abacus was no longer appropriate to support the triangular shape of such a profile, a new kind of capital was adopted (Figs. 90, 91, 96, 97), with a front angle jutting forward in the form of a beak (*chapiteau, tailloir à bec*). The adoption of this thinner transverse arch type and the beaked capitals disturb the harmony that had existed between the ribs, arches, and supports in the transept terminal bays. At C 6 and F 6 (Figs. 91, 97) the beaklike abacus used for the thin transverse arch looks much too narrow for the diameter of the shaft that supports it. The necking of the capital seems almost as wide as the abacus, and the graceful proportions of the capitals in the transept terminal bays have now been lost.[12] The diagonal ribs and the main transverse arches both share the same capitals in these bays. The angular projections of the abaci to accommodate the diagonal ribs add to the makeshift appearance of these capitals.

A last note must be added concerning these middle bays of the transept aisles. The keystone of the vault in the north transept arm (Fig. 88) has a cartouche that suggests a sixteenth-century date. The vault of this bay was restored after the collapse of the crossing tower in 1573. The keystone of the equivalent middle bay of the south transept aisle (Figs. 95, 96) is quite different from the simple O form in the bays at the extremities of the transept. Here the outer rolls of the rib do not simply disappear into the keystone but are carried on around it to create a lozenge shape enclosing the central circle.

At the innermost bay on each side, the transept aisle (Figs. 88, 90) turns at ninety degrees to join the choir aisles. The vault of this bay on the north side had been rebuilt in the sixteenth century, after the collapse of the crossing tower brought down the northeast crossing pier and the adjacent pier to the east. On the other (south) side the vault is a thirteenth-

---

[12] These capitals may have been reworked. There are signs that the necking may have originally existed at a lower level but was subsequently chiseled off.

century one, resembling its neighbor to the south.

As the transept aisle turns to join the inner aisle of the choir, some interesting formal and structural problems are encountered. The type of support, the *pilier cantonné*, had been borrowed from Amiens Cathedral, where it served in a straight arcade with a relatively slender wall. Where this wall turns at ninety degrees in the crossing at Amiens, appropriately massive crossing piers are used. At Beauvais, on the other hand, the same pier is used in conjunction with a thicker wall at points (C 6 and F 6) where that wall makes a ninety-degree turn to effect the transition from transept aisle to choir aisle (Fig. 90). In the transept aisles, this thick wall occupies the entire diameter of the body of the pier and is received on top of heavy, square-set capitals of the type noticed in the extremities of the transepts. The outer orders of the arches are received by angle corbels. The corresponding wall of the choir aisle is very thin—it has to be, since there is no more room left on the pier for a thick wall. The slender wall is expressed in the arcade of the inner aisle by means of a wedge-shaped profile like the one that had been used for the diagonal ribs. On the south side it is noticeable that the pier at the critical turning point (F 6) lacks the diamond points characteristic of the bases of its counterparts at F 5, C 5, and C 6, suggesting that while its shape may reflect the thinking of the first phase, its actual construction may have been delayed. The matching pier on the north side (C 6) has diamond points. The upper parts of this pier were entirely rebuilt in the sixteenth century and again in the nineteenth century. Nineteenth—century photographs show it pushed inward by the weight of the two arches it supports.

Thus, the choice of an inappropriate unit of support at this key position where the wall turns at ninety degrees has led to an amusing step-by-step sequence. The wall of the arcade of the inner aisle has been reduced in thickness for mechanical reasons (no room on the pier); the thinner arcade wall then determines a reduction in the mass of the next piers to be built at C 7 and F 7—work of the 1240s. Stylistic changes are often the result of internal problems of a formal kind rather than extraneous influences.

The Choir Aisles: North Side

Double aisles flank the central vessel of the choir (Figs. 120, 121). The lower outer aisle, with vaults some thirteen meters above the pavement, extends for two bays before ending abruptly (and somewhat uncomfortably) with the blind wall at the base of the crown of radiating chapels. This outer aisle forms a small pool of rather poorly illuminated and claustrophobic space. The inner aisle, on the other hand, tall and elegant, with vaults twenty-one meters above pavement level, continues for three bays before merging into the ambulatory.

It is in the choir aisles (Figs. 98–100) that we find the meeting point of two formal vocabularies: one associated with the transept (lower parts of outer walls) and one associated with the ambulatory and radiating chapels (pier C 7, vaults of outer aisle, and entirety of inner aisle). In the envelope of the building, the attached supports for the transverse arches and vaults are of the same type as those used in the envelope of the transept. However, the intermediary piers of the aisles have been reduced considerably in bulk. Whereas at bay divisions 5 and 6 the intermediary piers are substantial *piliers cantonnés*, at C 7 a much thinner unit is used, suggesting that this pier belongs to the second phase of construction.

The exterior wall of the outer aisle on the north side (Fig. 98) is blind because of the existence of the two chambers of the treasury and sacristy. The unrelieved masonry surface of bay B 6 7 is framed by a formeret, or wall arch. In the early fourteenth century a stone staircase was set against the wall to provide access to a clock. A change in the stone coursing is apparent just below the level of the capitals (Figs. 103, 104). The height of the average stone course becomes somewhat less in the upper part of the wall. It is probable that this change marks the extent of the first campaign, the cathedral of Miles of Nanteuil.

The lower part of the exterior wall of the outer aisle in the adjacent bay to the east (B 7 8) is pierced with a doorway leading to the eastern sacristy chamber that lies beyond (Fig. 98). Although the eastern sacristy chamber did not exist when the wall was built, it was certainly planned at that time, yet the decision was made to treat the wall surface as a window (Fig. 106). The surface is framed by a formeret, which is supported by shafts forming part of the attached piers at B 7 and B 8. A narrow strip of wall then flanks a "window"—but this window is rather a half-hearted one, since the lower part has to remain blind, blocked by the adjacent sacristy. The jambs and central mullion of the window are formed of slender shafts flanked by chamfered edges. Around the outer frame runs an undulating molding similar to the types found in the transept windows. The top part of the window rises above the sacristy roof and is glazed. The tracery embodies spherical triangles and certainly belongs to the period after 1284.

Did the builders not realize that a full window would be blocked by the sacristy? This seems improbable since the stone wall filling the lower part of the window was not added later—the stones are coursed in with the jambs and central mullion. The rather unhappy composition probably resulted from the growing realization that these bays of the outer aisle on the north side are dark, enclosed by solid masonry to the north and east. The window was an attempt to relieve the monotony of blank masonry.

Terminating the two bays of the outer aisle is another blind wall (Fig. 98), forming the base of the crown of radiating chapels. This terminal wall is pierced with a doorway into the staircase turret, above which is a sill and then a composition rendered in blind tracery. The forms used in the blind tracery are very different from those found in the almost useless window in the outer wall at B 7 8. In the latter work, the simple bases used for the

jambs and central mullion and the undulating moldings of the frame bear a general resemblance to the forms found in the windows of the transept, whereas in the terminal wall, the bases have a wide lower level, a narrower upper part, and a chamfered edge between the two. The mullions of the terminal wall are simple cylinders set on the surface of the wall, and the tracery has four lancets: two groups of two, topped by oculi with four cusps (turned diagonally), the total composition surmounted by an oculus with eight cusps, suggesting that the terminal wall was finished only in the second phase of construction, in the 1240s.

At the height of the vaults in the northern outer aisle of the choir (Figs. 98, 99), the thick, flat-surfaced transverse arches, characteristic of the terminal bays of the transept (and the aisles of the nave of Amiens Cathedral), have been abandoned, and instead, a narrow triangular profile has been adopted, similar in type to the form used for the diagonal ribs in the transept aisles (Fig. 13). In a certain sense, this constitutes a change of mode: a form is translated from a minor role to a major one. Similarly, the use of the thinner intermediary aisle pier at C 7 obviously reflects this shift of mode.

The use of thinner, sharper arches also necessitates a reconsideration of the type of capital used, since such a profile does not lend itself to the use of broad, square abaci. At bay division 7 in the northern outer aisle (Fig. 103–105), the designer has used beaked capitals for the main transverse arch and diagonal ribs, and square-set capitals for the wall arches. The main capital still has bold crockets arranged around a central "trumpet-bell" motif; the smaller capitals have crocket and other foliage forms. The most striking feature of the capitals, however, is the lack of a harmonious relationship between the size of the beaked abacus and the diameter of the neck and supporting shaft of the main transverse arch. The shaft belongs to the same vocabulary of forms as that isolated in the transept, and it has considerable bulk. It is obviously too large for the fine transverse arch and beaked abacus, which are characteristic of the eastern end of the choir and the upper parts. In this context, the thin arch and the beaked abacus are used with very slender shafts. The keystones of the two vaults of the outer aisle are little different. The western unit has a pronounced central O enclosed in a lozenge having its angles projecting out between the ribs. The eastern unit has the lozenge arrangement without the O.

The outer choir aisle may thus be seen as the meeting point between two different modes of articulation. In the lower, outer wall, the mode associated with the transept continues beyond division 7, suggesting that the envelope was laid out at the same time as the transept. In the capitals and vaults, however, the use of beaked capitals (not at home on the thick supporting shaft) and refined moldings for the transverse arches reflect elements of a vocabulary that is used in a mature form only in the ambulatory and radiating chapels. The inner aisle belongs entirely to the 1240s and will be examined later.

The Choir Aisles: South Side

Although similar in general terms to the northern aisles, the south choir aisles (Figs. 107–114) exhibit some important differences. The absence of a treasury or sacristy on this side rendered it possible to glaze the eastern window of the south transept arm and the two bays of the outer wall of the aisles at G 6 7 and G 7 8. However, the window at G 6 7 has been partially blocked by a fourteenth-century buttress inserted to strengthen the window frame (Fig. 108). This consolidation, completed after the collapse of 1284, was considered necessary since the window frame here partially supports the great buttress that would have ascended to form the corner of the south transept tower. When this work of con-

solidation was undertaken (Fig. 55), the tracery of the chapel window at G 6 7 was rebuilt, reusing certain elements of the old tracery, notably the mullion base in the east jamb of the window and the adjacent free-standing base. The original frame of the window is formed by two very slender shafts, one for the enclosing arch and an inner one for the transept lancet. Running parallel to the shaft is a concave molding framed by two rounded rims. At its lowest point, this molding curves gracefully into the base molding of the outermost shaft.

The wall of the adjacent chapel in bay 7 8 has not been modified in any way. The interior wall is enclosed in a wall arch of some projection (Fig. 111). The almond-shaped molding of this wall arch is carried by beaked capitals with well-developed foliage (the simple bell-shaped core is dominated by the foliage elements). A considerable expanse of wall surrounds the window opening. The window jambs are equipped with two small shafts to receive the inner and outer order of the window tracery. The same multiplicity of shafts is apparent in the central mullion. Parallel with the shafts runs a concave molding flanked by two rounded rims. The lowest part of the molding runs directly into the base molding of the shafts in a similar fashion to the adjacent chapel to the west. The tracery itself is composed of four lancets with uncusped pointed heads grouped into two major units. Each major unit is topped by a quatrefoil inside a rose. A large eight-cusped oculus crowns the whole composition. The closest parallels for this pattern can be found in the windows of the Sainte-Chapelle in Paris (Fig. 168) and in the eastern nave chapels of Notre-Dame in the same city (Fig. 162), suggesting a date in the 1240s. The intense linearity of the composition (produced by the multiplicity of shafts) can be found in works such as the chapel of Saint-Germain-en-Laye (Fig. 172).[13]

At division 7, the intermediary aisle pier, presumably a slender unit to match its coun-

[13] Branner, *Saint Louis and the Court Style*, Figs. 31, 32, 42. For Saint-Germain-en-Laye, see G. Houdard, *Les Châ-teaux royaux de Saint-Germain-en-Laye, 1124–1789*, 2 vols., Paris, 1909–1911.

terpart on the north side, has failed and has been replaced by a sixteenth-century undulating type (Fig. 110). The sixteenth-century restorers must have felt that this was an inherently weak spot in the building, since a solid wall was added, linking the pier with the outer wall. The continuous space of the outer aisle has thus been subdivided to form clearly defined individual chapels. Sixteenth-century work is also noticeable in both the aisle clerestory and triforium of bay 6 7 and in the triforium at 7 8.

As on the north side, we are led to distinguish between two sets of forms, one characteristic of the transept, and the other characteristic of the ambulatory and radiating chapels. In the envelope, the attached shafts and their bases (up to division 8) are of the same type as those found in the transept and belong to the first campaign of construction (Figs. 109, 114). However, the tracery pattern of the window of the chapel at G 7 8 (Fig. 111) and the tracery applied to the wall that forms the base of the radiating chapels (Figs. 112, 113) belong to a later phase. Similarly, at the level of the capitals and vaults, the beaked capitals and the slender transverse arches are later.

The exterior surfaces of the southern aisles (Fig. 50) are organized in two main levels following the pattern laid down in the transepts: an unrelieved lower wall capped by a heavily projecting molding for the windowsill and an upper wall framing the windows, where the surface is set back somewhat. The sill molding continues around the buttresses to form the lowest weather molding, or *glacis*. The mass of the buttress is reduced at this point on its front surface and sides. The upper level of the aisle wall is defined by the horizontal cornice of crockets that runs over the chapel windows. As the crocket band runs around the two great buttresses, two gargoyles slant inward from the corners of each buttress, as opposed to the single, central gargoyle in the transept buttresses.

In this upper level, the main buttresses are punctuated by two further *glacis*, which bring reductions in mass to the front surface. It has been seen that the thickness of the wall in the western chapel (G 6 7) was increased in the course of construction to help support the buttress above (Fig. 51). Despite this thickening, the enclosing arch of the window has been distorted by the weight of the buttress, an additional support has been inserted into the window, and the tracery was reworked at some date around 1300. The eastern jamb of this window is original; two slender shafts are placed to receive the tracery elements, and parallel to the shafts, and outside them, is the familiar undulating molding composed of a central concavity flanked by two rounded rims. At its lowest point, this molding turns and merges into the base of the jamb as a spur.

The lowest part of the wall of the adjacent chapel (G 7 8; Figs. 52, 53) continues through from the buttress H 7 into the buttress H 8 without any sign of dislocation. The mullion bases for the window tracery of chapel G 7 8 provide for double shafts in the window frame and the central mullion. Once again, these shafts are flanked by the familiar undulating moldings. On the east side of the window this molding turns into the base as a curved spur, whereas on the west it turns inward in a right-angled corner. A mural strip divides the window jamb from the flanking buttress on each side. On the left (west) side of the window the lower courses match those of the adjacent buttress and are neatly tongued in (Fig. 52). At a point several courses below the window capitals, this regularity is lost, however, suggesting that the upper wall, including the enclosing arch of the windows, was added at a point when the buttress already existed. The tracery of the window at G 7 8 is of a type that is considerably more developed than that found in the transept. The rosette-studded hood molding over the window frame (Fig. 53) is similar to the moldings used in the radiating chapels at the eastern extremity of the building (Figs. 56, 57). The two gargoyles placed in the spandrels of the window-enclosing arch, designed to evacuate any water that might collect in the vault pocket, also reflect the similar arrangement in the radiating chapels. All of these factors lead one to disassociate the upper part of this window from the work on the transept and choir straight bays (1225–1232; Fig. 55) and to suggest a rather later date (1240s).

The Sacristy and Treasury Chambers

The four chambers that served as sacristy and treasury nestle in the angle formed between the north transept arm and the northern flank of the choir. Seen from the exterior, the complex is three levels high on its west side and one level high on the east side (Figs. 47, 48). A jumble of different types of molding, different kinds of stone, and different wall planes presents itself, suggesting that the work was not executed as part of a single, unified campaign. Two main areas may be defined in the exterior surfaces. First, extending from the eastern buttress of the north transept to the bay division 7 is an area of wall extending above a prominent cornice. The wall is pierced by a tall window, which is divided by a transom into an upper and a lower part. The window has simple chamfered edges, no tracery, and is capped by a hood molding. The upper and lower parts of the window open into a vaulted upper chamber and an unvaulted lower chamber. The top edge of this first exterior zone is defined by a prominent weather-molding.

To the east and on top of this first zone are two further areas that seem to have been added at a slightly later date. To the east, the wall surface is inset, and a lighter, chalkier stone is used. A careful examination of the stones and coursing reveals that the first phase extends into the western jamb of the western window. The two windows piercing this area of wall are divided by a shallow pilaster. Whereas the wall on the west side of this pilaster is aligned with the transept, to the east the wall is angled inward toward the body of the church. The hood moldings used over the simple windows of this second zone differ slightly in profile from the types found in the first zone. The top of this second part of the complex is defined by a heavy band of crockets (mostly restored), which are considerably lower than the weather molding that topped the first area.

Finally, belonging to the same category of additions to the original structure, a third story was added over the western part of the complex. The eastern side of this uppermost chamber overhangs its substructure on the east side. The vaulted interior of the third story is lit with a simple window with chamfered jambs.

Seen on the plan (Fig. 6), the two chambers that constitute the ground level of the sacristy/treasury complex correspond to the bay divisions of the choir, the exterior buttress at division 7 constituting the massive wall between the two chambers, and the buttress at 8 being incorporated into the eastern wall. The western (older) of the two chambers is, in its interior, anonymous of stylistic features. It is unvaulted and its walls are entirely covered with wooden paneling and cupboards. It is lit by two windows, one pierced through the outer wall, and the other (considerably smaller) penetrating through the massive block that constitutes the buttress against the north transept façade.[14]

The eastern chamber is very different (Fig. 119). It is irregular in shape since the outer wall is not parallel to the inner wall, so that the depth of the chamber diminishes toward the east. The room is brightly lit by three windows, two in the northern wall and one in the eastern wall. The two northern windows are divided by a cylindrical shaft that receives the transverse arch of the two quadripartite rib vaults. All of the windows have simple chamfered edges.

The room is vaulted in two quadripartite bays, the transverse arch and the diagonal ribs being received on top of cylindrical shafts attached to the middle points of the north and south wall and to the four corners. The capitals have knobbed crockets supporting a star-

---

[14] A deep crypt exists under this chamber, accessible by means of a trap door in the floor.

shaped abacus.[15] The profiles of the ribs and arches, although wedge-shaped like the types used in the interior of the choir, are unique in the context of Beauvais Cathedral. A central almond-shaped molding is flanked directly by two rounded rolls and by two concavities. The keystones of the vaults are decorated with flat, rather sparse foliage.

The two upper levels are reached by means of stairs set in the thickness of the mass of masonry at division 7. Both upper chambers are vaulted with double quadripartite vaults with simple prismatic profiles for the ribs and arches, and crocket capitals. The walls are relieved by means of deeply recessed panels with pointed arches.

The Character and Extent of the Cathedral of Bishop Miles

The uniformity of the stylistic vocabulary in the parts of the building just described (eastern transept aisles and outer walls of the choir) indicates that this part of the building is the result of a single building campaign. The close links with the nave of Amiens Cathedral suggest that the campaign should be placed in the mid-1220s, directly after the fire of 1225. The main damage wrought by this fire was in the area of the wooden-roofed transept, which was immediately demolished to allow work to begin on the eastern aisles of the Gothic transept. The old choir, perhaps rebuilt in the 1190s with stone vaults, was left intact for as long as possible. High in the order of priority of construction was the eastern chamber of the sacristy/treasury complex, which would provide an admirable site office and deposit for the artisans' wages. The total extent of the first campaign is neatly defined by four staircase turrets, two in the buttresses at the base of the hemicycle and two in the buttresses to the west of the transept tower. The staircase in the southern transept was rebuilt in the sixteenth century, and the equivalent unit on the

north has been blocked in its lowest parts. Neither staircase has therefore been indicated on the plan (Fig. 6). It is significant to note that in all the original turrets the lowest steps are approximately one royal foot in width, whereas at a higher point (some six to eight meters) a wider step of 0.36 m is adopted. This suggests that the lowest part of each of the four staircases was begun at the same time.

The builders of the cathedral in the period between 1225 and 1232 hastened to complete the bases of the transept towers up to the vaults and to install the window tracery in these bays. The completion and vaulting of two towers at a height of twenty-one meters while the lower walls of the eastern parts of the choir had not yet been begun reveals the desire on the part of the administrators of the fabric to achieve the maximum possible showy effect.

One way to achieve such rapid progress was to employ two teams of masons who worked simultaneously on the two flanks of the choir. The southern team was the more progressive of the two and abandoned the simple chamfered edges of the window jambs used on the north side in favor of multiple shafts as found, for example, in the nave chapels of Notre-Dame in Paris. The presence of two distinct teams working on the two flanks of the choir and separated by the bulk of the old, half-demolished cathedral may explain the misalignment of the base of the hemicycle. The two teams developed a distinctly different approach to the handling of wall surfaces and the design of piers, the group on the north retaining a more three-dimensional and cumbersome approach. Thus, while the wall surface framing the window at B 7 8 is articulated in two orders, the equivalent surface on the other side (G 7 8) has only one order. On the north side (Figs. 16, 98, 104, 106, 113), additional shafts are incorporated at window level into the supports at B 7 and B 8, creating a more expansive kind of support. The existence of two different kinds of support at the

---

[15] Such abaci with star-shaped forms can also be found in the lower chapel of the Sainte-Chapelle and the church of Nogent-les-Vierges; see Branner, *Saint Louis and the Court Style*, Figs. 66, 72.

base of the hemicycle, expansive on the north (B 8) and more streamlined at the south (G 8) may have led to the error involved in the misalignment of the hemicycle. This error occurred at the point where one campaign stopped (1225–1232) and the next started (after 1238).

What of the overall intentions of the builders of the cathedral of Bishop Miles of Nanteuil? Certain aspects of these intentions will always remain unknown—for example, we can never be sure of the form intended by the original designer for the upper parts of the choir.[16] Similarly, it is impossible to determine whether the initial plan included a shallow hemicycle system, like the one that actually exists. While remaining aware of the speculative nature of our thinking here, it is certainly worth making a mental note of the fact that all the other great French churches with a pyramidal elevation (Bourges, Saint-Quentin, Le Mans, Coutances) employed a deep design for the east end, with either a double ambulatory or deeply projecting radiating chapels. Similarly, and in the same speculative vein, we might note that the broad spans of the Beauvais choir would find a more comfortable termination to the east in the slower rhythm of a five-segment hemicycle, rather than the staccato of the actual seven-part composition.

Embodied in the parts of the building completed in the first campaign is a five-aisled choir with a tall inner aisle continuing into the transept arms as an L-shaped corridor, flanked by a much lower outer aisle. The most important feature of the cathedral of Bishop Miles of Nanteuil was the lavish transept, equipped with towers, whose unified spaces were linked with the tall inner aisle.

The Stylistic Context of the Cathedral of Bishop Miles

Previous writers have found no place in their scheme of things for the cathedral of Bishop Miles of Nanteuil. This results from several factors: doubts about the chronology of construction, a failure to recognize the significance of the transept, and a preoccupation with the "classic" cathedrals of Chartres, Bourges, Reims, and Amiens.

Almost any commentary on High Gothic architecture will begin with Chartres and Bourges cathedrals.[17] The designers of Chartres Cathedral (Fig. 160), begun in 1194, created a massive three-story structure in which the height of the clerestory equals the arcade.[18] The great clerestory was made possible through the use of powerful flying buttresses. The choir has double aisles on each side, and the boldly projecting transept arms are flanked by towers. The articulation of the structure is appropriately massive, the most important innovation being the *pilier cantonné* composed of a central core flanked by four shafts where the core and the shafts alternate from octagonal to cylindrical.

Bourges Cathedral (Figs. 158, 159), begun

[16] Branner, "Maître de Beauvais," p. 78, suggested that the height of the choir central vessel was increased as part of a change of plan, but he adduced no archeological evidence for his assertion. It will be seen in Chapter v that evidence can be found for an increase in height introduced around 1250.

[17] See Grodecki, *Gothic Architecture*; and Bony, *French Gothic Architecture*. Kimpel and Suckale, *Die gotische Architektur*, provide a welcome alternative framework for the understanding of "High Gothic." Less emphasis is placed upon the power of certain paradigmatic "great buildings" and more attention is given to the dynamic relationship between architecture and patronage. Their treatment of the chronology of the Beauvais choir (350–361, 505–507) corresponds somewhat to the interpretation presented here. They are aware of the chronological priority of the northern

choir aisles and the historical importance of the struggle between bishop and king in the 1230s.

[18] Chartres Cathedral was constructed between 1194 and the 1220s, with work moving out from the crossing in a series of horizontal campaigns, the nave preceding the choir. The bibliography for Chartres is obviously immense; see esp. R. Branner, *Chartres Cathedral*, New York, 1969; M. J. Bulteau, *Monographie de la cathédrale de Chartres*, 3 vols., Chartres, 1887–1892; L. Grodecki, "Chronologie de la cathédrale de Chartres," *Bull. mon.*, CXVI, 1958, pp. 91–119; J. van der Meulen, "Histoire de la construction de la cathédrale Notre-Dame de Chartres après 1194," *Bull Soc. arch. Eure-et-Loir*, XXIII, 1965, pp. 79–126; and idem, "Recent Literature on the Chronology of Chartres Cathedral," *Art Bull.*, XLIX, 1967, pp. 152–172.

after 1195, is often presented as the antithesis to Chartres.[19] Chartres has a lavish transept; Bourges has none. Chartres has relatively limited spatial communication between central vessel and aisles; Bourges has more unified space. At Chartres the double aisles are the same height; at Bourges a tiered arrangement is used. Chartres is an architecture of mass; Bourges is an architecture of space.

High Gothic architecture is frequently interpreted in terms of a series of buildings that followed Chartres (notably Soissons, Reims, and Amiens cathedrals), a series of pyramidal structures following Bourges (Saint-Quentin, Le Mans, and Coutances), and then, finally, a group of buildings whose designers held out against the validity of these prototypes.[20]

This scheme can lead to an exaggerated assessment of the impact of the "classic" cathedrals of Chartres and Bourges. Soissons Cathedral provides a useful test of the validity of the traditional interpretation of High Gothic.[21] Was the choir of Soissons Cathedral a direct reaction to Chartres, or should it be understood as a parallel speculation? We are still ignorant of the exact starting date for Soissons—it might even predate Chartres. Certainly, there are enough striking differences between the two buildings (in plan, articulation of piers and molding profiles, mode of buttressing, etc.) to allow us to detach Soissons from Chartres and to see it as a parallel speculation, dependent upon local prototypes.

The Soissons choir provided inspiration for later generations in many different ways. This is particularly true of the purposeful double-rank flying buttress system, so much more economic than the cumbersome wagon wheels of Chartres. The builders of Reims Cathedral

may have studied the flyers of Soissons. Similarly, the streamlined exterior of the Soissons choir, with all the chapels of the same depth and the moldings of the buttresses coordinated to form horizontal bands swathing the exterior, anticipates the similar arrangement at Beauvais.

Reims Cathedral, begun in 1210, is much more than a variation upon the Chartrain theme and owes a considerable debt to the Soissons choir and a range of local monuments.[22] Its designers continued the structural speculations associated with the perfection of the flying buttress. The Reims flying buttresses are similar to those used at Soissons, except that the head of the flyer now butts the central vessel at the level of the *tas-de-charge* of the vault. At Chartres, Soissons, and Amiens the point of abutment is somewhat lower, corresponding to the vault capitals. The builders of the upper choir at Beauvais were to follow the pattern initiated at Reims. Also of significance for Beauvais, and particularly the cathedral of Bishop Miles of Nanteuil, is the sculptural quality of the walls at Reims. In the interior, this is expressed by means of a wall passage above the dado running around the aisles and ambulatory. The little rose windows set in the transept façades are framed by round arches of great depth, resembling the arrangement of the roses of the Beauvais transept. The window tracery of Reims Cathedral lies behind the forms employed at Beauvais, not only in the cathedral of Bishop Miles (the lower windows of the transept) but also in the later work in the radiating chapels. A small detail in the tracery at Reims provides confirmation for the west-to-east chronology at Beauvais. The earliest windows at Reims have two joints

[19] Bony, *French Gothic Architecture*, p. 198. For Bourges, see Branner, *La Cathédrale de Bourges*.

[20] J. Bony, "The Resistance to Chartres."

[21] C. Barnes, "The Cathedral of Chartres and the Architect of Soissons," *J. Soc. Arch. Hist.*, XXII, 1963, pp. 63–74; idem, "The Twelfth-Century Transept of Soissons: The Missing Source for Chartres?" *J. Soc. Arch. Hist.*, XXVIII, 1969, pp. 9–25; E. Lefèvre-Pontalis, "La Cathédrale de Soissons," *Cong. arch.*, LXXVIII, 1911, pp. 315–337; R. Pestell, "The Design Sources for the Cathedrals of Chartres and Soissons," *Art History*, IV, 1981, pp. 1–13; J. Ancien, *Contribution à l'étude archéologique: Architecture de la cathé-*

drals de Soissons, privately published, 1984. Carl Barnes is currently rethinking the chronology of Soissons Cathedral on the basis of newly discovered written sources.

[22] For Reims Cathedral, see H. Reinhardt, *La Cathédrale de Reims*, Paris, 1963. Aspects of the debate over the chronology of construction at Reims are discussed in R. Branner, "The Labyrinth of Reims Cathedral," *Soc. Arch. Hist.*, XXI, 1962, pp. 18–25; J.-P. Ravaux, "Les Campagnes de construction de la cathédrale de Reims au XIIIe. siècle," *Bull. mon.*, CXXXVII, 1979, pp. 7–66; and F. Salet, "Chronologie de la cathédrale [de Reims]," *Bull. mon.*, CXXV, 1967, pp. 347–394.

in the lower rim of the oculus between the heads of the two lancets, and the later windows have only one joint.[23] At Beauvais the windows in the transept have two joints and the windows in the radiating chapels only one.

The cathedral of Amiens (Figs. 142–148), begun in 1220, provided the most important single source of inspiration for the builders of Beauvais Cathedral at all periods of construction, both in terms of details and in the overall conception.[24] This is hardly surprising, given the close geographical proximity of the two cities and the fact that Amiens was begun only five years before Beauvais and therefore provided a ready source of up-to-date solutions to the problems of designing piers, rib and arch profiles, capitals, and so on. The similarities and differences between the two monuments can thus reveal much about the intentions of the designers of Beauvais Cathedral. The design of both buildings evolved significantly during the course of construction, and it is necessary to consider not only their relationship in their completed form, but also their interaction at various points of time during construction.

The completed Amiens, with vaults forty-two meters above the pavement, embodied not only unprecedented height but also a proportion that is steeper than Bourges, Chartres, or Reims. The relationship of width to height is almost 1:2 (pavement to keystone) at Chartres, 1:2.5 at Bourges, 1:2.6 at Reims, and very close to 1:3 at Amiens. It has been seen that Beauvais embodies this same (1:3) relationship. However, since the central span at Beauvais is wider, its height is commensurately greater. At Amiens new emphasis is placed upon the unified space of the lower central vessel and aisles. The sill of the triforium marks the halfway point of the elevation, and the soaring arcade is thus taller than the clerestory. At Chartres the arcade and the clerestory had been equal in height. The visual impact of the new spatial economy of Amiens is enhanced through the use of a *pilier can-*

tonné type that is much slenderer than the equivalent units at Chartres or Reims. The designers of the cathedral of Bishop Miles of Nanteuil at Beauvais have adopted an identical pier type and the same profile for arch and rib moldings. They have even fixed the sill of the high triforium at approximately the same height (about twenty-one meters) as at Amiens. We should try to envisage the half-finished Amiens nave as it looked around 1230, completed up to the triforium sill in its entire length, and turning at ninety-degree angles into the western aisles of the transept arms. The lofty arcades of the transept of Beauvais correspond with this initial work at Amiens both in terms of height and in many of the details. However, in the Beauvais transept and choir the span of the arches has been increased, and unlike Amiens, the earliest work at Beauvais already embodies a pyramidal elevation (tall inner aisle and low outer aisle). Moreover, in the Beauvais choir as completed, the relative expansion of the width of the central vessel at the expense of the inner aisle is evident.

The nave clerestory at Amiens (Fig. 146), which belongs to the 1230s and 1240s, may provide an idea of the intentions of the designers of the cathedral of Bishop Miles. The upper wall of the Amiens nave is conceived as a series of receding surfaces. The triforium is set back somewhat from the level of the arcade—the eye is able to read this from the fact that the bundle of three shafts that ascends to the high vaults from the arcade pier is increased to five at the level of the triforium sill. Similarly, the level of the glass of the clerestory window is set back behind the level of the triforium. The articulation of the upper elevation is achieved by means of a myriad of slender shafts. The triforium is linked to the clerestory with continuous mullions. Thus, the entire upper elevation above the triforium sill becomes a screen of tracery and glass. The use of only three shafts (not five) in the arcade reduces the bulk of the bay divisions and pro-

---

[23] For example, in the clerestory windows at the west end of the nave of Reims Cathedral.

[24] G. Durand, *Monographie de l'église Notre-Dame, ca-* *thédrale d'Amiens*, 3 vols., Amiens and Paris, 1901–1903; Erlande-Brandenburg, "La Façade de la cathédrale d'Amiens."

duces a more slippery surface over which the eye can glide.

The choir at Amiens, from the 1240s to 1260s, embodies important new features that allow us to draw close parallels with the contemporaneous work completed at Beauvais under Bishop Robert of Cressonsac and William of Grez. These similarities will be explored in Chapter V.

Thus, Amiens and Beauvais cathedrals both bear witness to a restless search for new forms, and both embody repeated modifications introduced to transform and update the original vision. Both buildings may have been increased in height during construction. The increase in height at Beauvais is particularly interesting, since it involved a building where the arcade was intended to have an enhanced importance in the spatial economy. There is thus an exaggerated clerestory superimposed on an exaggerated arcade.

Continued experimentation with the balance between the spatial economy of the lower and upper parts of the building and speculations that included the glazing of the triforium and the development of new types of flying buttress and window tracery mark the decades between 1220 and 1240 as a fertile period of invention and innovation rather than a phase where designers and their patrons were content to go on copying the great classic prototypes of Chartres and Bourges.

In many respects, the cathedral of Bishop Miles of Nanteuil was far closer to the choir of Le Mans Cathedral in design than to Bourges. The Le Mans choir was begun after 1217—recent scholarship has favored a date in the 1220s for the choir chapels.[25] The three straight bays of the central choir, flanked by double aisles, are terminated to the east by a seven-segment hemicycle. The pyramidal section of the choir (low outer aisle, tall inner aisle) is intersected by a transept, as at Beauvais. The actual transept at Le Mans is considerably later, but the idea was presumably part

of the original design. Another striking similarity between the two choirs is the progressive opening of the bays toward the east end, so that the hemicycle is preceded by an enlarged bay. Of course, notable differences also exist, especially in the use of a deep hemicycle system at Le Mans (double ambulatory and deep chapels), as compared with the very shallow composition at Beauvais. The buttressing system at Le Mans is much more solidly constructed than at Beauvais, especially as far as the outer uprights are concerned. In the hemicycle, the outer uprights are doubled, so that two flyers meet the intermediary upright, forming a Y shape. In the straight bays, a point of critical weakness at Beauvais, the Le Mans designers have filled in the spaces between the lateral apsidal chapels with solid masonry, making a formidable base for the outer uprights.

Coutances Cathedral, like Le Mans and Beauvais, has a pyramidal section, with a tall inner aisle. Mussat has proposed a starting date around 1230 for the Coutances choir,[26] but Herschman has argued for a date in the 1220s, at a time when it might have influenced the start of work at Le Mans.[27] For two buildings as close in general design principles (pyramidal section) and in time and geographical location, Coutances and Le Mans certainly display spectacular differences. Especially striking is the difference in the arrangement of the flying buttresses in the two buildings. Whereas Le Mans has intermediary uprights, at Coutances the flyers take a single leap from the outer uprights to the central vessel. The two alternative methods of buttressing a double-aisled structure were studied by the designers of the Beauvais hemicycle, who seem to have started out with a system similar to that found at Coutances, but then turned to a double-rank system with intermediary uprights. This question will be explored in Chapter V.

The collegiate church of Saint-Quentin is

[25] Salet, "La Cathédrale du Mans"; A. Mussat, *La Cathédrale du Mans*, Paris, 1981.
[26] A. Mussat, "La Cathédrale Notre-Dame de Coutances," *Cong. arch.*, CXXIV, 1966, pp. 9–50.

[27] J. Herschman, "The Norman Ambulatory of Le Mans Cathedral and the Chevet of the Cathedral of Coutances," *Gesta*, XX, 1981, pp. 323–332. Herschman expresses strong reservations about the idea of a "family" of Bourges.

often presented as a prototype for the Beauvais choir.[28] Most recently, Jean Bony has seen in the enlarged clerestory of Saint Quentin the same kind of "concentrated disproportion" as at Beauvais.[29] However, this observation does not have anything to do with the cathedral of Bishop Miles of Nanteuil, which probably would have had a relatively low clerestory. The characteristic pyramidal stacking of the spaces at Saint-Quentin is found only in the idiosyncratic billowing spaces of the ambulatory. The Saint-Quentin choir is intersected by a nonprojecting transept whose eastern arcade does not express the tiered arrangement of low outer space and tall inner space. Pierre Héliot also has argued for a connection between Saint-Quentin and Beauvais, especially in the arrangement of the triforium and clerestory windows of the ambulatory (stubby lancets).[30] Héliot also believed that the use of beaked capitals at Beauvais was related to the similar arrangement at Saint-Quentin (capitals of the freestanding piers of the chapel mouths). However, neither beaked capitals nor stubby lancets formed part of the cathedral of Bishop Miles of Nanteuil, but rather the beaked capitals belong to the second campaign (1240s) when they could have been derived from a host of other sources.

The designers of the cathedral of Bishop Miles of Nanteuil clearly had access not only to the recently constructed cathedrals of High Gothic, particularly Amiens, but also to more venerable prototypes. Thus, the considerable degree of mural plasticity inherent in the transept walls of Beauvais should be understood in the context of twelfth-century monuments such as Laon Cathedral, where the upper level of the transept has wall passages and windows framed by arches so deep that they resemble little barrel vaults.[31] The great wingspan of Beauvais (expansive transept) should be seen not only in the context of Laon, but also in relation to northern cathedrals such as Arras and Cambrai.[32] For the combination of pyramidal elevation with spacious transept we might look as far back as the third abbey church at Cluny. However, a more recent (and geographically closer) prototype existed for the peculiar spatial organization of the Beauvais choir with tall L-shaped corridors turning at ninety degrees from inner choir aisle to transept aisle—the galleries of Notre-Dame of Paris.[33]

In our preoccupation with Chartres and Bourges as paradigmatic Gothic churches, we sometimes tend to forget the enduring power of the cathedral of the capital city to influence the buildings of the area around the Ile-de-France. This influence resulted not so much from the fact that Notre-Dame offered compelling architectural solutions that no mason could manage to ignore, but more from the growing prestige and economic strength of the capital. Moreover, the workshops of Notre-Dame were active over a prolonged period, from Early to Late Gothic, and the cathedral thus provided a mine of architectural solutions that would have been considered up-to-date. Certain monuments have fairly literal interpretations of the elevation of Notre-Dame (for example, Saint-Sulpice at Chars and the collegiate church of Notre-Dame at Mantes).[34] Other designers might take a particular feature of Notre-Dame—for example, the double aisles, as at Saint-Laurent at Beaumont-sur-Oise, Saint-Séverin in Paris, or Saint-Pierre-et-Saint-Paul at Montreuil-sous-Bois. Theories of Gothic development as structural progress have led to the belief that the invention of the

[28] P. Héliot, *La Basilique de Saint-Quentin et l'architecture du moyen-âge*, Paris, 1967.

[29] Bony, *French Gothic Architecture*, p. 288.

[30] Héliot, *La Basilique de Saint-Quentin*, pp. 61–62.

[31] For Laon Cathedral, see most recently W. Clark and R. King, *Laon Cathedral, Architecture*, I, London, 1983. See also Bony, *French Gothic Architecture*, Figs. 162–165. William Clark kindly brought to my attention the similarity between the deep-set roses in the transepts of Beauvais Cathedral and the clerestory of the church at Boult-sur-Suippe;

see C.-H. Besnard, "L'Eglise de Boult-sur-Suippe," *Cong. arch.*, LXXVIII, 1911, pp. 170–185.

[32] L. Serbat, "Quelques Eglises anciennement détruites du nord de la France," *Bull. mon.*, LXXXVIII, 1929, pp. 367–435.

[33] Bony, *French Gothic Architecture*, Fig. 133.

[34] Ibid., Figs. 134, 147. For the influence of Notre-Dame, see Aubert, *Notre-Dame de Paris*. For Mantes, see J. Bony, "La Collégiale de Mantes," *Cong. arch.*, CIV, 1946, pp. 163–220.

flying buttress and the popularity of the tall clerestory had rendered the gallery obsolete, yet under the influence of Notre-Dame and the great galleried churches of Normandy and the northeast, many designers and their patrons continued to favor an elevation with a generously proportioned gallery as the middle level. Sexpartite vaulting was not rendered obsolete overnight by the use of quadripartite vaults at Chartres and Soissons.

The cathedral of Bishop Miles of Nanteuil was conceived in a milieu that had not fossilized into clearly defined "families" of related buildings. The attempt to impose clear lines of filiation on the monuments of the 1220s and 1230s tends to ignore the extraordinary inventiveness of the period. On the one hand, Beauvais was touched by the immediate past and close vicinity (especially Amiens), but on the other hand, the designers also drew on the more distant past. The great cathedrals of the north were close at hand (Normandy and Flanders).[35] Notre-Dame of Paris was also available as a prototype, as were the many buildings of the Ile-de-France that owed their inspiration to the Parisian cathedral.

Two significant details can be found in such structures. First, it is common to find that the "classic" relationship between the diameter of the support and the thickness of the arcade wall as employed at Chartres, Reims, and Amiens is entirely absent, and that supports are relatively slender, necessitating a bracket or corbel to support the bundle of shafts that ascends to the vaults. Alternatively, other designers reduced the mass of this bundle by pushing the shafts backward into the mass of the wall so that the full roundness is not expressed (for example, at Saint-Leu-d'Esserent and in the nave of Gonnesse).[36] The same relatively skinny piers used with a thick arcade

wall led to the same expedients at Beauvais (see Chapter v).

Another feature particularly favored by the designers of the region that may have been derived from buildings related to Notre-Dame of Paris was the oculus used in the Parisian cathedral at triforium level to aerate the gallery roof. There is a similar use of oculi in the upper level at Champeaux and Chars, but much more common was the combination of an oculus with a fairly depressed pointed arch to form a window lighting the aisle, gallery, or clerestory.[37] At Beauvais, such oculi were used to light the eastern aisle of the transept, and it is possible that they were to have been continued around the inner aisles and ambulatory, creating an impression much like Mantes or the choir of Saint-Etienne of Caen.[38]

The diamond points in the torus of the base moldings of the *piliers cantonnés* in the transept arms of Beauvais can be found in the western bays of the nave of Notre-Dame of Paris and in a host of other buildings, especially to the north and east of Paris, from Taverny to Saint-Leger of Soissons.[39] The fact that Saint-Leu-d'Esserent has both diamond points and a type of compound pier very similar to those used in the Beauvais transept suggests that this area just to the north of Paris exerted a particularly strong influence in the early work at Beauvais.

The cathedral of Bishop Miles of Nanteuil was conceived at a time when many designers and their patrons were speculating on various kinds of adaptation of the galleried elevation. These speculations included the running together of gallery and the aisle spaces, as can be seen in the neighboring cathedral of Rouen and in the collegiate church of Eu.[40] Meaux Cathedral provides a useful demonstration of continuing interest in the galleried elevation

[35] M. Anfray, *L'Architecture normande, son influence dans le nord de la France aux XIe. et XIIe. siècles*, Paris, 1939.

[36] D. Bontemps, "La Nef de l'église Saint-Pierre de Gonesse et ses rapports avec l'abbatiale de Saint-Denis," *Bull. mon.*, CXXXIX, 1981, pp. 209–228; Müller, *Le Prieuré de Saint-Leu-d'Esserent*.

[37] Bony, *French Gothic Architecture*, Figs. 134, 145.

[38] Ibid., Figs. 148, 292.

[39] Examples of such use of diamond points can be found at Auvers-sur-Oise, Bury (choir), Cambronne-lès-Clermont, Champagne-sur-Oise, Beaumont, Mello, Mouy, Taverny, etc.

[40] For Eu, see Dr. Coutan, "Eu: Eglise Notre-Dame-et-Saint-Laurent," *Cong. arch.*, IC, 1936, pp. 388–412. For Rouen, see Chanoine Jouen, *La Cathédrale de Rouen*, Paris, 1932.

and various ways in which such elevations could be modified.[41] The choir of Meaux Cathedral, begun in the last decades of the twelfth century, has a galleried elevation related to that of Notre-Dame of Paris. The non-projecting transept and the galleries forming L-shaped corridors of space turning into the transept arms lend to Meaux a general similarity to the Parisian cathedral. In the 1250s work began to transform this elevation through the suppression of the gallery floor. A very tall inner aisle thus resulted. Saint-Leu-d'Esserent provides another example of a church where the original plan involved a spacious gallery, but where the gallery was suppressed in course of construction and the openings were partially glazed.

The pyramidal elevation of Bourges Cathedral has sometimes been interpreted as a speculation upon the elevation of Notre-Dame of Paris with its gallery floor omitted. The wheel can be invented twice over—in other words, we should consider the initial plan for the choir at Beauvais with oculi lighting the inner aisle and ambulatory in relation to galleried choirs such as Mantes and Saint-Etienne at Caen. What sets the cathedral of Bishop Miles of Nanteuil apart from these galleried structures is the enormous height of the inner aisle. The gallery of Notre-Dame of Paris is about eighteen meters high, whereas the inner aisle at Beauvais, under the influence of Amiens, rises to about twenty-one meters.

The Unfinished Cathedral of Bishop Miles: Conclusion

Thus, we are able to gain a glimpse of the vision of the builders of the cathedral of Bishop Miles of Nanteuil. This vision was an ambitious one—of a five-aisled basilica with a pyramidal elevation intersected by a spacious aisled transept with towers. Such a building had never before been realized in High Gothic and had only been anticipated in buildings such as Notre-Dame of Paris and Cluny III. Bishop Miles's ambitious theocratic program is strikingly conveyed in his Gothic Cluny III. If the vision was glorious, the means of execution were questionable. The financing of the operation was beyond even the wealthy bishop-count and his chapter. Moreover, the workshop was not subject to a high level of centralized control. This is revealed both by the acceptance of forms from the Amiens nave that were not fully in accord with the elements of the outer envelope of the transept (i.e., the *piliers cantonnés*) and in the lack of complete coordination between the two teams of masons at work on the two flanks of the choir. Certain features of the unfinished cathedral of Bishop Miles were to cause considerable headaches for the builders of the next phase, especially the use of two different kinds of support at the base of the hemicycle (at B 8 and G 8), a factor that may have caused the misalignment of the east end of the building and also the arrangement of the windows of the southern chapel G 6 7 and the eastern flank of the south transept at a point where a major upright for the flying buttress system would be necessary. The builders of the second phase were forced to place their upright overhanging the window, anticipating the overhang (*porte-è-faux*) used in the intermediary upright of the flyers all around the choir.

The construction of the cathedral of Bishop Miles of Nanteuil was interrupted in 1232 with the profound crisis associated with the loss of the bishop's revenues and the interdicts.

The leading members of the workshop may have left Beauvais to seek employment elsewhere. Work was resumed only with the end of the dispute, and with the accession in 1238 of Bishop Robert of Cressonsac.

---

[41] P. Kurmann, *La Cathédrale Saint-Etienne de Meaux, étude architecturale*, Bibliothèque de la Société française d'archéologie, I, Geneva, 1971.

CHAPTER V

The Cathedral of Bishops
Robert of Cressonsac and William of Grez:
Rayonnant Architecture on a
Colossal Scale

The six-year struggle with the king of France having ended with the submission of the bishops of Beauvais, peace returned to the diocese. The bishop's revenues were restored, and construction on the Gothic cathedral was resumed. The builders of the 1240s–1260s favored a different kind of architecture, with thin walls, brittle supports, and forms of articulation that suggest a Parisian background. A similar Parisian invasion (polyphony from Notre-Dame) affected liturgical music in the same years, overlaying the more archaic local tradition.[1]

Although Bishops Robert and William did not adopt the position of proud independence of Miles of Nanteuil, they were powerful as well as wealthy, and there is every reason to believe that they and their chapter respected the financial arrangements defined in the charter of Bishop Miles. Very little is known of Bishop Robert, except that he agreed to pay Louis IX his *droit de gîte* and that in 1248 he left on crusade with that monarch and died in Cyprus. Bishop William (1249–1267) was a

generous patron of the fabric of the cathedral and an enthusiastic builder. The episcopal chapel that he built was equipped with stained glass said to resemble the glass of the Sainte-Chapelle.[2] It is to be expected that he would have been an active patron of the new work on the cathedral. However, in 1266 a renewed struggle with the bourgeois of Beauvais led to royal arbitration. Most of the upper choir must have been finished during his episcopacy, although the inauguration took place under his successor, Renaud of Nanteuil. There were thus some thirty years of intense activity with a very large workshop well-financed with funds drawn from the regular income of the bishop and chapter. Within this thirty-year period, two distinct phases of construction can be discerned.

The sequence of foundations and endowments of altars (Figs. 7, 21, 22; Appendix A) suggests that the radiating chapels were under construction in the 1240s—a date confirmed by a recent study of the stained glass.[3] On stylistic grounds it can be demonstrated that the

---

[1] D. Hughes, "Liturgical Polyphony at Beauvais in the Thirteenth Century," *Speculum*, XXXIV, 1959, pp. 184–200.

[2] Hermant, *Histoire ecclésiastique*, II, pp. 754–755.

[3] Cothren, "The Thirteenth-Century Glazing."

chapels were built from the base of the hemicycle toward the center, with the axial chapel the last to be constructed.

Simultaneously with this work on the chapels, the choir of the old cathedral was completely demolished to allow the piers of the central vessel to be constructed. Changes in the type of base molding employed and in the capital sculpture reveal quite clearly that these piers were built from west to east, with the hemicycle last of all. The slender piers of the aisles at C 7 and F 7 also belong to this campaign. These piers having been completed, it was possible to build the arcade of the inner aisle with its triforium and clerestory and to vault the aisles and ambulatory (1245–1250). The upper central vessel was then completed between 1250 and 1272 in the more lavish style that we associate with the patronage of Bishop William of Grez.

Each of these parts of the building must now be examined in some detail in order to define the vision of the builders of the cathedral of Bishops Robert and William and to determine their stylistic affiliations.

Ambulatory and Radiating Chapels

The ambulatory and radiating chapels (Figs. 115–117) embody the most coherent and fully developed stylistic vocabulary of any part of the lower choir.

The tall U-shaped corridor of the ambulatory linking the inner aisles of the choir opens on one side into the radiating chapels (Fig. 118) and on the other into the central vessel. The space of the ambulatory is organized in three levels: the chapel openings, a band triforium, and low clerestory windows. The supports between the chapels are elegant, even dainty (Fig. 12e). A slender central cylindrical core (not coursed in with the chapel dividing walls) is flanked on three sides by skinny detached shafts, one on the front edge to receive the transverse arches of the ambulatory, and

two more on either side for the arches framing the mouths of the radiating chapels. Thus the pier resembles an ordinary *pilier cantonné* with one of the four shafts (at the back of the pier) replaced by the thin wall dividing the chapels. Two tiny shafts on either side at the rear of the pier receive the ribs of the chapel vault. In plan, the pier could equally well serve as a division between chapels in straight or in turning bays. The function of the pier as a division between turning bays is expressed not by the body of the pier, but by the plinth. The central body of the pier sits on top of an octagonal plinth whose two levels are defined by a chamfered edge in the middle. Each of the three detached shafts has its own small octagonal plinth, and the plinths of the side shafts (for the arches of the mouths of the chapels) are turned to reflect the angle at which the two outer walls of the ambulatory meet. These supports have sometimes been likened to the equivalent units at Reims,[4] but such a comparison must take into account the very great difference in mass—the piers at Beauvais are incredibly attenuated.

The arches enframing the chapels have a sharpened profile with a central almond-shaped molding flanked by two right-angled "shoulders" and two rounded rolls. This essentially triangular section is received on top of elegantly proportioned beaked capitals. In these capitals, unlike the beaked capitals found in the transept and at division 7 on the outer wall of the north aisle, there is a harmonious relationship between the slender necks and the boldly projecting beaked abacus. The central shaft of each pier continues upward to support the elegant beaked capital of the ambulatory vault (Fig. 117). The arcade wall is so thin that it allows a small segment of the central cylindrical core of the piers to continue upward, thus providing a base for an adapted version of the angle corbel now used to support the diagonal ribs of the ambulatory vault.[5]

The beaked capitals, slender shafts, and

4 Bony, *French Gothic Architecture*, p. 292.
5 This segment of the cylindrical core of the pier is reminiscent of the similar arrangement in the main arcade of Bourges Cathedral.

thin arcade wall are elements in a vocabulary of forms expressing the desire on the part of the designer to employ two-dimensional membranes stretched tightly between brittle supports. The design of the triforium and clerestory is fully in accord with this tendency. The window is composed of an oculus with nine cusps surmounting two stubby lancets; the triforium is a band of six trilobed arches. The two units are linked together in a single plane, the central mullion of the window and the mullions of the window frames continuing down into the triforium. A band of framing wall remains on either side. The general effect is quite different from the muscular quality of the oculi in the transept tower bays. There, in the transept, the wall was thick enough to carry two passageways side-by-side, whereas in the ambulatory the wall is not even thick enough for a single passageway. The triforium is thus corbeled out behind the wall (Figs. 17, 20). The reverse wall of the triforium was pierced and glazed with two arched openings per bay. The overall effect of the triforium, closely linked with the stubby clerestory, is comparable to the arrangement of the dado and windows of the lower chapel of the Sainte-Chapelle from the 1240s (Fig. 169).[6]

The vaults of the ambulatory are quadripartite (Fig. 115). Because of the trapezoidal shapes of the bays, the diagonal ribs do not continue straight from corner to corner of each bay (which would result in a keystone pushed too far toward the center of the building) but are slightly broken at the point where they meet the undecorated keystone. The keystones have the same form as in the inner bays of the south transept aisle, namely a central O inside a lozenge. Transverse arches and ribs both have the same triangular-shaped profile as the diagonal ribs in the transept. Ribs and arches are received by beaked capitals, some of which embody well-developed foliage variations.

Opening between the slender piers, and enframed by the sharpened arches and thin walls described above, are the seven radiating chapels (Fig. 118), each defined by five enclosing walls, two blind and three glazed. A socle bench runs around the lowest part of each chapel wall. The unrelieved flatness of the lower wall is very different from the sculptured richness produced by the lavish dado found in the radiating chapels of Amiens Cathedral.[7] The rounded windowsill, at the top edge of the wall, splays upward to meet the surface of the glass. In the two side walls of the chapels, the mural surfaces are treated as blind windows. In the windows and blind tracery a generous-sized eight-foiled oculus surmounts uncusped lancets. The rim of the oculus merges with the enclosing arch of the window and with the heads of the lancets. The tracery pattern is thus quite similar to the form used in the transept windows, except that the chapel windows are much narrower, the oculus is relatively larger, and the coursing of the lower part of the oculus is different; in the transept two joints are used at this point, whereas in the chapel windows there is only one. The mullions are composed of a central rounded shaft applied to a body with chamfered edges. The plinths of the window mullions have two levels: a broad base, a chamfer, and a narrower top.

In the angles formed at the intersection of the chapel walls, the designer has achieved a particularly pleasing hierarchy of forms. The shaft for the chapel vault is flanked by narrow wall strips, thin shafts for the window jambs, and finally chamfered edges leading into the glass. The composition is a shallow one, and the plane of the glass is not recessed much behind the surface of the wall. The shafts placed in the angles of the chapel walls are capped by well-proportioned beaked capitals, which receive the chapel vault ribs. The keystones, decorated with delicate low-relief foliage sculpture, are placed well inside the space of the chapel. From the keystone descend six ribs with sharpened profiles. The overall effect is immediate, intimate. The beholder is content to admire from a vantage point in the ambulatory and does not feel drawn to enter the

[6] Branner, *Saint Louis and the Court Style*, Fig. 66.

[7] Ibid., Fig. 65.

chapel, where one would be too close to see the windows.

The chapel at the north side of the base of the crown of radiating chapels (dedicated to the Madeleine) was the first to have been constructed. There is evidence of extensive experimentation in the forms used in this chapel, especially in the mullion bases of the tracery, each one of which employs a slightly different design. One of the bases of the window mullions has a string of diamond points embedded in the scotia, a motif used by Branner to date the piers of the transept to a period around the middle of the thirteenth century.[8] The appearance of the motif at both the east as well as the west end of the building suggests that its usage extended, in fact, over a period of several decades. The thickness and projection of the exterior buttresses of the chapel of the Madeleine are slightly different from those of the other chapels.

The ambulatory and chapels (Figs. 115–118) should certainly be recognized as one of the supreme realizations of Gothic: unified prismatic spaces defined by membrane like walls that meet at clean-cut angles over brittle, cylindrical supports. The precise definition of the parts of the composition is enhanced by the sharpened profiles of the ribs and arches. Both in terms of space and of line, a hierarchy of forms results. The lancet of the window is the smallest planar form, magnified to form the overall window, magnified again to form the arch enclosing the chapel, and finally to form the total ambulatory bay. The chapel space defined by this brittle spider's web of lines forms a prism that is subordinated to, but closely unified with, the inner trapezoidal space of the ambulatory bay. The overall composition, with its wide-yawning arcade and reduced clerestory, points ahead to the spatial economy favored by Late Gothic designers. The vocabulary of articulation might be compared with other buildings of the 1240s: the use of *en-delit* shafts with the aisle piers of the choir at Amiens (Fig. 148) and the porch of

the Sainte-Chapelle (Figs. 169, 170), the beaked capitals with the ambulatory of Amiens, and the linked triforium and clerestory with the dado and windows of the lower chapel of the Sainte-Chapelle.[9] The total composition, however, is unique and should be recognized as the masterpiece of the unknown architect of the 1240s.

As befits an ambulatory, which is essentially a passage of circulation, the space is best appreciated as the visitor moves through it. The transition from straight bays to turning bays is subtle; the angle between the ambulatory upper walls at the base of the system is slight, and the full angle of turn is only achieved at the second pier. As one walks into the ambulatory from the aisle, the arches framing the chapels offer themselves to the viewer in a constantly changing variety of different degrees of foreshortening.

The visitor advancing into the ambulatory is at first oppressed by the extent to which the blind walls block his vision: terminal walls close off the outer aisles, and beyond that, the dividing wall between the first and second chapel presents itself squarely to the eyes, while the second dividing wall is seen more obliquely. The first chapel is perceived with some feelings of disappointment; only two of its five facets are glazed. The second chapel, more completely glazed, is also perceived as a distinct spatial entity. Farther around the ambulatory, however, the visual importance of the dividing walls diminishes as the colored light and space of more and more chapels burst upon the beholder, who at last reaches a point toward the center of the ambulatory where all of the seven chapels can be enjoyed at once.

If the spatial effects of the ambulatory and chapels are best described in terms of movement, when perceived from the central vessel (Fig. 122), this area of the building may be understood in more static terms. The central vessel is an inverted chasm; the beholder is drawn upward with a feeling of near vertigo.

---

[8] Branner, "Maître de Beauvais," p. 80.

[9] Branner, *Saint Louis and the Court Style*, Figs. 52, 66, 67.

The wide arcade openings and slender piers allow for free visual communication from central vessel to periphery. In this spatial economy, the ambulatory and radiating chapels serve as a stabilizing influence. The continuous band of the triforium and the rhythmic rise and fall of the aisle clerestory windows form a horizontal belt of light and texture around this intensely vertical central vessel, while the radiating chapels offer themselves widely to the gaze forming a multifaceted crown of colored light—an ambience fit for the meditations of Abbot Suger of Saint-Denis!

Exterior of the Hemicycle in the 1240s: Radiating Chapels

The eye tends to slide around the eastern chapels very easily, the result of the very shallow projection of the chapels, the rounded plinth on which they sit, and the emphatic horizontal accent created by the weather moldings (Figs. 33–36, 56, 57). Each of the seven radiating chapels is defined by two of the great buttresses that support the uprights of the flying buttresses. The chapel forms a trapezoidal or bow-shaped entity between these great enclosing buttresses. Two smaller buttresses jut from the two angles formed by the chapel wall. This basic composition is repeated seven times around the east end of the building. Despite the fact that the axial chapel of Notre-Dame housed a group of chaplains that was considerably more numerous than that found in any of the other chapels, it is identical in size to the others (unlike the axial chapels at Amiens, Reims, Troyes, etc.). The optical effect of such a regular repetition of identical forms is one of a bewildering series of surfaces: walls, buttresses, and windows meeting at a variety of angles.

The whole composition sits atop a continuous rounded plinth whose outline encloses all of the projecting buttresses. In the lower walls of the east end there is a marked contrast between the irregular junction of the crown of radiating chapels with the buttresses and tur-

rets at B 8 and G 8 and the mechanical regularity of the chapels themselves. The lower wall is topped by a heavy molding forming a windowsill. The stones of this sill turn the corners from the walls to the buttresses in a well-behaved fashion that indicates a single, rapid campaign of construction.

The chapel windows have been fitted into two different kinds of space (Figs. 56, 57). The central bay of each chapel is flanked by two buttresses that splay away from the window, whereas in the side bays the main buttress forms an acute angle with the chapel wall, thus impinging onto the space outside the chapel window. In somes cases, the imperfect calculation of the geometry of the design has forced the constructors to angle back the main buttresses so that their mass does not impinge into the space needed for the frames of the side windows of the chapels.

A most important feature of the east end is the way in which the designer has sought the effects of optical unity in his handling of the weather moldings and offsets. The same molding runs around both the main buttresses and the chapel buttresses at the level of the windowsill. Two more such moldings are applied to both types of buttress between the level of the sill and the upper band of crockets that defines the top of the chapels. Thus, the beholder is struck by the uniformity of major and minor forms and is led to read the composition in terms of horizontal levels: a continuous crown of many facets.

The arches enclosing the chapel windows are decorated with a band composed of two rolls flanking a concavity studded with small rosettes. The tracery in all seven chapels is uniform: a large eight-foiled oculus placed over two uncusped lancets, the mullions being formed of central cylindrical shafts flanked by chamfered edges, and the capitals and abaci being rounded in form.

The axial chapel of Notre-Dame (Fig. 57) exhibits some important variations. Here the rounded capitals of the window tracery have a more fully developed type of foliage sculpture, and the crockets of the upper cornice are thinner and more fussy than in the other chapels. This results from the fact that the radiating chapels were begun in the two units at the base of the system (the chapels of the Madeleine and Saint Denis) and that work advanced from the sides toward the center, so that the axial chapel was the last one to be completed.

At the top of the chapels a horizontal band of crockets runs above the chapel windows and around the main buttresses. The chapel buttresses are terminated at this point by pinnacles having triangular-shaped pediments at their bases. The small trefoils that occupy these triangles resemble the similar motifs found on the west façade of Saint-Nicaise at Reims.[10]

The shallow-pitched chapel roofs (Fig. 34), made of reinforced concrete covered with lead, date from around 1900. They replaced a roof formed of a series of pyramids. The original roofs were probably in the form of a stone terrace low enough to allow the reverse side of the ambulatory triforium to receive the light, since glazed openings existed at this level.[11] The ambulatory triforium, corbeled out behind the wall, creates a small exterior passage running round outside the great windows opening into the ambulatory. Each of these windows has an oculus cusped in nine lobes surmounting two uncusped lancets; the exterior mullion profiles are prismatic and strikingly simple. These windows are enclosed in flat walls that meet at angles behind the main buttresses. If this horizontal level of ambulatory windows existing above the level of the chapels reminds the beholder of Early Gothic monuments such as Notre-Dame at Mantes, the polygonality of the wall at Beauvais provides the faceted look of Gothic.[12]

The outer uprights for the flying buttress system of the hemicycle, sitting partly on the main buttresses between the chapels, and partly upon the interior chapel dividing walls, are linked with the ambulatory wall by a narrow arch. They continue as undecorated, rectangular blocks as far as the height of the cornice over the ambulatory windows. At this height they are diminished in thickness by means of weather molding, and in their upper parts (above the height of the ambulatory windows) their flanks are decorated with detached shafts forming panels that are topped by small arches and gables. It is evident that the quality of the masonry deteriorates in the upper parts, where the mortar joints become wider and more ragged. It is probable that the upper parts of the uprights belong to a later phase of construction, from the 1250s or early 1260s (Figs. 22, 55).

The Choir Aisles in the 1240s

The choir aisles (Figs. 98–114) are undoubtedly the unhappiest part of the choir of Beauvais Cathedral. The builders of the 1240s found the walls of the outer aisles completed up to a level somewhat below the capitals. They were forced to try to fit their slender transverse arches and beaked capitals on top of supports that were really too massive and that had been intended for thick arches like the ones found in the transept. At three different points (C 6, F 6, and B 7; Figs. 91, 97, 105) the builders of the cathedral of Robert of Cressonsac were forced to terminate these stocky supports with unfortunate looking beaked capitals where the abaci are much too small in relation to the necking.

The transition to a different mode is also marked in the design of pier C 7 in the north choir aisle (Figs. 98, 99, 100), which is much thinner than its counterparts to the west. The slenderness of this pier is fully in accord with the thin walls of the inner aisle. The organization of the space of the inner aisle is identical to the ambulatory, with the upper parts occupied by a band triforium linked to a stumpy lancet window surrounded by a considerable expanse of wall.

---

[10] Ibid., Fig. 22.

[11] For Branner ("Maître de Beauvais") this was the first glazed triforium in French Gothic, the work of the revolutionary *maître de Beauvais*. However, the chronology proposed here would allow this part of the building to be completed in the 1240s, after the glazed triforium had been introduced at Saint-Denis and Troyes Cathedral.

[12] Bony, *French Gothic Architecture*, Fig. 179.

Both the triforium and the clerestory (Fig. 100) strike one as somewhat monotonous, as if almost mechanically produced. This effect of mechanical mass-production of parts is only partly counteracted by the variety found in the form of the base moldings of the little columns of the triforium. A single bay may include several very different types, and it is hard to detect any signs of a progression from west to east or vice versa.

On the other hand, it is quite obvious that it was in the transept arms that the earliest *essais* were made in the aisle triforium and clerestory (Figs. 89, 96). It is thus probable that work on the aisle triforium and clerestory began in the transept arms and moved inward toward the central vessel and then eastward. Once the builders reached the main body of the choir (ca. 1245) they pierced and glazed two openings in the rear wall of the triforium.

The choir aisle are a veritable battlefield of repairs and rebuildings, which have detracted very greatly from the beauty of this part of the bulding (Figs. 100, 101, 107). Extra piers were interposed in the intermediary arcades after 1284, and the outer aisle vaults on the south side were transformed into quinquepartite vaults and the inner aisle into pseudosexpartite vaults. The work of repair on the north side is less complete; the outer aisle remained untouched, and the inner aisle has a quinquepartite and a sexpartite vault.[13] Pier C 7 in the north aisle was completely rebuilt. The massive block of the sacristy/treasury complex has contributed additional strength to the north side but has reduced the lighting. More rebuilding took place in the sixteenth century, when pier F 7 in the south aisle (Fig. 110) was replaced, a solid wall was added between the two bays of the outer aisle, and much of the clerestory and triforium was rebuilt. Again, in the nineteenth century, piers in the northern aisle were rebuilt. The obvious weakness of this part of the building can tell us much about the nature of the collapse that took place in 1284.

Interior of the Central Vessel

Although the ambulatory and radiating chapels are the masterpiece of design in the cathedral of Bishops Robert of Cressonsac and William of Grez, the central vessel (Figs. 120–124), because of its great height, has attracted more than its fair share of attention from visitors to the cathedral, as well as from art historians. This steep slice of space, three times taller than wide, is organized in three levels: a very tall arcade, and a linked triforium and clerestory that together occupy more than half the total height of the elevation.

The cathedral of Bishops Robert of Cressonsac and William of Grez had only three wide bays in the main arcade. In the campaigns of repair after 1284, however, additional piers were interposed between the original ones. The original piers of the main arcade (Fig. 12b) have a cylindrical body with a diameter of about 1.38 to 1.40 m, to which are applied two shafts (as in a *pilier cantonné*) placed on the east-west axis, in order to receive the inner order of the main arcade. Whereas in a traditional *pilier cantonné* (Chartres, Reims, Amiens, and Beauvais transept) the shaft toward the rear (aisle) of the unit is identical to the shaft toward the central vessel, in the Beauvais main arcade, the front shaft has been pushed in a somewhat playful manner into the body of the pier. As if to compensate for the loss of mass, the designer has added a substantial bundle of three shafts to the rear (aisle) side of the pier in order to receive transverse arches and diagonal ribs (Fig. 129). With the pushing inward of the front of the pier, and the pulling outward of the back, the total north-south thickness remains the same as the total east-west thickness. This peculiar arrangement served two purposes, structural and optical. The passageway of the high triforium is carried on a series of relieving arches that project out behind the arcade wall. The additional mass of masonry in the rear of

[13] Post-1284 modifications to the aisle vaults were piecemeal, leaving in place as much of the original fabric as possible. The original ribs had an almond-shaped central to-rus. In the post-1284 ribs the sharp front edge of the almond is square.

the main piers helps support these arches. In optical terms, we are seeing the work of a designer who was something of a mannerist—one who wanted to play with the accepted form of the *pilier cantonné* and to create a somewhat slippery optical effect in the central vessel. Thus the eye of the beholder moves over the front surfaces of the piers without being stopped by heavily projecting shafts. Such "slippery" shafts had been used before at the level of the arcade—one thinks particularly of the reduced bundles of three shafts in the arcade of Amiens and the flattened arrangement favored by designers influenced by Notre-Dame of Paris. Flattened bundles of shafts can be found at Saint-Leu-d'Esserent and in the nave of Gonnesse.[14] It is more difficult, however, to find a prototype for the use of the squashed shaft in pier design. It is also difficult to believe that this somewhat mannered and playful composition could have been conceived before the traditional *piliers cantonnés* of the transept (Fig. 12b, c).

To the west, the arcade was terminated by the great piers of the crossing (Figs. 120–121). Today, the northeastern pier of the crossing is an undulating type similar to the sixteenth-century western crossing piers designed and constructed by the architect Martin Chambiges. The northeastern pier of the crossing and the adjacent interpolated pier in the main arcade were damaged and rebuilt after the collapse of the crossing tower in 1573. The original crossing piers, with sixteen shafts applied to a core composed of a series of rectangular steps, were identical in design and dimensions to the tower-supporting piers in the terminal bays of the transept arms (Fig. 12a), although the surviving southeast crossing pier differs in some details from the transept piers. The founding of the crossing piers would demand the demolition of the choir of the *Basse-Œuvre*, and it is possible that this was delayed until the 1240s.[15]

The thickness of the wall of the main arcade of the choir central vessel, approximately 1.34 m, was determined by the design of the crossing piers. Thus, as noted earlier in the context of the transept, we are dealing with two pier types that are mismatched in their thickness. An arch of 1.34 m is really too wide to set on top of a column 1.38 m in diameter, since space is also needed on top of the abacus of the capital for the bundle of shafts (three or five) that ascends to the transverse arches, diagonal ribs, and wall arches of the high vaults. In the Beauvais main arcade, the problem was exacerbated by the fact that the shaft toward the central vessel, which normally helps to provide the platform necessary for the bundle of shafts, had been pushed inward toward the center of the pier.

The main arcade has two orders, both of them flat-surfaced and both edged by rounded rolls, exactly as in the transept. The inner order of the arcade is received by generously sized square capitals placed on top of the east-west shafts of the piers. The outer order perches on "angle corbels," formed by angular projections of the abacus with a spiky crocket underneath. The surface of the arcade wall is approximately level with the perimeter of the circle that forms the body of the pier. Very little space remains therefore for the bundle of shafts that ascends to the high vaults. To overcome this problem, two solutions have been applied. In one pier (D 6, at the west end of the north arcade; Fig. 125) the central shaft is allowed to cut through the capital and the abacus to ascend to the single high capital, which receives the ribs and arches of the vault. Since the shaft has been pushed inward toward the center of the pier, it also appears to be pushed into the surface of the wall. It is flanked by two smaller flattened shafts that sit (without bases) on top of the capital abacus. All three shafts have only a very shallow projection beyond the surface of the ar-

---

[14] Müller, *Le Prieuré de Saint-Leu-d'Esserent*; Bontemps, "La Nef de l'église Saint-Pierre de Gonesse."

[15] I would now offer an interpretation somewhat different from the one expressed in my *Art Bulletin* article of 1980 ("Choir of the Church of Saint-Pierre"), where I pro-

posed that the crossing piers belonged to the first campaign. In the southeastern crossing pier, the notches cut into the angles of the octagonal plinths are larger than in the transept piers, suggesting that the crossing piers may belong to the second campaign.

cade wall. A somewhat squashed, distinctly halfhearted bundle of shafts results—certainly displeasing to the eye, and possibly considered dangerous in the upper piers, in view of the reduction of mass.

In all of the other five original thirteenth-century piers of the choir straight bays (Figs. 126, 127) as well as the seven piers of the hemicycle (Figs. 128, 129) a different solution was applied; the central shaft is terminated by a heavy abacus, and above the abacus a generous-sized sculptured corbel provides a platform for a substantial bundle of three shafts. The existence of two different solutions to the same problem does not necessarily reflect stylistic influences from a progressive workshop elsewhere. The more "up-to-date" solution, which allows the shaft to continue unbroken through the capital and abacus, was not peculiar to the workshop of Saint-Denis, as proposed by Branner.[16] The same solution also could be found, for example, in the Romanesque nave of Saint-Etienne at Beauvais. Nor is it inherently likely (as Branner has argued) that the one pier with the continuous shaft was the last to be executed. Given the tendency of Gothic builders to experiment with potential design solutions at the beginning of a campaign, and given the evidence that construction of the Beauvais choir started in the northwest corner, it is much more likely that this single pier constitutes an initial experiment, later to be rejected for the optical and structural reasons defined above. The sculpture of the capitals in the main arcade becomes more lavish as we advance toward the east. When the piers at the base of the hemicycle are reached (Figs. 127–129), we are very far removed from the simple spiky crockets of the transept. The base moldings (Fig. 14) also change somewhat; the western piers of the main arcade have a more bulbous torus and the eastern piers a flatter one. The more bulbous forms may be associated with the piers of the transept, and the flatter ones with the ambulatory and radiating chapels.

The geometry of the three arches of the principal arcade (Fig. 129) reflects the problem of fitting pointed arches of differing width under the triforium sill, whose height remains constant. Whereas in the transept, the arches of the main arcade approximate to a two-point arch composed of two arcs struck from center points lying on the opposite springer, in the eastern bays of the choir, the wider spacing of the arcade has forced the designer to find his center points well within the space of the arch, in order to avoid making the arch too high. A shape closer to a rounded arch results in the widest bays at the east end of the arcade.

The addition of the extra piers to fortify the main arcade (Fig. 129) after the collapse of 1284 has divided each arcade space into two. The height of the arcade has been reduced with the addition of the spandrels forming the new arcade. The restorers of the cathedral after the 1284 collapse attempted to enliven and relieve the ugliness of this arrangement by means of delicate oculi bisected by the single shafts rising to the vaults. The wall of the main arcade is split by many alarming vertical fissures, which, in several places, extend down into the tracery of the oculus in the spandrel. Elements of the tracery must have started to pop, and, no doubt because of fears about the safety of the main arcade, the decorative oculi on the north side of the choir were filled in with plaster or cement.

The straight bays of the choir are terminated at the east by a seven-part hemicycle. As outlined earlier, the two bays at the base of the system are slightly larger than the other five, but because of the effects of foreshortening, one fails to notice the difference unless standing within the hemicycle itself. In its first bay, the hemicycle wall turns only slightly away from the plane of the arcade of the main part of the choir. The angle of turn is increased in the remaining five bays.

The piers of the hemicycle (Fig. 12d) have a central cylinder (1.38 m to 1.40 m) with a single shaft placed toward the central vessel and three shafts at the rear for the ambulatory

---

[16] Branner, "Maître de Beauvais."

arches and ribs. As in the choir straight bays, the single shaft is pushed inward toward the center of the pier. Since the inner order of the main arcade is greatly reduced in the hemicycle, it was possible to omit the shafts flanking the sides of the pier, thus allowing the gaps between the piers to remain more open. The piers at the base of the system of the hemicycle (division 8; Figs. 128, 129) still have lateral shafts, and the first bays of the hemicycle on either side (wider than the others) have a heavy inner order. Thus, it was necessary to add a small shaft sitting on top of a corbel to the second piers of the hemicycle in order to receive the inner order of this arch. The heavy stilting of the arches of the hemicycle arcade and the reduced inner order create more space to allow the beholder's gaze to penetrate to the windows of the ambulatory.

At a height of about twenty-two meters above the choir pavement, the prominent rim of the triforium marks a point somewhat less than halfway up the elevation (Figs. 129–132). The triforium is rather tall in proportion; its height almost equals the distance from the arcade capital to the triforium sill. All of the tracery of the triforium in the straight bays of the choir was rebuilt after the collapse of the choir in 1284. Only the hemicycle survives.

In the original choir (Figs. 122, 123) the three shafts ascending to the high vaults were increased to five at the level of the triforium sill, as in Amiens Cathedral. In the hemicycle the outermost shafts of the bundle of five ascend to receive the elements of the tracery of the clerestory windows. In the straight bays the equivalent shafts must have ascended to the formerets (enclosing arches) of the clerestory windows, but the arrangement has been suppressed by the rebuilders of the cathedral after 1284. The effect of the addition of the extra shafts at the level of the triforium sill is to recess the front plane of the triforium somewhat behind the surface of the arcade. In the triforium (Figs. 129, 130) a rectangular cage of tracery frames two pointed lancets in each bay. The small blind spandrels between the lancets and the rectangular frame are filled with trefoils. Inside each lancet is an oculus cusped with five petals surmounting two trilobed arches. A close inspection of the triforium reveals an incredibly delicate layered effect with no less than five planes. The outermost plane is expressed by the shafts ascending into the tracery of the clerestory windows at the sides of the bay and in the middle; then comes the enclosing arch of the lancet; recessed behind this is the plane of the two trilobed arches and the oculus; and behind this again are two more orders on the reverse side. The oculus does not merge into the enclosing frame; it is actually held in a concavity between the front and rear orders. All these different planes are expressed by tiny shafts in the jambs—these shafts are arranged in a shallow bundle that continues directly into the five shafts that ascend to the high vaults. The profiles used for the tracery elements and the mullions are unbelievably delicate (Figs. 131, 132). The tracery has a rounded front edge but is keeled in the center with a sharpened rectangular nose. The overall effect is that of fragile metalwork. The fourteenth-century restorers of the cathedral made no effort to reproduce these delicate forms. The oculi used in the restoration work are small and fat, with four cusps instead of five, and the arches of the triforium are cusped rather than trilobed (Figs. 122, 123). Heavy and rather awkward-looking spherical triangles fill the spandrels between the arches.

The clerestory windows in the hemicycle survived the collapse, whereas those of the straight bays were rebuilt after the disaster. In the hemicycle, the two lancets of the clerestory window are linked with the central mullion of the triforium (Fig. 122). In the head of each of the two lancets is a four-lobed oculus over a cusped arch, while the head of the window itself is occupied by a six-cusped oculus. The windows are framed by the shafts that have ascended from the level of the abaci of the main piers, while the shafts of the tracery have climbed from the level of the triforium sill. A chamfered edge flanking these shafts causes the glass to be recessed behind the level of the triforium. The elongated lancets are glazed with grisaille glass, with a band of colored glass in the middle echoing the other horizontal bands swathing the central vessel—the triforium and the band of arches in the inner aisle and ambulatory.

Only the hemicycle vault is original (Fig. 141); the others (Figs. 139, 140) were rebuilt after the 1284 collapse, when the three quadripartite vaults of the straight bays of the choir were transformed into sexpartite vaults through the addition of extra transverse arches supported by the piers that were interpolated in the main arcade. The hemicycle vault is composed of seven segments created by ribs radiating out from a pierced keystone located well to the east of the transverse arch of the last straight bay toward the east. Both transverse arch and ribs have the same profile (central almond-shaped molding flanked by square shoulders and round rolls) as that used in the lower parts of the building. At the springers of the vault, the stones are coursed in horizontally with the *tas-de-charge*. The concave surfaces of the severies are made up of rectangular *pendans*, which are barely visible through the coats of plaster and paint.[17] The elegantly proportioned beaked capitals of the hemicycle have crockets and more complex foliage. At the base of the hemicycle (bay division 8; Figs. 135–137) the capital has to receive diagonal ribs as well as transverse arches. A star-shaped abacus has therefore been adopted for these capitals. The capitals executed for the rebuilt vaults in the straight bays of the choir are easily distinguishable, for they have polygonal abaci (Fig. 138). On the north side of the straight bays three capitals do not conform to the fourteenth-century type. The capital of D 5/6 (Fig. 133) adjacent to the northeastern crossing pier has acanthus foliage and belongs to the sixteenth-century rebuild after the collapse of the crossing tower in 1573. At D 6 (Fig. 134) and D 7 star-shaped abaci are found, suggesting that these capitals are reused elements, or copies of the original capitals.

The rib type in the vaults of the straight bays (Fig. 140) is similar to that used in the hemicycle (Fig. 141), except that the sharpened front edge is now squared. The transition from pointed to square front edge can be seen in the diagonal springers to the east of the vault at bay 7 8. The springers forming part of the original work have a pointed front edge, whereas the ribs themselves, forming part of the rebuild, have a square edge.

A final word on the overall impact of the central vessel (Figs. 120–123). Beauvais Cathedral, like Bourges, is a "church within a church"—in other words, the central vessel is perceived as a three-story elevation, yet through the diaphanous screen of piers of the arcade can be seen the three levels of the ambulatory and inner aisle. An intriguing ambiguity results: should the building be read as a five-story structure or a three-story structure? The designers of Bourges Cathedral (Figs. 158, 159) conceived this play in terms of measured distance and space: the inner church is a restatement of the outer one. At Beauvais the play is conceived in terms of light and contrast. The presence of the shallow radiating chapels creates a brilliantly lit base to the composition. Each of the succeeding five levels was glazed. The elevation of the central vessel is not an echo of the elevation of the aisles and ambulatory but a contrast. In the former we find a horizontal emphasis, while in the latter the tall triforium is linked with the clerestory to form an elongated vertical cage. The designers of Bourges have placed a relatively restrained clerestory on top of a soaring arcade. The builders of the cathedral of Robert of Cressonsac and William of Grez inherited an unfinished choir, where the height of the arcade (ca. twenty-one meters) was already fixed. They had the temerity to build a superstructure that exceeded in height the arcade of Bishop Miles. In the ambulatory and aisles the limited height of the stubby triforium and clerestory was fixed by the existing work in the transept from the 1220s. In the central ves-

---

[17] A *pendan* is a roughly shaped stone used in a vault severy.

sel, however, no such restraints existed, and it is probable that its height was increased in course of construction.

The incredible delicacy of the main triforium with its rectangular cage of tracery certainly offers a striking contrast to the much simpler forms found in the ambulatory and inner aisles. It is probable that the central vessel was brought up to the level of the high triforium sill in the 1240s, under Bishop Robert of Cressonsac, and that the lavishly decorated upper choir should be associated with the patronage of Bishop William of Grez, 1250s and 1260s (Fig. 22). This hypothesis is confirmed by the study of the exterior upper parts.

Exterior Upper Parts, 1250s–1260s

The choir of Bishops Robert of Cressonsac and William of Grez was completed to the high vaults in all three bays before 1272 (Figs. 32–37). The slow rhythm of the three straight bays with their broad clerestory windows was changed into a staccato in the hemicycle with its tall narrow bays and a jungle of flying buttresses, much as in the choir of Le Mans Cathedral.[18] The flying buttresses at Beauvais are supported by two uprights, a massive outer upright and an attenuated inner one. In the straight bays of the choir the uprights are separated by the space of the outer aisle. In the hemicycle, however, no such outer aisle or outer ambulatory exists, and the outer uprights are shifted inward to a point where they almost touch the inner elements. The uprights are incredibly tall, lending a distinctly square emphasis to the exterior.

The collapse of the upper choir in 1284 led to a major rebuild in the straight bays, involving the reconstruction of all of the elements of the upper choir above the triforium sill and the transformation of the original three bays into six through the addition of extra piers in the main arcade. Only the hemicycle has been left intact. Further rebuilding took place after the collapse of the crossing tower in 1573 and

once more in the seventeenth century. In order to understand the forms of the original choir it is necessary to examine the rebuilt parts too, since they embody a certain amount of reused masonry. We will start with the hemicycle and proceed to the straight bays where the rebuilding has taken place.

The changing forms of the decorative details as well as changes in the masonry surfaces (Figs. 22, 55) suggest that the stumps of the flying buttress uprights around the hemicycle were begun simultaneously with the triforium and clerestory of the inner aisle and ambulatory. Up to a point level with the roof of the ambulatory the stumps of the outer uprights are undecorated and embody masonry with a smooth texture, yellowish color, and narrow mortar joints. Above this level the uprights are whitish in hue with wider mortar joints, and they carry more decoration. The stumps of the outer uprights together with the radiating chapels, the ambulatory, and the main arcade of the choir may be considered as belonging to the same phase. That these stumps were constructed in the same sequence as the radiating chapels is demonstrated by a significant detail. It has been seen that the radiating chapels were built from the base of the hemicycle toward the center, with the north side a little in advance of the south. The same is true of the stumps of the outer uprights. Thus, it is noticeable that the units flanking the earliest chapel, that of the Madeleine (chapel a), at the base of the hemicycle on the north side, have an additional tongue of masonry on their inner surfaces (Figs. 67–69). This feature is also found in the next upright on the north side and on the upright at the base of the hemicycle on the south side, but not in the units toward the center of the hemicycle. A further detail confirms that buttress G 8 was brought up to the level of the roof of the inner aisle as part of the first phase of the second campaign (Figs. 36, 37, 55, 66). The staircase turret was brought up to the level of the roof of the outer aisle, while the body of the buttress must have continued up to the height

---

[18] Bony, *French Gothic Architecture*, Figs. 246–247.

of the roof of the inner aisle. In the second phase it was decided to continue the staircase turret up to provide access to the roof of the inner aisle, and the upper part of the turret and the connecting bridge are set awkwardly against the existing work.

In the equivalent unit on the north side (B 8; Figs. 32, 33, 48) the arrangement is different because it had been realized that this unit was badly placed in relation to the transverse arches it was intended to support. Even in the lower parts of this buttress, it is evident that attempts had been made to shift the mass of the buttress to the east by means of offsets applied to its right (west) flank but not to its left flank. The staircase turret was continued directly up to the level of the roof of the inner aisle, since it was realized that this would form a useful base for the upper part of the buttress, which is shifted considerably to the east and which sits on top of the staircase turret (Fig. 61).

Thus, the builders of the cathedral of Bishop William of Grez in the 1250s (Fig. 22, 33–37) found the hemicycle completed to the roof of the inner aisle/ambulatory. At all points in the building as they continued the work upward they adopted much more elaborate and delicate forms. This same phase of work provides the extraordinary richness of the main triforium of the central vessel. The outer uprights of the flying buttresses of the hemicycle have been reduced in mass and decorated with cages of *en délit* shafts (Figs. 67–69). The moldings carrying the bases of these shafts mark the beginnings of the second phase of construction. The units are divided into three vertical panels in their lower parts and two panels in the reduced upper part. These panels are capped by delicate cusped arches and crocketed gables with fleurons. The composition is strongly reminiscent of the framing device used on Gothic ivories. The greater mass of the buttresses at the base of the hemicycle allows for four panels in the lower parts of each upright and three in the upper part. The front edge of the upper part of each upright projects forward as an angle

supporting a gargoyle that evacuates the rainwater channeled through the upper flyers from the choir roof. The tops of these uprights are protected by gabled roofs and capped by pinnacles. Most of these pinnacles have been restored, but one original unit takes the form of a delicate aedicule protecting a small crocketed pinnacle.

These outer uprights are linked with the central parts of the building at three points. At the level of the clerestory of the ambulatory a massive flying buttress bridges the narrow gap and provides a channel for the evacuation of rainwater from the ambulatory roof. This level still belongs to the 1240s. Two flying buttresses spring from the upper part of each of the hemicycle uprights across to the central vessel—a leap that is facilitated through the support of slender intermediary uprights. The flyers are inclined at an angle of about thirty degrees to the horizontal. The lower flyers, very slender in their proportions, support the outward thrust of the high vaults at a level about three meters above the capitals of these vaults. The soffit of each flyer has a chamfered edge, and the upper rim is decorated with crockets (as at Reims Cathedral, but not Chartres or Amiens). The upper flyers follow the same shallow trajectory. They lack the crockets on their crest and instead carry a gutter to evacuate the rainwater from the main roof.

The intermediary uprights form needlelike columns of masonry dividing the span of the flyers into two unequal parts (Figs. 67–69). These uprights are hexagonal in plan, with an added strip toward the inside to receive the tails of the flying buttresses. The flanks of these uprights are enlivened with cages of *en délit* shafts, the lower panels sitting on a molding at the level of the top of the main triforium and the upper panels occupying the space between the two flyers. There are significant differences between the decorative forms of these slender uprights and the forms employed in the more massive outer units. Whereas the arches capping the panels in the outer uprights are cusped, the comparable arches on the inner units are trilobed with little trefoils in the spandrels. In this respect the intermediary uprights may be matched with the main piers of the body of the hemicycle (Fig. 67), which also have trilobed decorative forms and trefoils.

The eight upper piers of the hemicycle (Figs. 67, 72–74) are the original ones, built around 1260. In the lower parts (below the head of the lower flyer) a squarish block of undecorated masonry has been set against the moldings of the window jamb. The stones are not coursed through, and an untidy vertical cement joint separates the buttress from the window jambs. The jambs are equipped with two shafts, one to support the enclosing arch and one for the tracery. A trilobed arch and sharply incised trefoils decorate the block of masonry (original thirteenth-century work) where the lower flyer abuts the pier. Above this point an openwork tabernacle shelters a statue set upon a plinth decorated with gables and sharp trefoils. The canopy of this tabernacle forms a block where the upper flyer abuts the pier. Viollet-le-Duc suggested that the unadorned solid masonry forming the lower part of the pier was added after the collapse of the choir in 1284 and that the lower pier took the form of an openwork tabernacle resembling the arrangement in the upper part (Fig. 24).[19] He suggested furthermore that the weakness of the construction at this point was the critical factor leading to collapse.

Viollet-le-Duc's interpretation is open to question, however, since the canopy that caps the lower pier at the head of the lower flyer is a solid one, unlike the voided upper canopy.[20] It is obviously quite impossible to be certain of the form of the original pier or when it was rebuilt. Two conclusions may, however, be reached. The hemicycle piers did not actually fail. There is little distortion evident in the window jambs, and it is quite possible that this reconstruction was undertaken in the very conservative atmosphere that existed after the great collapse. Such a rebuilding does not nec-

essarily tell us about problems that actually existed, but rather about problems that were feared. Second, we may assume that the original composition was more delicate than the existing one and that it embodied *en délit* shafts arranged as a cage around a solid or voided pier. It is obvious that Beauvais Cathedral did not collapse because of a weakness inherent in these piers. Had this been the case, the hemicycle would not have survived. The famous collapse of the upper choir in 1284 involved far more than the upper piers.

At clerestory level the seven segments of the hemicycle (Figs. 73, 74) survived the collapse. To the beholder familiar with Chartres and Reims cathedrals the upper wall at Beauvais seems incredibly thin. Whereas in these earlier monuments the clerestory wall provides a heavily projecting frame for the windows and casts deep shadows, at Beauvais the mural surface is on a plane not far in front of the tracery and glass. The entire depth of the composition is expressed in terms of the two slender shafts that form the window jambs, the outer shaft supporting the roll molding of the window frame. A second most important characteristic of the Beauvais clerestory wall is its rounded surface. Polygonality was, by the 1260s, a well-established feature of Gothic design. The radiating chapels and the exterior of the ambulatory at Beauvais are polygonal. In the upper choir, the triforium and glazed surface of the clerestory are also faceted. The transition from flatness to roundness is effected at the level of the enframing arches of the clerestory windows. The smoothly rounded surface of the upper wall is corbeled outward by means of a massive crocket band, thus providing enough width for an upper passage with a balustrade.

The smooth, rounded sweep of the balustrade is punctuated only by miniscule pinnacles at the base of the hemicycle. The eastern termination of the roof assumes the form of a continuous half cone, lending to the end of the

---

[19] Viollet-le-Duc, *Dictionnaire*, IV, pp. 179–182.
[20] As already proposed by M. Wolfe and R. Mark, "The

Collapse of the Beauvais Vaults in 1284," *Speculum*, LI, 1976, pp. 462–476.

choir a somewhat boatlike appearance similar to Bourges Cathedral and Notre-Dame of Paris.[21] A similar rounded treatment of the east end is present in many Romanesque and Early Gothic monuments—polygonality became standard only in the first decades of the thirteenth century. In the context of Beauvais Cathedral, however, this cannot be seen as merely an outdated feature but rather as a device used in order to gain a particular visual effect. The horizontal rim crowning the edifice provides an echo of the horizontality so predominant in the lower building, especially in the chapels with their moldings and cornices forming a series of horizontal levels.

We come last of all to the tracery elements of the hemicycle windows. The bays of the triforium at the base of the hemicycle were replaced after 1284 (three bays on the north side and two on the south), while the four panels of the triforium in the central bays of the hemicycle are original (Figs. 70, 71). The pattern of the outer skin of the triforium reflects the forms used inside: two twin-lancet units, each enclosing a five-lobed oculus. Each of the lancets is capped with an uncusped arch (unlike the trilobed arches used in the interior), which merges completely with the rim of the oculus. Trefoils fill the blind spandrels. The mullions embody rounded shafts to mark the main divisions, while prismatic forms (without capitals) are used for the minor elements.

The post-collapse elements of the hemicycle tracery are made up of four units per bay, each unit composed of a pointed cusped arch surmounted by a quatrefoil oculus, all executed in prismatic forms.

In the hemicycle clerestory (Figs. 73, 74) the original tracery patterns are preserved: a double-lancet window is surmounted by a six-foiled oculus. Each of the smaller units is topped by a quartrefoiled oculus, under which is placed a cusped arch. The main elements are rendered in rounded sticks of stone, while the minor ones (the small pointed arches and the cusps of the oculi) are prismatic.

The hemicycle was thus undisturbed by the collapse of 1284 and the subsequent rebuild. To what extent does this extraordinarily vertical composition with its precarious buttressing system express a unified vision? First, the contracted nature of the choir of Bishop Robert of Cressonsac (the radiating chapels of the 1240s) was not necessarily envisaged in 1225. This contracted plan caused the buttresses to be pulled inward, so that the outer uprights and intermediaries almost bump into one another. Second, it is probable that the intentions of the builders changed again soon after 1250 and that the slender intermediary uprights were added as part of a generally more grandiose program that we associate with the patronage of Bishop William of Grez. The evidence for this assertion is derived from a study of the pronounced difference in the decorative forms of the outer and intermediary uprights. Whereas the intermediaries have trilobed arches and trefoils, like the main piers of the central vessel, the outer uprights have cusped arches and no trefoils. Given the extraordinary slenderness of the main piers and intermediaries, it is unlikely that these could have been built first, without the support of the more massive outer props. Although the cusped arch is generally considered more "modern" than the trilobed form, it is interesting to see the same sequence (cusped to trilobed) in the lower and upper chapels of the Sainte-Chapelle (Figs. 169, 170).

It seems probable that the outer uprights were completed while the designers still debated the question of the best solution to reconcile the two different types of buttressing called for by the different types of ground plan—expansive in the body of the choir and contracted in the hemicycle. It must have occurred to these designers that a single flyer could bridge the gap from the outer upright to the hemicycle without the agency of an intermediary upright, much as in the similar pyramidal elevation of Notre-Dame of Paris, as rebuilt in the thirteenth century, or at Coutances.[22]

Viollet-le-Duc's drawings (Fig. 24) and the

[21] Bony, *French Gothic Architecture*, Fig. 192.

[22] Herschman, "The Norman Ambulatory of Le Mans

model of the Beauvais ambulatory in the Palais de Chaillot in Paris (Fig. 17) suggest that the inner edge of each intermediary, as it overhangs the clerestory wall of the ambulatory, received support from a series of corbels, projecting out and coursed in with the masonry of the walls.[23] In this way, Viollet-le-Duc wanted to persuade us that the feature was a "rational" one, intended deliberately to help provide an active prop for the outward thrust of the high vaults, transmitted by the flying buttresses. In fact, however, no such corbels exist, and it is perfectly evident that the intermediaries were a last-minute addition. The inner edge of each upright, as it overhangs the clerestory wall of the ambulatory, is supported on a narrow strip of masonry (Fig. 30), which is not coursed in with the clerestory walls of the ambulatory or with the walls dividing each bay of the ambulatory vaults. It will be demonstrated later that around 1250 a new plan was introduced to allow the superstructure of the choir to gain an additional five meters in height. The same new thinking is reflected in the addition of the intermediary uprights.

Despite these shifts in intention, the upper hemicycle exhibits a general uniformity that contrasts sharply with the choir straight bays, which were transformed in the wake of the disaster of 1284 (Fig. 37). At division 7, the middle bay of the choir, the units on both the north and south sides (Figs. 60, 64, 65) have been rebuilt from the level of the roof of the outer aisle. The outer upright on the south side (G 7) has recessed panels, continuous moldings, and tracery patterns typical for the decades around 1300 (Fig. 65). The intermediary upright (F 7; Fig. 64) has similar forms and a cruciform section quite unlike the hexagonal forms of the hemicycle.

The equivalent units on the north side (B 7 and C 7; Figs. 32, 33) have similar forms, but with a much higher degree of intensity in the decoration—they have clearly been rebuilt. The signs of distress that are so apparent on both the north and south sides of the choir at division 7 should be interpreted in conjunction with the evidence of extensive rebuilding and in the choir aisles, where the intermediary piers at both C 7 and F 7 have been entirely rebuilt. Division 7 was obviously a point of critical weakness in the choir of Bishops Robert of Cressonsac and William of Grez.

In the western bay of the choir (division 6; Figs. 32, 33, 37, 38, 58, 59, 62, 63) the outer uprights on each side were intended to form the corners of transept towers, and they are therefore equipped with shafts to frame the windows into the towers. The uprights have shallow recessed panels without moldings. These panels have simple square tops, which convey a Late Gothic appearance to the composition. It is most important to note, however, that the tops of these units were completed only in the sixteenth century in conjunction with the work on the transept (Fig. 55). The horizontal moldings of these uprights do not correspond with any of the main horizontals of the upper choir, and the unit on the north (B 6) is equipped with three flyers rather than two as elsewhere (Figs. 58, 59). Both the lower flyers have crockets and are clearly original. The lowest of the three flyers butts against the intermediary upright but is not continued across to the central vessel.

The intermediary uprights (C 6 and F 6; Figs. 59, 63) have *en délit* shafts and trilobed arches much like the comparable units around the hemicycle. However, whereas the hemicycle uprights are hexagonal in plan, the units at B 6 and F 6 are octagonal with additional projecting strips on their major axes. If it is fairly obvious that the intermediaries resemble the equivalent units in the upper hemicycle, the massive outer uprights at B 6 and G 6 are harder to interpret. Should they be assigned a date earlier than the hemicycle or later? The existence of the slender intermediaries provides a compelling reason for believing that the two tower buttresses must belong to a

---

Cathedral"; W. Clark and R. Mark "The First Flying Buttresses: A New Reconstruction of the Nave of Notre-Dame de Paris," *Art Bull.*, LXVI, 1984, pp. 47–64.

[23] Viollet-le-Duc, *Dictionnaire*, IV, p. 178.

slightly earlier phase, since if this part of the building had come down in 1284 and had been rebuilt, it is unthinkable that the massive outer buttresses could have collapsed without doing extensive damage, leaving the slender intermediaries upright.[24] The rather stark forms of the tower buttresses would be at home in the context of the work on the ambulatory and radiating chapels in the 1240s—the first phase of the second campaign (Figs. 22, 55). The use of recessed panels with no flanking moldings can be found in the intermediary uprights of the flying buttresses of the choir of Amiens Cathedral. We have thus identified an important part of the cathedral of Bishop Robert of Cressonsac (1240s) and have established that work on the upper choir began in the transept and followed a west-to-east sequence, just as in the lower choir.

The existence of the two low crocketed flyers springing from B 6 (Figs. 58, 59) may reveal that the cathedral of Bishop Robert of Cressonsac was to have been somewhat lower than the present choir, as actually completed under Bishop William of Grez. Had the lower crocketed flyer been continued up as the support for the high vaults, the superstructure would have been some five meters lower than the present one—in other words, about forty-one meters, close to Chartres and Bourges cathedrals.[25] Directly after the construction of these great tower buttresses, however, there was a shift toward greater height and the more decorative forms that we associate with the cathedral of William of Grez (1250s).

It has been seen that the collapse of the upper choir in 1284 led to the complete replacement of the flying buttresses at division 7 (Fig. 55) but that all the other buttresses predate the collapse. In the body of the central vessel straight bays, everything from the sill of the triforium to the high vaults was rebuilt. The junction between the old work and the post-collapse rebuild, with its thicker clerestory

wall, can be seen to the east of piers D 8 and E 8 (Figs. 67, 72, 73). The rebuild included all of the main piers on both sides of the choir and the addition of extra piers in between the existing ones. The additional piers are not supported by flying buttresses. The post-collapse piers (Figs. 33, 37) are composed of an undecorated rectangular block of masonry. The stone coursing of the pier runs directly into the moldings of the window jamb without a break. Some reused elements are visible in the jambs. The additional piers, interposed in the middle of each of the original bays, are similar to the piers at the main bay divisions, except that they are not supported by flyers and their front surfaces have two weather moldings applied to them. The main pier at D 6 on the north side has shallow panels on its flanks.

The tracery of the windows reconstructed after the collapse (Figs. 33, 37, 72) is organized as three lancets under an oculus with six cusps. A close inspection of these windows reveals two variations. In most units the outer lancets, rising higher than the central one, are topped with cusped spherical triangles over cusped pointed arches. The central lancet has a trefoil over a trilobed arch. Three windows do not conform to these specifications, however. At D 6/7 7, E 6/7 7, and E 7 7/8 the main oculus is significantly larger, no spherical triangles are used in the outer lancets, and the trefoil is missing from the central lancet. Spherical triangles are generally a trademark of the fourteenth-century work at Beauvais, and the absence of this element from the three windows suggests that they may be made up of elements of tracery that survived the collapse. If this were the case, then the original clerestory windows would have had six lancets organized in two groups of three.[26] Each triplet would be surmounted by an oculus, and the total composition would be surmounted by another oculus of considerable

[24] In a previous study, I assigned the entire buttresses at B 6 and G 6 to a period after the 1284 collapse; see S. Murray, "The Collapse of 1284 at Beauvais Cathedral," *Acta of the Center for Medieval and Early Renaissance Studies, State University of New York at Binghamton*, III, *The Thirteenth Century*, Binghamton, 1976, pp. 17–44.

[25] The change of plan must have been introduced even while these flyers were under construction. The upper flyer, which now props the main vaults, has been given increased mass.

[26] It should be remembered that the addition of the extra piers reduced the space available for the window. The

size. One of the groups of three lancets could be adapted and recut for use in a window that was half the size of the original one.

Extensive repair work also took place in the sixteenth century when the two piers and windows at the west end of the north side of the choir were completely rebuilt. Pier D 8 at the base of the hemicycle on the south side was reinforced through the addition of a spur of masonry and a small flying buttress, and the equivalent pier on the south side (E 8) was completely rebuilt in the seventeenth century.[27]

This survey of the forms of the exterior of the upper choir has allowed us to define the essentials of the structure as it existed by the collapse of 1284 and to propose a more complete chronology for the construction (Figs. 22, 55). It has been seen that the upper parts were begun at the same time that the ambulatory and radiating chapels were under construction, and we have associated the great tower buttresses at B 6 and G 6 with the cathedral of Bishop Robert of Cressonsac and work in the 1240s. At the same time the stumps of the outer uprights of the choir and hemicycle were constructed up to the level of the roof of the inner aisle and ambulatory. No intermediary uprights were planned for the choir hemicycle at this point. The work at this stage was reduced in both mass and decoration.

The accession of Bishop William of Grez brought increased funds for the fabric and a shift toward greater intensity of decoration and greater height. Progressing from west to east, work began on the completion of the uprights of the flying buttresses, intermediaries were added in the hemicycle, and work then continued with the upper superstructure of the main vessel.

A vertical glass box of incredibly delicate

construction soars upward to a smoothly rounded upper wall and balustrade uninterrupted by pinnacles or gables. In the straight bays, the effect of the three enormous clerestory windows, each with six lancets organized in two groups of three, must have been particularly striking. The supports have been reduced to openwork tabernacles, and the clerestory wall is paper-thin. The building flexes its muscles on the periphery with the massive outer uprights of the flying buttresses that create such a square silhouette as they march around the outside of the hemicycle.

This monument was not conceived as a single sublime vision; rather, it reflects the shifting intentions of its designers and patrons. These shifts in intention have been analyzed in three phases: an expansive vision in the 1220s (transept, outer walls of a five-aisled choir), a reduced or contracted vision of the 1230–1240s (radiating chapels, lower parts of central vessel), followed by a return to grandiose schemes in the 1250s (upper triforium and clerestory, with increased height and the addition of the intermediary uprights in the hemicycle). These shifts in intention have lent to the Beauvais choir forms that are unique in Gothic, especially the extraordinary flying buttress uprights that tower to heaven.

The Stylistic Context of the Cathedral of Bishops Robert and William

Some of the features of the work of the 1230s to 1260s (the cathedral of Bishops Robert and William) can be understood in the context of the Rayonnant architecture of the Ile-de-France.[28] This period saw a tendency on the part of patrons and designers to favor edifices with a reduced scale, with the optical effects of window tracery transferred to the

---

reused elements are installed in the broadest windows at the east end of the choir. These elements were taken from the narrower windows at the west end. The original pattern of the Beauvais clerestory is reflected in the great west window of Sens cathedral, rebuilt after the 1268 collapse.

[27] The profiles of the soffits of the small flyers added to strengthen the base of the intermediary upright at C 8 belong to the sixteenth century.

[28] For definitions of Rayonnant, see H. Bober, "A Reappraisal of Rayonnant Architecture," in *The Forward Movement of the Fourteenth Century*, ed. F. L. Utley, Columbus, 1961, pp. 9–30; R. Branner, "Paris and the Origins of Rayonnant Gothic Architecture down to 1240," *Art Bull*, XLIV, 1962, pp. 39–51; and H. Focillon, *The Art of the West in the Middle Ages*, II, London, 1969, p. 40.

structural framework of the building. Some of the precious effects of buildings of the 1170s and 1180s were revived, particularly the use of detached shafts. Plans were simplified and reduced, the double ambulatory, for example, becoming rare after 1220.

Within this context, the Cistercian church of Royaumont (Fig. 171) assumes considerable importance, particularly since the plan of the hemicycle of its choir is virtually identical to the hemicycle of the Beauvais choir, and since Bishop Miles of Nanteuil was involved (although indirectly) in this foundation in the southern tip of the diocese of Beauvais.

Before his death at Montpensier in November 1226, Louis VIII had stipulated that his jewels should be sold and the resultant funds should be put toward the foundation of a monastery and a church dedicated to the Virgin Mary.[29] It is thought that Louis VIII had envisioned a Victorine house, but the youthful Louis IX, almost certainly under the influence of his mother, Blanche of Castile, chose rather to found a Cistercian monastery. A piece of land was purchased close to the royal manor of Asnières-sur-Oise in the southern part of the diocese of Beauvais. The estate had previously been known as Cuimont and had been held by the priory of Saint-Martin of Boran.[30] The charter of the foundation for Royaumont, dated 1228, is a very generous one indeed, providing substantial rights and holdings for the new monastery.[31] The following decades also brought further gifts from the monarch. Louis took a strong personal interest in the construction of the monastery, visiting the site and performing symbolic acts of manual labor with the monks.

Unfortunately, the chronology of the construction work is far from clear. A group of monks from Cîteaux was established on the site in 1228, and an act of the Cistercian general chapter in 1229 has been interpreted as indicating that the internal organization of the community was complete.[32] The church was consecrated on October 25, 1235.[33]

Although existing buildings on the site might have offered immediate accommodation for the monks, it is reasonable to assume that early construction work would have been concentrated not only upon the church, but also on the extensive monastic buildings. Thus, despite the lavish funding provided by Louis VIII and Louis IX, it is questionable whether the entire church could have been finished in the seven-year period from 1228 to 1235.

The church, almost entirely demolished after the French Revolution, was a sizable one, with a central vessel of 12.20 m and vaults rising some 28 m above the pavement. A nine-bay nave extended into a transept that protruded two full bays beyond the nave aisles. The transept had aisles on both east and west sides, but the western aisle of the south transept was engulfed by the cloister. East of the transept existed a one-bay choir with double aisles terminating in a seven-segment hemicycle encircled by a single ambulatory and seven shallow five-sided radiating chapels. The east end bears a strong resemblance to the choir of the Cistercian church of Longpont (Fig. 161),[34] consecrated in the presence of Louis IX and Blanche of Castile one year before the foundation of Royaumont, and it is impossible to escape from the conclusion (already reached by Duclos and others) that in its plan, at least, Royaumont is Longpont "*corrigée et perfectionée.*"[35]

It has been seen that the eastern parts of the choir at the nearby cathedral of Beauvais were not begun until the late 1230s. It is thus of some importance to recognize in the plan of the church at Royaumont certain essential characteristics of Beauvais, namely an east

---

[29] Abbé H. Duclos, *Histoire de Royaumont, sa fondation par Saint Louis et son influence sur la France*, Paris, 1867; Lauer, "L'Abbaye de Royaumont"; Gouïn, *L'Abbaye de Royaumont.*

[30] Duclos, *Histoire*, p. 36, claimed that the purchase was approved by Miles, bishop of Beauvais.

[31] Ibid., pp. 37–42.

[32] Ibid., p. 77.

[33] Louis had given the monastery certain relics of the Holy Cross.

[34] For Longpont, see Bruzelius, "Cistercian High Gothic."

[35] Duclos, *Histoire*, p. 170.

end designed around a center point that has been pushed somewhat to the east of the last transverse arch, a double-aisled choir terminated in a single ambulatory, and seven radiating chapels of equal depth.[36]

It has been common to see in Royaumont a kind of "purified" Gothic, which had been modified to render it appropriate for Cistercian use.[37] In fact, the essential elements of Royaumont are interchangeable with other Benedictine and secular churches of the period. The elevation had three stories, an arcade carried by lofty cylindrical piers, and a blind triforium made up of two units each containing a pair of trilobed arches topped by a trefoil. The tracery of the tall clerestory comprised two lancets under an oculus. We need not see the cylindrical piers or the mural strips flanking the clerestory as evidence of a "resistance to Chartres" nor of Cistercian asceticism; they were both perfectly common in the Ile-de-France of the 1220s and 1230s.[38] The use of oculi piercing the wall of the southern nave aisle (above the cloister walk) is closely paralleled in Parisian churches such as Arceuil. The relatively low springing point of the arches and ribs of the high vaults can also be recognized as a standard local trait.

A study of the evolution of forms apparent in the church confirms a dating to the 1230s–1240s. Whereas a deep scotia is still present in the one surviving freestanding pier in the east end of the building, the bases attached to the fragment of the north and south transept façades have a reduced scotia, or none at all, bearing witness to a date toward the mid-century. The elegant beaked capitals of the nave confirm the suspicion that the consecration of 1235 saw only the choir and parts of the tran-

sept complete and that the construction of the nave continued into the middle and second half of the century.

The choir plans of Longpont, Royaumont, Amiens, and Beauvais are all very similar (Figs. 6, 142, 161, 171). The same formula was to be repeated at Cologne and Altenberg.[39] Is it possible to establish the filiation of the French versions of this choir type? Longpont was clearly first, but to place Royaumont, Beauvais, and Amiens in chronological order is impossible, since the last two cathedrals were built in a west-to-east sequence. Did Robert of Luzarches have a parchment plan at the start of work at Amiens in 1220 that included the entire building, or was the choir designed only at the time it was built, in the 1240s? The same question arises at Beauvais. Bishop Miles of Nanteuil was at the dedication of Longpont in 1227. If his masons took the Longpont plan and updated it, then Beauvais will provide the link between Longpont and Royaumont. This eventuality would make the cathedral of Bishop Miles seem all the more remarkable. All the other churches with a five-aisled pyramidal elevation have a deep hemicycle, with double ambulatory or deep chapels.[40] Beauvais is the only example of this kind of structure with a shallow east end. If we choose the other option, and see the design of the east end as belonging to the 1240s, then Beauvais will be later than Royaumont and contemporaneous with Amiens. The use of a plan type derived from Royaumont could be seen as an expression of the closer dependence of Beauvais upon the monarchy after the submission of Bishop Robert of Cressonsac to Louis IX. Of the two possibilities, the latter seems more plausible.

If Longpont and Royaumont provided the

---

[36] Double choir aisles reduced to a single ambulatory can be found at Reims, Saint-Remi, and Meaux, Troyes, Reims, and Amiens cathedrals.

[37] Branner, *Saint Louis and the Court Style*, pp. 30–31.

[38] The presence of a strip of wall flanking the windows can be found in the clerestory at Royaumont and in the windows of the inner aisle and ambulatory at Beauvais.

[39] For Cologne, see A. Wolff, "Chronologie der ersten Bauzeit des Kölner Domes, 1248–1277," *Kölner Domblatt*, XXVIII/XXIX, 1968. In most respects, the choir of Cologne

Cathedral was derived from Amiens, not Beauvais. However, the crown of seven shallow chapels of equal size and the arrangement of the staircase turrets at the base of the hemicycle are similar at Cologne and Beauvais. For the problem of filiation, see U. Schröder, "Royaumont oder Köln?" *Kölner Domblatt*, XLII, 1977, pp. 209–242, and M. Davis, "The Choir of the Abbey of Altenberg: Cistercian Simplicity and Aristocratic Iconography," *Cistercian Studies*, II, 1984, pp. 130–160.

[40] Including Saint-Quentin, Le Mans, and Coutances.

plan type for the cathedral of Bishops Robert and William, the choir of Amiens Cathedral (Figs. 145–48), dating, for the most part, to the 1240s and 1250s, offers not only a similar plan type, with seven chapels arranged in a shallow hemicycle system, but also many other close parallels in the forms of articulation.[41] In particular, the approach to the design of buttresses is very similar in the two choirs; buttresses have a rapid sequence of offsets combined with strong verticality. In other words, the buttress loses very little mass at each offset. The minor buttresses of the chapels are coordinated with the major buttresses bearing the flyers in a way that is new in Gothic. The weather moldings of the offsets line up to give a series of horizontal bands swathing the hemicycle and unifying it. Indeed, in every sense the Amiens choir provides the closest analogies for the forms used at Beauvais in the 1240s: beaked capitals (appearing in the Amiens ambulatory), sharpened moldings, and four-unit tracery patterns similar to the window at G 7 8 in the Beauvais choir. At Beauvais, we find the use of detached shafts in the piers between the radiating chapels; at Amiens, such shafts are used in the piers dividing the double aisles of the choir. Both buildings bear witness to an ongoing search for novelty. At Amiens this is expressed in the transition to a glazed triforium in the transept and choir and the adoption of tracery work in the flying buttresses of the choir. Certain aspects of the Amiens choir might strike us as "mannered" in the same way we might consider the squashed shafts in the Beauvais piers as expressing a play on well-established forms that had become clichés. Hugh Libergier's design for the west façade of Saint-Nicaise of Reims with its zigzag of gables sliding across the surfaces of the buttresses expresses the same readiness to play with existing forms.[42]

The links between the Amiens choir and Paris have been clearly documented by Robert Branner,[43] and in many respects the cathedral of Bishops Robert and William bears witness to the fact that Beauvais was being tugged inward toward Paris. This is reflected in the links between the Beauvais choir and the work of the master mason Pierre of Montreuil at Saint-Germain-des-Prés.[44]

A new cloister had been begun at Saint-Germain-des-Prés around 1227 under Abbot Eudes, heralding a series of projects aimed at the general reconstruction of the monastic buildings (Fig. 164). In 1239, under Abbot Simon, a new refectory was begun on the north side of the cloister walk, and in 1245, under Abbot Hugues of Issy, the old chapel dedicated to the Virgin was replaced. The new Virgin chapel was parallel with the choir of the church and somewhat to the north. Both the refectory and the Virgin chapel are attributed with some certainty to the master mason

[41] For the chronology of Amiens Cathedral, see Erlande-Bradenburg, "La Façade de la cathédrale d'Amiens."

[42] The church of Saint-Nicaise was demolished after the French Revolution; we know of the church only through graphic and written sources as well as fragmentary remains. Most recently, see M. Bideault and C. Lautier, "Saint-Nicaise de Reims: Chronologie et nouvelles remarques sur l'architecture," *Bull. mon.*, CXXXV, 1977, pp. 295–330.

[43] Branner, "Paris and the Origins of Rayonnant."

[44] On Saint-Germain-des-Prés, see Dom J. Bouillart, *Histoire de l'abbaye royale de Saint-Germain-des-Prez*, Paris, 1724; H. Verlet, "Les Bâtiments monastiques de Saint-Germain-des-Prés," *Paris et Ile-de-France, Mémoires*, IX, 1957–1958, pp. 9–69; R.-A. Weigert, "Plans et vues de Saint-Germain-des-Prés," *Paris et Ile-de-France, Mémoires*, IX, 1957–1958, pp. 105–137.
On Pierre of Montreuil, see H. Stein, "Pierre de Montereau, architecte de l'église abbatiale de Saint-Denis,"

Mém. Soc. nat. ant. France, ser. 7, LXI, 1902, pp. 79–104; idem, "Pierre de Montereau et la cathédrale de Paris." *Mém. Soc. nat. ant. France*, ser. 8, LXXI, 1912, pp. 14–28; Abbé J. de Launay, in *Nouvelle Revue*, XLVII, 1920, pp. 1–26; M. Minost and M. Aubert, "La Fenêtre occidentale du réfectoire de Saint-Germain-des-Prés, œuvre de Pierre de Montreuil," *Bull. mon.*, CXII, 1954, pp. 275–280; R. Branner, "A Note on Pierre de Montreuil and Saint-Denis," *Art Bull.*, XLV, 1963, pp. 355–357; Grodecki, "Pierre, Eudes et Raoul de Montreuil"; idem, "Le Moyen Age occidental," *Revue de l'art*, XLII, 1978, pp. 21–22; D. Kimpel, "Die Querhausarme von Notre-Dame zu Paris und ihre Skulpturen," Ph.D. diss., Bonn, 1971; A. Prache, "Pierre de Montreuil," *Histoire et archéologie*, November 1980, pp. 26–38; J. Moulin and P. Ponsot, "La Chapelle de la Vierge à l'Abbaye Saint-Germain-des-Prés et Pierre de Montreuil," *Archéologie*, CXL, 1980, pp. 49–55.

Pierre of Montreuil.[45] Pierre, who died in 1267, was buried together with his wife, Agnes, in the Virgin chapel.

We know that the refectory was a sizable eight-bay rectangular vaulted structure.[46] A reader's pulpit was incorporated into the wall in the second bay from the east end. In two important respects, Pierre of Montreuil's refectory departed from existing practice. First, the interior space was undivided by the central line of columns often used in refectories,[47] and second, whereas it had been customary to eschew finely finished details in utilitarian monastic buildings, this refectory was lavishly finished. This is evident from descriptions of the interior that speak of a mass of delicate columns and moldings. It is clear that the interior elevation was organized in two levels: an extensive lower wall, which was unarticulated and topped by a projecting molding, and the two-light tracery windows topped with cusped arches and quatrelobed oculi.[48] The mural shafts supporting the vaults comprised bundles of three shafts carried on consoles, leaving the lower wall entirely flat. Such an extensive wall surface and the absence of interior freestanding columns would create a somewhat horizontal emphasis. This horizontality is expressed in the exterior elevation by the complete absence of pinnacles or gables penetrating the upper balustrade.[49]

Some of these features are also present in the Virgin chapel (Figs. 164, 165), which was a very large structure with four straight bays and a seven-part apse.[50] The interior elevation was organized in two levels. The lower wall was articulated as a dado with each panel topped by a finely chiseled cusped arch. Although solid in the straight bays, the panels of the dado were voided in the apse in order to give the impression of freestanding tracery.[51] The mullions of the dado were linked with the tracery of the great windows, which, in the straight bays, comprised four lancets grouped in pairs surmounted by a quatrelobed oculus, the entire composition crowned by an oculus of the same form.

The exterior of the chapel shares the rather horizontal organization of the refectory. This horizontality is emphasized by the unbroken sweep of the upper wall and balustrade, which turned around the apse in a smoothly rounded curve much like the upper wall of Beauvais. The surviving gargoyles from the Virgin chapel indicate that the mass of the exterior buttresses was enclosed in a delicate cage of four detached shafts in an arrangement closely resembling the forms of the upper choir at Beauvais.

It is thus quite evident that the designers of the cathedral of Bishops Robert of Cressonsac and William of Grez were familiar with the work of Pierre of Montreuil. The main features derived from this source were the emphasis upon horizontal articulation, absence of gables, rounded hemicycle, and the use of a cage of detached shafts to lighten the mass of the buttresses. It is also amusing to draw a parallel between the use of square schematism in the organization of the Beauvais elevation and the refectory and Virgin chapel of Saint-Germain-des-Prés. In both the latter buildings, a square placed with its base on the pavement enclosed inside the walls will give the height

---

[45] The sources linking the refectory to the name of Pierre of Montreuil are late; see Verlet, "Les Bâtiments monastiques," p. 40.

[46] Measuring 115 by 32 feet and 47 feet high.

[47] For example, at Royaumont or Saint-Martin-des-Champs.

[48] Parts of the west wall of the refectory were rediscovered in the 1950s. The great window had four lights topped by oculi with six and eight lobes. See Minost and Aubert, "La Fenêtre occidentale."

[49] Branner published the key drawings for the understanding of the refectory, in *Saint Louis and the Court Style*, Figs. 77, 78, 83.

[50] The segments of the apse are organized in a way that resembles the hemicycle of Reims Cathedral and that contrasts with the arrangement found at the cathedrals of Beauvais and Amiens or at the Sainte-Chapelle.

[51] The evidence for this lies in the form of the reverse side of the dado supports, which are tongued to fit onto slender slabs of stone linking the arcade to the outer wall. Similar use of a voided dado side by side with a flat mural arcade can be found in the chapter houses of Westminster Abbey and Salisbury Cathedral.

of the capitals. It has been seen that the total cross section of the Beauvais choir can be inscribed inside a square.

The fact that Pierre of Montreuil was named in 1247 a mason (*cementarius*) of Saint-Denis has led some art historians to believe that he was involved in the reconstruction of the great abbey church in the years after 1231.[52] Given the lack of stylistic links between Saint-Denis and this master's documented work at Saint-Germain-des-Prés and Notre-Dame of Paris, and given the fact that he is not actually named as master mason of the abbey church, it would be best to preserve an attitude of scepticism. In a general sense, the rebuilt Saint-Denis provided a model for the treatment of the upper central vessel as a glass box, with glazed triforium closely linked with the mullions of the clerestory windows. This model was followed at Troyes, Strasbourg, Metz, and at Beauvais itself.[53] However, a study of the details of the thirteenth-century work at Saint-Denis and the upper choir at Beauvais fails to reveal any close links between the workshops.

Although on a much smaller scale, the chapel of the royal château of Saint-Germain-en-Laye (Figs. 172, 173) embodies a similar tracery cage and is not without similarities to the cathedral of Bishops Robert of Cressonsac and William of Grez.[54] Certain elements of the chapel also resemble the forms of Saint-Denis. In both monuments the dado arcade is set out somewhat from the lower wall surface, creating an interior passage. Moreover, the centripetal pattern of the rose used in the chapel resembles the form of the north transept rose at Saint-Denis. However, the organization of the windows is quite different in the royal chapel. Here the pointed arches of the window are inscribed inside rectangular frames, and the glazed spandrels are decorated with trefoils.[55]

The arrangement is one that was to lead to many important repercussions. The rose-inscribed-in-square was to become a standard formula for transept façades, while the double-skinned envelope peculiar to Saint-Germain-en-Laye was to be exploited many times over in the following decades.[56]

The royal chapel at Saint-Germain-en-Laye has sometimes been seen as a prototype for the Sainte-Chapelle in Paris (Figs. 167–170), begun toward 1240 and consecrated in 1248.[57] However, little seems to relate the two monuments, other than that both are single-vessel seigneurial chapels commissioned by King Louis IX. In plan, the Saint-Germain-en-Laye chapel has three bays of equal size, followed (toward the east) by a seven-segment apse. The thought processes involved in the planning of the apse refer mainly to the planning of the central vessel at Reims Cathedral, whereas the Sainte-Chapelle plan refers to the cathedrals of Beauvais and Amiens. Thus the four straight bays are terminated by a seven-sided apse designed around a center point pushed somewhat to the east of the last transverse arch. Similarly, the two works differ considerably in their respective elevations, the Parisian chapel having two stories and lacking the double-skinned wall treatment peculiar to Saint-Germain-en-Laye. When we study the exterior features of the two monuments we are struck by the relative horizontality of the Saint-Germain-en-Laye chapel (conferred by the square-topped windows), similar to the style of Pierre of Montreuil, as opposed to the greater insistence on verticality in the Sainte-Chapelle, resulting not merely from the greater height of the Parisian chapel, but also from the greater emphasis given to the pinnacles and the presence of gables breaking through the line of the upper balustrade.

In the lower chapel of the Sainte-Chapelle

---

[52] Stein, "Pierre de Montereau." For the thirteenth-century work at Saint-Denis, see C. Bruzelius, *The Thirteenth-Century Church at Saint-Denis*, New Haven, 1985.

[53] Bony, *French Gothic Architecture*, pp. 391–396.

[54] Houdard, *Les Châteaux royaux de Saint-Germain-en-Laye.*

[55] The weight of the clerestory wall and roof are carried by the interior arches framing the windows. A narrow gap

exists between these arches and the window plane. The windows thus remain a delicate screen of tracery and glass, free from any weight-bearing function.

[56] As at Saint-Sulpice-de-Favières, the lady chapel at Saint-Germer-de-Fly, and at Saint-Urbain, Troyes.

[57] L. Grodecki, *La Sainte-Chapelle*, Paris, 1962; F. Gébelin, *La Sainte-Chapelle et la Conciergerie*, Paris, 1931.

(Fig. 169) the designer has chosen the format of a hall church with three vessels of equal height. The presence of the freestanding columns that divide the space into three vessels has been explained in functional terms; if the vaults had spanned a unified space of this size, the springing point of the vault would have been at floor level. Of course, other considerations may also have intervened: the prestige to be gained from a three-aisled composition; the impression of lightness lent by the slender columns. This impression of lightness is enhanced by the fine dado, which bears a close resemblance to the one used in the radiating chapels of the cathedral of Amiens. Whereas at Saint-Germain-en-Laye and in the nave of Saint-Denis, trilobed arches were used in the dado, at the Sainte-Chapelle we find the pointed cusped arch also used by Pierre of Montreuil in the Virgin chapel of Saint-Germain-des-Prés. The moldings of the arches and vaults of the lower chapel are wedge-shaped or sharpened in profile and are received on top of beaked abaci. In the freestanding piers, those beaked abaci run together to make a star-shaped form. The total composition embodied in the elevation of the lower chapel might be compared to the triforium and low clerestory windows of many of the smaller churches in the area around Paris, for example, at Champagne-sur-Oise. It also resembles the triforium and clerestory of the ambulatory of Beauvais Cathedral.

In the upper chapel of the Sainte-Chapelle (Fig. 170) the designer seems to deny some of the propositions enunciated so brilliantly downstairs. Thus in the dado he reverts to the more conservative trilobed arch rather than the pointed cusped arch.[58] Similarly, whereas the dado arcade and window tracery of the lower chapel are almost on the same plane, upstairs the designer takes care to prevent us from reading the dado as a "triforium." Thus, in the normal bay the dado has six units and the clerestory four, and the window plane is set back behind that of the dado by means of a rather obtrusive ledge. The space provided by this windowsill allowed the designer to add to the number of shafts that ascend to the upper parts of the edifice; a bundle that had begun as three shafts is thus increased to nine. For his tracery, the Sainte-Chapelle designer has adopted the form used by Pierre of Montreuil in the Virgin chapel at Saint-Germain-des-Prés, but for the narrow eastern bays he has demonstrated his own interesting inventiveness in a new form: three unframed trefoils piled in pyramidal fashion.

The jagged silhouette of the Sainte-Chapelle (Fig. 168), bristling with gables and pinnacles, contrasts sharply with the more peaceful massing of Pierre of Montreuil's Virgin chapel, with its smooth horizontality. In this respect, the Beauvais choir is closer to the Virgin chapel. However, two features of the exterior of the Sainte-Chapelle are reflected in the forms of the Beauvais choir: the steeply vertical articulation of the buttresses (as also in the Amiens choir) and the use of cages of detached shafts. At the Sainte-Chapelle, such shafts enclose the polygonal flanks of the staircase turrets at the west end.

The mid-thirteenth-century work at Notre-Dame of Paris (Figs. 162, 163)—the addition of lateral chapels between the buttresses of the nave and the transept façades—may be considered as the epitome of the brittle, two-dimensional articulation of structure peculiar to Rayonnant.[59] The metallic preciousness of the Notre-Dame transept façades is expressed, above all, in the parts of the Beauvais choir above the triforium sill, designated here as the cathedral of Bishop William of Grez. Since Pierre of Montreuil worked at Notre-Dame, and since we have recognized in the cathedral of Bishop William certain signs of influence from Pierre's work at Saint-Germain, it is not surprising to find some direct links between the upper choir at Beauvais and Notre-Dame. Thus, the use of a cage of detached shafts, peculiar to all the buttresses around the Beauvais choir, can also be found in the buttress upright

---

[58] Is this a play on the forms of Hugh Libergier?

[59] Aubert, *Notre-Dame de Paris*, pp. 137–176; Kimpel, "Die Querhausarme."

immediately to the east of the south transept of Notre-Dame.[60]

The Cathedral of Bishops Robert and William: Conclusion

It is thus quite evident that the eastern end of the Beauvais choir and the entirety of the upper superstructure should be considered in relation to Rayonnant architecture of the 1240s and 1260s. This conclusion allows us to deepen our understanding of the peculiar forms of the Beauvais choir, and also casts significant light on the essence of the style we have called "Rayonnant." It is generally much easier to draw parallels between the Rayonnant parts of the Beauvais choir and contemporary monuments than had been the case in the High Gothic choir of Beauvais. This tells us something about the eclectic, highly inventive designers of the cathedral of Bishop Miles, and it also tells us much about the way we have chosen to define High Gothic and Rayonnant. The former may be defined in terms of an overall structural framework in which many variations were possible. The cathedral of Bishop Miles was a unique synthesis of structural elements that had never before been attempted in Gothic (five-aisled pyramidal basilica intersected by an aisled transept). Rayonnant, on the other hand, is generally defined not so much in terms of the total structural framework, but more in terms of the way in which surfaces are handled. Formulas for the design of a window or the surfaces of a buttress travel much more easily than solutions for the total structure of a cathedral. Thus, we might expect to see certain similarities between the forms employed by the designers of the upper choir of Beauvais Cathedral and the forms found in many other monuments of the Ile-de-France of the 1240s to 1260s.

Our study of the cathedral of Bishops Robert and William may also allow us to gain an insight into the economic dimension of the Rayonnant style. In the atmosphere of financial crisis that must have prevailed in the aftermath of the struggle between bishop and king, it is not surprising to find the use of forms that appear somehow reduced. The designers of the cathedral of Bishop Robert of Cressonsac were working under severe artistic and economic restraints. It is most significant that they referred to a Cistercian prototype, Royaumont, for the ground plan of the choir. The elevation of the Beauvais ambulatory, with its band triforium and stubby clerestory windows, was fixed by the design of the eastern aisles of the transept arms completed between 1225 and 1232 under Bishop Miles of Nanteuil. The designers of the Beauvais ambulatory and radiating chapels referred above all to the Amiens choir and the Sainte-Chapelle for the forms of their buttresses, piers, and capitals. However, certain forms used at Beauvais during this phase of construction are unique—one thinks particularly of the mannered piers of the main arcade, with the central shaft pushed into the body of the pier. The nave at Fécamp (1220s) provides an example of a parallel speculation upon the traditional form of the *pilier cantonné*, but at Fécamp triple shafts were added to the front and the rear of the pier.[61] The use of flattened shafts has been observed in the wall surfaces under the towers flanking the choir at Saint-Leu-d'Esserent and in the south nave arcade at Gonnesse.

The cathedral of Robert of Cressonsac was a structure where forms were streamlined, simplified, and reduced. This trend belongs to the period of uncertainty that followed the struggle between bishops and king in the 1230s. In the 1240s, moreover, it is clear that the resources of the diocese and county were being drawn away toward the Crusade; Bishop Robert of Cressonsac set out on crusade in 1248, and he died soon after on the island of Cyprus. He left the cathedral com-

---

[60] It should be recognized that this unit has been subject to restoration work.

[61] For Fécamp, see Abbé J. Daoust, *Fécamp, l'abbatiale de la Trinité*, Fécamp, 1956.

plete in its lower parts, with a start made on the buttress uprights at the extreme west end of the choir (Fig. 22).

The new bishop, William of Grez (1249–1267), was an enthusiastic builder. He is known to have rebuilt the episcopal chapel and to have equipped it with stained glass similar to that of the Sainte-Chapelle. The upper parts of the central vessel of the choir belong to his period and bear witness to structural adventurousness and a taste for lavish decoration. It seems probable that Bishop William, like his predecessor, Bishop Miles of Nanteuil, financed his building efforts partly through heavy taxes imposed upon the bourgeois of Beauvais. This would explain the renewed tension between bishop and commune in the 1260s. The builders of Beauvais Cathedral in the 1250s enjoyed more financial support and artistic freedom than in the previous decade. This increased level of funding is reflected in the decision made soon after 1250 to increase the height of the superstructure by about five meters. We thus find a monument whose scale surpasses the greatest works of High Gothic, but whose structural elements (piers, buttresses, etc.) have been reduced in the manner appropriate for Rayonnant.

For the design of the high triforium at Beauvais (groups of two trilobed arches under a five-cusped oculus with trefoils in the spandrels) there are prototypes in and around Paris. The extremely fine moldings compare only in general terms with the forms used by Pierre of Montreuil. The five-cusped oculus was used, perhaps by this master, in the eastern nave chapels on the north side of Notre-Dame. The rectangular panels framing the composition and the trefoils in the spandrels compare with the windows in the chapel of Saint-Germain-en-Laye (1230s) and the triforia of Saint-Sulpice-de-Favières (Figs. 175, 177) and Meaux Cathedral (1250s–1260s).[62] Similar trefoils placed in spandrels can be found in the dado of the Sainte-Chapelle (Figs. 169, 170) and in the chapel of Saint-Germer-de-Fly, a work inspired directly from Parisian sources.

The key element in the tracery pattern used in the clerestory of the Beauvais hemicycle involves the placing of a polyfoiled unit directly above a cusped or trilobed lancet. Prototypes for this unusual pattern can be found in the decorative screen at the base of the towers of the west façade of Notre-Dame of Paris,[63] and a pattern similar to the three-lancet units that were clumped in pairs in the clerestory of the choir straight bays can be seen at the east end of the choir aisles of Saint-Sulpice-de-Favières (Fig. 176).

If the masters of the second campaign were very dependent upon Parisian monuments, and particularly on the work of Pierre of Montreuil, this is not to deny the extraordinary originality of their work. A great part of this originality lay in the application of forms that were conceived in the context of relatively small monuments to a structure that had been conceived on a vast scale. In a certain sense, however, this very characteristic rendered these achievements somewhat irrelevant as far as the architecture of the following generation was concerned. We find that certain details of Beauvais are repeated in the smaller churches of the surrounding area (for example, angle corbels were used at Saint-Barthélemy and Agnetz, and simplified forms of tracery patterns from Beauvais can be found at Saint-Martin-aux-Bois and Chambly).[64] The church at Agnetz, situated to the east of Beauvais and constructed in the middle and second half of the thirteenth century, serves both to provide a context for the style of the cathedral of Bishop Robert of Cressonsac (compare the considerable expanses of wall and the tight linkage of triforium and clerestory at Agnetz with the similar arrangement in the ambulatory of Beauvais Cathedral) and

[62] Y. Sjöberg, "Saint-Sulpice-de-Favières," *Cong. arch.*, CIII, 1944, pp. 246–264.

[63] Branner, *Saint Louis and the Court Style*, Fig. 25.

[64] Abbé A. Barraud, "Description de l'ancienne église collégiale de Saint Barthélémy," *Mém. Soc. acad. Oise*, IV, 1859, pp. 734–747; for Saint-Martin, Chambly, and Agnetz, see Bony, *French Gothic Architecture*, Figs. 412–414, 417, 418.

also to remind us of the general irrelevance of the total program of the Beauvais choir as far as the architecture of the surrounding churches was concerned.

Thus, there was no "family of Beauvais Cathedral." The monument has to be evaluated on its own terms, not in relation to its impact on following generations. The towering superstructure of the cathedral of Bishops Robert of Cressonsac and William of Grez was imposed on top of the massive lower walls of the cathedral of Bishop Miles of Nanteuil, producing a unique edifice. Unfortunately, however, both campaigns contributed different kinds of weakness to the building: the first campaign, with its very elongated bays and poor coordination of north and south flanks, producing (in the second campaign) a misaligned hemicycle. The reduction of mass, increased height, and the extraordinary arrangement of the uprights of the flying buttresses in the second campaign may also have contributed to this weakness.

What force propelled the builders of the cathedral of Bishop William of Grez to reach toward the unprecedented height of 46.75 m? The breaking of established norms in the relationship of width to height in Early Gothic architecture is, of course, announced first in details of articulation, especially the shafts that ascend to receive the ribs and arches of the high vaults. These shafts are generally equipped with bases and capitals, expressing a beginning and an end, but the middle, namely the shaft itself, was capable of almost indefinite elongation. The intense interest in towers in Early Gothic announces the same readiness to search for new relationships between width and height. Towers expressed both secular and spiritual authority, and with increased height, the body of the church itself would be-

gin to take on the appearance of a tower. Certainly, at Beauvais, the transept towers intended under Miles of Nanteuil were subsumed in the additional height introduced under William of Grez.

Extreme height at Beauvais should be understood in the context of the urban site, set in a deep basin, and in light of the desire to go beyond certain significant prototypes in order to reach a new order—an order that might seem to us to express sheer madness, but that may have been based upon geometric and iconographic principles that were very important to the builders. The prototypes to be surpassed were found both in Antiquity and in the recent past; the model to be emulated may have come from Biblical sources. The recently completed nave of Amiens Cathedral (about 42 m in height) provided an obvious incentive. Less obvious is the fact that the Beauvais choir is the only Gothic monument to surpass the Pantheon in height.[65] The "perfect" proportions embodied in the tall Beauvais central vessel allowed it to assume the same relationship of height to width (3:1) as that embodied in the already-constructed inner aisle. Moreover, the increased height brought the total section (including the double aisles) very close to a square.[66] The idea of square schematism, which was deeply rooted in medieval design, was derived partly from Biblical descriptions of the Ark of the Covenant and the New Jerusalem seen in the vision of Saint John in the Book of Revelation.[67] The vision of the New Jerusalem is particularly important in this context, since Saint John tells us not only that it was as high as it was wide (like the Beauvais choir) but also that the upper wall rose to a height of 144 cubits. Now if we translate the Biblical cubits into royal feet, this would give a height of 46.80 m. Is it purely a coincidence

[65] Most recently on the Pantheon, see R. Mark and P. Hutchinson, "On the Structure of the Roman Pantheon," *Art Bulletin*, LXVIII, 1986, pp. 24–34, with bibliography. The height of the dome of the Pantheon equals its span, which is here given as 43.4 m. W. Macdonald, *The Architecture of the Roman Empire*, New Haven and London, 1982, p. 111, gave the height of the oculus (to the exterior surface) as 45 m.

[66] For the use of the square and triangle in Gothic design,

see J. Ackerman, "Ars Sine Scientia Nihil Est," *Art Bull.*, XXXI, 1949, pp. 84–111.

[67] Revelation 21. See the interesting discussion of the relationship between the Tabernacle of Moses and church design in A. Prache, *Saint-Remi de Reims: L'Œuvre de Pierre de Celle et sa place dans l'architecture gothique*, Bibliothèque de la Société française d'archéologie, VIII, Geneva, 1978.

that the keystones of the vaults of the Beauvais choir are placed 46.75 m above the pavement? Otto von Simson has written a brilliant commentary on the interpretation of the Gothic cathedral as a vision of the Heavenly Kingdom.[68]

This image of the celestial city was made possible through the enormous temporal resources of the diocese of Beauvais. It was realized at a time when the authority of the established secular clergy was being challenged by the doctrines of the mendicants. In this context, it is obviously most significant to note that a canon of the Beauvais chapter, William of Saint-Amour, led the seculars in their attempt to check the growing power of the mendicants. Beauvais was ever the home of lost causes, for William was no match for Saint Thomas Aquinas and Saint Bonaventure, who enjoyed the support of the king himself.

Twelve years after the inauguration of this spectacular new choir, disaster intervened. It is hard to escape from the symbolic significance of the collapse of this great expression of the power of the established church.

[68] O. von Simson, *The Gothic Cathedral*, New York, 1962.

CHAPTER VI

Collapse of the Upper Choir in 1284 and the Subsequent Reconstruction

"On Friday November 29, 1284, at eight o'clock in the evening, the great vaults of the choir fell and several exterior pillars were broken; the great windows were smashed; the holy *châsses* of Saint Just, Saint Germer, and Saint Evrost were spared; and the divine service ceased for forty years. Several pillars were interposed in the choir arcade in order to fortify it."[1] Various versions of this text are recorded by the local antiquarians of the seventeenth and eighteenth centuries.[2] The original source, no doubt the deliberations of the chapter, is lost. The antiquarians who compiled the Bucquet-aux Cousteaux Collection suggested that two collapses occurred, but as we have seen, this myth resulted from the belief that the present (Gothic) choir was begun in the tenth century. Some catastrophe had to be invented to explain the rebuild of 1225, and therefore it was suggested that a collapse took place in that year, followed by a second one in 1284.

This collapse was clearly a major one, involving much more than a partial fall of the vaults. The cathedral was still not completely repaired in 1338/39. We have a copy of a text from the chapter deliberations for that year, which relates that William of Raye, master of the masonry at Beauvais Cathedral, Aubert of Aubigny, stonecutter, and Jean of Maisonchelle, chaplain and master of the works, had recently considered the works that were to be done in the cathedral—the church would be completely rebuttressed (*réconfortee*) and vaulted, the scaffolding would be removed, and the church would be made ready for the divine service—without which the church could not continue to stand.[3] The author of the text then went on to specify work on raising a great pillar (*pillier* can mean buttress, or flying buttress upright, as well as interior pier), installing the flyers, reseating the sick arches, remaking the windows, and closing in the body of the church. Purchases of materials are recorded, including seven hundred *pendans*, or stones for the severies of vaults, four hundred of which were said to have been old," or in other words, reused, and therefore were

---

[1] Bucquet-aux Cousteaux, XXIII, p. 1.
[2] Louvet, *Histoire et antiquitez*, II, p. 474.

[3] Bucquet-aux Cousteaux, XXVII, p. 34, cited in Murray, "The Collapse of 1284 at Beauvais Cathedral," p. 40.

not paid for. Such reuse of material suggests that although the collapse was a serious one, parts of the vaults may have remained intact and could be demolished and the stones reemployed.

The work of repair and consolidation of the damaged choir took even longer than the initial construction of the monument. The historical factors that explain the very slow progress were partly of a personal nature, for with the exception of Jean of Marigny, the bishops seem to have been reluctant to sink their own resources and efforts into the reconstruction. Other broader historical issues were also involved. For much of the first part of the period the bishops of Beauvais were in conflict with the commune and also at times with the chapter. In the second part of the period, the economic impact of the Hundred Years' War began to be felt.

Bishops and Commune

The collapse took place during the episcopate of Thibaud of Nanteuil (1283–1300).[4] His predecessor, Renaud of Nanteuil, had clashed with the commune over the definition of the role of bishop and commune in the placing of guards for the defense of the city. Violence on the part of the commune was met with interdict on the bishop's part. The settlement, negotiated by the commissioners of King Philip, known as the *Grande Composition*, was ill-conceived, and tension and conflict continued much as before.

The same tension seems to have characterized relations between Renaud of Nanteuil and his chapter. In 1281, when the bishop refused to recognize the newly elected dean (Gautier of Saumur), the chapter exercised its right to impose a cessation of the divine service.[5] The difference was resolved only through the intervention of papal commissioners.

The episcopate of Thibaud of Nanteuil, the nephew of the former bishop, Renaud, was uneventful as far as relations with the commune were concerned. The taxes imposed by Philip the Fair must have had a negative effect upon the financial ability of the bishop and chapter to repair their shattered cathedral,[6] but there is no reason to believe that the work of clearing out the debris and consolidation could not have been begun immediately.

However, the episcopate of Simon of Clermont (also called "of Nesle") saw a recrudescence of civil disorder. The election that followed the death of Thibaud of Nanteuil failed to produce a clear consensus, and Pope Boniface VIII intervened to impose a bishop who was not among the candidates favored by various factions of the chapter. Simon of Clermont, bishop of Noyon, was the son of the seigneur of Nesle, count of Breteuil, formerly regent of France (during the second Crusade of Louis IX).

In 1302 Simon of Nesle was sent, along with his two brothers, on a military expedition against the Flemish. He was present at the defeat of Courvrai, where he saw both brothers killed. Relations between Philip the Fair and Pope Boniface VIII were degenerating, and Simon found himself subject to claims and counterclaims from the pope (Councils of Compiègne, 1301 and 1304) and king (assembly at the Louvre, 1303).

In 1305 yet another uprising took place in the city of Beauvais, directed primarily against the bishop. At Whitsun 1305 a certain number of the inhabitants of Beauvais rose against the requirement that they grind their grain and bake their bread in the episcopal mills and ovens. The mayor seems to have incited the *communiers* to violence, declaring (unilaterally) that they were henceforth free of the duty to attend the bishop's mills and ovens, and free of his jurisdiction in general. A mob destroyed the offensive mills and ovens and attacked the bishop's palace with surprising ferocity. The guards were massacred and the palace and chapel pillaged, the bishop escap-

---

[4] Delettre, *Histoire du diocèse*, II, pp. 351–367.
[5] Ibid., p. 347.

[6] Ibid., p. 356.

ing to one of his residences outside the city. The bishop proceeded to attack the city with weapons both spiritual and physical; he imposed an interdict and attempted to prevent the supply of the town of Beauvais with provisions from the surrounding country. In the latter respect, the bishop was infringing upon royal prerogatives, and Philip the Fair intervened to hold an inquest, arresting both the mayor and the bishop's bailiff. A new mayor, Jean of Coudon from Pont-Sainte-Maxence, was imposed upon the city, and the bishop's temporalities were seized.

The royal settlement, reached in 1306, involved a massive fine imposed upon the commune (eight thousand pounds) and the requirement that the bishop should hold an inquiry into improper exactions on the part of the farmers of his mills.[7]

The strain upon the episcopal budget must have been considerable. The episcopal temporalities were seized by the king for a while, and the expense of rebuilding the damaged palace and the cathedral property (including canons' houses) may have exceeded the reparation that had been allowed. After his unhappy experiences, Simon of Clermont constructed the massive gateway to the bishop's palace, which still exists, to the southwest of the cathedral. The threatening bulk of this twin-towered fortified gate provides a powerful symbol of the turbulent relationship between the bishops and the bourgeois of Beauvais. Bishop Simon died in 1312. It is reported that he did not wish to be buried in the cathedral of Beauvais and that he was buried at Beaupré, beside his father. Delettre suggested that his remains were divided between Beaupré and Beauvais.[8] It is unlikely that much progress was made on the reconstruction of the damaged choir during the episcopate of Simon of Clermont.

His successor, Jean of Marigny (1313–1347), presided over a more harmonious situation but was unfortunate in that he saw his diocese turned into a battlefield with the

opening phase of the Hundred Years' War.[9] The very longevity of this bishop was a positive factor as far as the reconstruction of the cathedral was concerned. His thirty-five-year tenure as bishop saw a succession of four popes and five kings.

At the beginning of his episcopate, Jean of Marigny saw his brother Enguerand, who had been intendant general of Philip the Fair's finances, hanged when the accession of Louis X produced a backlash against the former regime. For the sake of more peaceful relations with his chapter, Bishop Jean ceded in 1325 all jurisdiction over the clergy of the cathedral, including chaplains, vicars, and the like. In 1328 he was appointed chancellor by Philip VI. Hereafter, his movements were determined, to a considerable extent, by affairs of state. In the 1330s we find him sent on a mission to England in connection with plans for a crusade and to the Near East to assess the potential difficulties of such a crusade. In 1340 he was appointed governor of Languedoc.

The 1340s saw the first ravages of the war in the Beauvaisis. In 1346 Edward landed at Honfleur and advanced toward Paris, sacking Vernon, Mantes, Meulan, and Saint-Cloud. The English army turned toward Beauvais, using the monastery of Saint-Lucien as a base. The monasteries of Saint-Quentin and Saint-Lucien and parts of the suburbs were burned, but the city of Beauvais remained intact behind its recently consolidated walls. A contingent of troops from the commune of Beauvais was utterly destroyed in the ensuing battle of Crécy.

In 1347 Jean of Marigny was transferred to the see of Rouen. The work of repair on the damaged choir was substantially completed during his episcopate, although doubtless the campaign continued into the 1350s, a period when Guillaume Bertran occupied the see (1347–1356).[10] It was during this time that the first devastating effects of the Black Death were felt.

It is thus relatively easy to understand why

---

[7] Ibid., p. 392.
[8] Ibid., p. 399.
[9] Ibid., pp. 401–431; C.-L. Doyen, *Histoire de la ville de Beauvais, pour faire suite à l'histoire politique, morale et*

religieuse de M. E. de la Fontaine, Beauvais, 1842, pp. 18–25.
[10] Delettre, *Histoire du diocèse*, II, pp. 432–440.

the reconstruction of the shattered cathedral took as long as sixty years. To ascertain exactly what collapsed and why poses many more problems, however.

Theories of the Collapse

The disaster of 1284 has caught the imagination of modern historians of the cathedral and students of Gothic architecture, and numerous explanations have been devised. It has been tempting to slip into a moralizing frame of mind and to associate the collapse with the excessive pride of the builders who wanted to erect a new Tower of Babel. Similarly, the construction of the Beauvais choir provides writers with the symbolic expression of the end of the structural speculation we call High Gothic—the "end of a system."[11]

Very few writers have been able to escape the deeply ingrained belief that there must be a link between the disaster and the status of the Beauvais choir as the tallest Gothic cathedral ever constructed, and that the limits of the strength of materials and human ingenuity had been reached. In one respect, this belief is obviously incorrect; stone can be piled as high as a mountain, and yet the material at the base will not be crushed. It is naive to consider the collapse as a punishment for the *hubris* of the builders. Yet there is an element of truth in the explanation linking sheer height to structural failure. A cathedral is not a mountain; it contains space. This space-enclosing function is made possible by the structural repertoire of the Gothic architect: a skeletal system with rib vaults and flying buttresses. The calculation of mass to void and the planning of the geometry of an arch or the trajectory of a flying buttress were learned in the workshop, and where formulas existed to fix the thickness of a buttress in relation to the span of a vault or to establish the spatial framework of the edifice, we may assume that they were based upon abstract notions of a Platonic nature. It is certainly correct to see the masons of the Beauvais choir at all stages of construction as designers who departed from the formulas developed by their predecessors, both in terms of details (for example, the form of the main arcade piers) and in overall structural solutions.

The proportions of the Beauvais central vessel (ratio of three to one in the relationship of height to span) were matched only at Amiens, which had a much more solidly constructed buttress system. The great height of the Beauvais choir should not be considered as a High Gothic phenomenon, since the original plan involved a superstructure some five meters lower. The change of plan, introduced in the 1250s, brought a towering superstructure surpassing all previous monuments, yet a superstructure where the key structural elements (piers and buttresses) were rendered in a delicate mode characteristic of Rayonnant.

Thus, it is not inappropriate to make a connection between the fact that the Beauvais choir was the tallest cathedral ever constructed and that it collapsed. In particular, it should be remembered that the additional weight of this lofty superstructure might exacerbate problems already existing in the design of the lower parts of the building.

Returning to the views of previous commentators on the collapse, we find that the oldest sources blame the disaster upon the very wide spacing of the piers of the main arcade.[12] This theory resulted simply from the fact that the rebuilders of the cathedral doubled the piers of the main arcade. It was therefore assumed that this must have been an area of weakness. The arcade itself did not fail, however, and it is tempting to dismiss this theory as oversimplistic. However, it is important to note that the wide spacing of the piers coupled with the great span of the central vessel produced very large main vaults—in fact, the largest vaults of any French Gothic cathedral. The great span of these vaults would call for

---

[11] H. Gardner, *Art through the Ages*, New York, 1970, p. 373.

[12] Thus, the unknown eighteenth-century antiquarian who compiled the manuscript history of Beauvais, now in the Bibl. Nat., Collection de Picardie, CLXII, fol. 30, wrote:

"*La veille de St André 1284 que les piliers boutants tombèrent, ce qui causa l'ecartement des gros murs et la chute de la voute, car les piliers du chœur qui auroient dû la retenir etaient trop éloignés les uns des autres.*"

extremely substantial buttressing at the main points of support. However, it will be seen that the flying buttress system of the Beauvais choir was inadequate for several different reasons.

A theory for the collapse of the Beauvais choir that found wide acceptance among architectural historians is the one propounded by Viollet-le-Duc, who suggested that the detached shafts of the exterior buttresses at the clerestory level settled at a different rate than the coursed masonry of the body of the pier, causing a rotational movement (Fig. 24).[13] This theory was recently endorsed by Jacques Heyman, but has been convincingly refuted by Robert Mark.[14] There is another theory that attempts to relate the collapse to the alleged failure of the upper piers. It has been suggested that the flying buttresses were placed too high, allowing the upper piers to bulge outward at a point just below the head of the flyer.[15] This deformation, it is claimed, led to the addition of iron bars between the buttress uprights and the piers of the central vessel. These bars would be intended not as ties (capable of resisting tension or elongation) but as stays or props, to resist the pressure caused by the tendency of the upper piers to buckle outward.[16]

Another theory for the collapse involves the possibility of settlement at foundation level.[17] It is, of course, impossible to prove or disprove this particular theory. Such settlement has undoubtedly taken place, but it is impossible to demonstrate that this was the major cause of the structural failure of 1284. Signs of such settlement are evident in the undulations of the horizontal rims of the triforia of the inner aisle and central vessel and in the dramatic fissuring of the massive wall of the main arcade.

The most recent collapse theory, generated through the use of photo-elastic modeling, has brought our attention to the undoubted weakness existing at the base of the very slender intermediary uprights of the flying buttresses.[18]

All of the theories summarized above contain elements of truth, yet none of them was based upon a careful analysis of the building itself, and none of the previous commentators has made an attempt to consider the cathedral as process—in other words, as the product of successive building campaigns of very different character. Since the building survives, although in a somewhat rebuilt state, it is possible to use the edifice itself as a model, defining the extent and nature of the collapse through a discussion of the rebuild.[19] It is obviously most important to identify the part of the choir that was most affected by the disaster.

A survey of the forms of tracery, capitals, molding profiles, and similar details confirms that in the main body of the choir everything has been rebuilt from the level of the sill of the high triforium to the vaults. The hemicycle remained intact, as did the main arcade, which was fortified by the addition of extra piers dividing each bay into two, and inviting the rebuilders of the choir to resort to sexpartite vaults. The written sources hint at the possibility of the reuse of material in the high vaults, suggesting that parts of the original vaults might have survived; such reuse of elements of the original tracery of the clerestory windows has been noticed in three of the present windows. It is probable that the original windows in the narrower bay at the west end of the choir may have survived the disaster, and that elements from these windows could have been recut and reused after 1284.

On the exterior of the building, it is quite evident that the outer and inner uprights of the flying buttress system have been entirely rebuilt in the middle bay of the choir at division 7 (Fig. 55). The uprights here lack the de-

---

[13] Viollet-le-Duc, *Dictionnaire*, IV, pp. 177–182.

[14] Heyman, "Beauvais Cathedral"; Mark, *Experiments in Gothic Structure*; Wolfe and Mark, "Collapse of the Beauvais Vaults."

[15] Delatouche, "La Cathédrale de Beauvais."

[16] In fact, iron rods probably were used both as ties and props; they were installed at the time of construction in or-

der to stabilize the masonry.

[17] P. Frankl, *Gothic Architecture*, Harmondsworth, 1962, p. 101.

[18] Mark, *Experiments in Gothic Structure*.

[19] See Murray, "The Collapse of 1284 at Beauvais Cathedral."

tached shafts and simple bases of the original units around the hemicycle. This is the only bay where the flying buttress uprights have been rebuilt—in the adjacent bay to the west, it has been seen that the main uprights were specially thickened units, designed to form the corners of towers, and that they probably belong to the 1240s. The intermediaries at this point (division 6) are also original.

Significant rebuilding is evident at the base of the hemicycle, but this belongs to a much later period. In the exterior of the hemicycle itself (Figs. 67, 68), all the major elements including the flying buttress system predate the collapse. Only the exteriors of the upper hemicycle piers were rebuilt, replacing an arrangement that Viollet-le-Duc reconstructed (on paper) as openwork tabernacles, with fully detached shafts (Fig. 24). The fact that this feature of the otherwise intact hemicycle was rebuilt, presumably after the 1284 collapse (although the masonry is anonymous in terms of stylistic identifying forms), led Viollet-le-Duc to his theory that it was precisely this element in the design of the upper superstructure that caused the collapse. If we follow Viollet-le-Duc's thesis, then we must view the source of the weakness as essentially a longitudinal one, running on the east-west axis of the building. For Viollet-le-Duc, moreover, this was a faulty detail in an otherwise well-conceived structure, the "Parthenon of French Gothic."

The extent of the rebuild suggests, however, that the collapse occurred not because of a faulty detail in the upper superstructure, but rather because of a critical lack of lateral buttressing at a point in the choir that is easily ascertainable. There is only one bay in the choir where all the vertical members have been rebuilt, including the piers of the central vessel (in their upper parts), the intermediary piers dividing the double aisles, the intermediary uprights on top of these piers, and the massive outer flying buttress uprights from which the entire buttressing system is generated—namely, the middle bay of the choir, at

division 7. What were the special characteristics of the plan and elevation that would combine to produce unusual weakness at this point in the building? First, it is evident from the plan that the central vault at 7 8 was the largest vault in the building, measuring about 15.30 m by almost 9.00 m. There is an obvious lack of balance between this oversized central vault and the undersized spans of the transverse arches of the aisles—spans that would be expressed by undersized flyers, lacking the weight and inward thrust of a more conventional unit. A flyer acts as a strut as well as an active agent with its own inward thrust, and at Beauvais the former function must have been much more significant than the latter, given the reduced spans and weight of the flyers. Acting as rigid struts, the flyers would thus transmit the thrust of the massive central vault at division 7 to the uprights over the intermediary piers and to the outer uprights. Reference to the plan reminds us that this exceptionally heavy load was delivered at the point of the choir least able to support it. Division 7 is the only point where the lateral thrust of the high vaults was not countered by exceptionally heavy masonry—either in the more massive uprights at the base of the hemicycle, nor in the great buttresses intended to support the corners of towers at division 6. It is of interest to find an analogous situation in the very well-documented building history of Troyes Cathedral, where it was necessary in the 1360s and again in 1402 to consolidate the lateral buttressing in the middle bay of the choir, at a point exactly corresponding to this.[20]

Thus, the problems experienced at division 7 resulted from certain basic characteristics of the plan. When we turn from a study of the plan to the elevation we find that the main problems encountered in bay 7 8 affected the piers dividing the double aisles of the choir rather than the piers of the main arcade, which remained intact. Piers C 7 and F 7 may be associated with the second campaign of construction in the 1240s, and they lack the

[20] Murray, *Building Troyes Cathedral.*

mass of their counterparts to the west. These slender piers have failed not once but repeatedly. The base of the unit on the north side (C 7; Fig. 100) reveals that it was rebuilt around 1300, but the present pier dates almost entirely from the nineteenth century. The pier on the other side (Fig. 110) was presumably rebuilt around 1300, but in its present form it dates from 1517, at which time it was also found necessary to add a solid wall dividing the bays of the outer aisle.[21] This wall was continued right up to the little flying buttress supporting the vault of the inner aisle, and there is extensive sixteenth-century work in the triforium and clerestory of the inner aisle at this point.

The problems experienced with aisle piers C 7 and F 7 resulted from a variety of different causes, including their reduced mass and the fact that they helped support the west end of the largest and heaviest vault in the choir, in bay 7 8. What of the aisle piers at the other side of this vault, at division 8? These piers also have the reduced mass that is associated with the second campaign and the work of the 1240s. Drawings preserved in the archives of the Monuments Historiques in Paris indicate that these piers began to fail toward the end of the nineteenth century. Photographs of the cathedral taken at the time reveal that the piers were bending inward at a height corresponding to the capitals of the arches into the radiating chapels. The restoration drawing by Sauvageot (Fig. 23) also shows a plumb line running parallel with the pier, with measurements to show the extent of the bending. In the drawing, the masonry of the solid wall of the radiating chapel at the base of the hemicycle is full of gaping joints, indicating that the pier was pulling away toward the interior of the building.

What caused this inward bending in the aisle piers of the Beauvais choir? Several factors probably contributed, but the most important problem was certainly created by the existence of a lower outer aisle and chapels whose vaults and arches exerted an inward thrust on piers whose cross section had been reduced excessively and that received no support or buttressing on their inner sides—hence the provisional wooden braces that appeared in the inner aisle at this time. Other factors also intervened. The flying buttress uprights helped support the heaviest vault of the choir and transmitted that weight to the aisle piers and outer buttresses. While the rebuild has swept away the key evidence, it seems probable that these uprights were carried eccentrically—in other words, that a significant part of their mass projected beyond the support. Such eccentric loading can produce bending, resulting from pressure on the side of the support where the overhang exists and tension on the other side.[22] This would cause the upper parts of the aisle piers to bend inward.

This is pure speculation, however, since we cannot be sure that the original uprights at division 7 were placed eccentrically. What is certain, however, is that the reduced mass of the aisle piers was subject to various kinds of bending, producing significant settlement and deformation at the base of the intermediary uprights of the flying buttresses. This problem resulted not only from the pyramidal massing of the Beauvais choir (no prop for the inward thrust of the vaults and arches of the outer aisle) but also from the weight of the largest central vault, transmitted by the uprights of the flyers. The solid masonry embodied in the chapel walls at the base of the hemicycle at division 8 allowed this part of the edifice to survive for six centuries after the collapse of the choir; the absence of such masonry and the more slender form of the outer upright at division 7 were the critical factors leading to the failure of the buttressing system at division 7, which in turn led to the sequential collapse of the upper choir.

Previous studies of the collapse of the Beauvais choir have been founded upon the assumption that a basically well-conceived structure failed because of a particular faulty

[21] For the chronology of this work, see Chapter VII.
[22] For an explanation of bending in a support under ec-

centric load, see Mark, Alexander, and Abel, "The Structural Behaviour of Medieval Ribbed Vaulting."

detail. However, it is most important to consider the disaster in the context of a building where several conflicting artistic visions had been grafted together. The initial vision (the cathedral of Bishop Miles of Nanteuil) already embodied potential problems: enlarged spans and bending in the intermediary piers of the aisles. These problems were exacerbated by the decision of the designers of the second campaign to reduce the mass of the aisle piers, to place the intermediary uprights of the flying buttresses in an eccentric position, and to increase the height of the central vessel. It is particularly significant to note that the collapse affected the building in the middle bay of the choir, at 7 8, where the two campaigns of construction met, and moreover, that this bay had been enlarged as a result of the poor coordination of the two campaigns. This recognition adds historical dimension to our understanding of the collapse and also provokes a series of speculations about what might have been. What if the builders of the cathedral of Bishop Miles of Nanteuil had continued their work, uninterrupted by the crisis of the 1230s? Would they have realized that the supports at the eastern edge of bay 7 8 were poorly aligned? It seems highly probable that they would have refrained from reducing the mass of the aisle piers, and thus they might have avoided the bending problems that have plagued this part of the building. Similarly, they might have refrained from placing the uprights of the flying buttresses in an eccentric position, and they would have constructed a lower superstructure.

Thus, in a very real sense, the collapse may be seen as the result of the funding crisis of the 1230s, which in turn resulted from the struggle between Miles of Nanteuil, the bishop who was "as proud as Nebuchadnezzar,"[23] and the king and his mother. We thus have an "accidental" theory for the collapse in terms of the attendant historical circumstances—it would not be altogether nonsensical to insist that the Beauvais choir collapsed because a proud bishop accused the mother of the king of having sexual relations with the papal legate.

The collapse took place on a November evening when the awesome spectacle would have been shrouded by the gathering dusk. When the dust cleared, beholders might have been able to see the choir still standing, but with much of the central vessel down and the lateral buttresses dislocated down to the level of the aisle vaults. Did the master mason witness the catastrophe? Did his contract with the bishop and chapter contain a clause making him responsible for financial loss incurred through his mistakes? Was he punished? The lack of documents deprives us of the answers to these questions. We may be fairly certain that one or more *expertises* followed the collapse, with visiting master masons asked to suggest plans for the rebuilding of the shattered structure. In the increasingly troubled political and economic circumstances, the funding of the new work constituted a real problem. The campaigns were prolonged, probably comprising two main phases, one immediately following the collapse and a second one during the episcopate of Jean of Marigny. A number of different master masons probably participated. Structurally, the solutions adopted seem to suggest considerable conservatism, especially in the doubling of the piers of the main arcade and in the thickening of the clerestory wall. Certain elements of the new work strike one as being somewhat gauche, notably the tracery designs employed in the reconstructed triforium and clerestory. However, the new work was not without its optical refinements. The additional piers of the main arcade were designed to match the existing ones (Figs. 122, 123). However, instead of having a circular central core, they were designed around a series of ellipses in order to reduce their bulk and to prevent them from completely blocking the diagonal vistas into the aisles.

In 1338 the clergy asked a certain Enguerrand Le Riche to draw up plans for the completion of the church.[24] In 1341 the final

---

[23] See Chapter II, note 49, above.

[24] Bibl. Nat., Collection de Picardie, CLXII, fol. 16–17:

stages of the work were entrusted to three master masons from Paris. It is tempting to associate the elaborately decorated buttresses on the north side of the choir with these masons.[25]

With the completion of the work of repair on the shattered cathedral, construction ceased for a period of about a century and a half.

"*Enguerrand Le Riche fut chargé en 1338 de faire un Dessein pour finir l'Eglise.*"

[25] Bucquet-aux Cousteaux, XXVII, p. 37: "It was ordained in the chapter that the silver that was left to the treasury by Bishop Miles should be sold as advantageously as possible and the money that accrued should be used for the work that three master masons from Paris have ordered to be done in the church and that from the residue the canon's stalls should be covered because of [the droppings of] the pigeons and from the remaining balance windows should be made for the upper parts [of the choir]."

CHAPTER VII

The Late Gothic Transept of Martin Chambiges

Beauvais Cathedral has a transept *de luxe*, extending a full bay beyond the five-aisled choir and provided with aisles on each side (Figs. 31, 32, 38, 39). Towers were originally intended to flank the façades. The transept was constructed between 1500 and 1550, and the work included the beginnings of a five-aisled nave. Thirteenth-century campaigns of construction had stopped short at the eastern piers of the crossing and included the eastern transept aisles. The designers of the cathedral of Bishop Miles of Nanteuil (after 1225) had already envisaged an edifice whose spacious transept and relatively short choir and nave would produce a distinctly cruciform shape.

The upper transept dates entirely from the sixteenth century. However, it is quite possible that the clerestory of the eastern side of the transept arms (Figs. 76, 77) had been begun in the thirteenth century to provide abutment for the eastern crossing piers (as at Cologne Cathedral) but that this work was demolished in the sixteenth century for the sake of stylistic uniformity.

The architect of the Late Gothic transept inherited a situation where most of the decisions relating to plan and elevation were prejudiced by the form of the existing building. The transept crossing had to be square, and the aisle bays to the west of the transept arms had to match their counterparts to the east. The major decisions facing the architect, Martin Chambiges, were whether to continue the transept towers already begun over the eastern aisles, whether to begin a five-aisled nave to match the choir, and how much of the existing work should be retained and how much demolished in order to allow him to achieve the effects he wanted. Chambiges showed himself to be both bold and conservative at the same time. He wisely decided against any attempt to continue the towers, and in order to achieve interior abutment for his façades, he introduced clifflike solid walls in the outermost bays. He took a bold step in anticipating a five-aisled nave and in abandoning the pyramidal elevation of the choir; the west aisle of the transept announces that the nave was to have two aisles of the same height (Fig. 31), much like the nave of the church of Saints-Gervais-et-Protais in Gisors. One wonders whether Chambiges was aware of the bending problems in the intermediary aisle piers of the choir, and that these problems resulted partly from the use of two aisles of different heights. Are we dealing with a Late Gothic architect able to perceive and correct the faults of High Gothic? He certainly rebuilt one of the defective aisle piers of the choir (F 7, rebuilt in 1518). In the transept and first bay of the nave (Figs. 120, 121) the height of the aisles has been considerably reduced in relation to the very tall inner aisle of the choir. A truly colossal clerestory results from this arrangement.

In elevation the transept arms and the first bay of the nave have three stories: arcade, triforium, and clerestory. The piers have a smoothly undulating surface with four large shafts and four smaller ones, received on top of hexagonal plinths (Figs. 75–77). The triforium (an oddly archaic feature) is blind to the east side of the transept arms and glazed to the west and in the first bay of the nave. The use of the triforium is probably to be explained through the designer's desire to avoid the enormous unarticulated expanse that would result from the choice of a two-story elevation. The immense height of the clerestory is subdivided by means of tracery arches halfway up—a device that had been used earlier by Martin Chambiges in the transept arms at Sens Cathedral.[1] The transept arms at Beauvais are vaulted with quadripartite bays over the extremities and sexpartite vaults adjacent to the crossing, making use of the alternation of piers on the east side of the transept and echoing the vaults of the choir. These sexpartite bays as well as the wooden vault of the crossing itself were rebuilt after the collapse of the crossing tower in 1573.

In its interior the work embodies the effects of sheer height (inherited from the choir) coupled with the smooth sophistication of the undulating piers. The projection of the attached colonnettes in the High Gothic and Rayonnant choir had already been reduced to a minimum, producing a rather "slippery" optical effect. This effect is gained to an even greater

degree in the undulating surfaces of the piers of the transept. This is Gothic reduced to its bare bones; the streamlined shafts of the piers take a single leap from floor to vault without the interruption of capitals. Such is the coldly rational quality of the interior that it is tempting to apply the epithet "doctrinaire Gothic."[2] The decorative niches in the interior walls of the transept façades help to relieve the austerity of the interior, as do the rich colors of the stained glass.

The bishop and chapter had waited for three centuries for a ceremonial entrance to the cathedral, and Martin Chambiges gave them all they could have hoped for. There is a striking contrast between the restrained articulation of the interior and the ebullience of these transept façades (Figs. 38, 39).

The towering south transept is the cathedral's face toward the outside world, looking on the place Saint-Pierre. Such is the overall height of the façade that all idea of transept towers has been abandoned, and the composition is thus made up of two lower lateral segments constituting the ends of the transept aisles flanking the steeply vertical central vessel. Little attempt was made in the sixteenth-century western transept aisle to match the forms of the thirteenth-century aisle to the east. The lofty central segment is made up of four main levels flanked by elegant staircase turrets. The turrets perform a variety of contortions as they ascend. In their lowest parts, which are deeply pierced by niches that echo the indentations of the portal jambs, they form a continuation of the portal embrasures; they then turn cylindrical for a time; and toward the top of the façade they become octagonal, presenting an angle toward the front of the façade. In their decoration, consisting of niches and panels, they provide a reflection of the forms used in the central area of the façade, while their plastic, three-dimensional bulk contrasts with the sea of flat tracery in the central vessel.

The lowest horizontal level of the central

[1] For Sens Cathedral, see esp. C. Porée, "Les Architectes et la construction de la cathédrale de Sens," *Cong. arch.*, LXXIV, 1907, pp. 559–598.

[2] The idea of "doctrinaire Gothic" is explored by W. Gross, *Die Abendländische Architektur um 1300*, Stuttgart, 1948.

segment of the façade is the portal, capped by a straight-sided gable intersected by a horizontal balustrade. In the embrasures of the portal a series of concave scooped-out forms gives the impression that the space of the portal has eaten into the surrounding mass. The embrasures continue across onto the lowest parts of the flanking turrets. The sharp-edged fillets of the jambs rise unbroken by capitals into the archivolts of the portal, enclosing sculptured scenes from the life of Saint Peter.[3] The tympanum is relieved with vertical panels and niches. The flat area of the gable and balustrade also has vertical panels, the lines of which descend to invade the outermost order of the portal as vertical pendant cusping, and ascend to form spiky candelabra protruding above the balustrade. The vertical moldings are linked by round-headed cusps, which are distorted to fit the varying angles formed with the curving molding of the portal. Very fine, almost indiscernible free-flowing lines have been added to link the verticals with the diagonal lines of the gable. The flat, calligraphic effect of this screen of paneling provides a foil for the recession of the cavernous portal below.

Above the portal is a middle "triforium" level of glazed tracery panels. The setbacks in the surface of the façade at this middle level allow circulation passages to be introduced and break the monotony of the huge expanse of glass and tracery. The upper part of the window features the six-petaled rose that is characteristic of all of Chambiges's works, each unit consisting of a soufflet enclosed between two mouchettes. The wall over the main arch of the window is decorated with a gable and vertical paneling, and the same device is repeated again in the uppermost level of the façade, the gable of the roof. Above the level of the balustrade of the passageway under the rose the decoration of the turrets changes in character, becoming less bold and distinctly more fussy. This change marks the point of transition between the work of two different master masons.

The north transept façade (Figs. 32, 41) has the same general disposition as the southern unit but is very different in details. The key to this difference may be found in the fact that on the south side the old buttress to the east of the portal was demolished and replaced with a lavishly decorated staircase turret. The equivalent buttress on the north side has been left intact, and the designer has been forced to match it with a similar unadorned, flat-faced buttress on the other (west) side of the portal. The portal jambs (Fig. 41) are not arranged in terms of a series of concave scooped-out forms, as on the south side, but instead have three blocky square pilasters, which seem to echo the forms of the simple enclosing buttresses. Many details on the north transept façade have remained unfinished, suggesting shortage of funds or excessive haste.[4]

To the west of the transept the cathedral remains unfinished (Fig. 31). Only one bay of the nave was completed to its full height, and massive provisional buttresses support the west end of the building in the absence of a nave. A provisional wall made of rubble in its lower parts and slate-covered timber in its upper parts closes the building to the west. What a paradox that the cathedral intended to be the greatest Gothic edifice ever constructed should have been terminated in this way!

It seems clear that whereas the choir was begun as a monument to the wealth and power of the bishop-counts, the chapter was the main driving force behind the construction of the transept. It is hardly necessary to ask why the transept was built—the unfinished state of the cathedral in the fourteenth and fifteenth centuries must have been a source of worry and frustration to all concerned. An engraving (based upon a medieval drawing) of the unfinished cathedral published by Gustave Desjardins gives a general impression of the appearance of the building during these years (Fig. 26). The extreme verticality of the choir without transept or nave must have created a rather shocking silhouette and feelings of vertigo in the interior. The west end was closed

---

[3] These sculptured scenes were heavily damaged by iconoclasts during the French Revolution.

[4] A financial crisis brought on by the refusal of the bishop to make his due contribution affected the fabric at the time of the construction of the north transept; see later in this chapter.

in with a lofty wall pierced by a rose window and surmounted by a gable.[5] A small wooden spire in which bells were suspended rose above the west end of the roof. This spire was in a damaged state and was reconstructed in 1408.[6] A porch, or *parvis*, extended along the length of the west end of the choir.[7] Massive provisional buttresses, probably of stone, prevented the western piers of the unfinished choir from being pushed outward by the thrust of the arches and vaults that they supported. The absence of a transept or nave must have been a real nuisance in liturgical terms, since the portals and interior space of the transept would facilitate processions and entrance into the choir. The deliberations of the chapter include some discussion as to how best to use this awkward space.[8] Signs of serious structural disorder were apparent, as, indeed, they always have been at Beauvais Cathedral. Thus, in 1486 we find the *proviseur* of the fabric, Jean Danse, charged to look into the problem of a pier on the south side of the choir that was "threatening ruin."[9]

Awareness of the fact that the construction of the transept and nave was a task that would, at some point, have to be undertaken must have hung over the clergy like a leaden weight through the difficult years of the fifteenth century. A brief review of the history of the city in the fifteenth century confirms our impression that these were not years for cathedral construction.

Beauvais in the Fifteenth Century

The early fifteenth century had seen the city of Beauvais aligned with the Burgundian faction, against the followers of the house of Orléans known as the Armagnacs. The pro-Burgundian movement in Beauvais manifested

itself particularly with the episcopate of Bernard of Chevenon (1413–1420) and Pierre Cauchon (1420–1432).[10] The former bishop was nominated by the pope—the king and the Burgundian party attempted to impose Henry of Savoisy. Two years later the disastrous battle of Agincourt brought renewed pressure to refurbish the decaying fortifications of the city. In 1417 the duke of Burgundy was received in the city, and the canons of the cathedral found themselves forced to contribute a substantial tax for the profit of the duke. The tax did not, however, bring indemnity from the ravages of troops, both Burgundian and English, in the following years.

On the death of Bernard of Chevenon in 1420 there was a short period of vacancy. Local historians tell of great devastation and suffering in the diocese: properties and fields ravaged, the land uncultivated, and endemic disease.[11] In the situation where the properties designated to meet the requirements of certain prebends were unable to produce the necessary grain, the chapter, as an emergency measure, decided in 1420 to centralize all funds into a consolidated account.[12]

The election of Bishop Pierre Cauchon in 1420 was probably the result of Burgundian pressure on the chapter.[13] The new bishop was certainly an enthusiastic supporter of the duke. This was the year of the Treaty of Troyes, which allowed Henry V, king of England, to succeed to the French throne on the death of Charles VI, an event that ensued in 1422. Pierre Cauchon supported the English king; he witnessed the induction of the duke of Bedford as duke of Anjou and count of Le Mans, and he was among the clergy consecrating Jacques of Chastellier, an English candidate, as bishop of Paris.

Delettre, the sometimes prejudiced historian of the diocese of Beauvais, tells us that the

[5] Bucquet-aux Cousteaux, XXVII, p. 196.

[6] Ibid., p. 227; XXVIII, p. 48.

[7] S. Murray, "An Expertise at Beauvais Cathedral," *J. Brit. Arch. Assoc.*, CXXX, 1977, Fig. 3.

[8] Bucquet-aux Cousteaux, XXVII, p. 427; XXVIII, pp. 105, 109.

[9] Ibid., XXVII, p. 439. This was probably pier F6/7, which

shows signs of having been rebuilt in an indeterminable style.

[10] Delettre, *Histoire du diocèse*, II, pp. 530–545; III, pp. 1–24.

[11] Ibid., II, p. 547.

[12] Bucquet-aux Cousteaux, XXVIII, p. 69.

[13] Delettre, *Histoire du diocèse*, II, pp. 548–553.

people of Beauvais remained, at heart, anti-Burgundian.[14] The late 1420s saw the success of the anti–Anglo-Burgundian movement associated with the name of Joan of Arc. In 1429 Charles VII was consecrated king of France in Reims Cathedral. Beauvais followed the example of so many other French cities—Troyes, Laon, Soissons, Château-Thierry, Provins—in submitting to the king, upon which Pierre Cauchon fled to the English. He later played a memorable role in the trial and execution of Joan of Arc.

Jean Juvénal des Ursins succeeded as bishop (1432–1444). His episcopate saw the Beauvaisis still occupied, in part, by English and Burgundian troops. Under his successor, William of Hellande (1444–1462) the English were finally driven out of Gerberoy.[15] Normandy was recaptured by French forces in the 1450s.

The Beauvaisis did not, however, immediately see the return of a peaceful prosperity conducive to cathedral building. During the episcopate of Jean of Bar (1462–1488)[16] the city was beseiged by the Burgundians—a seige that has left an indelible imprint upon the urban consciousness of Beauvais. Jean of Bar was a royal nominee, formerly *maître des requêtes*. Louis XI, threatened by the duke of Burgundy and his allies, had every interest in cementing the towns of Picardy to his cause. He visited several Picard towns, including Beauvais in 1471, where he attended mass and prayed in the cathedral.

The following year saw the attempt of the duke of Burgundy to gain control of Picardy. He concentrated particularly upon a prolonged siege of Beauvais, which began on June 27, 1472. The bishop, Jean of Bar, made every effort to leave the besieged city. Prevented from doing so a first time, at the Porte de Paris, he succeeded the second time by choosing an escape over the wall of the episcopal palace.[17] A missile launched by the Burgun-

dian artillery during the siege is said to have penetrated the clerestory of the choir and to have crashed into the canons' stalls.[18] The siege was raised, and the subsequent defeat of the duke of Burgundy restored peace to the Beauvaisis.

Louis XI developed a special affection for Beauvais Cathedral as a symbol of the strength and loyalty that had led to the defeat of the Burgundian cause. He donated 2,000 pounds to the cathedral in connection with a vow that he had made, stipulating that the money be used for the honor of the Virgin, to be known under the title of Notre-Dame-de-la-Paix.[19] The chapter thereupon instituted an altar of Notre-Dame-de-la-Paix (Fig. 25), placed in the central vessel of the choir, to the left of the high altar. A statue of the Virgin was set upon the altar, while on the wings or doors were painted images of King Louis XI on the right and his son Charles VIII on the left. The money donated by the king was used to institute an anthem to the Virgin, sung in front of this altar just before the high mass.

The register of chapter deliberations provides some interesting details of this altar. In February 1471 Bishop Jean of Bar announced his wish to use some of the money donated by the king to make a capital (*chapiteau*) for the altar of Notre-Dame-de-la-Paix.[20] In March 1472 an order was issued that the statue should be painted.[21] Of course, differences arose between the bishop and chapter over the use of the money given by the king, and in March 1473 we find the chapter attempting to constrain the bishop to make good the 972 pounds that he had already spent.[22] In July 1475, upon the request of Louis XI, the office of Sainte Anne was also instituted. Associated with this new office was a new altar, with an image of Sainte Anne, placed to the right side of the high altar. Under the date October 1475 is recorded the text of a letter from Louis XI to the chapter of Beauvais confirming that the

---

[14] Ibid., III, pp. 1–25.
[15] Ibid., pp. 25–56.
[16] Ibid., pp. 57–103.
[17] Bucquet-aux Cousteaux, XXIII, pp. 14–15.
[18] Ibid., p. 15.

[19] Ibid., pp. 16–17.
[20] Ibid., XXVIII, p. 114.
[21] Ibid., p. 119.
[22] Ibid., p. 123.

king had made a vow in the cathedral of Beauvais to Notre-Dame-de-la-Paix, and that in honor of that vow he was now making 3,000 pounds available, through the bailiff of Vermandois.[23] In November 1475 a statue of Sainte Anne was commissioned in the city of Rouen.[24] In January 1476 a new *chapiteau* was made for the tabernacle of the image of Notre-Dame-de-la-Paix. The statue of Sainte Anne was placed on the altar on the right side of the hemicycle at Easter 1476.[25] In the years 1476 to 1478 there was an intensification of interest in reliquaries: several relics of Saint Germer were placed upon the altar, and a new reliquary was made for Saint Germer's head, at the expense of a member of the bourgeoisie.[26] In 1486 a new *chapiteau* was made for the altar of Sainte Anne, to match the one already made for the Notre-Dame-de-la-Paix altar.[27] Jean Bernard, a canon of the church, in his sermon to the synod of parish priests, emphasized the need for generous donations to the fabric.[28]

Jean of Bar died in 1488, and a disputed election resulted in a prolonged vacancy, from 1488 to 1497.[29] A combination of outside powers, including the marshall of Esquerdes, governor of Picardy, King Louis XI, and the pope, attempted to impose Anthoine of Bois, the nephew of the aforementioned marshall. The chapter elected Louis of Villiers, and a prolonged stalemate ensued, during which Louis XI held the episcopal temporalities. The final success of Louis of Villiers resulted from the death of the marshall and the findings of an inquest charged to look into the affair.

In 1493 the choir of the church was repaved with a hard stone similar to marble, since the stone floor was in a state of disintegration and clouds of dust were spoiling the ornaments.[30]

With the embellishment of the church, the endowment of new altars, and the hint of royal patronage, it is not surprising to find that thoughts would turn to the completion of the envelope of the building. One of the contributors to the Bucquet-aux Cousteaux Collection put the decision as early as 1484, when it was noticed that the choir, which was not accompanied or supported by transept or nave, was threatening ruin.[31] However, the death of Bishop Jean of Bar and the ensuing interregnum rendered immediate action impossible.

The financial implication of the disputed election and interregnum were obviously unfortunate as far as the fabric was concerned; episcopal revenues would be diverted, *sede vacante*, into the coffers of the king. The decision to designate funds for urgent repairs to the cathedral, "and even for completing the rear part," was taken in May 1496, during the period of vacancy.[32] In view of the financial losses incurred by the bishopric through the prolonged vacancy, as well as the considerable expenses involved in the repairs to the episcopal palace and wall resulting from the hostilities of 1472, the chapter agreed to make over to the newly consecrated bishop, Villiers of l'Ile-Adam, a certain sum of money as "retribution."[33] The exact terms of the transaction are ambiguous. It seems that the chapter understood that a loan was involved and that it was to be used in accordance with the testament of Jean of Bar, but the bishop took the money as a gift.[34] He went ahead and had the episcopal palace rebuilt on a sumptuous scale. The work was completed in the first decade of the sixteenth century, and the great bell, named "Louyse," was dated 1506.[35]

During the episcopate of Louis of Villiers of l'Ile-Adam (1497–1521) and that of his successors, the transept of Beauvais Cathedral was completed. It is interesting to note that like Miles of Nanteuil, Louis was also from a

[23] Ibid., pp. 129–130.
[24] Ibid., p. 130.
[25] Ibid., p. 135.
[26] Ibid., pp. 135–136.
[27] Ibid., p. 169.
[28] Ibid., p. 165.
[29] Delettre, *Histoire du diocèse*, III, pp. 104–128.

[30] Ibid., p. 191.
[31] Bucquet-aux Cousteaux, XXIII, p. 22.
[32] Ibid., XXVIII, p. 195.
[33] Ibid., p. 195.
[34] Ibid., pp. 198–199.
[35] Delettre, *Histoire du diocèse*, III, pp. 132–133.

local family (he was son of Jacques of Villiers, seigneur of Ile-Adam in the southern part of the diocese of Beauvais) and was elected by the chapter, not imposed by king or pope. In addition to his background in the chapter of Beauvais Cathedral, he had also been a canon of the Sainte-Chapelle—a significant fact in light of the choice of a Parisian architect for the work on the transept.[36] However, as we shall see, under the financial pressure imposed by his lavish building projects, relations between the bishop and chapter very soon became acrimonious.

Chronology for the Construction of the Transept

Despite the almost total loss of the fabric accounts and the original records of the chapter deliberations of the cathedral, texts from surviving sources, and from various copies of lost documents, coupled with an analysis of some of the changing forms used in the cathedral transepts provide a fairly closely defined chronology for the work.

The decision to undertake campaigns aimed at the completion of the transept arms was reached by the bishop and chapter in the 1490s. Despite the existence of provisional stone buttresses against the west sides of the piers, which constituted the western termination of the choir (and between which a provisional wooden wall doubtless existed), the building was beginning to settle in an alarming way toward the west.[37] Funds were allocated in 1496 for the urgent repair of the building and "even for finishing the western part."[38] The formal structure of the fabric fund seems to have been established by 1499.[39] The next year saw the invitation extended to the Parisian master mason Martin Chambiges to come to Beauvais in order to give his advice on the laying of the foundations.[40] His initial presence at Beauvais was probably as visiting expert with special knowledge in the question of adding new work onto much earlier edifices, and in the question of digging foundations. He is found in the company of Pierre Tarissel, master mason of Amiens Cathedral, with whom he had already worked as consultant to the Bureau de la Ville de Paris on the problem of the foundations for the Pont Notre-Dame.[41] It is clear

[36] The west rose of the Sainte-Chapelle, from the 1480s, bears a strong resemblance to roses designed by Martin Chambiges.

[37] This was apparent from the 1480s: "*Le chœur menaçoit ruine des l'année 1484*" (Bibl. Nat., Collection de Picardie, CLXII, fol. 31). The fact that imminent ruin threatened the cathedral is confirmed in the opening sentence of a fabric account for 1499–1500, now in the Archives de la Seine, Paris (provisional code no. Cartes et Plans 4942): "*Compte de Jehan Thourin presbytre chanoine de l'eglise de Beauvais commis par messeigneurs de chappitre de ladite eglise a faire les receptes despenses et mises pour l'edifficacion d'une croisee neufve ordonnee estre faicte a ladite eglise pour obvier a la ruyne du cueur qui est de long temps estayé de pierre lequel est dangereux au moyen de ce qu'il n'y a croisee ne nef qui le appuye et soustienne.*" The assessment of the structural dangers threatening the cathedral that is given in the 1518 Indulgence issued by Pope Leo X is even more gloomy: "*Iceluy cueur est sans croisée ne nef, au moyen de quoy est en danger de totale ruyne et trébuchment, s'il n'est contrebouté par le secours desdictes croisée et nef*" (cited in Leblond, *Le Cathédrale de Beauvais*, p. 16).

[38] Bucquet-aux Cousteaux, XXVIII, p. 195: "*Fonds assignés pour reparations urgentes et considerables a l'Eglise et meme pour achever la partie anterieure*" (May 9, 1496).

[39] This decision is recorded in a gloomy passage that is preserved in ibid., p. 203: "*Nonobstant la guerre que le Roi porte en Italie pour recouvrer l'etat de Milan envahi par Louis Sforcia, la mauvaise recolte detruite cette année par la grele et les orages et la peste qui regne en plusieurs endroits on arrete de continuer le batimen de l'Eglise et de faire la croisée, deputés nommés a cet effet, on y emploira les crementum, on prendra meme sur les distributions, et l'argent qui est dans le tresor. On dira une messe du St Esprit*" (August 19, 1499). The presence of Martin Chambiges in Beauvais is recorded in the fabric account for 1499–1500, now in the Archives de la Seine, Paris. At this time, he was not yet master of the workshop.

[40] V. Leblond, *L'Art et les artistes en Ile-de-France au XVIe. siècle (Beauvais et Beauvaisis), d'après les minutes notoriales*, Paris, 1921, p. 13. After mentioning the 1499–1500 fabric account in Paris, Leblond writes: "*Après quoi on fit venir de Paris Martin Chambiche et d'Amiens Pierre Tharissel, lesquels avec Jean Vast maître maçon de l'église firent leur rapport aux chapitre de sorte que, le 20 mai 1500 le terrain aient eté trouvé bon et suffisant pour jeter les fondemens de la croisee sans piliers*" (i.e., it was decided not to use wooden piles).

[41] Martin Chambiges was consulted on the question of the reconstruction of the collapsed Pont Notre-Dame in Paris; see F. Bonnardot, *Registres des délibérations du bureau de la ville de Paris, publiés par les soins du Service historique. Histoire générale de Paris, collection de documents*

that Martin Chambiges impressed the bishop and chapter with his judgment and ideas, for they requested him to take over direction of the workshop and gave him a house in which to live and an annual stipend of twenty pounds, with a daily wage of five sous.[42]

The foundation stone of the south transept façade was laid on May 20, 1500. The stone had inscribed upon it a cross with the arms of the chapter on one side, and on the other, those of the bishop, Villiers of l'Ile-Adam.[43]

In 1505 (1506 according to the unidentified authority of V. Leblond) Martin Chambiges presented a plan for the demolition of an old pillar that had formerly provided access to the belfrey, in order to substitute the new work as

skillfully as possible.[44] The word "pillar" is often used in order to designate an exterior buttress, and in this case there can be no doubt that the unit that was being demolished was the buttressing to the south and west of the pillar that had existed at the extreme south-west corner of the unfinished building (H 5 on the plan). In the present cathedral (Figs. 38, 39, 55), it can be seen that most of the old masonry in this upright has been demolished in order to allow the designer a free hand to shape the right turret of the transept façade as he wished. There is, indeed, a staircase in the buttress just as defined in the text.

Thus, work began on the façade of the south transept arm. Despite a slow start, prog-

publiée sous les auspices de l'édilité parisienne, I, 1499–1526, Paris, 1883. L. Brochard (*Saint-Gervais: Histoire du monument d'après de nombreux documents inedits*, Paris, 1938), suggested that Martin Chambiges was the master mason who designed the church of Saints-Gervais-et-Protais. His evidence includes the observation that the Chambiges family had a house in the parish (Pierre Chambiges was, apparently, buried in this church) and the fact that the name of Martin Chambiges was included in a list of seventy-five notable parishioners summoned in 1500 in order to approve the foundation of a new chapel. Chambiges is not named as master mason in that list, however, and it would seem extremely unlikely that the master directing the work would be listed with the other parishioners without any title attached to his name. Stylistically the church is quite unlike any of the firmly documented works of Martin Chambiges, and it therefore seems necessary to detach this building from the master's oeuvre. Other attributions to Martin Chambiges in the city of Paris include the west rose of the Sainte-Chapelle (E. Gavelle, *Notice architecturelle sur l'église Rumilly-les-Vaudes*, Arcis, 1896), a portal attached to the church of the Dominicans (R. Nelson, "A Lost Portal by Martin Chambiges?" *J. Soc. Arch. Hist*, XXXIII, 1974, pp. 155–157), and the tower of Saint-Jacques-de-la-Boucherie (M. Vachon, *Une Famille parisienne d'architectes maistres-maçcons aux XV, XVI, XVII siècles: Les Chambiges, 1490–1643*, Paris, 1907, p. 85). The lack of documentation renders it impossible to be certain about the authorship of the Sainte-Chapelle rose. On the other hand, the resemblances between the portal of the Dominicans and Chambiges's documented portals are not strong enough to support the claim that this is the work of that master. There was a fairly generalized set of Parisian decorative forms current around 1500 that tend to lend a certain family likeness to many of the portals designed in this period. The Tour Saint-Jacques, which shares many of these forms, has now been firmly attributed to the brothers de Felin, who also worked with Martin Chambiges in the consultations regarding the Pont Notre-Dame (J. Meurgey de Tupigny, *Saint-Jacques de la Boucherie et la Tour Saint-Jacques*, Paris, 1960). L. Gonse (*L'Art gothique*, Paris, 1891, p. 280)

attributed three further nondocumented works to Martin Chambiges: the façade of Saint-Maclou, Pontoise; the nave of Saints-Gervais-et-Protais, Gisors; and the church of Chaumont-en-Vexin. There is absolutely no evidence, either documentary or stylistic, to support these attributions.

In 1504, Martin Chambiges visited Senlis Cathedral; see E. Couard-Luys, "Note sur une mission de Martin Chambiges à Senlis en 1504," *Bulletin archéologique du comité des travaux historiques et scientifiques*, 1884. The quittance for this visit by Martin Chambiges is preserved in the Departmental Archives at Beauvais (Arch. Oise, G 2717, Titres Généraux, Cote 22). The fact that Martin Chambiges did not sign his name but merely made his mark led Couard-Luys to believe that the master was illiterate. However, another example of a signature by Martin Chambiges was published by V. Leblond, "Les Artistes de Beauvais et du Beauvaisis au XVIe. siècle et leurs œuvres," *Mém. Soc. acad. Oise*, XXIV, 1923, pp. 85–138.

[42] Bucquet-aux Cousteaux, XXVIII, p. 205: "*Sur la requete presentée par magistrum Cambiche operarium architectorem latomia mandatum de longinquis partibus pour conduire le batimem de l'Eglise et qu'il est necessaire qu'il demeure a Beauvais pour ce magnifique ouvrage, on lui accorde la maison de la charpenterie 20 livres tournois de pension annuel 4 sous tournois par chaque jour de travail et chaque jour un pain de chapitre*" (May 29, 1500). Leblond (*L'Art et les artistes*, p. 14) gives a Latin version of the same text, citing as his source the Troussures Collection. The Troussures source gives Chambiges a daily wage of five sous, which seems more probable than the four sous mentioned in the Bucquet-aux Cousteaux text.

[43] Leblond, *La Cathédrale de Beauvais*, p. 14.

[44] Bucquet-aux-Cousteaux, XXVIII, p. 214: "*Sur le devis de Me. Martin Cambiche architecte, de Pierre Lefebvre et Jean Vast massons on resout la demolition en partie d'un vieux pilier par lequel on montoit aux befroy pour y substituer le nouvel œuvre le plus habilement que faire se poura*" (February 18, 1505; this would be 1506, New Style). For Leblond's dating, see "Les Artistes de Beauvais et du Beauvaisis."

ress after 1505 was rapid, although the master was forced to take some time off in order to visit his workshop at Troyes. The chapter of Beauvais Cathedral was clearly not entirely happy with this arrangement, and when he overstayed his leave of absence in 1508/9 he was sent a sharp request that he send his plans back to Beauvais, for fear that they might be lost.[45] At the same time, the excessive expense of the elaborate stone cutting involved in the south portal led the chapter to bring pressure upon the bishop for a larger contribution toward the masons' wages.[46] The completion of this portal was announced by the placing of an image of the Madeleine in May 1509.[47]

In 1510 efforts were transferred away from the south transept façade toward the north transept.[48] Difficulties were obviously still being experienced in persuading the bishop to make an appropriate contribution; on May 8, 1510, the chapter informed the bishop of the necessity of laying the foundations of the "left aisle" (the north transept). In the same month, the bishop made a contribution of one hundred pounds, and Martin Chambiges inspected the foundations and the quarries that were to be exploited.[49]

Whereas on the south side work had concentrated on the façade alone, on the north side work began on the western piers of the transept arm at the same time as the façade. Evidence for this is found both in documentary sources and from an analysis of the base moldings of the piers. On May 24, 1510, the parishioners of the *Basse-Œuvre*, the church that exists to the west of the Gothic cathedral and that was progressively demolished in order to make way for the new work, were allocated the Chapelle des Anges in the cathedral, indicating that the demolition of the choir of the *Basse-Œuvre* was imminent.[50] This demolition would be occasioned by the digging of the foundations of the interior piers of the northern transept arm (Figs. 80, 81). An analysis of the molding forms of the pier bases confirms this impression. Each base has three different kinds of moldings, one for the plinth of the large shafts, one for the plinth of the diagonal shafts, and one for the pier itself. This pier base molding provides a clear chronological criterion, since two types are found, a simple type consisting of two concave scoops meeting in a sharp ridge, and a more complex type with deep indentation under a rounded rim in the lower parts of the molding. The former type, the earlier chronologically (Fig. 5), may be found attached to the interior of the south transept façade and in all of the piers in the north transept (including the northwest crossing pier). The other type can be found in the interior of the south transept arm.

Chambiges directed work on the north transept in person, and the chapter refused to consider a request from the cathedral chapter at Troyes for the master's presence.

In May 1511, with work on the north tran-

[45] Bucquet-aux-Cousteaux, XXVIII, p. 219: "*Apres avoir representé a Martin Cambiche le dommage infini causé par son absence on lui accorde encore cependant un mois de congé, et on lui redemande le plan ou dessein du nouvel œuvre de peur qu'il ne se perde*" (February 8, 1509).

[46] Ibid., pp. 219–220: "*Deputés vers M. l'Eveque pour lui representer le grand detroit du chapitre au sujet du nouvel œuvre, attendu les grandes depenses faittes cette année pour autres emplois, on attend la reponse de M. l'Eveque pour regler l'etat des ouvriers que l'on emploiera*" (February 15, 1509).

[47] Ibid., p. 219: "*Permis a Sr. Poulain de choisir avec l'avis du Me. architecte une place au nouveau portail pour y mettre l'image de Ste Madelaine qu'il a fait faire a ses despenses pour le decorer*" (September 17, 1509).

[48] Ibid., p. 221: "*Deputés vers l'Eveque pour lui annoncer qu'il falloit bientot poser les fondemens de l'aile gauche de la croisée ou nouvel œuvre*" (May 8, 1510). When work began on the south transept façade, the bishop and chapter

had the financial resources necessary to be able to demolish the old, flat-faced buttressing to the east of the present south portal, so that Chambiges could substitute his own richly decorated polygonal turrets flanking the central vessel (see note 44, above). When work reached the north transept, however, the lack of money and the difficulties between the bishop and chapter led to the decision to preserve the corresponding buttress to the east of the north portal. The unfinished appearance of many of the details on this side was, no doubt, the result of the same difficulties.

[49] Ibid.: "*100 livres donnés par M. l'Eveque pour le nouvel œuvre. Deputés pour conferer avec Cambiche sur les fondemens de la partie gauche de la croisée pour visitter les carrieres de l'Eglise et s'assurer d'un certain nombre d'ouvriers*" (May 22, 1510).

[50] Ibid.: "*On assigne aux paroissiens de la basse œuvre la chapelle des anges pour y faire l'office pendant qu'on fera les fondemens du nouvel œuvre dans la basse œuvre*" (May 24, 1510).

sept arm fully under way, the confrontation between the bishop and chapter over contributions to the work became more embittered. The chapter, taking advice from experts in Paris, decided to file a case against the bishop with the parliament in Paris.[51] An attempt was made to reach a compromise solution, by which the bishop would contribute eight hundred pounds instead of the twelve hundred demanded by the chapter, on the condition that he give one thousand pounds in each of the two following years. The bishop, on his side, attempted to influence the chapter by means of the presence of his puppets among them, so that the chapter was forced to consider the exclusion of his *commensaux* and *familiers* from their meetings.[52] By March 1511 the case against the bishop was well under way, and an order issued on March 14 gave strict instructions to canons and officers of the chapter not to collaborate with the bishop while the case was being heard.

The decision of the parlement of Paris, issued before September 12, 1512, was that the bishop and chapter should both contribute one thousand pounds per annum to the new work.[53]

Between 1512 and 1517 there is a gap in the documentary evidence. Work must have been going ahead in these years on the north transept façade and interior piers.

By 1517 the north transept portal had been finished (payment had been made for the stat-

ues of the Transfiguration to set in the portal), and Chambiges was involved in repair work on certain "large pillars in the choir."[54] There are clear signs of Late Gothic repair work in the south choir aisle, where parts of the tracery of the clerestory windows opening into the inner aisle and the triforium below these windows have been replaced with Flamboyant tracery. One of the piers between the lateral chapels of the south side aisle was entirely replaced (F 7 on the plan; Fig. 110), and a wall was added between the chapels.[55] The molding of the pier base is without indentation, placing this work in association with the work in the north transept arm.

In 1518 Martin Chambiges requested that his son, Pierre, be accepted as comaster of the workshop, at the same wages as himself.[56] There was an outbreak of the plague in Beauvais that year, and the fabric accounts of Troyes Cathedral record the fact that Martin Chambiges was sick. The chapter of Beauvais Cathedral at first refused to accept Pierre, on account of the drunkenness and bad reputation of the young man, but was later persuaded to accept him as comaster.

The piers inside the south transept, with their later type of base molding, may be dated after 1518. In 1521 Martin Chambiges is found visiting the vaults of the *chapelle des orgues*, to the east of the south transept arm, and there is thus every reason to suppose that work had been transferred back to this side.[57]

---

[51] Ibid., pp. 225–226: "*M. l'Eveque donne 100 livres pour le nouvel œuvre . . . ne veut s'engager a paier un contingent, persiste dans sa disposition le 13 juin, et ce jour sur les consultations de Paris messieurs deliberent de le poursuivre licet dolentes, et on lui donne le devis fait par Cambiche et Marin Vaast de ce qui restoit a faire*" (May 26, 1511).

[52] Ibid., pp. 227, 232: "*M. le chantre a dit qu'il avoit proposé a M. l'Evesque par le conseil de Paris, de consentir un arret conforme a l'accord pour sa contribution au nouvel œuvre . . . qu'il avoit conferé avec des chanoines de Paris et de Tours au sujet de l'exclusion des commensaux et familiers de l'Eveque, lorsquon traite quelque chose qui le concerne, qu'ils avoient dit que c'etoit un usage et une pratique constante parmi eux. . . . Deffenses tres rigoureuses a tous chanoines ou officiers du chapitre qui auroient chez eux des titres, memoires, comptes, ecritures, ou enseignemens, d'en rien communiquer qui put favoriser en aucune sorte M. l'Eveque dans le procez que l'on a contre lui et ce sous peine de la perte des distributions pendant 10 ans.*"

[53] Ibid., pp. 233–234: "*Suivant l'arret rendu nouvelle-*

ment au parlement pour la provision sur la continuation du nouvel œuvre, chapitre paiera chaque année 1000 lb en 4 termes egaux et M. l'Eveque pareille somme" (December 27, 1512).

[54] Ibid., p. 240: "*Mention de 20 ecus au soleil legués par Pierre Lebastier lieutenant de capitaine pour faire les images de la transfiguration au grand portail. Martin Cambiche fait son rapport de certains gros pilliers du chœur qui n'etoient pas encore achevés et dit qu'il falloit les reparer pour prevenir plus grand danger*" (September 1, 1517).

[55] The corresponding pier in the north aisle had already been replaced in the campaigns of repair that followed the 1284 collapse.

[56] Bucquet-aux Cousteaux, XXVIII, p. 243: "*Martin Cambiche demande de recevoir son fils aux memes gages que lui pour la direction de la construction de l'Eglise. Refusé a cause des mœurs de son fils ob vanitates, ebrietates et ludibria. Cependant le 23 juillet on le prit jusqu'a la St. Remi a condition qu'il se corrigeroit*" (July 19, 1518).

[57] Ibid., p. 252: "*Visitte de la voute de la chapelle des orgues, avec Martin Cambiche*" (January 23, 1521); and p.

Money problems continued to trouble the chapter, however, despite the indulgence granted in 1518 by Pope Leo X.[58] To the rescue came King Francis I, who in 1522 agreed to retain five masons to work at Beauvais alongside the six masons and Chambiges, who were paid by the chapter.[59]

Martin Chambiges died on August 29, 1532, and was accorded the honor of a tomb to the west of the transept crossing. His place was taken by Michel Lalie, who had worked as subordinate in the workshop for many years. At the time of the death of the master, the lower parts of both transept arms had been completed, and it seems probable that work was going ahead on the interior piers of the south transept. A tapestry from the *History of the Gauls* series (Fig. 27), at present conserved in the tapestry museum in Beauvais, shows the building as it was in 1530, with the north transept façade completed up to the sill of the great window, and the four great buttresses of the façade up to roof level. The flyer on the east side of the transept is shown as already in position. This would probably have been possible, given the massive nature of the masonry of the façade buttress at this point. The south transept had been finished up to the level of the balustrade under the great rose. Documentary evidence for the completion of both transept arms exists in the form of the dates painted on the vaults inside the two transept façades: 1537 on the north side and 1550 on the south.

The Work of Martin Chambiges and Flamboyant Architecture

Thus the massive and lavishly decorated transept arms of Beauvais Cathedral were completed in a period of fifty years, after the plans of the greatest architect of French Late Gothic, Martin Chambiges. It seems certain that Chambiges was chosen by the bishop and chapter to direct the workshop for two reasons: because of his expertise as an engineer and because of his inventiveness as an artist. The engineering problems faced by Chambiges involved the addition of new parts to a building that had been conceived on a gigantic scale over two hundred and fifty years previously, that had seen a major collapse, and that was, by 1499, showing severe signs of settlement toward the west. There can be no question about the success of Martin Chambiges as an engineer. The severity of the structural problems in the old cathedral may be illustrated by means of one example. The triforium on the east side of the north transept arm over pier C 5 shows a remarkable degree of distortion (Fig. 76). The rear wall of the triforium is not parallel with the surface of the wall over the arcade below. This distortion has been commonly interpreted as having resulted from the collapse of the crossing tower in 1573. Such a collapse would cause cracked stones and gaping masonry joints, but not wholesale shifts in walls, however. In fact the "distortion" is deliberate, resulting from the fact that pier C 5 has a very marked lean to the west (because of centuries of inadequate support from this side). The master had wanted to avoid continuing the line of the leaning pier directly upward, and instead had pushed the rear wall of the triforium as far as possible to the east. The sacrificing of the idea of transept towers, and the blind bays on the inside of both transept façades seem to show the kind of prudence that placed a greater degree of importance on the virtues of solidarity rather than effect.

Martin Chambiges faced a problem that would have been familiar to all master masons of Late Gothic—he had to decide whether to reproduce the forms of the older parts of the

---

253: "*On travaillera aux reparations de l'Eglise, on y commettra Martin Cambiche, ou Pierre son fils*" (April 23, 1522). The chapel on the west side of the south transept arm has window tracery turned at a slight angle to the axis of the window. Thus, the beholder approaching the chapel at an angle will see each mullion from directly in front. This piece of optical illusionism may reflect the hand of Pierre Chambiges.

[58] Leblond, *La Cathédrale de Beauvais*, p. 16.

[59] Bucquet-aux Cousteaux, XXVIII, p. 255: "*Arreté que l'Eglise retiendra de son coté 6 maçons avec Martin Cambiche et qu'il y en aura encore cinq autres employés sur le compte du Roi*" (October 29, 1522).

building or to break the unity of the building through the introduction of more up-to-date forms. Modern critics have tended to blast the unfortunate Late Gothic master whether he made one choice or the other—as being excessively conservative and uninventive, or as responsible for the adulteration of the stylistic purity of the building with forms that were somehow no longer "valid."

The formula that allowed a previous generation to understand the relationship of Late Gothic to High Gothic was based upon the belief that High Gothic was essentially "rational," that form and function were harmoniously reconciled, and that the researches of master masons into the purely optical impact of forms from the mid-thirteenth century onward led to mannerism and the loss of the meaningful relationship between form and structural function.[60] Thus, whereas the rounded quality of the applied shafts of High Gothic symbolized the support function of the piers and walls, in Late Gothic these forms were often transformed into sharp edges or soft undulations. The effects of brittle linearity on the one hand, or the undulating piers on the other, would render impossible the visual symbolization of the support function of the building. Certain details, moreover, became the vehicle for speculations that were entirely free of the restraints imposed by structural considerations. The fantastic inventions produced by these researches were then transposed into a variety of other media, including the graphic arts, stained glass, and sculpture. We might see this as a preoccupation with architecture for its own sake, rather than as a mere receptacle for the liturgy.[61]

One of these inventions provided the style label by which the architecture of this period became known. In the late thirteenth century the geometric forms of the tracery window began to merge together to form sinuous, undulating lines.[62] Far from being "irrational," the flickering "Flamboyant" forms that resulted provided real benefits, both practical and aesthetic. Many of the awkward interstices characteristic of geometric tracery were now eliminated. Flamboyant designs may actually have been more resistant to structural distortion than were geometric patterns. They certainly allowed the rainwater to drain off more easily. Most important, the sinuous patterns reflected the more sculptural quality inherent in Late Gothic design.

Although "Flamboyant" provides a useful label for fifteenth-century architecture, it tends to suggest a rather limited interpretation of the architectural style of the period in terms of pure speculation on tracery. Needed is a conceptual framework that takes into account a much broader range of concerns; one that will recognize the dependence of many of the basic design principles of Flamboyant upon High Gothic prototypes, yet also will realize the validity of the new forms produced.[63] The intellectual atmosphere of our age of postmodernism provides obvious incentives to look again at the eclectic and inventive speculations of Late Gothic masons. Similarly, we should question the assumption that High Gothic was "rational" at all, either in its structural framework or in its forms of articulation.

A recent study of Flamboyant sets out to isolate the characteristics of "individualism" and "détente" in the architectural design of the fourteenth and fifteenth centuries.[64] Individualism implies that the various parts of the building were allegedly no longer bound to-

---

[60] Focillon, *Art of the West*, II, p. 146: "The architecture of the fifteenth century . . . bears witness to a great confusion of thought."

[61] F. Bucher, "Micro-Architecture as the 'Idea' of Gothic Theory and Style," *Gesta*, XV, 1976, pp. 71–89.

[62] Such double curves are already visible in an incipient form in the tracery of the choir of the church of Saint-Urbain of Troyes from the 1260s. In England curvilinear tracery matured by around 1300, whereas in France fully mature curvilinear patterns were not produced until the end of the fourteenth century. Such patterns were produced until the decades after 1500.

[63] J. Bialostocki, "Late Gothic, Disagreements about the Concept," *J. Brit. Arch. Assoc.*, XXIX, 1966, pp. 76–105, attempted to provide a more positive framework for the assessment of Late Gothic and Flamboyant. See also L. S. Adelman, "The Flamboyant Style in French Gothic Architecture," Ph.D. diss., University of Minnesota, 1973.

[64] R. Sanfaçon, *L'Architecture flamboyante en France*, Quebec, 1971.

gether with the same rigid discipline found in High Gothic. Thus, sharp prismatic forms in the ribs and arches of the vaults might contrast with the massive rounded forms of the walls and piers. A logic was then found in this very contrast. Individualism is also applied to the many regional options open to Flamboyant designers. The overall thought process involved here is one that is still dependent, to some extent, upon Foçillon's "life of forms,"[65] with the pejorative stigma removed. We thus have a dialectic triad: thesis (High Gothic), antithesis (individualism: experiments made especially in the fourteenth century), and synthesis (Flamboyant logic).

While such a formula provides a useful conceptual matrix, it is always best to return to the realization that architectural design results from human factors: the training and vision of the master mason, and the taste and demands of the patron. In church design other factors also intervene: the need to make the building a vehicle for didactic cycles of imagery and to provide, using material means, a mirror of the Transcendental. Late Gothic masons would often receive their training in workshops charged with the completion or maintenance and repair of High Gothic edifices. This is especially true of Martin Chambiges, whose three major commissions at the Sens, Beauvais, and Troyes cathedrals all involved the completion of great monuments of Early and High Gothic. The power of High Gothic formulas to survive over a period of centuries might thus be explained less in terms of the "life of forms" and more in terms of the conditions of training and apprenticeship in the masons' profession. There might also have existed a certain nostalgia for the past in the period after the Hundred Years' War, a nostalgia that could be expressed visually through frank references to High Gothic prototypes.

Church building projects in the fifteenth century would often be on a relatively small scale, often involving parish or collegiate churches or chapels. Patrons and architects tended to shy away from the complex plan types favored in High Gothic; in particular, the cumbersome system of ambulatory and radiating chapels found very little favor. High Gothic east end planning involved something of a paradox, in that, although curving wall surfaces were generally avoided, the overall design would often involve segments of circles, as we have seen in the plan of the Beauvais choir. Thus, the polygonal, faceted look of High Gothic does not express the essence of a design based upon curves. Late Gothic plans, on the other hand, tend to be reduced, streamlined, and angular. East ends are often designed around a square, a trapezoid, or sometimes even a triangle. The latter solution would produce the dramatic interior effect of a pier placed in the axis of the east end (as at Caudebec-en-Caux). Other aspects of the church plan might also be reduced in comparison with the lavish quality of thirteenth-century cathedral design. This might involve the suppression of a projecting transept and the avoidance of ambitious towered façades.

In the structure of the church, its mass and its articulation and decoration, Flamboyant presents some intriguing paradoxes (hence the term "individualism"). In structure, some edifices are pared down to a minimum (for example, Saint-Ouen in Rouen, or Saints-Gervais-et-Portais in Paris; Fig. 166), while others emphasize mural surface and mass (particularly rustic churches, for example those in southern Champagne). Side-by-side existed a drive to achieve great light and steep proportion (Saint-Jean-au-Marché, Troyes; Fig. 180) and modest proportion or even a hall church arrangement, with aisles the same height as the central vessel (Saint-Nizier, Troyes, and Saint-André-les-Vergers, near Troyes).[66] Fantastic Flamboyant inventions, for example the hanging keystone (porch at Louviers, porch of the Marmousets, Saint-Ouen, Rouen choir screen of the Madeleine, Troyes) or flying ribs (Saint-Florentin, Aube) accompanied the coldly rational drive to reduce and streamline

[65] H. Focillon, *La Vie des formes*, Paris, 1934.
[66] S. Murray, "The Choir of Saint-Etienne at Beauvais,"
J. Soc. Arch. Hist., XXXVI, 1977, pp. 111–121, esp. pp. 120–121.

interior articulation, bringing it into closer harmony with the structure. Late Gothic masons were inclined to reduce the diameters of the applied shafts that formed the interior articulation, eventually creating almond-shaped profiles or fillets. These sharpened forms were of particular interest to the designers, since they reflected profile types already used in ribs and arches. By omitting the capital altogether, it was possible to avoid a problem that had produced some awkward solutions in High Gothic design and to allow the forms of the arches and ribs to continue downward without a break into the moldings applied to the surface of the supports.[67] Thus it was possible to express, for the first time in Gothic design, the fact that no single point (that is, a capital) can separate the function of support from the role of being supported. An alternative solution was also applied, whereby the moldings of the ribs and arches might simply disappear into the smooth surfaces of walls and piers without the agency of a capital.

There is no denying the logic of these modes of articulation. Late Gothic architecture is an architecture of space. Space is a seamless entity, and this seamlessness is expressed in the continuous forms of the arches and moldings. Fifteenth-century churches such as Saint-Maclou at Rouen and Saint-Germain at Amiens embody a harmonious relationship between space and the forms of articulation of a kind that had not been seen before.

The Style of Martin Chambiges

The key to the understanding of Flamboyant is provided by our ability to come to grips with the design vocabulary of a known master mason working within a well-documented historical context. Martin Chambiges, with major commisions at Sens, Beauvais, and Troyes, was one of the most prolific architects of Late Gothic, and his work embodies an easily recognizable vocabulary of forms expressing a personal style.[68] This vocabulary was developed partly through references back to High Gothic and Rayonnant prototypes, and partly through inventions made by himself or borrowed from a closely knit circle of colleagues working in and around the capital city.

In the structural envelope of Beauvais Cathedral, Chambiges departed from the model of the choir only in one important respect—he reduced the height of the arcade and abandoned the pyramidal massing of the choir (Fig. 31). In the first bay of the nave he gave the two aisles an equal height. The magnificent spatial unity of the choir was thus compromised, although it is probable that the nave, had it been completed, would have been sounder in structural terms than the High Gothic and Rayonnant choir. In his design of the various parts of the transept—vaults, portals, piers, etc.—Chambiges, while not obliged to follow existing prototypes, sometimes chose forms that appear to us as traditional.

In the design of his vault forms, Chambiges certainly appears as somewhat conservative. All of the vaults at Beauvais and Sens are simple quadripartite or sexpartite types, with the exception of the vaults of the chapels to the west sides of the transept arms of Beauvais Cathedral. It should be emphasized, however, that the northern aisle vaults (Fig. 78), including the chapel of the baptismal fonts, are the only ones built under his personal supervision. The vaults of Sens Cathedral were erected after his departure, the high vaults at Beauvais were completed only after the death of the master, and this is also true of the vaults of Troyes Cathedral. The decorative vault of the chapel of Saints Peter and Paul in the south transept (Fig. 79) was installed only after Pierre Chambiges had assumed codirection of the workshop and may show signs of influ-

---

[67] The omission of the capital occurs in details as early as the mid-thirteenth century (Saint-Urbain at Troyes). The general omission of the capitals of the main arcade became standard in the later fourteenth century.

[68] The question of the style of Martin Chambiges was addressed in doctoral dissertations by Robert J. Nelson, "Martin Chambiges and the Development of French Flamboyant Architecture," Johns Hopkins University, 1973, and Stephen Murray, "The Work of Martin Chambiges," London University, Courtauld Institute, 1973.

ence from him. Both decorative vaults have the overall design of a quadripartite vault with added tiercerons. Instead of the tiercerons being linked by straight barlike liernes, however, curving ribs form petallike patterns. In the northern chapel, built around 1512, the petal shapes fit inside the segments created by the basic rib pattern. In the matching chapel on the south, however, the sinuous lines cross the borders of these segments to run in a free-flowing way across the surface of the vault. This vault, completed in the 1520s, reveals the interest of Martin Chambiges and his son, Pierre, in connecting together elements of a composition that had previously been separate. Comparable free-flowing lines, almost like a doodle, can be found in the design of the panels at the level of the gables and balustrades over the portals. These panels are linked with the gables and outer orders of the portals by means of a similar kind of calligraphy (Fig. 39).

One assumes that the ribs and arches of a Gothic vault were normally centered over rigid wooden forms. It has been demonstrated that the webbing or severies of some Late Gothic vaults in France were built over heaps of dirt, humped up to give the necessary domical shape.[69] How were the sinuous ribs of the Beauvais vaults constructed? Dirt centering would certainly have provided the flexibility needed. These were expensive units. The other vaults of the western aisle of the transept arms were simple quadripartite units. Few comparable examples of petal vaults can be found in contemporary French edifices.[70]

Flamboyant architecture in France is often seen as the direct continuation of Rayonnant, but with geometric tracery replaced by double curved forms. What really seems to distinguish the exterior forms favored by Martin Chambiges from a comparable Rayonnant work like the transept façades of Notre-Dame of Paris is the plasticity and relief provided by the decorated staircase turrets that flank the central segment of the southern façade at Beauvais (Figs. 39, 163). These turrets resulted from the merging together of the concept of buttress and polygonal staircase in a way that appears only in a very tentative form in High Gothic or Rayonnant.[71] Chambiges was not alone among designers of the fifteenth and early sixteenth centuries in his interest in the heavily articulated turret. The west façade of Tours Cathedral and the transept of Saint-Maclou in Rouen provide important prototypes.[72] In the decades around 1500 the form became common property, shared among a considerable number of master masons. One thinks especially of the central segment of the west façade of Rouen Cathedral, of the north transept façade of Evreux Cathedral, the tower of Saint-Jacques-de-la-Boucherie in Paris, the west façade of Saint-Riquier, and the north transept façade of the church of Saints-Gervais-et-Protais in Gisors.[73]

Martin Chambiges's well-documented work allows us to watch him develop the forms of the decorated staircase turret. In his earliest work on the south transept of Sens Cathedral the polygonal turret appears haltingly—the turrets are placed on top of the flat-sided buttresses belonging to a project for a new transept that had been begun in the fourteenth century. The master's forms for his portals result very much from his work on the unfinished Rayonnant portal of the same transept. Niches do not appear in his work at this point. It is at Beauvais that Chambiges developed his fully mature formula for the combination of portal and staircase turret richly articulated with panels and niches. A similar

---

[69] The use of dirt centering was explored by S. Murray, "Master Jehançon Garnache (1485–1501) and the Construction of the High Vaults and Flying Buttresses of Troyes Cathedral," *J. Soc. Arch. Hist.*, XIX, 1980, pp. 37–49.

[70] Petal vaults are found in the churches of Saints-Gervais-et-Protais and Saint-Germain-l'Auxerrois in Paris. For German petal vaults, see G. Fehr, *Benedikt Reid*, Munich, 1961, Figs. 81–85.

[71] For example, in the western turrets of the Sainte-Cha-

pelle in Paris.

[72] For Tours, see Sanfaçon, *L'Architecture flamboyante*, Fig. 84. For Saint-Maclou, most recently, see L. Neagley, "The Parish Church of Saint-Maclou: A Study of Rouennais Flamboyant Architecture," Ph.D. diss., Indiana University, 1983.

[73] Sanfaçon, *L'Architecture flamboyante*, Figs. 118, 180, 216.

composition is repeated in the later north transept façade of Sens Cathedral, designed by Martin Chambiges, but executed under the direction of the resident master mason, Hugh Cuvelier. Although the west façade of Troyes Cathedral, begun by Chambiges after 1506, may bear a general resemblance to the south transept of Beauvais and the north transept of Sens Cathedral, a playful adaptation has been introduced. The turrets flanking the central portal at Troyes look like staircase turrets, but the staircases have been shifted to the much more massive, flat-sided buttresses at the outer edges of the façade.

In his treatment of the decorative niches that provide such extraordinary richness to his façades, Martin Chambiges shared a vocabulary of forms with several other designers working in and around the capital city. We know that Chambiges was a consultant for the Bureau de la Ville in connection with the reconstruction of the Pont Notre-Dame; the meetings to discuss the form of the bridge would provide an ideal forum for the sharing of ideas.[74] In his niche canopies Chambiges favored the use of two verticals cutting through the enclosing frame that was often in the form of a tightly pointed arch designed around arcs of circles whose center points lay outside the composition. Such canopies can be found on the church of Saint-Nicolas-des-Champs, the portal of the church of Saint-Benoît, the church of Saints-Gervais-et-Protais, and the fragments from the demolished Hôtel le Gendre, all in the capital city.[75]

If the exterior decorative forms used by Chambiges were shared by a number of contemporaries, his pier forms seem unique. The piers of the Beauvais transepts (Figs. 80, 81) have eight symmetrically arranged shafts whose contours are allowed to merge together to form a sinuous, undulating outline. The ef-

fect is that of a cylindrical pier with eight shafts (Amiens choir aisles), which has been cloaked in a heavy, clinging blanket, half revealing and half concealing the geometry of the forms underneath. If the streamlined character of the pier results in a certain loss of clarity in the sense of the distinct individuality of the component elements, this is more than adequately compensated for by the design of the plinth, which is a model of academic thinking. Each of the eight shafts is received on top of a regular hexagonal molding, whose form is continued downward into the plinth.[76] The sides of the hexagons merge into the sweeping surfaces of concave scoops that exist between the individual plinths. The role of the shafts within the total structure of the building is reflected in the placing of the hexagonal plinths; the plinths for the main shafts have their flat sides presented toward the outside of the pier, whereas the plinths of the minor shafts reflect the diagonality of the ribs that they support by presenting their angles. The same overall design is used both for the smaller piers in the transept arms as well as for the great piers to the west of the crossing. The effect achieved in the two different sizes of pier is rather different, however, since the larger piers have much more of a gap between the shafts, causing the balance resulting from a more-or-less equal alternation of concave and convex surfaces to be lost.

A measured drawing of one of the smaller piers in the Beauvais transept (Fig. 28) allows us to investigate the nature of the design process that lay behind the formulation of the plan.[77] The drawing shows that the center points of the shafts coincide with the centers of the hexagonal plinths and lie upon the circumference of a master circle. It is of some interest to note that the relationship between the two different sizes used for the hexagonal

[74] Bonnardot, *Registres des délibérations.*

[75] For Saints-Gervais-et-Protais, see Brochard, *Saint-Gervais.* For the Hôtel le Gendre, see Y. Christ, "Les Vestiges de l'ancien Musée des Monuments français à l'Ecole des Beaux-Arts et leur sort," *Gaz. des Beaux-Arts,* LXVI, 1965, pp. 167–174.

[76] The hexagonal plinth does not occur in the attached piers of the Sens Cathedral south transept, Chambiges's first

documented work. In the north transept, begun after the master had departed for Beauvais, hexagonal plinths are found. It seems certain, therefore, that he first used this idea in his work at Beauvais.

[77] The pier sections were prepared using an indirect system of measurement generated from a square pegged out on the pavement around the pier base.

plinths seems to be a fixed one in both the large and the smaller piers of the Beauvais transept. If smaller units are inscribed inside the larger hexagon used for the main shaft of each pier, it will be found that the third such unit will give the dimension of the plinth used for the smaller shaft. In the smaller piers the relationship seems to go even further, to include the overall circle around which the pier was planned. If this unit is taken as the starting point, the sixth inscribed hexagon will give the size of the larger plinths of the pier, and the ninth hexagon will give the size of the smaller ones. Thus the whole unit may be expressed in terms of the ratio of 1:6:9. This relationship between the main circle of the pier and the dimensions of the plinths of the shafts is only valid for the smaller piers in the Beauvais transepts and does not apply to the great piers of the crossing.

The idea of hexagons was nothing new. Hexagonal designs had been traditional in rose window tracery from the beginnings of Gothic, and hexagonal bases had begun to replace the traditional octagonal type in the second half of the thirteenth century.[78] In the piers in the ambulatory of Notre-Dame, Paris, constructed around 1300, at the time when the chapels were being added around the choir, hexagonal plinths linked by concave surfaces can already be found. What is new in Martin Chambiges's piers, however, is the coherent, fluent way in which these various elements are used. In optical terms the pier becomes a unit that interacts with the surrounding space, in that the curves of the pier are determined both from within (the shafts are based on circles that have their center points inside the mass of the pier) and from without (the concave surfaces, although not perfect arcs of circles, imply a center of design that lies outside the mass of the pier in space.

Although we know that Martin Chambiges

was a Parisian, no real prototype can be found in the architecture of the capital city for the pier type found in the transept of Beauvais Cathedral. The closest analogies can be seen in the piers of the porch of the church of Saint-Germain-l'Auxerrois, Paris. This porch is generally attributed to Jean Gaussel and dated to the 1430s.[79]

The successive campaigns of construction at Saint-Séverin, Paris, serve to illustrate the development of taste away from solid, rounded forms toward sharp linearity.[80] The ambulatory and radiating chapels are considered to have resulted from construction campaigns in the 1490s. In the piers flanking the mouths of the chapels the sharp fillet moldings of the ribs run directly down into the body of the pier. Deep concavities separate the fillets, and the abrupt transition from light to shadow lends to these units an appearance of brittle linearity. The freestanding piers of the ambulatory, on the other hand, embody the system of disappearing moldings, where the profiles of the ribs and arches are swallowed up by the mass of the piers.

Saints-Gervais-et-Protais in Paris (Fig. 166), begun in the 1490s, has actually been attributed to Martin Chambiges, the architect of the Beauvais transept.[81] It is certain that he owned a house in the parish but most unlikely that he directed the construction of the church.[82] In planning the church, the designer has speculated with a combination of a polygonal and a flat-ended choir. The articulation is reduced to a series of lines formed by the angles between concavities.

The Choir of Saint-Etienne Beauvais

Martin Chambiges's pier type is a distinctly personal expression, dependent in a distant way upon thirteenth-century prototypes and

---

[78] Pierre of Montreuil pioneered the use of hexagonal plinths in his Grande Chapelle de la Vierge at Saint-Germain-des-Prés in Paris, and later in the south transept of Notre-Dame. Martin Chambiges, a Parisian, was almost certainly familiar with the latter work.

[79] A. Lesort and H. Verlet, *Saint-Germain-l'Auxerrois: Epitaphier du vieux Paris*, v, Paris, 1974. The porch is clearly not the work of a single period. The two outermost

bays, with their more massive supports and low vaults, might belong to the 1430s, but the central bays of the porch were surely added at a date closer to 1500.

[80] Sanfaçon, *L'Architecture flamboyante*, pp. 91–95.

[81] Brochard, *Saint-Gervais*.

[82] Had he been master mason of the church, he would certainly have been named as such in the list of "notable parishioners" in which his name is recorded.

developed by the master as a result of a series of experiments at Sens and Beauvais. Although undulating forms were used by Martin Chambiges in the south transept at Sens, he had not yet invented his characteristic base with hexagonal plinths. The first use of this feature was probably in the parish and collegiate church of Saint-Etienne and Saint-Vast in Beauvais (Figs. 149–157), where the choir was completely rebuilt after the collapse of the crossing tower in 1480.[83] The date normally given for the start of the work is 1506, when the ceremony of laying the foundation stone of the ambulatory (*pourtour*) took place. However, it seems fairly certain that the actual beginnings of the work on the new choir may be placed somewhat earlier than this. The small sepulchre chapel opening on the north choir aisle adjacent to the transept is dated by inscription to the year 1502,[84] and the chapel already embodies architectural forms (for example, the petal vault; Fig. 156) characteristic of the main body of the choir. Thus, there is every reason to believe that work was already under way before 1502. We have very little in the way of documentary evidence to allow us to fix the stages of construction of the choir. The unfinished edifice was consecrated in 1522. In 1525 Michel Lalie, Martin Chambiges's subordinate in the cathedral workshop, was named master of Saint-Etienne. The year 1526 saw the glazing of certain windows in the chapels, and the date 1546 is painted on the high vaults.

The plan (Fig. 149) embodies the characteristics of streamlining and simplification typical of Late Gothic. The four rectangular bays of the central vessel end in a trapezoidal hemicycle. Flanking the central vessel is an aisle made up of square bays. At the east end this aisle continues around the hemicycle in the form of irregular parallelograms flanking the central trapezoid and a rectangular bay in front of the five-sided axial chapel.

The choir is a steep two-story basilica (Fig. 152). The tracery and glass of the clerestory windows are recessed only a little way behind the plane of the arcade, producing an overall impression of flatness. The arrangement of the east end, with its great rose window, contributes to this rather flat, boxlike effect.

The piers of Saint-Etienne are of two types, a larger one in the arcade and a smaller one between the side aisles (Figs. 150, 151). In their design they are very similar to the piers of the cathedral, having eight shafts arranged symmetrically around a central core and an undulating profile. The pier plinths attached to the envelope of the choir (probably the first part of the structure to be erected) consist of a continuous "trumpet" molding intersected by small fillet bases (Fig. 153). The molding resembles the pier base forms used by Martin Chambiges in his earliest work at Sens Cathedral. The period of usage of this form at Saint-Etienne may probably be dated to the years around 1500. Like the piers of the cathedral, most of the freestanding piers of Saint-Etienne have hexagonal plinths for each one of the individual shafts, and three different moldings: for the main shafts, the diagonals, and the body of the pier itself. The moldings used for the body of the pier may be divided into two different types, a simple type with no indentation in the lower parts of the molding (Fig. 154), and a more complex type with a deep indentation under a rounded rim (Fig. 155). This observation leads to two conclusions, one relating to the chronology of the work, and the other to the mind behind the design process. It seems certain that work must have progressed from the envelope to the piers of the north choir aisles, and then advanced at a later date into the southern side. The piers at Saint-Etienne cannot have been based upon a single copy of the type found in the cathedral, because we find a similar change affecting the units in both buildings,

[83] Henwood-Reverdot, *L'Eglise Saint-Etienne de Beauvais*; Leblond, *L'Eglise Saint-Etienne de Beauvais*; V. l'Huillier, *La Paroisse et l'église de Saint-Etienne de Beauvais*, Beauvais, 1896.

[84] "*Icy dedens gist ung poure pecheur*

Guy de Hodene nommé qui en l'honneur
De JhesuChrist et de la passion
A faict construire par grand devotion
Ce beau sepulchre en l'an Vc. de grace
Mil aveuc deux. Jhs pardon luy face."

implying that a single mind lay behind the designs of both sets of piers.

The hypothesis that Martin Chambiges himself was the designer of the choir of Saint-Etienne and that he directed the initial stages of the work may be tested by means of a study of measured drawings of the Saint-Etienne piers, and by a reconsideration of the chronology of the two works. It is quite evident that despite their similar external appearance, the Saint-Etienne piers do not share the same kind of "skeleton" as their counterparts in the cathedral. A different principle of design is applied, which provides two main circles for the center points of the shafts, a larger one for the main shafts and a smaller one for the diagonals. This means that the main shafts seem to be thrust outward, making for a very vigorous undulation. This is entirely appropriate in a smaller pier, where only a relatively narrow gap can separate the shafts, and therefore a deep concave depression is impossible.

Thus, both the change in the molding forms that appears in the Saint-Etienne choir piers as well as the basic design itself seem to suggest that we are not dealing with a simple case of copying. Two further factors suggest that a very close relationship exists between the two groups of piers. First, there is a simple arithmetic relationship between the dimensions of the hexagonal plinths in the cathedral crossing piers and the larger piers in Saint-Etienne; the former are exactly twice as large as the latter. Second, echoes of the idea of inscribed hexagons can be found in the Saint-Etienne piers.[85]

The argument advanced here might seem paradoxical. It is partly because of the very degrees of dissimilarity between the piers of Saint-Etienne and those in the cathedral that the probability emerges that they were designed by the same master. Copies they certainly were not, both because of the control over the principles of design, which is evident, and because a careful consideration of the chronology of the two works reveals that the Saint-Etienne piers might even have provided the prototypes for their counterparts in the cathedral. The first freestanding piers in the cathedral transept arms were not constructed until after work had begun on the north transept in 1510 (Fig. 5). It has been seen that work at Saint-Etienne probably began as early as ca. 1500, and thus the design for the piers at Saint-Etienne must have been made long before the similar piers in the cathedral had been constructed.

There is also a significant relationship between the forms of the vaults of the two buildings. For the most part, the Saint-Etienne aisle vaults are of the simple quadripartite type, although a lozenge vault is used in the central vessel, and some more complex types are found in the sepulchre chapel opening into the north choir aisle and in certain bays in the south aisle. The vault of the sepulchre chapel (Fig. 156) is a petal type, which provides a prototype for the vault of the chapel in the north transept of the cathedral (Fig. 78). The decorative vaults of the south aisle (Fig. 157), however, which may be placed in the 1520s, have the same boldly flowing lines linking the segments of the vault as the chapel in the south transept of the cathedral (Fig. 79). One of the vaults of the south aisle has an elaborate form of pendant wheel vault that is almost identical to a vault in the cathedral of Senlis, to the east of the south transept, work that may be attributed to Pierre Chambiges, Martin Chambiges's son.[86]

If the design of the choir of Saint-Etienne is, indeed, to be attributed to Martin Chambiges, the work will take on considerable importance as the only instance where that master was able to undertake a major project where the proportions of the existing building did not compromise the possibility of achieving a new design. Despite the existence of slight irregularities in the layout, the plan of the choir of Saint-Etienne seems to possess a high degree of coherence. The central vessel is around

---

[85] In the smaller piers a sequence of 1:6:9 can be detected, whereas the larger piers of the main arcade follow a ratio in the order of 1:9:10.

[86] The rebuilding of Senlis Cathedral after the 1504 fire does not seem to have been directed by Martin Chambiges. Pierre's activity at Senlis in the 1530s can, however, be documented.

10.40 m in width (almost exactly 32 royal feet), the inner aisle consists of bays that are almost perfectly square (having sides of around 6.10 m), and the outer aisle has bays of around 6.10 by 4.30 m. It is readily apparent that the width of the central vessel has been given by the simple addition of the widths of the two aisles. The relation of the dimensions of the aisles themselves is given by a simple root two calculation.

The realization of the strong probability that Martin Chambiges was the designer of the choir of Saint-Etienne should provoke a reconsideration of the context of this work within the total oeuvre of that master, particularly in relation to the cathedral transepts. An initial reaction to the two works tends to lead to an unfavorable assessment of the Saint-Etienne choir. Despite the freedom of planning enjoyed in this project, it would seem that Martin Chambiges was unable to rival the effects of his own work on the cathedral transepts. Of course, at Saint-Etienne the concentration is upon interior effects, whereas in all of Chambiges's other works he was able to design dazzling façades. The rather stark two-dimensional effect of the Saint-Etienne elevation certainly does seem somewhat arid in comparison with the sculptured exuberance of the cathedral transept façades.

On the other hand, the soaring verticality, the svelte form of the piers, and even the flattened east end of Saint-Etienne invite comparison with the cathedral transept interior. In assessing the impact of the Saint-Etienne choir, moreover, it must be remembered that Martin Chambiges's architectural forms were intended to be accompanied by sculpture and stained glass. Whereas the absence (through noncompletion or destruction) of statues does not seriously detract from Chambiges's façades, the absence of stained glass in the clerestory of Saint-Etienne certainly has a most damaging effect upon the lighting of the interior. Around 1500 there took place a con-

siderable revival in the art of stained-glass making in many areas of France. In the 1490s the clerestory windows of the nave of Troyes Cathedral were filled with glass that is characterized by brilliant colors with an overall heavy degree of saturation. The Troyes glaziers were later summoned to Sens to glaze the clerestory of the transept of the cathedral. The windows of the chapels of Saint-Etienne, glazed by such artists as Engrand le Prince, have a similar brilliance. Thus, whereas the calligraphic sharpness of a Rayonnant interior, equipped with grisaille glass, was intended to be flooded with clear light, the softer, simpler forms of the Saint-Etienne interior were to be illuminated with a light that was warmer and more suffused. The very design of the church, with its flattened east end and hemicycle piers widely spaced in order to open up the vista to the windows of the axial chapel, seems calculated to serve the purpose of presenting as many large windows to the viewer as possible.[87]

In constructing an elevation that consisted of a skeleton of stone (Fig. 152), intended to provide a framework for glass of deeply saturated colors, the master of the Saint-Etienne choir was obviously placing himself in line of descent from the master masons of High Gothic and Rayonnant. Saint-Etienne has nothing of the more specifically "Late Gothic" characteristics of concentration on mural surfaces, diminution of the clerestory, and intensified spatial unity. Certain elements in the vocabulary of forms used in the cathedral transepts also seem to reflect a conscious decision to go back to thirteenth-century prototypes: for example, the academic thinking that characterizes the pier planning, the three-story elevation, and the use of straight gables intersected by balustrades over the portals, rather than curvilinear ogee gables.

The problem of the role of the Saint-Etienne choir as a model must now be considered.[88] Three of the city churches in Troyes may owe

[87] For the question of the flat east end, see M. L. Régnier, "Une Particularité architectonique du chœur de Saint-Etienne de Beauvais," *Cong. arch.*, LXXII, 1905, pp. 530–534.

[88] The style of Martin Chambiges had some impact in the city of Beauvais, the churches of Saint-Nicholas and Saint-Sauveur (both now demolished) receiving additions in the new style. Outside the city, the church of Marissel has a

their plan and elevation to this source. In southern Champagne most rural parish churches built in the last decades of the fifteenth century and the first decades of the sixteenth were of the hall-church type, or else had a very reduced clerestory (for example, Saint-André-les-Vergers and Sainte-Savine, both near Troyes).[89] The first decades of the sixteenth century saw the construction of a different type of church in Troyes, having a steep two-story elevation and a flattened east end. These churches might possibly owe their inspiration to a Parisian monument such as Saints-Gervais-et-Protais (Fig. 166), but given the close connections between the masters of the Troyes churches and the workshop of Martin Chambiges engaged in the construction of the façade of Troyes Cathedral, it seems more probable that Saint-Etienne, Beauvais, provided the model.

It has been claimed that Martin Chambiges himself was consulted in the planning of two of these parish churches (Saint-Pantaléon and Saint-Jean-au-Marché; Fig. 180).[90] The texts that have been advanced to support this hypothesis do not, however, make any mention of Martin Chambiges, and the personal involvement of that master is unlikely. These above-named churches, as well as the church of Saint-Nicolas in Troyes, all have steep two-story elevations, three-sided apses enclosed inside flat east ends, and piers that have undulating shafts received on top of hexagonal plinths like Saint-Etienne, Beauvais. At Saint-Pantaléon[91] all of the plinths have their flat sides toward the exterior, whereas at Saint-Jean the angles of all of the hexagons are presented toward the outside. The geometric clarity of the Saint-Etienne piers is entirely missing, however. If the churches of Saint-Pantaléon and Saint-Jean cannot be attributed to Chambiges himself, they were certainly the work of his followers from the cathedral workshop in Troyes. Another group of churches exists in the city of Troyes with choir plans that embody three interlocking hexagons. The identity of the master masons of these buildings has still not been established with any degree of certainty, though there is a strong likelihood that the choir of the church of La Madeleine, begun in the 1490s by the master Jehan Gailde, provided the prototype.[92]

Thus, the choir of the church of Saint-Etienne, Beauvais, stands at the head of a small family of parish churches in the city of Troyes in terms of plan and elevation, while in terms of pier design, the family tree that springs from the Saint-Etienne design is immense. In following this family tree, one finds both the playful adaptation of forms that characterizes Pierre Chambiges's piers in the transepts of the cathedral of Senlis (Figs. 178, 179)[93] and the rather mindless copying of

---

nave and west façade that show influence from the same source, and the nave of Saints-Gervais-et-Protais, Gisors, may be a copy of the choir of Saint-Etienne. The church at Allonne has a decadent version of the undulating type of pier.

[89] E. Lefèvre-Pontalis, "L'Architecture gothique dans la Champagne méridionale au XIIIe. au XVIe. siècle," *Cong. arch.*, LXIX, 1902, pp. 273–349.

[90] F. Salet, "Saint-Pantaléon de Troyes," *Cong. arch.*, CXIII, 1955, pp. 153–165. Salet repeats an argument that was first put forward by A. Babeau, "L'Eglise Saint-Pantaléon de Troyes," *Annuaire de l'Aube*, 1881, p. 33, where the latter writer states that a text for the year 1516, which records a visit by the master mason of Saint-Pierre (Troyes Cathedral) at the commencement of work at Saint-Pantaléon, indicates that Martin Chambiges was consulted on the plans for the church. Such an argument is invalidated for two reasons: the text makes no mention of plans, but merely of a visit; and Martin Chambiges did not go to Troyes in 1516, his last visit to that city having been in 1512. The master mason referred to in the text is Jehan de Damas (de Soissons), Martin Chambiges's son-in-law, and resident master of the Troyes Cathedral workshop. Piétresson de Saint-Aubin, "L'Eglise Saint-Jean-au-Marché à Troyes," claimed that Martin Chambiges was involved with the planning of Saint-Jean, but his argument is invalidated for the same reasons.

[91] Saint-Pantaléon was begun by Jehan Bailly, a mason from the Troyes Cathedral workshop, and continued by his former assistant, Maurice de Favereau. Bailly was also involved in the beginnings of the reconstruction of the choir of Saint-Jean-au-Marché, but in 1517 his place was taken by Martin de Vaulx, who is thought to have been a Parisian. The master of Saint-Nicolas, Gerard Faulchot, came from a family whose name is found in the cathedral accounts in the late fifteenth century. Jehan Bailly seems to have been a key man in the appearance of the steep two-story flat-ended basilica in Troyes, but we have no information concerning his background before he appeared in the Troyes Cathedral workshop in 1501–1502.

[92] F. Salet, "La Madeleine de Troyes," *Cong. arch.*, CXIII, 1955, pp. 139–152.

[93] The word "mannerism" inevitably springs to mind in connection with the style of Pierre Chambiges, both because

forms that are not really understood in many of the smaller churches in southern Champagne, built under the influence of the Troyes city churches. We seem to be dealing with a cycle that takes us from the "orthodoxy" of Martin Chambiges's designs to the stages of decline represented by the many attempts to adapt and copy those forms that were made by countless rustic masters in Champenois churches in the first decades of the sixteenth century. The same cycle characterizes the use and adaptation of Chambiges's niche canopies, which appear for the first time at Beauvais, and which are transmitted via the Troyes Cathedral workshop to scores of Champenois churches.

The last decades of Gothic architecture in France should not be viewed as the decadent end of an artistic movement that had begun with the Early Gothic architecture of the twelfth century. On the one hand, the work of Martin Chambiges should be judged on its own merits, as a powerful personal vision that inspired a series of copies and adaptations embodying a cycle of change from orthodoxy to mannerism (the piers of Pierre Chambiges at Senlis) and decline. On the other hand, Martin Chambiges should also be seen as a master who, although separated by a gap of some two hundred and fifty years from the period of construction of the Beauvais choir, was yet able to understand it in structural terms and to continue the construction in a style that was simultaneously "contemporary" and yet in perfect harmony with the existing work. His architectural forms thus embody both the brittle calligraphy of Rayonnant and the sculptural mass of High Gothic.

---

of his rather overrefined adaptations of his father's formulas (the studied asymmetry of the Senlis piers), and because of his playful use of forms that had been used by his father for minor units in a more monumental context (for example, the gables over the portals of Senlis Cathedral, which consist of broken ogee arches formed of inverted curves, much like Martin Chambiges's niche canopies).

CHAPTER VIII

The Crossing Tower

The construction of the Gothic cathedral of Saint-Pierre ended as it had begun—with the frustrated attempt to build a bell tower. It has been seen that the very first work on the choir after 1225 was concentrated upon the two towers to the east of the transept façades. The unprecedented, and unexpected, height of the central vessel caused the body of the building to take on a towerlike quality, and the transept towers begun under Bishop Miles were never completed. The cathedral thus lacked a belfrey, although a small steeple had existed at the west end of the choir roof. The main bells of the cathedral must have hung in the great freestanding tower that stood to the southeast of the south transept.

More important than these purely functional concerns were considerations of prestige. Since Beauvais Cathedral is set in a basin, the construction of a tower would allow the edifice to dominate the surrounding countryside. It is said that the spires of Paris were visible from the top of the completed tower at Beauvais. It is amusing to speculate that the great height of the choir of Saint-Pierre expresses the Gothic attempt to surpass the Pantheon in Rome and that the sixteenth-century crossing tower was intended as a rejoinder to the dome of Saint Peter's. References to the tower in the deliberations of the chapter suggest that its builders had in mind a prototype more venerable still, for the tower is described as a "pyramid."[1]

The second part of the sixteenth century was not a period particularly conducive to cathedral construction. The Concordat of Bologna of 1518 had given the king the right to nominate bishops. The candidates nominated by the king were often pluralists, holding several benefices *in absentia*. Without local ties, such bishops often lacked the commitment necessary to devote large sums of money to building. Protestantism was gaining strength in France, and active persecution of Protestants began in the 1530s. Tension and violence escalated, and by the 1560s France was

[1] Bucquet-aux Cousteaux, XVIII, p. 338: "*On examine les modeles du clocher autrement de la piramide. . . .*" The comparison with Saint Peter's in Rome was first made by Etienne de Nully, "Notice," p. 233.

in a state of civil war. The war was accompanied by atrocities on both sides. In 1563 the Catholic Duke of Guise was assassinated, and in 1572 the Protestant leader Coligny was murdered together with thousands of others in the massacre of Saint Bartholomew's Eve. One of the visible manifestations of Protestantism was the destruction of statues and other images decorating churches.

In Beauvais, the bishop responsible for the start of construction on the transept, Louis of Villiers of l'Ile-Adam, died in 1521.[2] A short interregnum ensued before the accession of Anthoine Lascaris of Tende (1523–1530), who was nominated by Francis I at the request of the candidate's uncle, the Bastard of Savoye, Grand Master of France. Anthoine was an absentee bishop. During this period extensive riots took place in Beauvais on account of the high price of food.

Charles of Villiers of l'Ile-Adam (1530–1535) was the nephew of Louis of Villiers. He had been bishop of Limoges but exchanged his see with Anthoine of Tende. Serious epidemics took place in Beauvais in those years. Charles had some difficulty in gaining control of his revenues, some of which Anthoine of Tende continued to receive, but nevertheless contributed substantial sums for the completion of the transept.

The next bishop, Cardinal Odet of Coligny (1535–1569), was also nominated by the king. Odet had been made a cardinal at the age of seventeen and archbishop of Toulouse at eighteen. A favorite of the Constable Anne of Montmorency, Odet held sixteen abbeys (including Saint-Lucien, Saint-Germer, and Froidmont) as well as four priories and the position of canon at the Saint-Chapelle in Paris. Naturally, Odet of Coligny spent very little time in Beauvais.

In the 1550s Odet's family was converted to the doctrines of Calvin. Odet attempted to act as a mediator, still speaking for the Catholics at the Council of Poissy in 1561, but by 1562 the bishop was openly Calvinist. He dropped the title "bishop of Beauvais," preferring to retain the title "count." He began to celebrate the Protestant office in his episcopal chapel. We are told that the people of Beauvais remained, for the most part, faithful to Rome. An uprising took place in the city on account of the presence of the Protestant priest Adrien Fourré. A Huguenot, Jean of Bury, pursued by the mob, took refuge in the bishop's palace, which was then attacked. In April 1563 the bishop was excommunicated by Pope Pius IV. On December 1, 1564, Odet married Isabella of Hauteville, and some four years later he fled to England. He was convicted of *lèse-majesté*, and the see was declared vacant. He is said to have been poisoned by his *valet-de-chambre* in 1571.

Charles of Bourbon (1569–1575) was chosen bishop of Beauvais by King Charles IX. Son of the Duke of Vendôme, Charles was seventeen when he became bishop. He was simultaneously bishop of Nevers, Saintes, and Rouen and abbot of Saint-Lucien, Saint-Germer, Froidmont, Corbie, Ourscamp, and several other abbeys. During his period as bishop the crossing tower was completed and collapsed. It is appropriate, therefore, to turn to an account of the construction.

Construction of the Crossing Tower

In 1534, with work in progress on the upper parts of the transept, the bishop, Charles of Villers of l'Ile-Adam, donated a sum of money for the construction of a new bell tower.[3] This is the first reference in the written sources to the project that was to be initiated some thirty years later.

In January 1543 an *expertise* was conducted in order to determine whether the tower should be constructed of wood or of stone.[4] In March 1546 masons and carpenters submitted models for alternative projects in

---

[2] The following information on the sixteenth-century bishops of Beauvais is taken from Delettre, *Histoire du diocèse*, III, pp. 164–272.

[3] Bucquet-aux Cousteaux, XXIII, p. 65; XXVIII, p. 297.

The former source specifies three hundred pounds and the latter source four hundred.

[4] Ibid., XXVIII, p. 329.

masonry or wood.[5] In the following month experts examined the four great crossing piers in order to determine whether the foundations were strong enough to support a stone pyramid.[6] The piers themselves were inspected by masons from the churches of Saint-Etienne and Saint-Sauveur in the city of Beauvais.[7] In 1557 commissioners were sent to the quarries of Saint-Leu-d'Esserent to purchase the necessary stone, and in 1562 skilled carpenters were hired.[8]

In 1563 purchases of timber and rope were made and a model of the tower was sent from Paris.[9] Work seems to have begun at this time and to have progressed remarkably quickly. We may assume that although the plans had been sent from Paris, the direction of the work lay in the hands of the principal architect, Jean Vast.[10]

By 1565 the great masonry lantern that formed the lowest three levels of the tower must have been nearing completion. A model for the wooden spire was approved,[11] and a canon was commissioned to work with experts to render the design more beautiful.[12] Work on the spire must have progressed very swiftly, for we are told that the great iron cross worked by Nicolas of Louvencourt was affixed to the summit on April 2, 1565 or 1566.[13] The wooden spire was then covered with lead bought at Rouen, glass was installed, and the painters Nicolas Nitard and Thomas le Pot decorated the vaults.[14] All was finished by late in the year of 1569.

We know something of the appearance of the tower from a contemporary description preserved in the Oise archives and from a drawing, later engraved by Desjardins (Fig. 29), which dates from the subsequent period.[15] The lowest part of the tower comprised a masonry lantern that rose some eighty-two feet above the top of the clerestory wall. In its general proportions, this part of the tower would have approximated two cubes, one placed atop the other. The sides of the lantern were pierced with great windows. The second level was in the form of an octagon, sixty-three feet high, also pierced by windows, and then came a second octagon, fifty feet high. Finally, a timber spire crowned the edifice, towering up another ninety-six feet. The total height of the tower itself was thus about two hundred and ninety-one feet, about twice the height of the body of the church. The tip of the steeple was about four hundred and thirty-eight feet above floor level.

It is especially interesting to note the relationship between the octagonal levels of the tower and the square base. Instead of placing the octagon with its sides aligned with the sides of the square in the traditional mode, the designers have centered an angle of the octagon at the midpoint of each side of the base. The details (tracery, canopies, medallions, etc.) are in the transitional style characteristic of the last gasp of Gothic. The general composition must have had the rather flimsy and theatrical appearance of an eighteenth-century Gothic folly.

The view up into the interior of the tower with its multiple levels of windows and painted decoration must have been spectacu-

---

[5] Ibid., p. 338.

[6] Ibid., pp. 338–339.

[7] Ibid., p. 339.

[8] Ibid., pp. 353, 356–357.

[9] Ibid., pp. 357–362.

[10] Ibid., p. 413. Jean Vast, who died in 1581, is described as "principal architecte de l'église." However, none of the sources consulted by our eighteenth-century copyist (of the Bucquet-aux Cousteaux Collection) actually mentions Vast as the mason in charge of work on the tower.

[11] Ibid., p. 361. On June 8, 1565, the canons discussed the construction of the wooden spire "following the little model that had been presented."

[12] Ibid., p. 362: "chanoine député pour reformer et rendre plus beau le clocher ou piramide."

[13] Desjardins, Histoire, p. 86.

[14] Bucquet-aux Cousteaux, XXVIII, p.368.

[15] Arch. Oise, G 707, "Le memoire de ce que contient le cœur de l'église de St. Pierre de Beauvais. . . ." The drawing of the elevation of the tower was published in Woillez, Description de la cathédrale de Beauvais (conveniently available in Bonnet-Laborderie, Cathédrale Saint-Pierre, p. 70). The original of this drawing is conserved in the cathedral treasury. Leblond also published a view of the tower (La Cathédrale de Beauvais, p. 19), but the original of this drawing is unknown to me. The drawings published by Leblond and Woillez are closely related. In its overall proportions, the tower depicted corresponds quite closely with the dimensions given in the manuscript cited above, and we may therefore assume that the drawing may be based upon a reliable source. See also Desjardins, Histoire, frontispiece.

lar. Although the plan was sent from Paris, it is hard to escape from the conclusion that the inspiration for the idea of a great central lantern tower came from the north and northwest. One thinks especially of the great crossing towers of England and Normandy; in the latter area, moreover, lantern towers were particularly popular.

The thrill to be derived from the tower was not merely from the contemplation of the extraordinary interior effects peculiar to the lantern, or the distant prospect of the edifice, now surmounted by a steeple of highly decorated masonry and wood, towering twice as high as the body of the church itself. The adventurous might also climb up into the tower and survey the city, the vineyards and gardens on the sides of the surrounding hills, and in the distance, the towers and steeples of Paris. The ascent into the tower soon became so popular that the chapter had to close the door that provided access "in order to prevent the people (especially lay people) who wanted to climb."[16]

Structural Problems and the Collapse of the Tower

Structural problems were experienced even before the tower had been completed. In 1567 an *expertise* was conducted.[17] In January 1572 the heavy iron cross was removed from the steeple,[18] and on April 8, 1572, a major *expertise* was conducted by two Parisian masons, Gilles of Harlay and Nicolas Tiersault.[19] They found that the four great crossing piers that supported the tower had begun to rotate outward, propelled by the great weight of the tower. They suspended plumb lines from the tops of the piers at a height of sixty feet, and they noted that the northeastern pier was two inches out of a true vertical position, the southeastern pier four inches, the northwestern pier five to six inches, and the southwest-

ern pier eleven inches. The presence of the choir to the east and the absence of the nave to the west caused the two sides of the crossing to behave in a different fashion. Thus, the western piers were pushed out of a vertical position but were not broken; the eastern piers yielded little, but we are told that certain stones were actually fractured. This is significant in light of the fact that the tower, when it finally collapsed, seems to have fallen in an easterly direction.

The surviving manuscript source provides an indication that at least one bay of the central vessel of the nave had already been completed at that time, since we are told that the pillars to the west of the crossing were also leaning for lack of adequate support.

It is important to gain a correct understanding of the solution proposed by the visitors, since this reveals something of their understanding of Gothic structure. The secondary sources tell us that the visiting masons proposed to construct four solid masonry walls under the four great arches of the crossing.[20] If one pauses to consider the implications of this project, it will become evident that this would be entirely impractical. A massive amount of masonry would be involved, the effect of the interior space would be entirely ruined, and the problem of the outward buckling of the piers would not be solved. In fact, the sixteenth-century text has been generally misunderstood, and the solution proposed by the visitors was rather a different one. They recommended a rapid completion of the remaining piers (i.e., of the nave) and, as an immediate measure, the construction of a great wall of ashlar masonry "from the floor to the great arches [arcade] behind the great [crossing] piers." Furthermore, they suggested that the masons should "leave in each wall a passage and opening to allow access to the aisles. And above the arcade, the openings and windows must also be blocked." The walls specified were clearly not in the crossing itself, but

[16] Bucquet-aux Cousteaux, XXVIII, p. 367.
[17] Desjardins, *Histoire*, p. 92.
[18] Ibid., p. 93; see also Bucquet-aux Cousteaux, XXVIII, p. 373.

[19] Arch. Oise, G 707.
[20] For example, Leblond, *La Cathédrale de Beauvais*, p. 24; Bonnet-Laborderie, *Cathédrale Saint-Pierre*, p. 72.

at arcade level to the west of the crossing (the first nave bay) and in the triforium and clerestory of the same bay.

Once these walls had been constructed and the crossing had been propped up on the west side, it would have been possible to repair the cracks that were beginning to show in the arches of the crossing and the base of the lantern. It would also have been possible (and necessary) to found four more nave piers, two in the nave of the *Basse-Œuvre* and two more to the south of the *Basse-Œuvre* where the masons' lodge was located.[21] These piers, it was specified, should be linked by sleeper walls beneath pavement level. The piers, together with the vaults and arches that they would support, should follow the forms of the counterparts in the transept.

The visitors went on to recommend other repairs of lesser importance: certain flyers were not properly linked with their uprights, the terraced roofs of the ambulatory were leaking, and the steps of the "small staircase above the aisle roofs" were in need of repair.[22]

On June 9, 1572, another *expertise* was conducted by Jean Etienne, a skilled architect from Laon, and Jean Baudry from Mello.[23] In July 1572 the chapter commissioned several colleagues to confer with the master of the works to expedite the start of work on the nave piers, and on April 17, 1573, laborers were hired to work "very promptly" to prop up the new work. On April 29 carpenters were also procured "to prop up the edifice."[24]

However, on April 30, the day of Ascension, at seven o'clock in the morning, just after a great procession had left the church, the tower collapsed, blowing out the doors and injuring two people who were saying mass at the altar of the Holy Sacrament.[25] Gustave Desjardins described the sequence of the collapse thus: "All at once the pillars toward the episcopal palace and the *Basse-Œuvre* [in the west] gave way, the pillar of the crossing to

---

[21] The stone (chalk) for the footings of these piers had already been ordered from the quarries at Bongenoult; see Bucquet-aux Cousteaux, XXVIII, p. 372.

[22] The reference to the terraced roof of the aisles and ambulatory is important since it documents the fact that the double-sloped wood-and-slate roof system over the aisles and chapels that existed until the nineteenth century must have dated from after the 1570s.

[23] Bucquet-aux Cousteaux, XXVIII, pp. 376–377.

[24] Ibid., pp. 377, 380.

[25] Ibid., pp. 380–381: "1er. mai 1573, le chapitre se tient a l'heure des primes dans le chapitre de St. Nicolas a cause de la chûte de la grande piramide arriveé la veille, jour de l'Ascension. On fit l'office a St. Nicolas et le 4. mai le chapitre fit donner par le pannetier 50s a André Martine qui entendoit la messe a St. Pierre lors de la chute de la piramide et qui fit blessé. ... On donne cent sols a Simon Hoste prestre habitué de l'Eglise qui avoit eté blessé au bras lors de la chute de la piramide." Hermant, *Histoire ecclesiastique*, IV, pp. 1731–1732, provides the most detailed description of the collapse: "Deux jours avant la feste de l'Ascension de l'an 1573 la chûte de quelques petites pierres qui s'estoient détachées du corps de la voûte et du clocher fut un avis que Dieu donna par sa providence de se précautionner contre le peril dont on estoit menacé. On differa neanmoins d'y pourvoir jusques au jour de cette grande feste, ou on a accoustumé depuis plusieurs siecles de faire une procession fort solemnelle autour de l'Eglise, et d'y porter les chasses des trois saints patrons que l'on y conserve comme un precieux depost. La procession marchoit déja lorsqu'un maçon qui estoit monté au clocher pour s'informer du peril, s'estant apperçu d'une ruine eminente [sic], et estant descendu avec toute la diligence possible, pour pourvoir luy mesme a la conservation de sa vie, cria de haute voix que

chacun se hastast de se sauver comme l'on pourroit. Dans cet instant mesme il s'eleva dans l'Eglise un vent si impetueuse qu'il en ferma les portes et obligea ceux dont les épaules estoient chargées des chasses de S. Just de S. Germer et de S. Evrost de doubler le pas pour se sauver avec ces saintes reliques. Quelques momens de retardement auroient accablé le clergé et le peuple sous une ruine generale; mais Dieu permit que l'on fust déja sorti lorsque deux piliers du chœur se lascherent et firent tomber le clocher sur la voûte laquelle estant ecrasé succomba elle mesme sous ce fardeau. Et fist detoure l'Eglise une si grande masse de pierres et de poussiere qu'elle se déroba longtemps à la veüe de ceux qui en estoient sortis. Il n'y estoit resté qu'un seul Prestre qui celebroit actuellement la messe a l'autel du Saint Sacrement dans le temps de ce fracas si horrible et celuy qui servoit a l'autel. Et cet Ecclesiastique a ecrit sur le 30 Avril jour de l'Ascension qu'il y eüt bras cassé. J'ay ce Breviaire parmy les livres de ma Bibliotheque. Autant que le peuple de Beauvais eüt de sujet de rendre graces a Dieu de sa conservation dans un accident capable de depeupler la ville en un seul instant, autant fut il affligé la de la ruine d'un si excellent ouvrage qu'il estoient comme impossible de reparer. Sa chûte ne fit pas seulement trembler l'Eglise et les maisons des environs, mais la consternation qu'elle causa dans le cœur de tant de personnes dura longtemps, et s'accrut encore lorsque la maçonnerie qui estoit restée menaçoit d'une seconde ruine que personne n'avoit la hardiesse d'empescher. On s'avisa enfin de se demander a un criminel s'il vouloit bien l'entreprendre. Il le fit parceque la mort luy estoient meritable, et dés qu'il eut mis le pied sur ce reste de maçonnerie elle tomba sans autre effort, et il sauva sa vie en se jettant a une corde qui estoit suspenduë le long de l'echaffaudage. Ainsi la corde qui devoit estre la supplice de ce miserable fut son salut."

the right [southeast] moved, and all the weight was left on the fourth pillar. It gave way in its turn."[26] This description, implying that the tower began to go toward the west but then finally fell in an easterly direction, sounds fanciful. Yet there are probably certain elements of truth involved. Desjardins certainly knew that the major problem arising from the deviation of piers involved the west side of the crossing. Masonry will obviously fall vertically. A large wooden structure like the steeple, on the other hand, could topple in one direction or the other, and the damage inflicted on the lower parts of the building confirms that it fell toward the northeast. Whereas the western piers could continue to shift outward, on the east the presence of the choir reduced this potential for movement. The outward thrust of the crossing arches, moreover, was not buttressed by the arches of the clerestory windows, since the latter would be somewhat too high.[27] The visiting masons had observed that certain stones were beginning to fail in the eastern piers. These stones must have been at a level approximately halfway up the clerestory window. The sequence of collapse was probably initiated by failure of the eastern crossing piers at this point.

An analysis of the masonry of the crossing area reveals the extent of the damage caused by the collapse. The most serious damage was inflicted on the east side of the north transept arm. Here the main crossing pier was completely rebuilt together with the triforium and clerestory in the adjacent bays of the transept and choir. In the transept itself, the clerestory tracery of bay B C 5 was also rebuilt. In the northern arcade of the choir, the pier adjacent to the northeast crossing pier (D 5/6) was rebuilt. Two aisle vaults in the angle of the transept and choir were rebuilt. On the east side of the south transept, damage was more limited. Here the main crossing pier was rebuilt

only in the upper parts, and the tracery of the great transept and choir clerestory windows was reassembled.

The sexpartite vaults of the transept arms were rebuilt. The southern vault has the date 1577 painted on it, while the northern vault is dated 1578. On the west side of the transept arms, it is hard to distinguish the new work from the old since the same templates would have been used in each case. We may assume that the upper parts of the crossing piers have been rebuilt, as well as the tracery of the clerestory windows of the first nave bay. The vault of the crossing itself was replaced in the form of a wooden star vault.

On May 8, 1573, a week after the collapse, the ruin was visited by a group of local artisans: Guillaume Petit, Anthoine Fournier, Jacques David, and Martin Candelot, masons, and Guillaume Regnault, carpenter.[28] They recommended steps for the removal of the fallen masonry and for the protection of the surviving parts of the edifice from damage inflicted by falling stones. They observed that it would be necessary to rebuild the great (northeastern) crossing pier together with an adjacent pier in the choir (D 5/6). They also observed that the aisle pier in front of the clock (C 6) had been damaged by the falling masonry and timber and that it would be necessary to rebuild it.[29] Two flyers on the west side of the south transept as in the first nave bay were also to be rebuilt. Two other flyers on the west of the north transept were also in need of attention, including the installation of iron ties.

Not content with this advice, the bishop and chapter invited on June 1, 1573, an outside mason, Bauldry from Mello, to add his opinion.[30] His recognition of the three piers to be reconstructed corresponded with the earlier *expertise*. He stressed that the new northeastern crossing pier should be cut using the

---

[26] Desjardins, *Histoire*, p. 95.
[27] See Delatouche, "La Cathédrale de Beauvais." It has also been suggested that one of the main crossing piers originally enclosed a staircase turret (Bibl. Nat., Collection de Picardie, CLXII, fol. 31).
[28] Arch. Oise, G 707.

[29] Nineteenth-century photographs show this pier with an acanthus capital: obvious evidence from the sixteenth-century rebuild. This capital was removed when the pier was again rebuilt in the nineteenth century.
[30] Arch. Oise, G 707.

same template as that used in the western crossing piers. Scaffolding should be erected to facilitate the stone-by-stone demolition of the remains of the lantern. He then recommended the consolidation of the nave. He estimated the cost of the work at forty-seven thousand pounds, of which twenty-two thousand was for labor and twenty-five thousand for materials.

Desjardins suggested that the outlay of this sum of money would have been sufficient for the completion of the nave. Certainly, if the cost of the construction of the tower is included, this might, indeed, have been an accurate assessment of the situation. To find the money necessary for the repair work, the chapter sold many of the precious objects in the treasury and a small organ. The bishop sold, for thirty thousand pounds, the Hôtel de Beauvais in Paris and donated one thousand écus, and the king offered timber from his forest at La Neuville en Hez.[31] Certain residents of Beauvais lent fifteen thousand pounds for the campaign of repair. Thus financed, the work progressed rapidly, and by 1576 the reconstruction was substantially complete and the crossing had been repaired. The wooden vault of the crossing was complete by 1579.

The unfinished end of the cathedral continued to pose problems. In 1576 the great provisional west wall was blown down by strong winds. It was rebuilt but again damaged in 1587 and 1599.[32]

In 1600 an attempt was made to continue the work on the upper part of the first bay of the nave. A contract was made with Rochefort the carpenter and Martin Candelot, mason, for the erection of the vault of the first nave bay.[33] It might have made more sense to continue with the aisle walls, the flying buttress uprights, and the interior arcade of the rest of the nave before venturing such a step. In the absence of these elements, abutment for the high vault would certainly constitute a problem. The construction of the vault advanced slowly, and in 1604 two *expertises* were conducted.[34] By late 1604 the vault was threatening ruin and was propped up with the great provisional wall.[35] It was subsequently demolished; the present vault is a wooden one. In 1605 the decision was made to constitute the great provisional wall that closed off the first nave bay—a provisional wall that the passing of time has rendered definitive (Fig. 31).[36]

Attempts to complete Beauvais Cathedral thus ended both with a bang and with a whimper. The structural impasse that had been reached was rather different from the two great collapses. The collapse of 1284 was the result of major errors in the planning of the elevation and poor coordination of the two campaigns. The collapse of the tower in 1573 was not so much occasioned by the absence of the nave, but more by the excessive mass and weight of the masonry lantern. The fiasco of 1604 was one involving an incorrect sequence of construction (aisle walls and buttresses must precede high vaults) and unpropitious historical circumstances. These circumstances may be understood both in terms of personalities of the builders and patrons of the cathedral and in the broad sweep of history. When we consider three of the leading masons of the period, Martin Chambiges (died 1532), Jean Vast (died 1581), and Martin Candelot (died 1604), we are struck by the progressive falling off in standards of skill and engineering. When we consider the general historical, economic, and cultural background, we cannot but agree with Gustave Desjardins, "*le temps n'était plus à bâtir des cathédrales.*"[37]

---

[31] Desjardins, *Histoire*, pp. 101–102; Leblond, *La Cathédrale de Beauvais*, pp. 25–26.

[32] Bucquet-aux Cousteaux, XXVIII, pp. 403, 426, 445.

[33] Ibid., p. 448.

[34] Ibid., pp. 456–457.

[35] Ibid., p. 458.

[36] Ibid.; see also Desjardins, *Histoire*, pp. 109–110.

[37] Desjardins, *Histoire*, p. 110.

CHAPTER IX

Conclusion

Beauvais Cathedral is a truncated giant—a building where tantalizing glimpses of the nearly sublime vision of its designers are seen through the tangle of later additions and consolidations. The choir, begun at the west end in 1225, was an ambitious new synthesis of a type never before realized in Gothic—the combination of a five-aisled pyramidal basilica with a spacious aisled transept. Previous studies have attempted to place this choir either in the family of Bourges (Branner) or in the family of Chartres (Grodecki, Bony). When Beauvais was begun, these prototypes were already thirty years old. In a certain sense, such an interpretation of High Gothic tends to lead to a reduced appreciation of the inventiveness of the master designers of the early thirteenth century. A study of the forms of the Beauvais choir reveals no direct links with Chartres or Bourges, but instead suggests that Amiens Cathedral, begun five years earlier, provided the major source for key design elements such as piers, molding profiles, and so on. However, the overall vision embodied in the cathedral of Bishop Miles of Nanteuil was not derived from Amiens, but brought a new kind of combina-

tion of spaces, for which a distant prototype existed in the third abbey church at Cluny, with its spacious transept intersecting a five-aisled pyramidal basilica. Although it is impossible to demonstrate that the Beauvais designers were familiar with Cluny III, many links exist with Notre-Dame of Paris. The peculiar disposition of L-shaped corridors of space arranged around the Beauvais crossing (tall inner aisles running into transept aisles) finds a distant precedent in the similar arrangement of the galleries of Notre-Dame.

Hopes of realizing this initial vision were dashed by the violent confrontation between Bishop Miles of Nanteuil and King Louis IX and the civic uprising of 1232/33. The relationship between the construction of the cathedral and social change was a reciprocal one—the riots led to the cessation of work on the cathedral and affected its form, and the excessive taxes levied by the bishop to pay for the construction helped to provoke the riots. Urban riots accompanied the reigns of all three energetic building bishops of the thirteenth century.

The second campaign (late 1230s–1240s) saw the lower choir completed in a Parisian

Rayonnant style with a streamlined east end (based on Longpont and Royaumont), with walls and supports reduced to a minimum, and with a mannered play on traditional forms, such as in the adaptation of the *pilier cantonné* used in the main arcade. In this phase of construction the choir was first taken up to the level of the sill of the main triforium and covered with a provisional roof, and a start was made upon the great uprights of the flying buttresses. With the accession of Bishop William of Grez a major change of plan was introduced around 1250. With the new plan came intensified decoration (for example, in the tracery of the high triforium and in the upper flanks of the flying buttress uprights) and the addition of some five meters to the total height of the clerestory.

The collapse of the upper choir in 1284 should be seen in the context of a monument that embodied certain inherent weaknesses (the tendency of the slender aisle piers to bend inward) and the gigantic scale of High Gothic, yet with structural elements reduced to conform to the metallic brittleness of Rayonnant. The collapse cannot be attributed to any one particular faulty detail (upper piers, intermediary uprights of the flying buttresses, etc.) but resulted from the failure of the buttressing system and intermediary aisle piers in the middle bay of the choir (7 8), where the two main building campaigns met. There is thus an intriguing "might-have-been" situation. If the choir had been completed by the first workshop, would it have been more solidly constructed? The evidence of the massive masonry in the transepts suggests that this would, indeed, have been the case.

The late Middle Ages brought multiple disasters to the Beauvaisis. The city tended to decline in importance, left far behind by its burgeoning neighbours, Amiens and Paris. The transept of Beauvais Cathedral was not undertaken until 1500. Completed by 1550 only through the dogged persistence of the chapter and with the direct assistance of the king, this part of the building is one of the greatest expressions of French Late Gothic. It embodies a style that reflects current taste and the recognizable handwriting of its designer, Martin Chambiges, and also involves frank borrowings from prototypes in the High Gothic and Rayonnant architecture of more than two hundred years earlier. Whereas the choir of Beauvais Cathedral is the expression of a unique vision and spawned no family of descendants, the transept should be understood in the context of the numerous buildings associated with Martin Chambiges and his followers.

Why was this, the most ambitious cathedral-building project of French High Gothic, generated at Beauvais, of all places? Into the web of narrative around this question are woven a combination of the "forces" of political and economic development in this strategic area to the north of Paris, the incentive provided by the achievement of Chartres, Reims, and Amiens cathedrals, the pretensions of the higher clergy in the years after the fourth Lateran Council, and the apparently accidental interplay of human personalities. The multiple structural disasters experienced in the cathedral seem to have been matched by the penchant of members of the clergy for fighting lost causes. Thus, the sequence of bishops who presided over building operations began with a proud prelate, Miles of Nanteuil, whose tenure was abruptly interrupted by a violent struggle with the powerful king of France and ended with a bishop, Odet of Coligny, who apostatized, fled his country, and was poisoned by his *valet-de-chambre*.

The Written Sources Relating to the Chronology of Construction of the Choir of Beauvais Cathedral

Whereas building accounts, contracts, and other documents can provide an astonishing wealth of information about Late Gothic construction, including names of masons and enough details about their work to allow us to establish a firm chronology, such sources simply do not exist for High Gothic, and the evidence that we have is often ambiguous and circumstantial in nature. An exception is the charter of the founding bishop of the Gothic choir of Beauvais, Miles of Nanteuil, given here under item 4.

The general significance of the written sources in relation to the interpretation of the chronology of the choir has been discussed in Chapter III, "Toward a Chronology for the Construction of the Gothic Choir." The purpose of this appendix is to allow the reader direct access to a transcription of each source. The transcriptions are accompanied by brief commentaries on problems of interpretation.

1. 1180 and/or 1188, fires at Beauvais Cathedral

En ladite année 1180, le vendredy vingthuictiesme jour de May la ville de Beauvais fut embrasee et presques entierement bruslée, les Eglises de S. Pierre, de S. Martin, de S. Sauveur, de S. André, de S. Marie Madelaine, S. Estienne, S. Thomas, de S. Iean furent bruslées, ie ne sçai si les autres eurent meilleure composi-

tion, iay veu un tiltre de S. Lazare qui appelle "incendium generale" cet ambrasement. (Louvet, Histoire et antiquitez, II, p. 308.)

Plusieurs historiens rapportent aussi qu'il y eust si grande secheresse en France en l'an 1188 que la pluspart des villes de Tours, Chartres, Amiens, Beauvais, Auxerre, Troye, Provins furent bruslees. (Ibid.)

Anno 1180 urbem Bellovacensem ignis edax in favillas pene redegerat: alter ignis an. 1225 basilicae S. Petri tam ingentem ruinam intulit, ut in ea canonici divina officia instaurare non potuerint ante an. 1272. (Gallia Christiana, IX, cols. 740–741.)

Commentary

The reference by Louvet to the 1180 fire suggests that he had at his disposal not only generalized chronicle sources (for example, William of Nangis) but also a more specific local text, in the form of a document from the hospital of Saint-Lazare. It is thus probable that there is a basis of truth in the list of churches (including the cathedral) that Louvet claimed were burned in the fire. The excavators of the *Basse-Œuvre* have, indeed, found evidence of several successive fires dating from the eleventh to twelfth centuries. Of course, when Louvet says of the churches that they were "burned," he does not necessarily mean that they were totally destroyed. The transept and nave of Saint-Etienne, for example, predate the fire. The high vaults of the nave of Saint-Etienne, as well as its two westernmost nave bays, are commonly dated to the period immediately after the fire(s).

Louvet and several other sources report another fire in 1188. It is impossible to determine whether we are dealing with two different fires, or whether a mistakenly transcribed date has rendered one fire into two.

In themselves, the texts relating to fires in the 1180s would have to be treated with caution. Another important group of texts relates to the foundation of several altars in the decades following the fire(s). These foundations may have been associated with repairs to the choir and the completion of the new chapel facilities. Without such an addition of chapel spaces, it is difficult to explain the sheer number of foundations in these decades.

2. 1188–1225, foundations of chapels and altars

1188, Saint Paul

Eodem anno [1188] *fundasse dicitur in ecclesia cathedrali capellaniam S. Pauli.* (Gallia Christiana, IX, cols. 732–733.)

1208, Saint-Etienne

Copie collationnée de la fondation d'une Chapelle à l'Autel St. Estienne par Jean De Clermont Doyen, pour être nomée par le seul Doyen et être possedée par un pretre a l'exclusion de tout autre et qui n'aura point d'autre benefice, en 1208. (Arch. Oise, G 2468, p. 60.)

1212, Saint-Sepulchre

Fondation par Guillaume dit Le Turk d'une Chappelle a l'autel du St. Sepulchre, pourquoy il a donné le tier dans les dixmes de Liancourt et au Chapitre 40s. de Cens avec toute justice sur huit maisons proche l'Eglise de Liancourt. Acceptation de la ditte fondation par Le Chapitre 1212. (Ibid., pp. 58–59.)

1221, Saint-Jean

Fondation par le Sr. Bernard souschantre d'une Chapelle a l'Autel St. Jean l'Evangeliste, tant en son nom qu'au nom de Philippe Eveq. de Beauvais, pourquoy il a donné la dixme d'Auregy, et plusieurs cens a prendre sur differentes maisons, 1221. (Ibid., p. 58. For this foundation, see also Bibl. Nat., Collection de Picardie, CCCXI, item 6.)

[1] Arch. Oise, G 751 and G 753.
[2] The Manuscrits Fabignon (eighteenth-century notes conserved in the municipal library) confirm the 1222 consecration. Further confirmation is provided by a copy of the text of the plaque attached to the Easter Candle in 1684

1221, Saint-Denis

Acquisition du tier de la dixme de Vandelicourt. . . . Ratification de la ditte acquisition par le Seigr. Suzerain, 1221. Acquisition par le Chappellain des 6s. de rente düe sur sa maison a St. Lazare au quel il avoit été aumoné par Henry de Braicel en 1226. Acquisition de 65s. de rente par le Chapitre sur la veuve Barthelemy Begnet pour augmentation de la ditte Chappelle, 1238. (Arch. Oise, G 2468, pp. 62–63.)

1222, master altar

L'eglise de N.D. de la Basse-Œuvre a ésté sans difficulté l'Eglise Cathédrale de Beauvais jusqu'en l'an 1222 auquel temps fut consacré le grand autel de la nouvelle église. (Bucquet-aux Cousteaux, XXIII, p. 2.)

. . . il paroit que le maître autel avoit été consacré en 1222. (Ibid., p. 3.)

A puto est cepandant par le tablet que le grand autel de la cathédrale fut consacré en 1222. (Ibid., p. 21.)

Commentary

The sources for the foundation of chapels in the thirteenth-century cathedral of Beauvais are surprisingly full. This is mainly due to the survival of an eighteenth-century inventory of the chapter archives (Archives Départementales de l'Oise, G 2468). In the *layette des chapelles* were preserved the documents that provided for the foundation of most of the chapels of the cathedral. Since we are dealing with an inventory, we can be fairly sure that our control over the documents is complete. In the case of the chapels of Saint-Sepulchre and Notre-Dame, the original charters themselves survive, enabling us to confirm the accuracy of the details of the inventory.[1] In the case of the texts relating to the consecration of the high altar in 1222, it is necessary to recognize that our source is late. The original source for this date is reported to be the "tablet" of the choir, a plaque upon which were recorded the names and periods of tenure of canons and dignitaries. If it were not for the confirmatory evidence of the chapel and altar foundations, it would be tempting to dismiss the 1222 date altogether.[2]

The evidence of the foundations has to be used with the greatest caution. As will be seen later, it is certain that the 1225 fire and the ensuing campaigns of construction led to a complete replace-

(Bibl. Nat., Collection de Picardie, CLVIII, fol. 56): "*Annus a consecratione majoris Altaris in alto opere CCCCLXII.*" The consecration is said to have taken place four hundred and sixty-two years ago, putting it in 1222.

ment of the earlier edifice. Thus, although most of the chapels named in our texts are synonymous with chapels existing in the present choir, these existing chapels are not the ones actually founded in those years.[3] It is clear that the endowment of the chaplains attached to the altars in question was retained after the disaster of 1225 and that the various altars were reassigned new locations in the Gothic choir.

The sheer number of new foundations in those years does suggest that some major change had taken place in the fabric of the cathedral, perhaps associated with the addition of new spaces appropriate for chapels, providing some stimulus for pious patrons to endow altars with chaplains to celebrate mass. The almost universal formula for a foundation was the gift in perpetuity of a rent in money or in kind or of a legal right of some description that would provide an annual income for one or more chaplains who would celebrate daily or weekly masses at the altar of the chapel, according to the stipulations laid down in the charter of foundation. Thus, the foundation of a chapel need not relate directly to the fabric, and the evidence of the foundations must be considered "circumstantial." We can only conclude that our texts are not incompatible with (but do not prove) the hypothesis that the cathedral was damaged in a fire in the 1180s, and that subsequent work of reconstruction had added to the space available for chapels and had provided incentive for pious donors to make new foundations.

3. 1217, *testament of Bishop Philip of Dreux*

Item, do, lego, Ecclesiae B. Petri, decimam de villa S. Pauli, et quicquid habeo in eadem villa, et decimam de Pomponio . . . et decimam de Chivieres . . . sub tali forma quod ad matutinas distribuantur: ita quod singuli Canonici habeant duos denarios, et tres Capellani qui interfuerint ad altare B. Mariae iuxta Crucem, et alii duo ad Capellas meas in domo mea similiter duos denarios habeant. (Louvet, *Histoire et antiquitez,* II, pp. 347–348.)

Item, do, lego Ecclesiae B. Mariae decem libras ad fabricam Ecclesiae. (Ibid., p. 352.)

Item, do, lego quatuor quadrigas, quamlibet ad duos equos, cum harnesio, unam Beatae Mariae ad ducen-

dos lapides: aliam leprosis: tertiam hospiti Clericorum: quartam maiori hospitali pauperum. (Ibid., p. 355.)

Commentary

The testament of Philip of Dreux is a detailed document specifying donations not only to the chapter of Saint-Pierre, but also to a wide range of religious houses in the diocese. Various tithes were given to provide an annual income that was to be distributed to the three chaplains of the altar of the Virgin near the crucifix; in other words, a chapel of Notre-Dame already existed and was functioning in the pre-Gothic cathedral in 1217. It is of interest that the ten pounds left to Notre-Dame (presumably the collegiate church of Notre-Dame-du-Châtel) was specifically designated for the fabric of the church, and the donation of a two-horse cart for carrying stones would suggest that masonry work was in progress. On the other hand, no gifts were made to the fabric of Saint-Pierre. Though the argument is obviously one based upon silence, it is here postulated that were major constructional campaigns under way at the cathedral, we might have expected to find similar donations for the fabric of the cathedral. Finally, we must note that Philip of Dreux was buried in the old pre-Gothic choir, only to be translated to the present choir in the late thirteenth century.

4. 1225, *charter of Bishop Miles of Nanteuil*

Milo Dei gratia Episcopus, et G. Decanus, et Capitulum Belvacense, omnibus Christi fidelibus praesentes literas inspecturis, salutem in Domino. Noverit universitas vestra, quod cum casu miserabili contingente, combusta esset Ecclesia nostra invitatis omnibus Canonicis Beluac. qui fuerant evocandi, ad tractandum de reedificatione dictae Ecclesiae in Capitulo convenissemus: Tandem post multos tractatus de dicta reedificatione habitos, Capitulum videlicet tam personae quan Canonici vnanimiter et concorditer ordinationi mei Milonis Episcopi se commiserunt, promittentes quod quicquid supra dicta reedificatione, tunc in ipso Capitulo bona fide ordinaremus, tam de meis rebus et redditibus, quam de redditibius Capituli et personarum eiusdem Ecclesiae ad dictam

---

[3] Godefroy Hermant may have been aware of the foundations made during the episcopate of Bishop Philip of Dreux, and he assumed that some of the existing chapels may have been constructed at this time: "*Il n'y a pas grande apparance que ce feu* [1188] *ait ruiné entièrement la Cathé-*

drale puis que l'on voit que plusieurs de ses chapelles ont esté construites en l'etat ou nous le voyons presentement sous l'Episcopat de Philippe de Dreux" (*Histoire ecclesiastique,* II, p. 572).

Ecclesiam pertinentibus, ad dictam reedificationem conferendum fuerit inviolabiliter observarent. Ego vero necessitati dictae Ecclesiae compatiens et devotionem dicti Capituli attendens de reedificatione dictae Ecclesiae ita ordinavi. Imprimis de consensu et unanimitate totius Capituli, omnium Parochialium Ecclesiarum de coetero vacantium quocumque modo vacent cedente vel decedente Presbytero in Dioecesi Belvac. annualia integre usque ad decem annos percipienda fabricae dictae Ecclesiae confero: omnes etiam succursus Parochialium Ecclesiarum totius Dioecesis Belvacensis, ad hac die usque ad decem annos integre percipiendos similiter fabricae dictae Ecclesiae concedo, quod II.c. mihi II.c. dicto Capitulo, II.c. de annualibus, II.c. de dictis succursibus licebit ad aliam relaxare. Insuper omnium reddituum et proventuum meorum tam spiritualium quam temporalium, tam Belvaci quam extra, et venditionum nemorum praepositurae Belvac. et aliorum omnium, exceptis forefactis de Comitiva mea (nisi in firma fuerint comprehensa cum aliis) decimam partem usque ad decem annos fabricae dictae dono: itaquod de hac decima fideliter et integre reddenda, omnes baillivi mei dicto Capitulo singulis annis fidelitatem, per sacramentum facere tenebuntur. De redditibus autem Capituli ita ordinavi, quod tam personae, quam Canonici decimam partem personatuum et praebendarum fabricae dictae Ecclesiae singulis annis, usque ad decem annos conferre tenebuntur. Exceptis quotidianis distributionibus, quae fiunt in Ecclesia, quae non decimabuntur, et exceptis Archidiaconis, qui pro eo quod tertia partem succursuum, usque ad decem annos dictae Ecclesiae praestant, cum ipsi succursus integraliter fuerint fabricae dictae Ecclesiae deputati, a decima suorum Archidiaconorum erunt immunes. Hanc antem [sic] ordinationem nostram a toto Capitulo approbatam firmiter et inviolabiliter me observaturum promisi. Actum anno Domini 1225, 3 Nonas Novembris. (Louvet, *Histoire et antiquitez,* II, pp. 363–365.)

Commentary

The contents of the charter may be analyzed under six headings:

1. The cathedral has burned. The evidence of the excavations of the *Basse-Œuvre* is entirely consistent with the destruction by fire of the pre-Gothic choir. The initiative for the measures to provide for the rebuilding has come from the bishop, Miles, who has summoned all available canons to a meeting.
2. At the command of the bishop, the chapter has agreed to follow any plan he might ordain for the reconstruction.
3. Annates from all vacant parish churches in the diocese conceded to the fabric for a period of ten years.
4. All the revenues (*succursus*) of the parish churches of the diocese were granted to the fabric for a period of ten years. The *succursus* was an income normally received by the archdeacons.
5. The bishop conceded one-tenth of his income (spiritual and temporal) for a ten-year period. This does not include the profits of justice from his county court.
6. The chapter is ordered to concede one-tenth of its annual income each year for ten years. This is not to include distributions made during offices. Archdeacons, since they have lost their *succursus*, are immune from this clause.

The inventory of the chapter archives reveals that this charter was still in the possession of the chapter in the eighteenth century.[4] This patronage of the bishop constituted an important precedent for the chapter, since it involved the bishop taxing his income to the same extent as the chapter for the profit of the fabric. In the sixteenth and seventeenth centuries the bishop argued that it had never been the custom for episcopal revenues to be taxed in this manner. Not only does this charter provide evidence as to the sources of funding for the campaigns of construction undertaken after 1225, it also demonstrates without a doubt that the initiative was taken by Miles of Nanteuil; the bishop constrained the chapter to agree to the tithe, not vice versa, as was the case in the later Middle Ages. The resulting revenue for the fabric was of the type that we might term "regular" funds, as opposed to the purely voluntary contributions of pious donors. If the stipulations defined in the charter were implemented (and there was no reason to believe that they were not), a regular and probably substantial income would have resulted. Such an income could only be threatened by a catastrophe of an economic or political nature. There is reason to believe, as the following texts show, that such a catastrophe did, in fact, intervene: the bitter struggle between the bishop and the king, and the resultant confiscation of the bishop's temporalities.

---

[4] Arch. Oise, G 2468, p. 163: "*Copie collationnée de la destination faite par Miles de Nanteüil Eveq. conjointement avec le chapitre d'une partie du revenu des benefices pour être employées a la reedification de l'Eglise qui avoit été bruslée 1225.* [In a different hand] *L'original est dans la Layette.*"

5. 1228, *charter of Bishop Miles of Nanteuil to the goldsmith Ivo*

Milo dei gratia Belvacensis Episcopus omnibus qui presentes litteras viderunt in domino salutem. Ad noticiam omnium volumus pervenire quod nos dedimus et concessimus magistro Ivoni aurifabro civi Belvacensis. . . . [A list of fiefs and quantities of grain in return for work on a variety of metal objects. . . .] *Sciendum est preterea quod nos damus eidem Ivoni unum modium bladi de redditu Thesauravii nepotis nostri et ipse debet resarcire Thurribula de ecclesia beati Petri et reficere de novo cathenas si opus fuerit. Et debet resarcire cruces et omnorum librorum tectos argenti vel auri si opus fuerit. Et debet resarcire filateria quae dependent ante altare et urceolas argenti et pomellos de capis pallei. . . .* (Bibl. Nat., Collection de Picardie, 311, item 14; original charter on parchment.)

Commentary

Ivo the goldsmith is here commissioned to repair the incense burners of the cathedral, together with its chain, and also to repair the crosses and bookcovers and the candles that hang in front of the altar. We can either dismiss the words of the charter as empty formulas, repeated from earlier charters but without real significance in the actual context of 1228, or else we must admit that the altar of the cathedral preceding the present one was still in existence. This altar might have been in the provisional choir of the *Basse-Œuvre*, or alternatively, it might be the altar dedicated in 1222. The hypothesis presented here involves the partial destruction by fire of the old cathedral in 1180/1188 and the subsequent reconstruction of the choir, with a dedication of the main altar in 1222. It is unthinkable that this refurbished choir would have been left with a wooden roof; the vaults of the choir may have protected it from the ravages of the fire of 1225, which would have been concentrated upon the transept and nave. The new work was begun in 1225 outside the body of the choir, on the arms of a new transept. The old choir was thus still intact in 1228, the altar was still in place, and Miles is here found repairing the liturgical equipment for that altar.

6. 1232–1239, *loss of episcopal temporalities and interdicts*

The wider implications of the struggle between Bishop Miles and King Louis IX and Blanche of Castile have already been discussed. Here we are interested in presenting the evidence relating specifically to the fabric of the cathedral. The funding program of the fabric, and thus the sequence of construction itself, might be adversely affected in three different ways. The charter of Miles of Nanteuil indicates not only that the initiative for the campaigns of reconstruction came from the bishop, but also that a major source of funding was provided by the tithe imposed upon the bishop's income. This source might have dried up if the bishop were dispossessed of all or a part of his normal revenues. Moreover, the struggle forced Bishops Miles and Geoffrey of Clermont to direct their efforts and attention toward the series of church councils that took place in the 1230s, rather than allowing them to concentrate upon the work in hand at the cathedral. Moreover, the two interdicts imposed upon the diocese (the second one prolonged) might affect the other three sources of funding defined in the 1225 charter: the tithe paid by members of the chapter, the annates from vacant parishes in the diocese, and the subsidy from parishes in the diocese normally paid to the archdeacons. Finally, the cessation of the divine office associated with the interdicts would hardly encourage potential donors to contribute money to the fabric or to endow new chapels or altars. It is necessary now to examine the evidence upon which these suppositions are based.

The loss of the revenues of the bishop in February 1233 is recorded by Louvet:

> *. . . le Roy . . . feit saisir l'Hostel Episcopal et tous les meubles et ustancilles appartenans audit Evesque, laissa en la ville pour la garde d'icelle, Messires Simon de Poissy, et Pierre de la Halle Chevaliers.*
>
> *Pendant la saisie, les Commissaires et Sergens du Roy demeurerent en l'Hostel Episcopal, lesquels vendent le vin qui s'y trouve, et reçoivent le revenu dudit Evesché. De sorte que pendant icelle, l'Evesque est constraint de se retirer en la maison du Tresorier.* (*Histoire et antiquitez*, II, p. 370.)

The occupation of the episcopal palace and the seizure of the episcopal revenues took place in February 1232/33. The royal accounts show that income from the episcopal regalia was still being enjoyed by the king in May 1238,[5] but it is difficult to ascertain whether all episcopal revenues were held by the king throughout that five-year period and whether the royal sergeants remained in the bishop's palace. Certainly, at the synod held at

---

[5] Magna Recepta et Magna Expensa, 1238, reproduced in *Recueil des historiens des Gaules et de la France*, XXI, ed.

J. D. Guigniaut and J. N. Wailly, Paris, 1855, pp. 251–260, esp. p. 255: "*De veteri recepta regalium Balvacensium*

Noyon on February 20, 1233, Miles's complaint implies that the royal agents were still in occupation. The admonition sent to the king by the ecclesiastics of the province of Reims, assembled at the synod of Laon on March 13, 1233, specifically requested the king to restore the bishop's regalia: *". . . et ut regalia que tenetis et quibus ipsum dissaisivistis, restituatis eidem."*[6]

The appeal of Bishop Miles to the synod assembled at Saint-Quentin on December 18, 1233, indicates that despite the interdict that had been thrown upon the diocese of Beauvais starting June 1233, and on the whole province of Reims from November to December 1233, the bishop had not been able to recover any of his lost rights: *"Domine archiepiscope, vos scitis quod auctoritate concilii, vos et suffraganei vestri, posuistis interdictum in vestras dioeceses, pro injuriis ecclesie belvacensi irrogatis, de quibus in nullo adhuc satisfactum est. . . ."*[7]

After this council, Miles placed himself, his church, and his possessions in the hands of the pope and left for Rome. He died on the road south on September 6, 1234. The necrology of the cathedral of Beauvais recorded various gifts and concessions made by Miles, but nothing specifically for the cathedral fabric or for the endowment of new chapels.[8] This point seems worth emphasizing, since existing reconstructions of the chronology of the Beauvais choir have suggested that the radiating chapels were complete by 1234. These chapels offer the most desirable spaces for altars, and were they complete, the absence of charters of foundation and endowment between 1225 and 1234 would seem odd indeed. Moreover, were the axial chapel complete, we might have expected Miles to have been buried there. Instead, he was translated into the new building only at a much later date.

There is some evidence that although the struggle with the king had originally been mainly the affair of the bishop, the chapter became increasingly involved. The election of the new bishop was protracted because a majority of the chapter insisted that the new bishop continue to maintain the case of the diocese against the king. The new bishop, Geoffrey of Clermont (December 1234–August 1236) had been dean of the chapter and a close friend of Miles. Soon after his consecration he left for Rome to continue the struggle. In the

absence of the bishop of Beauvais, and in view of the increasingly serious situation in the city of Reims, the interest of the ecclesiastics was drawn away from the injuries that had been inflicted on Beauvais Cathedral. Geoffrey died in August 1236, and his death would cause any remaining episcopal revenues that he had still been able to enjoy to fall into the hands of the king, where they would remain until the consecration of the new bishop, two years later.

The significance of all this as far as the fabric fund is concerned seems obvious. The initiative for the endowment of the fabric came from Bishop Miles. The tenth part of the episcopal income committed to the fabric would probably have constituted the largest single source of income. We have already seen that Miles's budget was heavily burdened at the time he left for Italy in 1230; the contributions to the cathedral fabric would have constituted one of his main commitments. Any further substantial loss of revenue would certainly have rendered it very difficult for the bishop to maintain his contributions to the fabric. Moreover, it is quite certain that for at least two years (1236–1238 or 1239) all episcopal revenues were diverted *sede vacante* into the royal coffers. It is reasonable to assume that the results would have been a sharp reduction of revenue for the fabric and a halt or slowing down of the construction.

If we widen the scope of our review to the diocese as a whole, we face the problem of attempting to define the effects of the two interdicts on the diocese, the first one imposed by Miles (June 1233–July 1234) and the second one by Geoffrey of Clermont (June 1235) and maintained *sede vacante* until May 1238. The interdict would, in principle, at least, entail the cessation of all services and the administration of the sacraments such as baptism, mass, the ordination of priests, and so on. Such a freeze imposed upon the day-to-day activities of the church might affect the collection of the annates and subsidies that also formed part of the fabric fund. The chapter would also be affected, since the major part of a canon's income came from the distributions received at various offices, which, during an interdict, would no longer take place.

An entry in the inventory of the chapter archive confirms that an interdict imposed by the bishop

---

1000. De Petro Hale, de veteribus regalibus Balvacensibus 340. De Nicholao Harode, de novis regalibus Belvacensibus, 1147."

[6] Quoted by Pontal, "Le Différend," p. 14. The same

source may be referred to for other details relating to the church councils and interdicts of the 1230s.

[7] Ibid., p. 18.

[8] Louvet, *Histoire et antiquitez*, II, p. 377.

on the cathedral would apply to all of the churches in the city: *"Accord entre le Sgr. Eveq. et le Chapitre portant que l'interdit etant mis pour la Cathedrale les autres Eglises de la ville sont seront [sic] aussi censées interdites, que meme les Eglises parroissiales ne pourront sonner ni faire aucun office public, 1212."*[9]

The chapter of Beauvais Cathedral was jealous of its privileges and did not consider itself bound to observe any interdict launched by the bishop in an unilateral fashion: *"Liasse de Declarations faites par les Evéques que les interdits portéz contre les Eglises de Beauvais ne doivent point s'etendre sur l'Eglise Cathedrale ni donner atteinte aux Privileges du Chapitre depuis 1228 jusqu'a 1273."*[10]

Given the jealous protection of rights that characterized the attitude of the chapter toward the episcopal interdict, it is important to cite the text of the charter of interdict itself: *"Milo divina miseratione Belvacensis Episcopus omnibus praesentes literas inspecturis in Domino Salutem. Notum facimus universis, quod super hoc quod cessare incoepit Capitulum Belvacense anno Domini 1233, mense Iunii die Lunae post festum S. Barnabae Apostoli, volumus et concedimus, quod nullum fiat eidem Capitulo propter hoc praeiudicium."*[11] Thus, it is made clear that the chapter had ceased (divine office) in June 1233. The bishop was obliged to assure the chapter that its rights would be in no way compromised.

This interdict of Bishop Miles lasted for about one year, until prior to the departure of that bishop for Italy. The charter of interdict in 1235 of his successor, Godfrey of Clermont, is explicit in defining that the chapter was in full support: *"Noverit universitas vestra quia cum nos in Dioecesi nostra interdictum posuissemus, et Decanum et Capitulum rogaremus, ut nobis compatiendo cessaret a divinis, Fidem Decanus et Capitulum authoritate propria ad preces nostras cessavit à divinis."*[12]

The chapter's role in the interdict is further defined by certain documents in the (now lost) chapter archives: *"Liasse de reconnoissance et certificat faisants foy pour que le Chapitre a souvent cessé le Service Divin de son autorité privée et l'a fait quelque fois a la priere de L'Evéque depuis 1235."*[13]

It is thus certain that the chapter was also in-volved in the interdicts of the 1230s. As defined above, the cessation of the divine service would have caused considerable financial difficulties for an individual canon, since the larger part of his income would come from distributions. These financial difficulties would have affected the canon's ability to maintain the tithe defined in the charter of Bishop Miles.

For the third supposition, loss of revenue through loss of good will, no documentary evidence can be adduced. *Anniversaires* and foundations and endowments of altars and chapels were made on the understanding that a certain bequest (often an annual rent) would bring prayers and remembrance of the donor. The interdicts did away (temporarily) with the entire framework in which such prayers could be made. Pious donors would hardly be encouraged to lend their financial support to the church or the fabric in a situation where no benefits accrued.

7. 1238, endowment of the chapel of Saint Denis

Omnibus presentes litteras inspecturis. Officialis Belvacensis salutem in domino. Universitati vestre notum facimus quod constituta in presentia nostra Maria Bequette relicta Bartholomei Bequet civis Belvacensis recognovit se vendidisse imperpetuum capitulo beati Petri Belvacensis ad opus capellanie Sancti Dyonisii quam tenebat dominus Guillelmus dictus matricularius in ecclesia Belvacensi sexaginta et quinque solidos annui et perpetui census quos habebat ut dicebat super domum Rogeri Morel sitam in Coleiseria Belvacensi de quibus redduntur domino episcopo Belvacensi de fundo terre sex denarii in festo Sancti Remigii et semiconsuetudo ad Natale domini pro sexaginta et quinque libris Parisiensibus sibi persolutis ut coram nobis recognovit, fidem prestans corporalem quod decetero in dicto censu nichil reclamabit vel reclamari faciet per se vel per alium ratione alicuius juris, sed ipsum dicto capitulo et capellano dicte capellanie contra omnes ad usus et consuetudines civitatis Belvacensis garandizabit. In cuius re testimonium presentes litteras sigillo curie Belvacensis fecimus communiri. Actum anno domini m.cc.xxx. octavo in crastino decollationis Sancti Johannis. (Arch. Oise, G 744; original charter on parchment.)

---

[9] Arch. Oise, G 2468, p. 331.
[10] Ibid., p. 120.
[11] Louvet, *Histoire et antiquitez*, II, p. 373.

[12] Ibid., p. 378.
[13] Arch. Oise, G 2468, p. 122.

Commentary

The chapel of Saint Denis (the first of the radiating chapels on the south side; see Fig. 9) was already in existence in the pre-Gothic cathedral. We have seen that a charter dated 1221 recorded the donation of one-third of the tithe of Vandelicourt for the needs of the chapel. These needs would include the money necessary to pay the stipend of the chaplain(s) and the distributions of cash made at the celebration of offices at the altar of Saint Denis, as defined in the charter of foundation. In 1226 the chaplain of Saint Denis acquired a further six sous of annual rent.

Two more charters, both dated 1238, record further acquisitions for the same chapel. Mary Bequette, a widow from Beauvais, ceded to the chapter sixty-five sous per annum of the rent that she held on the house of Roger Morel. This money was to be applied "*ad opus capellanie sancti Dyonisii.*" It is possible to translate *ad opus* as meaning "for the needs of," or "for the construction of" the chapel, but if the latter translation is favored, then the question arises as to why an annual rent would be acquired for construction work, when the masons and carpenters involved in construction and the necessary supplies of stone, glass, and timber would be paid for in cash out of the fabric fund. It would probably be best to translate *ad opus* as "for the needs of" the chapel. These needs would include stipends and maintenance, which could be paid out of an annual rent of the kind defined in the charter.

> *Omnibus presentes litteras inspecturis. Officialis Belvacensis salutem in domino. Universitati vestre notum facimus quod in nostra constituti presentia Walterus Palechon et Odelina eius uxor burgenses de Gornaco contulerunt in puram, perpetuam et irrevocabilem elemosinam capellanie Sancti Dyonisii fundate in ecclesia Beati Petri Belvacensis quinque solidos annui et perpetui census de triginta et quinque solidis censualibus quos habebant ut dicebant super domum presbiteri Beate Marie Magdalene de Belvaco ad opus dicte capellanie pro triginta tribus libris Parisiensibus sibi plene persolutis ut coram nobis recognoverunt. Dicta vero Odelina doti sue si quam in dicto censu habebat sponte et expresse renuntiavit, et tam ipsa quam dictus Walterus maritus eius fidem coram nobis prestiterunt corporalem quod decetero in dicto censu nichil reclamabunt vel reclamari facient per se vel per alium ratione alicuius iuris sive dotis titulo ex parte dicte Odeline sive alia ratione sed ipsum censum dictis capitulo et capellano capellanie predicte contra omnes ad uses et consuetudines civitatis Belvacensis garandizabunt, supponentes se super*

hoc iurisdictioni nostre; renuntiaverunt autem in hoc facto omni exceptioni et omni iuris auxilio et omni eo quod contra factum vel instrumentum istud possent obicere et quod sibi posset prodesse et dictis capitulo et capellano nocere. In cuius rei testimonium presentes litteras sigillo curie Belvacensis fecimus communiri. Actum anno domini m.cc.xxx. octavo mense Septembris in festo Sancti Egidii. (Arch. Oise, G 744; original charter on parchment.)

Commentary

A second charter of 1238 records the gift of five sous annual rent for the chapel of Saint Denis to be taken from the rent that Walter and Odelina, his wife, held on the house of the priest of the church of the Madeleine in Beauvais. The remainder of the rent was sold to the chapter to be used *ad opus*, for the needs of the chapel of Saint Denis.

Whether the formula *ad opus* actually means "for the construction" or "for the needs" of the chapel is not the most important consideration. More significant is the indication that one of the radiating chapels in the Gothic cathedral was now receiving its endowment.

8. *The endowment of the axial chapel of the Virgin Mary by Bishop Robert of Cressonsac (1238–1248)*

> *Les anciens Obituaires de S. Pierre portent, que ". . . redemit omnia gista Regis uno excepto de centum libris parisiensibus: dedit fabricae mille libras Turonenses: ad Capellam beatae Mariae centum quoque libras Parisienses ad emendos redditus."* (Louvet, Histoire et antiquitez, II, p. 392.)

> *In necrologio S. Petri fit mentio Roberti his verbis: "cal. Octobr. obiit Robertus hujus ecclesiae episcopus, qui dedit nobis quidquid habebat apud Villiacum, tam in hospitibus quam reditibus, justitia et censu. Item octo modios frumenti in grangia monachorum S. Luciani apud Fontanas. Item redemit omnia gista quae habebat rex in civitate, excepto uno gisto de centum libris Parisiensibus. Dedit fabricae mille libras Turonenses ad capellam B. Mariae; centum quoque libras Parisienses ad emendos reditus."* (Gallia Christiana, IX, col. 744.)

Commentary

The two readings of the text of the necrology concerning the gifts of Robert of Cressonsac to the fabric of the cathedral carry rather different meanings. The punctuation of the first text (Louvet) suggests that the bishop gave one thousand pounds to the fabric and one hundred pounds to purchase rents for the endowment of the chapel of the Virgin. The second text (*Gallia Christiana*) states that the one thousand pounds was for the chapel of the Virgin. Abbé Delettre favored the second reading, adding that the bishop's testament specified that the one thousand pounds should be employed to pay for the celebration, each day before primes, of a mass in honor of the Virgin in the chapel dedicated to her in the new cathedral. In the pre-Gothic cathedral, the altar of Notre-Dame had been staffed by three chaplains. This was now increased to ten. The one thousand pounds would presumably have been used to acquire rents to pay the chaplains' stipends.

The endowment of the Virgin chapel provides more evidence that the radiating chapels were being used by the late 1230s into the 1240s.

9. The patronage of Bishop William of Grez, 1249–1267

Sex millia librarum Parisiensium legaverat in fabricam majoris campanae. Plurima autem alia ecclesiae suae largitus est, quae enumerat necrologium his verbis. . . . Item dedit DCCC libras Parisienses ad fundandas quatuor capellanias in ecclesia Belvacensi. (*Gallia Christiana*, IX, col. 746.)

Il donna à la fabrique de S. Pierre six mille livres parisis et la grosse cloche selon que portoient les carmes qui estoient gravez sur icelle avant sa cassation seconde. . . . Cet Evesque trespassa de ce siecle en l'autre le jour et feste de la Chaire S. Pierre au mois de Fevrier l'an 1266 [i.e., 1267] et fut ensepulturé en la chapelle de nostre Dame derriere le cœur de ladite Eglise, où son tombeau se voit, sur lequel se trouve gravé cet Epitaphe. . . .

> *"G. Belvacensis Praesul, patriaque Briensis.*
> *Subiacet huic Petre cum pulvere qui tibi Petre,*
> *Cultu syncero servivit, cordeque vero*
> *Muneribus, cuius ferè fabrica dicitur, huius*
> *Ecclesia facta, vel magna parte peracta."*

(Louvet, *Histoire et antiquitez*, II, pp. 434–435.)

Commentary

The above passages say that William of Grez gave six thousand pounds and/or a great bell to the fabric, that he founded four chapels (or chaplaincies), that he was buried in the chapel of the Virgin behind the choir (the axial chapel of the Gothic cathedral), and that the church was, for the greater part, completed during his tenure as bishop.

The first text cited (*Gallia Christiana*) defines that the six thousand pounds were for the manufacture of the great bell, whereas the second text (Louvet) suggests (probably correctly) that the bishop gave both the money and the bell. It is curious to find the donation of a great bell at a point in time when the Gothic choir, in its unfinished state, did not offer a place where the bell could be suspended; although transept towers were certainly begun at this date, they had not been taken up as high as the belfrey. It is therefore probable that the great bell would have been suspended in the freestanding tower (sometimes called the Tour César) to the southeast of the south transept façade.

There is some ambiguity over the "four chapels" of William of Grez, probably because confusion between *capellania* (chapel) and *capellanus* (chaplain) began already as early as the eighteenth century. The bishop is said to have founded the chapels of Saint Maur and Saint Loup in the cathedral.[14] In 1258 he purchased an annual rent worth twenty pounds a year from Lady Philippa of Gerberoy,[15] and in 1262 he applied this rent to the endowment of the chapel of Notre-Dame.[16] Robert of Cressonsac had already provided for a group of ten chaplains who were charged to say the mass of the Virgin every day before primes. William, noting that the endowment that would allow for the necessary distributions to be made was incomplete, added two additional chaplains to the group, bringing the total to twelve. Thus, he was responsible for endowing two chaplains of Notre-Dame, one of Saint Maur, and one of Saint Loup; these, presumably, were the "four chaplaincies" of William of Grez.

It is worth noting that William of Grez was the first bishop to be buried in the Gothic choir, which, at the time of his death, was said to have been substantially complete. A charter issued by his executors in 1270, three years after the bishop's death, allowed the residue of the former bishop's estate, including a considerable number of unpaid debts, to be paid to the fabric of the cathedral, "which will remain incomplete, except through divine help."[17]

[14] Ibid., p. 55: "*Chapelle St. Loup, St. Maur, Fondation de 4 Chapelles par Guillaume Des Gréz.*"
[15] Arch. Oise, G 756.

[16] Ibid., G 753 and G 756.
[17] Ibid., G 691.

10. *1230s–1260s, further foundations and endowments*

1234, unidentified chapel

Accord entre les executeurs testamentaires de Berenger Boitel et Jean Rosselly par lequel le dit Rosselly consent payer 60 s. de cens pour aider a la fondation faite par le dit Boitel d'une Chapelle dans la cathedrale, en 1234. (Arch. Oise, G 2468, p. 53.)

1256, the Madeleine

Fondation de la Chappelle Sainte Madeleine ditte du four par le Sr. Leger souschantre, pourquoy a donné six muids de terre et un four a Noyers pour le produit appartenir deux tiers au Chapellain et un tiers au Chapitre avec le droit de Champart et de Justice, 1256. (Ibid., p. 64.)

1256, chapel of the Virgin Mary

Ste Vierge ou la Haute Œuvre [glossed in margin]. *Fondation par Renault de Nanteüil d'une messe pour être acquittée tous les jours par un Chappellain de la Haute Œuvre et des vespres de la Vierge tous les vendredys et pour la ditte messe être ditte au premier coup de la messe de la Vierge qui se celebre tous les jours, lequel sera sonné par le Chappellain meme . . . 1256.* (Ibid., p. 66.)

1270, chapel of the Virgin Mary

Donation par Renault de Nanteüil Evêque de Beauvais de 30 lb. de rente a prendre sur le sceau de l'Evesché pour fondation de l'office de la veille et du jour de l'Assomption en la Chapelle de la Vierge, 1270. (Ibid.)

Commentary

The most significant item among these further endowments is the reference to the foundation of the chapel of the Madeleine in 1256. We thus have a group of dates between the late 1230s (chapel of Saint Denis), 1240s (endowment by Robert of Cressonsac of the mass of the Virgin in the axial chapel), 1250s (augmentation of this endowment by Renaud of Nanteuil), and 1260s (the four chaplaincies of William of Grez) for the organization of the chaplaincies of the altars of the radiating chapels.

11. *1272, the entry into the new choir*

. . . les Chanoines ne peurent commencer a celebrer le divin service en iceluy, qu'en l'an mil deux cens septante deux, le Lundy veille de tous les saincts à Vespres. (Louvet, *L'Histoire de la ville*, pp. 368–369.)

Eodem anno [1272], *prid. cal. Novembr. in choro recens extructo mirae altitudinis et amplitudinis canonici Bellovacenses divina officia celebrare coeperunt.* (*Gallia Christiana*, IX, col. 747.)

Commentary

The date of 1272 for the celebration of the first mass in the Gothic choir should cause no difficulties. It is given by several sources, the contributor to the relevant passage in the Bucquet-aux Cousteaux Collection referring to the "tablet" of the choir as the ultimate source.[18] The formal celebration of the first mass would require the presence of the canons' wooden stalls, aligned with their backs against the piers of the central vessel. It is unlikely that these stalls would have been placed in position before the high vaults had been decentered on account of the falling debris.

[18] Bucquet-aux Cousteaux, XXIII, p. 2.

APPENDIX B

Restorations

The work of restoration on a great cathedral begins almost as soon as the work of construction itself. At Beauvais,[1] this was doubly true, since the collapse of 1284 necessitated prolonged campaigns of repair, and structural problems inherent in the building again produced a situation of near collapse in the late fifteenth century. The architect Martin Chambiges consolidated certain parts of the existing edifice and constructed the new transept. He was responsible for pier F 7 in the south aisle and the wall attached to it, the Flamboyant tracery in the inner aisle triforium and clerestory of the nave piers, as well as the strengthening applied to the base of the uprights of the flying buttresses at division 8 on the north side. A third flying buttress was added here. The collapse of the tower brought new campaigns of consolidation. The main northeast crossing pier was completely rebuilt, as well as the adjacent pier (D 5 6). The triforium and clerestory tracery in bay D 5 6 were entirely rebuilt, as were the vaults over the aisle bays B C 5 6 and C D 5 6, over the central vessel at D E 5 6, and in the transept at B D 4 5 and E G 4 5. It is probable that the *pilier cantonné* at C 6 was entirely reconstructed at the same time. Photographs from the early nineteenth century show this pier with a sixteenth-century acanthus capital

at the level of the arcade of the outer aisle. Campaigns of repair continued into the seventeenth century, when the upper parts of pier E 8 were consolidated and an additional flying buttress added.

In the nineteenth and twentieth centuries three main types of restoration have been effected: one intended to correct deformation resulting from severe structural problems in the edifice, the second to make good the effects of water damage and to correct the defective roofs and gutters, and the third, an extensive program of repairs to the structure of the edifice and the windows necessitated by the bombardments of June 1940. In addition to all this, we find the progressive replacement of weathered stones on the exterior of the edifice, particularly on the south side, where the close proximity of houses caused rainwater to drain inward toward the cathedral, damaging the stones of the lower walls.

The extreme seriousness of the structural problems inherent in the cathedral is witnessed by the decision to give this work priority over the repairs to the weather-damaged exterior. We know little of the work of the architect F. Beauvais, but Abbé Marsaux's short account indicates that it involved repairs to the very foundations of the choir. The work of the architect P. Vital (*entrepreneur de tra-*

[1] The written sources for the restoration of Beauvais Cathedral are in the Archives Départementales de l'Aube, Fonds Vital, esp. items 320–375, and dossier 963 in the Monuments Historiques, Rue de Valois, Paris.

vaux publics, Troyes, Aube) is very fully documented in the extensive series of drawings preserved in the Fonds Vital, Archives de l'Aube, Troyes. Vital, under the general direction of Sauvageot, was responsible for the reconstruction of all of the intermediary aisle piers on the south side, including C 8 (at the base of the system of radiating chapels), the fourteenth-century pier at C 7/8, C 7, and probably C 6/7 and C 6. At C 8, 7, and 6 the new work extended from the pavement to the vaults, and in the case of C 7, it was also necessary to repair the broken sleeper wall immediately to the east. Vital also restored the sacristy door and the "window" in bay B 7 8. In the south aisles, the work was less extensive; F 8, at the base of the radiating chapels, was entirely rebuilt, but F 7/8 was left. F 7 had already been rebuilt in the sixteenth century and F 6/7 at an undetermined point in time, perhaps in the fifteenth century. The fact that the repairs after the 1284 collapse had been taken farther in the south aisles than in the north perhaps saved this side from excessive disruption visible in the northern aisles. Work was also undertaken on a linkage arch under the pavement of the south aisles. In contrast to the intermediary piers of the aisles, the piers of the central vessel were hardly touched. Vital was also responsible for repairs to the lower triforium of the south transept; his name is still visible engraved upon the rear wall of the triforium.

In 1906 the same architect, working with G. Degaine, began the installation of reinforced concrete roofs over the inner aisle. H. Chaine, then diocesan architect, has left us valuable interpretations of the situation; he remarked that the interior of the edifice was in good condition, but not the exterior: "As almost always, it is the poor system for the evacuation of rainwater that is the principal cause of harm. But here the situation is exacerbated by the very defective disposition of the roof of the aisle (a double-pitched roof), whose continuous inner surface directs the water toward the center of the building."[2] He noted that the very narrow gutter between this roof and the triforium now received the water from the high roof of the central vessel. On wet days or during periods of snow, the system was unable to evacuate the volumes of water that accumulated, causing infiltrations into the masonry of the walls and vaults. Although Chaine considered that the double-sloped roof represented the original solution, he proposed an en-

tirely new remedy, similar to that found at Clermont-Ferrand: a shallow-pitched roof made of reinforced concrete. The work was begun in 1906 by P. Vital and sons, but the architect died two years later, and things seem to have been mismanaged. In 1906 an accident occured in the wooden scaffolding constructed to assist in the raising of stones to the level of the inner aisle roof, and a mason, Albert Duplant, was crushed by a fall of masonry. In July 1907 the men of the Beauvais workshop registered a complaint that they were not being paid. Work on the concrete roof was still not complete at the onset of hostilities in the First World War.

After the war, extensive restorations were carried out in the fourteenth-century cloister and attendant buildings to the west of the cathedral. Under the direction of the architect A. Collin, several flying buttresses on the south side of the choir and hemicycle were restored. Work on the northern flyers was interrupted by the renewed onset of hostilities. Much of the medieval glass had already been taken down before the bombardment of the city in June 1940. The remaining glass was removed in a damaged state, thereafter. The windows were filled with wooden screens into which small areas of translucent glass were set. The removal of these wooden screens and the reglazing of the windows is still not complete, thirty-five years after the termination of hostilities. Discussions concerning the replacement of the thirteenth-century glass in the axial chapel are recorded in 1949. Unfortunately, the damaged state of the glass has necessitated the manufacture of a considerable amount of entirely new glass. The explosion of some six or eight bombs on the cathedral also caused considerable structural harm; window tracery was blown away and the aisle roofs damaged. In the postwar period, moreover, we seem to be witnessing an acceleration in the general decay of the structure through failure of the stone, partly from the effects of weathering. In the late 1960s stones were falling from the upper parts of the south transept arm, both inside and on the exterior of the edifice. A massive scaffold tower was erected, then left abandoned for years, creating extensive rust stains on the stones of the south transept façade. Eventually the vaults of both transept arms were consolidated.

In the late 1970s and into the 1980s work has continued on the replacement of stained glass and

---

[2] H. Chaine, Monuments Historiques, dossier 963, 1.

the repair to damaged tracery elements (1980: chapel G 7 8; transept window G H 6). A new organ has been installed inside the provisional west wall, and the old instrument (sixteenth century, restored in the nineteenth century), which had been extensively damaged in the bombardment of 1940, has been removed, leaving the east aisle of the north transept free from encumbrances.

A program is now under way for the restoration of the hemicycle flyers and uprights not completed in the campaigns of repair of the 1930s–1950s and for the installation of stained glass into windows of the choir aisles, ambulatory, and eastern aisles of the transept. These windows had been blocked with provisional wooden screens.

BIBLIOGRAPHY

Primary Sources

Alberic (Aubry) of Trois-Fontaines. *Chronicle, Recueil des historiens*, xxi Paris, 1855, pp. 595–630.

Archives Départementales de l'Aube (Troyes). Fonds Vital.

Archives Départementales de l'Oise (Beauvais). G 691, 744, 751, 753, 756, 813, 2353, 2468.

Bibliothèque Nationale, Paris. Collection de Picardie.

Chronicles of the Crusades: Contemporary Narratives of the Crusade of Richard Cœur de Lion by Richard of Devizes and Geoffrey de Vinsauf and of the Crusade of Saint Louis by Lord John de Joinville. London, 1848.

La Chronique de Rains, publiée sur le manuscrit unique de la Bibliothèque du Roi par Louis Paris. Paris, 1851.

Collection Bucquet-aux Cousteaux. Municipal Library, Beauvais.

Etienne de Nully. "Notice de la cathédrale en 1685 par Etienne de Nully, chanoine de Beauvais." In Desjardins, *Histoire*, pp. 229–233.

Fabric account (fragmentary) for 1499–1500. Archives de la Seine, Paris. Provisional code no. Cartes et Plans 4942.

Fragment d'une chronique anonyme dite Chronique de Reims, Recueil des historiens, xxii. Paris, 1865, pp. 301–329.

Hermant, Godefroy. *Histoire ecclésiastique et ci-vile de Beauvais et du Beauvaisis.* 5 vols. Bibliothèque Nationale, Paris MS fr. 8579–8583.

John of Joinville. *Histoire de Saint-Louise, Recueil des historiens*, xx. Paris, 1840, pp. 190–304.

Paris, Matthew. *Chronica Majora, Rolls Series (Rerum Britannicarum Medii Aevi Scriptores)*, lvii, iii, ed. H. R. Luard. London, 1876.

Recueil des historiens des Gaules et de la France, xx, ed. J. Naudet and P.C.F. Daunou. Paris, 1840.

Recueil des historiens des Gaules et de la France, xxi, ed. J. D. Guigniaut and J. N. Wailly. Paris, 1855.

Vincent of Beauvais. *Speculum Historiale.* Reprint, Graz, 1965.

William of Nangis. *Chronicon, Recueil des historiens*, xx. Paris, 1840, pp. 543–646.

———. *Gesta Sanctae Memoriae Ludovici, Recueil des historiens*, xx. Paris, 1840, pp. 309–465.

Secondary Sources

Ackerman, J. "Ars Sine Scientia Nihil Est." *Art Bull.*, xxxi, 1949, pp. 84–111.

Adelman, L. S. "The Flamboyant Style in French Gothic Architecture." Ph.D. diss., University of Minnesota, 1973.

Adenauer, H. *Die Kathedrale von Laon.* Düsseldorf, 1934.

Aegerter, E. "L'Affaire du De Periculis Novissimorum Temporum." *Revue de l'histoire des religions*, CXII, 1935, pp. 242–272.

Ancien, J. *Contribution à l'étude archéologique: Architecture de la cathédrale de Soissons.* Privately published, 1984.

Anfray, M. *L'Architecture normande, son influence dans le nord de la France aux XIe. et XIIe. siècles.* Paris, 1939.

Armi, C. E. *Masons and Sculptors in Romanesque Burgundy: The New Aesthetic of Cluny III.* University Park, Pa., and London, 1983.

Aubert, M. *Notre-Dame de Paris, sa place dans l'histoire de l'architecture du XIIe. au XIVe. siècle.* Paris, 1920.

———. "A propos de l'église abbatiale de Saint-Lucien de Beauvais." In *Gedenkenschrift Ernst Gall.* Munich, 1965, pp. 51–58.

Babeau, A. "L'Eglise Saint-Pantaléon de Troyes." *Annuaire de l'Aube*, 1881, p. 33.

Barnes, C. "The Cathedral of Chartres and the Architect of Soissons." *J. Soc. Arch. Hist.*, XXII, 1963, pp. 63–74.

———. "The Twelfth-Century Transept of Soissons: The Missing Source for Chartres?" *J. Soc. Arch. Hist.*, XXVIII, 1969, pp. 9–25.

Barraud, Abbé A. "Description de l'ancienne église collégiale de Saint Barthélémy." *Mem. Soc. acad. Oise*, IV, 1859, pp. 734–747.

Bautier, R. H. *The Economic Development of Medieval Europe.* London, 1971.

Belperron, P. *La Croisade contre les Albigeois et l'union du Languedoc à la France (1209–1249).* Paris, 1945.

Benouville, L. "Etude sur la cathédrale de Beauvais." *Encyclopédie d'architecture et des arts qui s'y rattachent*, ser. 4, IV. Paris, 1891–1892.

Besnard, C.-H. "L'Eglise de Boult-sur-Suippe." *Cong. arch.*, LXXVIII, 1911, pp. 170–185.

Bialostocki, J. "Late Gothic, Disagreements about the Concept." *J. Brit. Arch. Assoc.*, XXIX, 1966, pp. 76–105.

Bideault, M., and C. Lautier. "Saint-Nicaise de Reims: Chronologie et nouvelles remarques sur l'architecture." *Bull. mon.*, CXXXV, 1977, pp. 295–330.

———. *Ile-de-France gothique, I, Les eglises de la vallée l'Oise et du Beauvaisis.* Paris, 1987.

Bloch, M. *La France sous les derniers Capétiens, 1223–1328.* Paris, 1958.

Bober, H. "A Reappraisal of Rayonnant Architecture." In *The Forward Movement of the Fourteenth Century,"* ed. F. L. Utley. Columbus, 1961, pp. 9–30.

Bongartz, N. "Die frühen Bauteile der Kathedralen in Troyes." Ph.D. diss., Freiburg-im-Breisgau, 1973.

Bonnardot, F. *Registres des délibérations du bureau de la ville de Paris, publiés par les soins du Service historique. Histoire générale de Paris, collection de documents publiée sous les auspices de l'édilité parisienne*, I, 1499–1526. Paris, 1883.

Bonnet-Laborderie, P. *Cathédrale Saint-Pierre, Beauvais.* GEMOB. Beauvais, 1978.

Bontemps, D. "La Nef de l'église Saint-Pierre de Gonesse et ses rapports avec l'abbatiale de Saint-Denis." *Bull. mon.*, CXXXIX, 1981, pp. 209–228.

Bony, J. "La Collégiale de Mantes." *Cong. arch.*, CIV, 1946, pp. 163–220.

———. "The Resistance to Chartres in Early-Thirteenth-Century Architecture." *J. Brit. Arch. Assoc.*, XX–XXI, 1957–1958, pp. 35–52.

———. "La Genèse de l'architecture gothique, 'accident ou nécessité?' " *Revue de l'art*, LVIII, 1982, pp. 9–20.

———. *French Gothic Architecture of the 12th and 13th Centuries.* Berkeley, 1983.

Bouillart, Dom J. *Histoire de l'abbaye royale de Saint-Germain-des-Prez.* Paris, 1724.

Branner, R. *Burgundian Gothic Architecture.* London, 1960.

———. "Historical Aspects of the Reconstruction of Reims Cathedral, 1210–1241." *Speculum*, XXXVI, 1961, pp. 23–37.

———. *La Cathédrale de Bourges et sa place dans l'architecture gothique.* Paris, 1962.

———. "The Labyrinth of Reims Cathedral." *Jour. Soc. Arch. Hist.*, XXI, 1962, pp. 18–25.

———. "Le Maître de la cathédrale de Beauvais." *Art de France*, II, 1962, pp. 77–92.

———. "Paris and the Origins of Rayonnant Gothic Architecture down to 1240." *Art Bull.*, XLIV, 1962, pp. 39–51.

———. "A Note on Pierre de Montreuil and Saint-Denis." *Art Bull.*, XLV, 1963, pp. 355–357.

———. *Saint Louis and the Court Style in Gothic Architecture.* London, 1965.

———. *Chartres Cathedral.* New York, 1969.

Brayet, M. *Beauvais, ville martyre . . . juin-août, 1940.* Beauvais, 1964.

Brochard, L. *Saint-Gervais: Histoire du monument d'après de nombreux documents inédits.* Paris, 1938.

Bruzelius, C. "Cistercian High Gothic: The Abbey Church of Longpont and the Architecture of the Cistercians in France in the Early Thirteenth

Century." *Analecta Cisterciensia*, XXXV, 1–2, 1979.

———. *The Thirteenth-Century Church at Saint-Denis*. New Haven, 1985.

Bucher, F. "Design in Gothic Architecture: A Preliminary Assessment." *J. Soc. Arch. Hist.*, XXVII, 1968, pp. 49–71.

———. "Micro-Architecture as the 'Idea' of Gothic Theory and Style." *Gesta*, XV, 1976, pp. 71–89.

Bulteau M. J. *Monographie de la cathédrale de Chartres*. 3 vols. Chartres, 1887–1892.

Bur, M. *La Formation du comté de Champagne: v.950–v.1150*. Nancy, 1977.

Campbell, G. J. "The Attitude of the Monarchy Towards the Use of Ecclesiastical Censures in the Reign of Saint Louis." *Speculum*, XXXV, 1960, pp. 535–555.

———. "Temporal and Spiritual Regalia during the Reigns of Saint Louis and Philip III." *Traditio*, XX, 1964, pp. 351–383.

Chadwick, O. *The Pelican History of the Church*, III, *The Reformation*. Harmondsworth, 1964.

Chami, E. Notices in *Archéologie médiévale*, I, 1971, pp. 277–280; III/IV, 1973/4, p. 403; VI, 1976, pp. 339–341; VII, 1977, pp. 259–261; and XI, 1981, p. 275.

Chédeville, A. *Chartres et ses campagnes (XIe.–XIIe. siècles)*. Paris, 1973.

Christ, Y. "Les Vestiges de l'ancien Musée des Monuments français à l'Ecole des Beaux-Arts et leur sort." *Gaz. des Beaux-Arts*, LXVI, 1965, pp. 167–174.

Clark, W., and R. King. *Laon Cathedral, Architecture*, I. London, 1983.

Clark, W., and R. Mark. "The First Flying Buttresses: A New Reconstruction of the Nave of Notre-Dame de Paris." *Art Bull.*, LXVI, 1984, pp. 47–64.

Cothren, M. W. "The Thirteenth-Century Glazing of the Choir of the Cathedral of Beauvais." Ph.D. diss., Columbia University, 1980.

Couard-Luys, E. "Note sur une mission de Martin Chambiges à Senlis en 1504." *Bulletin archéologique du comité des travaux historiques et scientifiques*, 1884.

Coutan, Dr. "Eu: Eglise Notre-Dame-et-Saint-Laurent." *Cong. arch.*, IC, 1936, pp. 388–412.

Daniel, Dr. "De l'ancienne cité de Beauvais." *Mém. Soc, acad. Oise*, II, 1852, pp. 9–53.

Daoust, Abbé J. *Fécamp, l'abbatiale de la Trinité*. Fécamp, 1956.

Davis, M. "The Choir of the Abbey of Altenberg: Cistercian Simplicity and Aristocratic Iconography." *Cistercian Studies*, II, 1984, pp. 130–160.

Deladreue, Abbé L. E. "Les Maisons canoniales du chapitre de Beauvais et leurs possesseurs." *Mém. Soc. acad. Oise*, VII, 1868, pp. 291–347.

Delatouche, J. "La Cathédrale de Beauvais: L'Effondrement des voûtes, l'écroulement de la tour lanterne, les fondations." Unpublished manuscript, n.d.

Delettre, Abbé F. A. *Histoire du diocèse de Beauvais depuis son établissement au IIIe. siècle jusqu'au 2e. septembre 1792*. 3 vols. Beauvais, 1842–1843.

Desjardins, G. *Histoire de la cathédrale de Beauvais*. Beauvais, 1865.

Desjardins, G., and A. Rendu. *Inventaire-sommaire des archives départementales antérieures à 1790: Archives ecclésiastiques, série G*, I. Beauvais, 1878.

Dictionnaire de la spiritualité, VI. Paris, 1967.

Dictionnaire d'histoire et de géographie ecclésiastique, VII. Paris, 1934.

Dollinger, P., and P. Wolff. *Bibliographie d'histoire des villes de France*. Paris, 1967.

Douie, D. L. *The Conflict between the Seculars and the Mendicants at the University of Paris in the Thirteenth Century*. London, 1954.

Doyen, C.-L. *Histoire de la ville de Beauvais, pour faire suite à l'histoire politique, morale et religieuse de M. E. de la Fontaine*. Beauvais, 1842.

Duby, G. *L'Economie rurale et la vie des campagnes dans l'Occident médiévale*. Paris, 1962.

———. *Le Dimanche de Bouvines, 27 juillet, 1214*. Paris, 1973.

———. *Le Temps des cathédrales*. Geneva, 1976.

Duclos, Abbé H. *Histoire de Royaumont, sa fondation par Saint Louis et son influence sur la France*. Paris, 1867.

Dufeil, M.-M. *Guillaume de Saint Amour et la polemique universitaire parisienne*. Paris, 1972.

Dufour, C. "Situation financière des villes de Picardie sous Saint Louis." *Mém. Soc. ant. Pic.*, XV, 1858, pp. 583–681.

Dupont-White. "Les Antiquaires de Beauvais." *Mém. Soc. acad. Oise*, I, 1847, pp. 1–53.

Durand, G. *Monographie de l'église Notre-Dame, cathédrale d'Amiens*. 3 vols. Amiens and Paris, 1901–1903.

Erlande-Brandenburg, A. "La Façade de la cathédrale d'Amiens." *Bull. mon.*, CXXXV, 1977, pp. 253–293.

Fawtier, R. *The Capetian Kings of France*. London, 1960.

Fehr, G. *Benedikt Ried*. Munich, 1961.

Félibien, M. *Histoire de l'abbaye royale de Saint-Denis en France*. Paris, 1706.

Focillon, H. *La Vie des formes*. Paris, 1934.

———. *The Art of the West in the Middle Ages*. 2 vols. London, 1969.

Fontaine, E. de la. *Histoire politique, morale, et religieuse de Beauvais*. 2 vols. Beauvais, 1840.

Fossard, A. *Le Prieuré de Saint-Leu-d'Esserent*. Paris, 1934.

Fourquin, G. "La Population de la région parisienne aux environs de 1328." *Le Moyen Age*, 1956, pp. 63–91.

———. *Les campagnes de la région parisienne du milieu du XIIIe. siècle au début du XVIe. siècle*. Paris, 1964.

———. *Les soulèvements populaires au Moyen Age*. Paris, 1972.

Frankl, P. *Gothic Architecture*. Harmondsworth, 1962.

Gallia Christiana, IX. Paris, 1751.

Gardner, S. "Notes on a View of Saint-Lucien at Beauvais." *Gaz. des Beaux-Arts*, XCVI, 1980, pp. 149–156.

Gavelle, E. *Notice architecturelle sur l'église Rumilly-les-Vaudes*. Arcis, 1896.

Gébelin, F. *La Sainte-Chapelle et la Conciergerie*. Paris, 1931.

Géraud, H. "Le Comte-évêque." *Bibl. Ecole Chartes*, 1st ser., V, 1843–1844, pp. 8–36.

Gilbert, A.P.M. *Notice historique et descriptive de l'église cathédrale de Saint-Pierre de Beauvais*. Beauvais, 1829.

Gillingham, J. "The Unromantic Death of Richard I." *Speculum*, LIV, 1979, pp. 18–41.

Gonse, L. *L'Art gothique*. Paris, 1891.

Goubert, P. *Cent mille provinciaux au XVIIe. siècle, Beauvais et le Beauvaisis de 1600 à 1730*. Paris, 1968.

Gouïn, H. *L'Abbaye de Royaumont*. Paris, 1932.

Griffe, E. *Le Languedoc cathare au temps de la croisade (1209–1229)*. Paris, 1973.

Grodecki, L. "Chronologie de la cathédrale de Chartres." *Bull. mon.*, CXVI, 1958, pp. 91–119.

———. *La Sainte-Chapelle*. Paris, 1962.

———. "Pierre, Eudes et Raoul de Montreuil à l'abbatiale de Saint-Denis." *Bull. mon.*, CXXII, 1964, pp. 269–274.

———. *Gothic Architecture*. New York, 1977.

———. "Le Moyen Age occidental." *Revue de l'art*, XLII, 1978, pp. 21–22.

Gross, W. *Die Abendländische Architektur um 1300*. Stuttgart, 1948.

Guenée, B. "Le Temporel du chapitre cathédral de Beauvais à l'époque de la guerre de cent ans (1333–1444)." Diplôme d'études supérieures d'histoire, n.d.

Hallam, E. *Capetian France, 987–1328*. London, 1980.

Hauser, A. *Social History of Art*. 2 vols. New York, 1951.

Heitz, C. *L'Architecture religieuse carolingienne*. Paris, 1980.

Héliot, P. "Remarques sur l'abbatiale de Saint-Germer et sur les blocs de façade du XIIe. siècle." *Bull. mon.*, CXIV, 1956, pp. 81–114.

———. "La Famille monumentale de la cathédrale de Bourges et l'architecture de l'Europe au moyen âge." In *Gedenkenschrift Ernst Gall*. Munich, 1965, pp. 143–170.

———. "Sur les tours de transept dans l'architecture du moyen âge." *Revue archéologique*, 1965, I, pp. 169–200; II, pp. 57–95.

———. *La Basilique de Saint-Quentin et l'architecture du moyen-âge*. Paris, 1967.

———. "La Diversité de l'architecture gothique à ses débuts en France." *Gaz. des Beaux-Arts*, LXIX, 1967, pp. 258–306.

Héliot, P., and M.-L. Chastang. "Quêtes et voyages de reliques au profit des églises françaises du moyen âge." *Revue d'histoire ecclésiastique*, LIX, 1964, pp. 789–822; LX, 1965, pp. 5–32.

Henriet, J. "Saint-Lucien de Beauvais, mythe ou réalité?" *Bull. mon.*, CXLI, 1983, pp. 273–294.

Henwood-Reverdot, A. *L'Eglise Saint-Etienne de Beauvais*. GEMOB. Beauvais, 1982.

Herschman, J. "The Norman Ambulatory of Le Mans Cathedral and the Chevet of the Cathedral of Coutances." *Gesta*, XX, 1981, pp. 323–332.

Heyman, J. "Beauvais Cathedral." *Transactions of the Newcomen Society*, XL, 1967–1968, pp. 15–36.

Houdard, G. *Les Châteaux royaux de Saint-Germain-en-Laye, 1124–1789*. 2 vols. Paris, 1909–1911.

Hughes, D. "Liturgical Polyphony at Beauvais in the Thirteenth Century." *Speculum*, XXXIV, 1959, pp. 184–200.

Huillier, V. l'. *La Paroisse et l'église Saint-Etienne de Beauvais*. Beauvais, 1896.

James, J. *The Contractors of Chartres*. 2 vols. Wyong, 1979–1981.

Jantzen, H. *High Gothic*. New York, 1962.

Jouen, Chanoine. *La Cathédrale de Rouen*. Paris, 1932.

Kerisel, J. "Old Structures in Relation to Soil Conditions." *Géotechnique*, XXV, 1975, pp. 449–451.

Kimpel, D. "Die Querhausarme von Notre-Dame zu Paris und ihre Skulpturen." Ph.D. diss., Bonn, 1971.

———. "Le Développement de la taille en série dans l'architecture médiévale et son rôle dans l'histoire économique." *Bull. mon*, CXXXV, 1977, pp. 195–222.

Kimpel, D., and R. Suckale. *Die gotische Architektur in Frankreich 1130–1270*. Munich, 1985.

Kraus, H. *Gold Was the Mortar: The Economics of Cathedral Building*. London, 1979.

Kurmann, P. *La Cathédrale Saint-Etienne de Meaux, étude architecturale*. Bibliothèque de la Société française d'archéologie, I, Geneva, 1971.

Labande, L.-H. *Histoire de Beauvais et de ses institutions communales jusqu'au commencement du XVe. siècle*. Paris, 1892.

Labarge, M. W. *Saint Louis: The Life of Louis IX of France*. London, 1968.

Lauer, P. "L'Abbaye de Royaumont." *Bull. mon.*, LXXII, 1908, pp. 215–268.

Launay, Abbé J. de. Notice in *Nouvelle Revue*, XLVII, 1920, pp. 1–26.

Launay, M.-M., C. Fauqueux, and A. Launay. *Essai d'histoire régionale: Département de l'Oise et pays qui l'ont formé*. Beauvais, 1925.

Leblond, V. *Inventaire-sommaire de la collection Bucquet-aux Cousteaux*. Paris and Beauvais, 1907.

———. *L'Eglise et la paroisse Saint-Etienne de Beauvais au XVe. siècle d'après des comptes des marguilliers et chanoines*. Beauvais, 1914.

———. *L'Art et les artistes en Ile-de-France au XVIe. siècle (Beauvais et Beauvaisis), d'après les minutes notoriales*. Paris, 1921.

———. "Les Artistes de Beauvais et du Beauvaisis au XVIe. siècle et leurs œuvres." *Mém. Soc. acad. Oise*, XXIV, 1923, pp. 85–138.

———. "L'Eglise de la Basse-Œuvre et la cathédrale Saint-Pierre de Beauvais, leur date de construction." *Mém. Soc. acad. Oise*, XXV, 1925, pp. 139–143.

———. *La Cathédrale de Beauvais*. Paris, 1926. Reprint, Paris, 1956.

———. *L'Eglise Saint–Etienne de Beauvais*. Paris, 1929.

Lefèvre-Pontalis, E. "L'Architecture gothique dans la Champagne méridionale au XIIIe. au XVIe. siècle." *Cong. arch.*, LXIX, 1902, pp. 273–349.

———. "Abbaye de Longpont." *Cong. arch.*, LXXVIII, 1911, part I, pp. 410–422.

———. "La Cathédrale de Soissons." *Cong. arch.*, LXXVIII, 1911, pp. 315–337.

Lemaire, R. *Une Construction urbaine de défense au IIIe. siècle: Le Castrum de Bellovacis*. Centre Départementale de Documentation Pédagogique de l'Oise. Beauvais, n.d.

———. *Beauvais hier et aujourd'hui*. Le Coteau, 1986.

Le Nain de Tillemont. *Vie de Saint Louis, roi de France*, ed. J. de Gaulle. 6 vols. Paris, 1847–1851.

Lenoir, A. *Statistique monumentale de Paris*, I. Paris, 1867.

Lesort, A., and H. Verlet. *Saint-Germain-l'Auxerrois: Epitaphier du vieux Paris*, V. Paris, 1974.

Levett, A. *The Black Death on the Estates of the See of Winchester*. Oxford Studies in Social and Legal History, V. Oxford, 1916.

Loisel, A. *Mémoires de l'evesché et évêques de Beauvais*. Paris, 1617.

———. *Mémoires des pays, villes, comté et comtes, evesché et évesques, pairrie, commune, et personnes de renom de Beauvais et Beauvaisis*. Paris, 1617.

Lopez, R. S. "Economie et architecture médiévales: Cela aurait-il tué ceci?" *Annales. Economies-Sociétés-Civilizations*, VIII, 1952, pp. 433–438.

———. *La Naissance de l'Europe*. Paris, 1962.

———. *The Commercial Revolution of the Middle Ages, 950–1350*. Englewood Cliffs, 1971.

Louvet, P. *L'Histoire de la ville et cité de Beauvais et des antiquitez du pays de Beauvaisis*. Rouen, 1614.

———. *Histoire et antiquitez du diocèse de Beauvais*. 2 vols. Beauvais, 1631–1635.

Luchaire, A. *Les Communes françaises à l'époque des capétiens directs*. Paris, 1890.

Macdonald, W. *The Architecture of the Roman Empire*. New Haven and London, 1982.

Madaule, J. *The Albigensian Crusade*. London, 1967.

Mango, C. *Art of the Byzantine Empire, 312–1453*. Englewood Cliffs, 1972.

Mark, R. *Experiments in Gothic Structure*. Cambridge, 1982.

Mark, R., K. D. Alexander, and J. F. Abel. "The Structural Behaviour of Medieval Ribbed Vaulting." *J. Soc. Arch. Hist.*, XXXVI, 1977, pp. 241–251.

Mark, R., and P. Hutchinson. "On the Structure of the Roman Pantheon." *Art Bulletin*, LXVIII, 1986, pp. 24–34.

Marsaux, Abbé L.-H. "Cathédrale [de Beauvais]." *Cong. arch.*, LXXII, 1905, pp. 4–15.

McGee, J. D. "The 'Early Vaults' of Saint-Etienne

at Beauvais." *J. Soc. Arch. Hist.*, XLV, 1986, pp. 20–32.

Meulen, J. van der. "Histoire de la construction de la cathédrale Notre-Dame de Chartres après 1194." *Bull. Soc. arch. Eure-et-Loir*, XXIII, 1965, pp. 79–126.

———. "Recent Literature on the Chronology of Chartres Cathedral." *Art Bull.*, XLIX, 1967, pp. 152–172.

———. *Chartres, Biographie der Kathedrale.* Cologne, 1984.

Meurgey de Tupigny, J. *Saint-Jacques de la Boucherie et la Tour Saint-Jacques.* Paris, 1960.

Millet, H. *Les Chanoines du chapitre cathédrale de Laon, 1272–1412.* Collection de l'école française de Rome, LVI. Paris, 1982.

Minost, M., and M. Aubert. "La Fenêtre occidentale du réfectoire de Saint-Germain-des-Prés, œuvre de Pierre de Montreuil." *Bull. mon.*, CXII, 1954, pp. 275–280.

Morel, E. "Le Mouvement communal au XIIe. siècle dans le Beauvais et aux environs." *Mém. Soc. acad. Oise*, XVII, 1899, pp. 481–499.

Moulin, J., and P. Ponsot. "La Chapelle de la Vierge à l'Abbaye Saint-Germain-des-Prés et Pierre de Montreuil." *Archéologie*, CXL, 1980, pp. 49–55.

Müller, E. *Le prieuré de Saint-Leu-d'Esserent.* Pontoise, 1901.

Murray, S. "The Work of Martin Chambiges." Ph.D. diss., London University, Courtauld Institute, 1973.

———. "The Completion of the Nave of Troyes Cathedral." *J. Soc. Arch. Hist.*, XXXIV, 1975, pp. 121–139.

———. "The Collapse of 1284 at Beauvais Cathedral." *Acta of the Center for Medieval and Early Renaissance Studies, State University of New York at Binghamton*, III, *The Thirteenth Century.* Binghamton, 1976, pp. 17–44.

———. "An Expertise at Beauvais Cathedral." *J. Brit. Arch. Assoc.*, CXXX, 1977, pp. 133–144.

———. "The Choir of Saint-Etienne at Beauvais." *J. Soc. Arch. Hist.*, XXXVI, 1977, pp. 111–121.

———. "Master Jehançon Garnache (1485–1501) and the Construction of the High Vaults and Flying Buttresses of Troyes Cathedral." *J. Soc. Arch. Hist.*, XIX, 1980, pp. 37–49.

———. "The Choir of the Church of Saint-Pierre, Cathedral of Beauvais: A Study of Gothic Architectural Planning and Constructional Chronology in Its Historical Context." *Art Bull.*, LXII, 1980, pp. 533–551.

———. *Building Troyes Cathedral: The Late Gothic Campaigns.* Bloomington, 1987.

Mussat, A. "La Cathédrale Notre-Dame de Coutances." *Cong. arch.*, CXXIV, 1966, pp. 9–50.

———. *La Cathédrale du Mans.* Paris, 1981.

———. "Les Cathédrales dans leurs cités." *Revue de l'art*, LV, 1982, pp. 9–22.

Neagley, L. E. "The Parish Church of Saint-Maclou: A Study of Rouennais Flamboyant Architecture." Ph.D. diss., Indiana University, 1983.

Nelson, R. J. "Martin Chambiges and the Development of French Flamboyant Architecture." Ph.D. diss., Johns Hopkins University, 1973.

———. "A Lost Portal by Martin Chambiges?" *J. Soc. Arch. Hist.*, XXXIII, 1974, pp. 155–157.

Newman, W. M. *Les Seigneurs de Nesle en Picardie (XIIe.–XIIIe. siècle). Leurs chartes et leur histoire: Etude sur la noblesse régionale ecclésiastique et laïque.* 2 vols. Philadelphia, 1971.

Pacaut, M. *Louis VII et les élections épiscopales dans le royaume de France.* Paris, 1957.

———. *Louis VII et son royaume.* Paris, 1964.

Panofsky, E. *Abbot Suger on the Abbey Church of Saint-Denis and Its Art Treasures.* Princeton, 1979.

Pennington, K. "Pope Innocent III's Views on Church and State: A Gloss to 'Per Venerabilem.' " In *Law, Church, and Society: Essays in Honor of Stephan Kuttner*, ed. K. Pennington and R. Somerville. Philadelphia, 1977.

Perrod, M. "Etude sur la vie et sur les œuvres de Guillaume de Saint Amour, docteur en théologie de l'Université de Paris et chanoine de Beauvais et de Mâcon (1202–1272)." *Mémoires de la Société d'émulation du Jura*, ser. 7 II, 1902, pp. 61–252.

Pessin, M. "The Twelfth-Century Abbey Church of Saint-Germer-de-Fly and Its Position in the Development of First Gothic Architecture." *Gesta*, XVII, 1978, p. 71.

Pestell, R. "The Design Sources for the Cathedrals of Chartres and Soissons." *Art History*, IV, 1981, pp. 1–13.

Petit-Dutaillis, C. *Etude sur la vie et le règne de Louis VIII.* Paris, 1894.

———. *Les Communes françaises: Caractères et évolution des origines, au XVIIIe. siècle.* Paris, 1947.

Piétresson de Saint-Aubin, P. "L'Eglise Saint-Jean-au-Marché à Troyes." *Bull. mon.*, LXXXIX, 1930, pp. 47–111.

Pihan, Abbé, L. *Beauvais, sa cathédrale, ses principaux monuments.* Beauvais, 1885.

———. "Notice sur M. le chanoine Marsaux." *Mém. Soc. acad. Oise*, XX, 1907, pp. 5–26.

Pontal, O. "Le Différend entre Louis IX et les

évêques de Beauvais." *Bibl. Ecole Chartes*, CXXIII, 1965, pp. 5–34.

Porée, C. "Les Architectes et la construction de la cathédrale de Sens." *Cong. arch.*, LXXIV, 1907, pp. 559–598.

Prache, A. *Saint-Remi de Reims: L'œuvre de Pierre de Celle et sa place dans l'architecture gothique.* Bibliothèque de la Société francaise d'archéologie, VIII. Geneva, 1978.

———. "Pierre de Montreuil." *Histoire et archéologie*, November 1980, pp. 26–38.

Prak, N. L. "Measurements of Amiens Cathedral." *J. Soc. Arch. Hist.*, XXV, 1966, pp. 209–212.

Ravaux, J.-P. "Les Campagnes de construction de la cathédrale de Reims au XIIIe. siècle." *Bull. mon.*, CXXXVII, 1979, pp. 7–66.

Régnier, M. L. "Une Particularité architectonique du chœur de Saint-Etienne de Beauvais." *Cong. arch.*, LXXII, 1905, pp. 530–534.

Reinhardt, H. *La Cathédrale de Reims.* Paris, 1963.

Rénouard, Y. *Etudes d'histoire médiévale.* Paris, 1968.

Rome, Chanoine. "Henri II de Braisne, archévêque de Reims (1227–40), Blanche de Castille et Saint Louis." *Trav. Acad. nat. Reims*, CLIV, 1941–1946, pp. 71–92.

Rousset, E., and M. J. Estienne. *Inventaire-sommaire des archives départementales antérieures à 1790: Archives ecclésiastiques, série G, II, Evêché de Beauvais.* Beauvais, 1942.

Salet, F. "La Madeleine de Troyes," *Cong. arch.*, CXIII, 1955, pp. 139–152.

———. "Saint-Pantaléon de Troyes." *Cong. arch.*, CXIII, 1955, pp. 153–165.

———. "La Cathédrale du Mans." *Cong. arch.*, CXIX, 1961, pp. 18–58.

———. Review of Branner's "Le Maître de la cathédrale de Beauvais." *Bull. mon.*, CXX, 1962, pp. 78–79.

———. "Chronologie de la cathédrale [de Reims]." *Bull. mon.*, CXXV, 1967, pp. 347–394.

———. Review of Bonnet-Laborderie's *Cathédrale Saint-Pierre. Bull. mon.*, CXXXVIII, 1980, pp. 351–353.

Sanfaçon, R. *L'Architecture flamboyante en France.* Quebec, 1971.

Schröder, U. "Royaumont oder Köln?" *Kölner Domblatt*, XLII, 1977, pp. 209–242.

Serbat, L. "Quelques Eglises anciennement détruites du nord de la France." *Bull. mon.*, LXXXVIII, 1929, pp. 367–435.

Seymour, C. *Notre-Dame of Noyon in the Twelfth Century: A Study in the Early Development of Gothic Architecture.* New York, 1968.

Shelby, L. "The Geometrical Knowledge of Medieval Master Masons." *Speculum*, XLVII, 1972, pp. 395–421.

Simon, D. *Supplément aux mémoires de l'histoire civile et ecclésiastique du Beauvaisis de M. Anthoine Loisel et de M. Pierre Louvet.* Paris, 1704.

Simson, O. von. *The Gothic Cathedral.* New York, 1962.

Sjöberg, Y. "Saint-Sulpice-de-Favières." *Cong. arch.*, CIII, 1944, pp. 246–264.

Stanislas de Saint-Germain. *Notice historique et descriptive sur l'église Saint-Etienne de Beauvais.* Beauvais, 1843.

Stein, H. "Pierre de Montereau, architecte de l'église abbatiale de Saint-Denis." *Mém. Soc. nat. ant. France*, ser. 7, LXI, 1902, pp. 79–104.

———. "Pierre de Montereau et la cathédrale de Paris." *Mém. Soc. nat. ant. France*, ser. 8, LXXI, 1912, pp. 14–28.

Thiebaut, J. *Les cathédrales gothique en Picardie.* Amiens, 1987.

Tierney, B. *The Crisis of Church and State, 1050–1300.* Englewood Cliffs, 1964.

Vachon, M. *Une Famille parisienne d'architectes maistres-maçons, aux XV, XVI, XVII siècles, Les Chambiges, 1490–1643.* Paris, 1907.

Vallery-Radot, J. *L'Eglise de la Trinité de Fécamp.* Paris, 1928.

Vercauteren, E. *Etude sur les civitates de la Belgique seconde.* Brussels, 1934.

Verlet, H. "Les Bâtiments monastiques de Saint-Germain-des-Prés." *Paris et Ile-de-France, Mémoires*, IX, 1957–1958, pp. 9–69.

Viollet-le-Duc, E. *Dictionnaire raisonné de l'architecture française.* 10 vols. Paris, 1854–1868.

———. *Entretiens sur l'architecture.* 2 vols. Paris, 1863–1872.

Warnke, M. *Bau and Überbau: Soziologie der Mittelalterlichen Architektur nach dem Schriftquellen.* Frankfurt am Main, 1976.

Watteeuw, F. *Beauvais et les Beauvaisiens des années 40.* GEMOB. Paris, 1980.

Weigert, R.-A. "Plans et vues de Saint-Germain-des-Prés." *Paris et Ile-de-France, Mémoires*, IX, 1957–1958, pp. 105–137.

Woillez, E. *Description de la cathédrale de Beauvais.* Beauvais, 1838.

Wolfe, M., and R. Mark. "The Collapse of the Beauvais Vaults in 1284." *Speculum*, LI, 1976, pp. 462–476.

Wolff, A. "Chronologie der ersten Bauzeit des Kölner Domes, 1248–1277." *Kölner Domblatt*, XXVIII/XXIX, 1968.

ILLUSTRATIONS

Le vray pourtraict de la Ville de Beauuais.

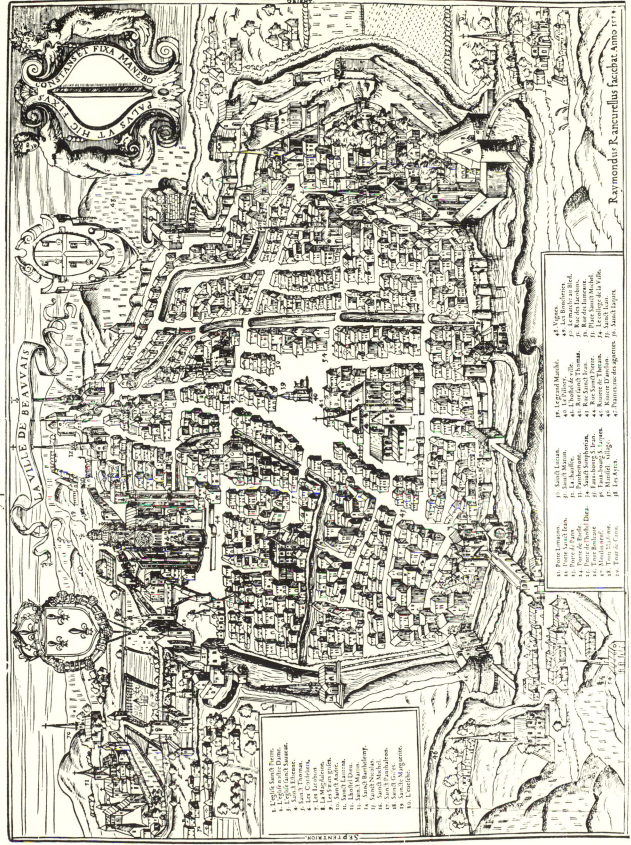

1. Beauvais. Plan of the medieval town, by Raymondus Rancurellus, 1574.

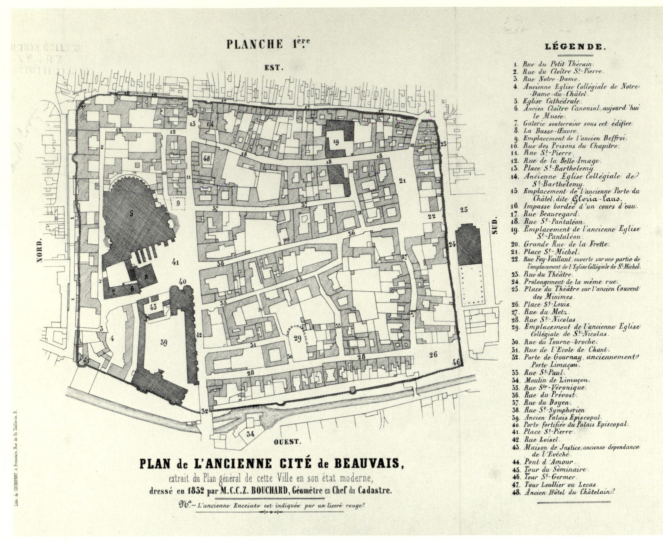

Lith. de COCHERET, à Beauvais. Rue de la Taillerie 3.

PLANCHE 1ère

EST.

NORD.

SUD.

OUEST.

LÉGENDE.

1. Rue du Petit Thérain.
2. Rue du Cloître St.-Pierre.
3. Rue Notre-Dame.
4. Ancienne Eglise Collégiale de Notre-Dame-du-Châtel.
5. Eglise Cathédrale.
6. Ancien Cloître Canonial, aujourd'hui le Musée.
7. Galerie souterraine sous cet édifice.
8. La Basse-Œuvre.
9. Emplacement de l'ancien Beffroi.
10. Rue des Prisons du Chapitre.
11. Rue St.-Pierre.
12. Rue de la Belle-Image.
13. Place St.-Barthélemy.
14. Ancienne Eglise Collégiale de St.-Barthélemy.
15. Emplacement de l'ancienne Porte du Châtel, dite Gloria-laus.
16. Impasse bordée d'un cours d'eau.
17. Rue Beauregard.
18. Rue St.-Pantaléon.
19. Emplacement de l'ancienne Eglise St.-Pantaléon.
20. Grande Rue de la Frette.
21. Place St.-Michel.
22. Rue Foy-Vaillant, ouverte sur une partie de l'emplacement de l'Eglise Collégiale de St.-Michel.
23. Rue du Théâtre.
24. Prolongement de la même rue.
25. Place du Théâtre sur l'ancien Couvent des Minimes.
26. Place St.-Louis.
27. Rue du Metz.
28. Rue St.-Nicolas.
29. Emplacement de l'ancienne Eglise Collégiale de St.-Nicolas.
30. Rue du Tourne-broche.
31. Rue de l'Ecole de Chant.
32. Porte de Gournay, anciennement Porte Limaçon.
33. Rue St.-Paul.
34. Moulin de Limaçon.
35. Rue Ste.-Véronique.
36. Rue du Prévost.
37. Rue du Doyen.
38. Rue St.-Symphorien.
39. Ancien Palais Episcopal.
40. Porte fortifiée du Palais Episcopal.
41. Place St.-Pierre.
42. Rue Loisel.
43. Maison de Justice, ancienne dépendance de l'Evêché.
44. Pont d'Amour.
45. Tour du Séminaire.
46. Tour St.-Germer.
47. Tour Leullier ou Lecas.
48. Ancien Hôtel du Châtelain.

PLAN de L'ANCIENNE CITÉ de BEAUVAIS,

extrait du Plan général de cette Ville en son état moderne,

dressé en 1832 par M.C.C.Z. BOUCHARD, Géomètre en Chef du Cadastre.

Nᵃ.—L'ancienne Enceinte est indiquée par un liseré rouge.

2. Beauvais. Plan of the episcopal *cité*. (From *Mém. Soc. acad. Oise*, II, 1852–1855, pp. 12–13.)

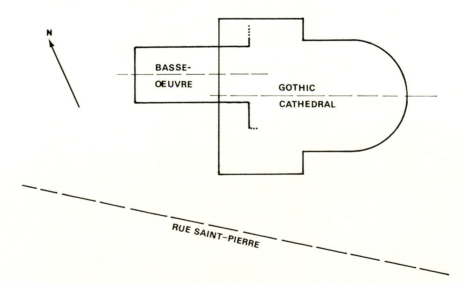

N

BASSE-OEUVRE

GOTHIC CATHEDRAL

RUE SAINT-PIERRE

3. Beauvais Cathedral. Schema of cathedral site.

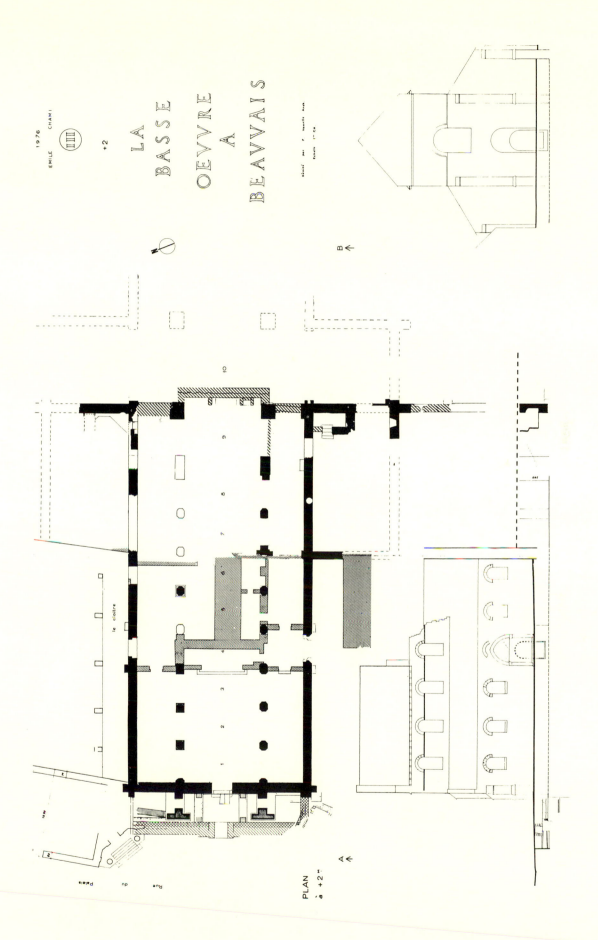

4. Beauvais Cathedral. Plan and elevation of the *Basse-Oeuvre*, by E. Chami, 1976.

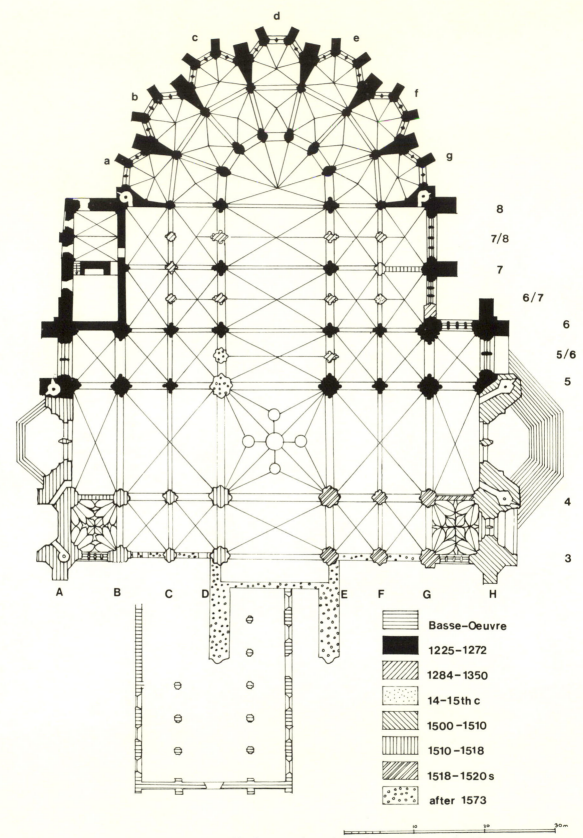

d

c

e

b

f

a

g

8

7/8

7

6/7

6

5/6

5

4

3

A B C D E F G H

	Basse-Oeuvre
	1225–1272
	1284–1350
	14–15th c
	1500–1510
	1510–1518
	1518–1520s
	after 1573

10   20   30 m

5. Beauvais Cathedral. Plan of the ensemble showing chronology of construction and grid system of reference.

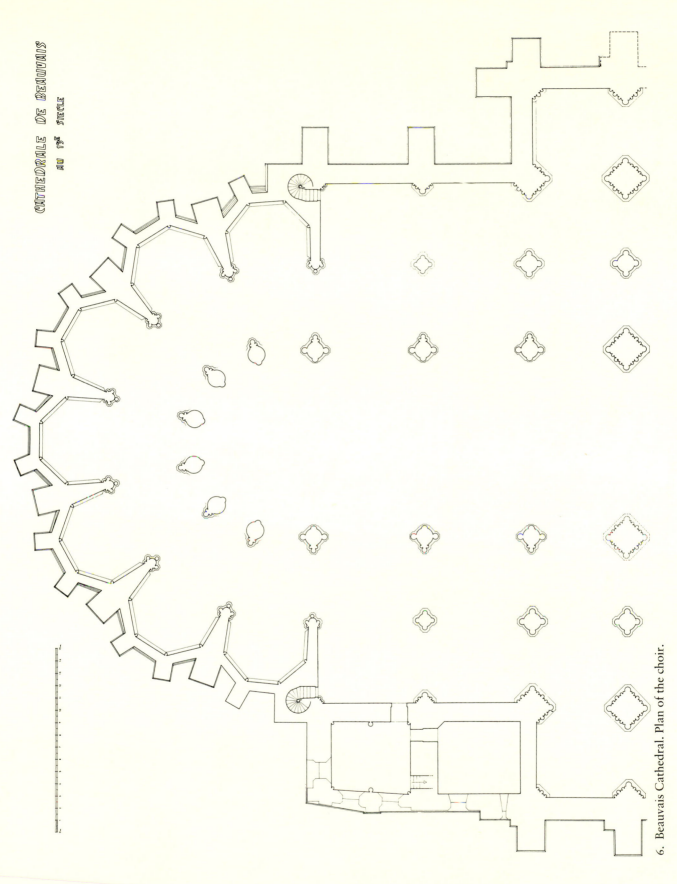

CATHEDRALE DE BEAUVAIS AU 13^e SIECLE

6. Beauvais Cathedral. Plan of the choir.

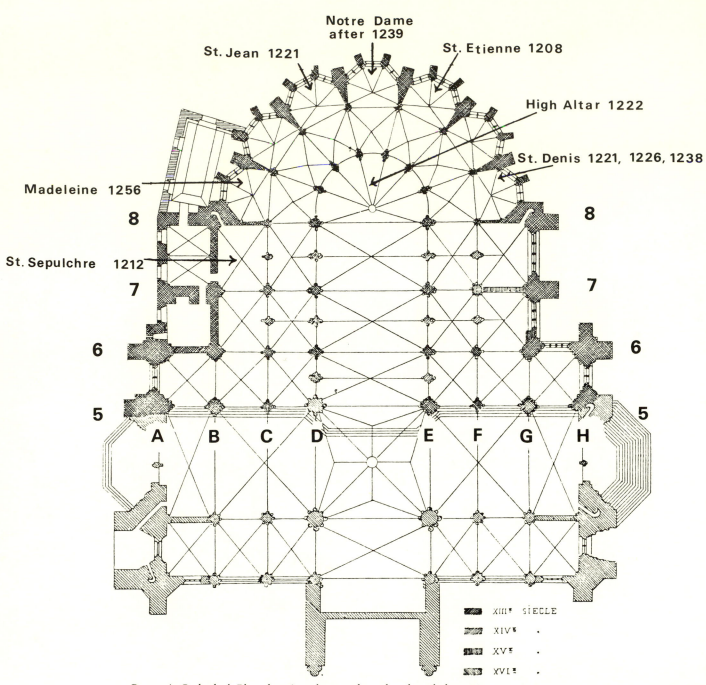

7. Beauvais Cathedral. Plan showing altars endowed or founded, 1188–1272.

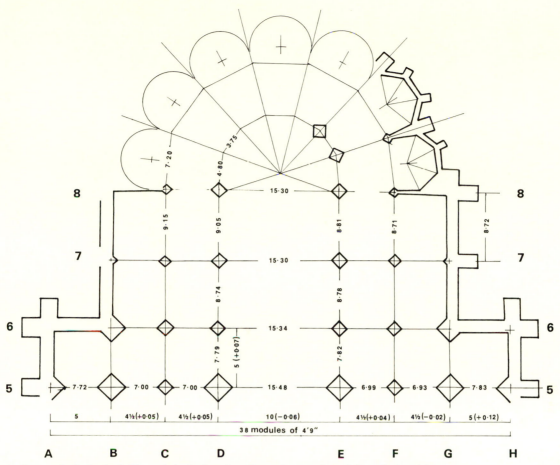

8. Beauvais Cathedral. Plan of choir showing dimensions and modular relationships.

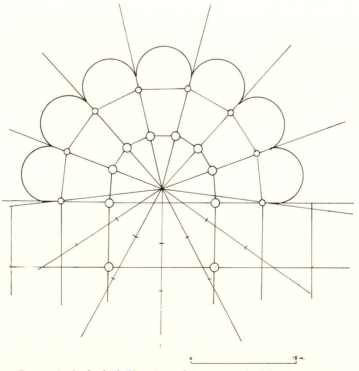

9. Beauvais Cathedral. Planning of the east end of the choir.

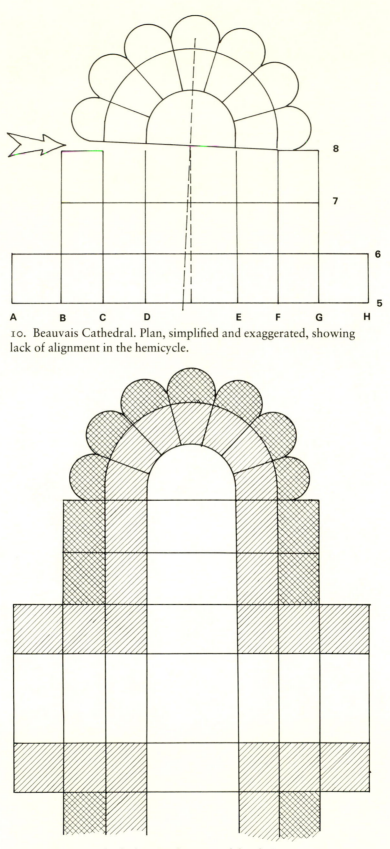

10. Beauvais Cathedral. Plan, simplified and exaggerated, showing lack of alignment in the hemicycle.

11. Beauvais Cathedral. Spatial system of the choir.

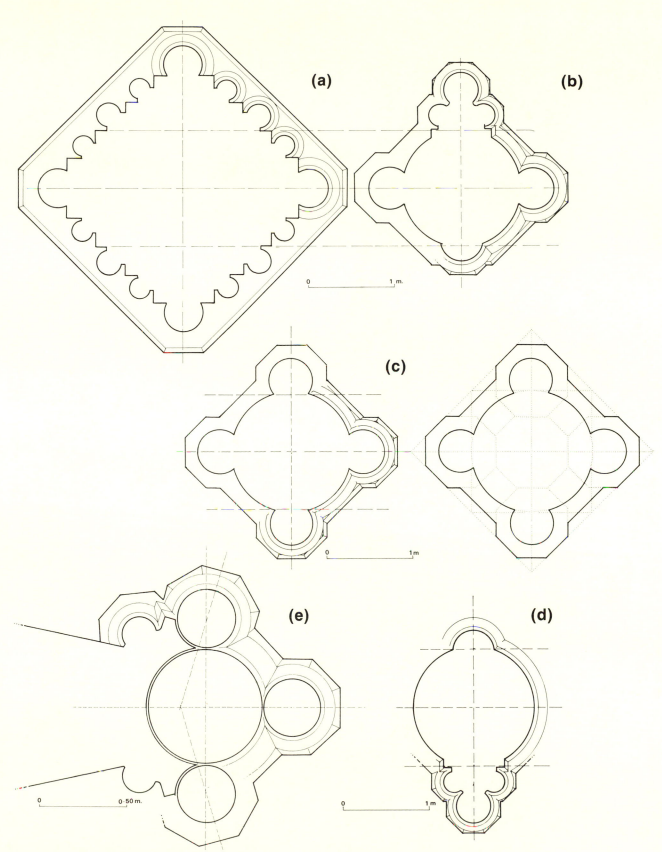

(a)

(b)

0   1 m.

(c)

0   1 m

(e)

(d)

0   0·50 m.

0   1 m

12. Beauvais Cathedral. Pier sections. (a) Compound pier (transept towers and crossing);
(b) Choir main arcade; (c) *Pilier cantonné* (transept); (d) Hemicycle; (e) Ambulatory
(between radiating chapels).

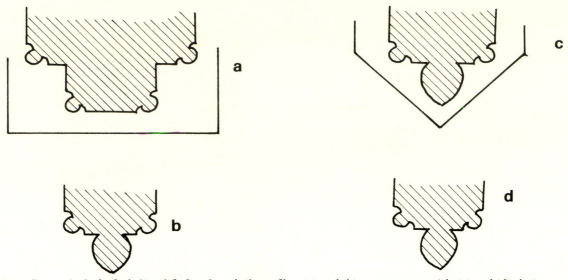

13. Beauvais Cathedral. Simplified arch and rib profiles; (a) and (b) transept, east aisle (c) and (d) choir aisles and ambulatory.

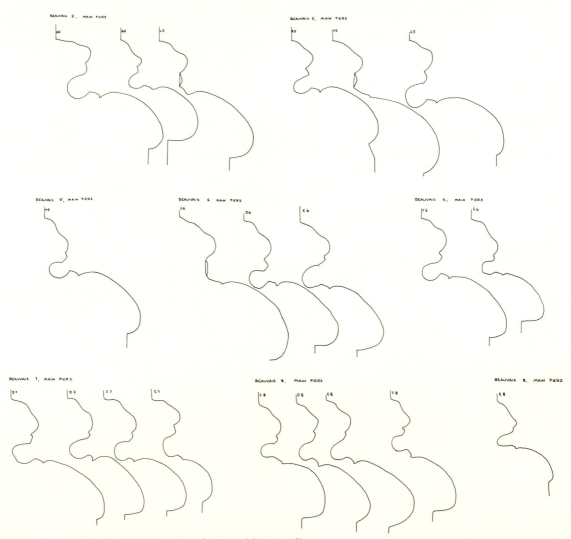

14a. Beauvais Cathedral. Main piers base molding profiles.

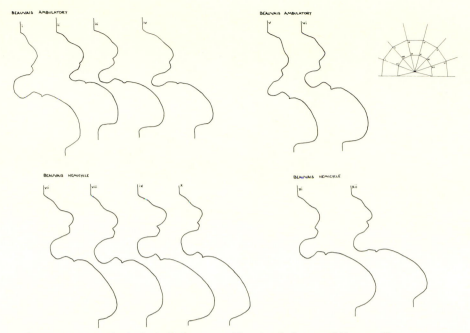

14b. Beauvais Cathedral. Ambulatory and hemicycle base molding profiles.

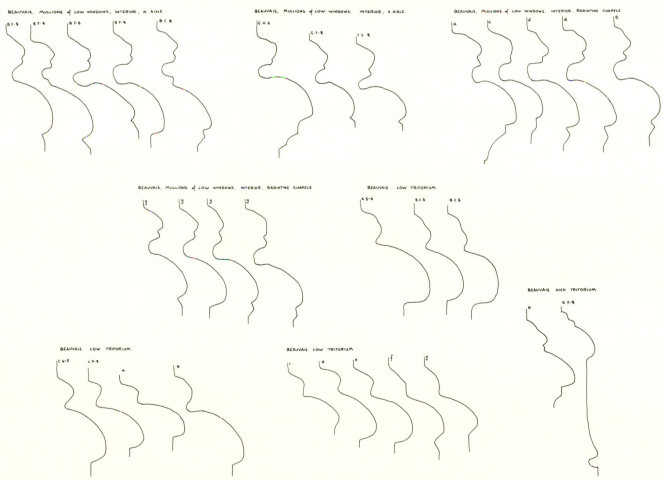

14c. Beauvais Cathedral. Low windows, low and high triforium base molding profiles.

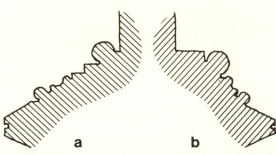

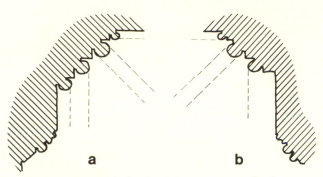

15. Beauvais Cathedral. Sections (not measured) of window jambs. (a) North transept; (b) South transept.

16. Beauvais Cathedral. Sections (not measured) of applied shafts. (a) North choir aisles, B 8; (b) South choir aisles, G 8.

17. Beauvais Cathedral. Model of the hemicycle, in the Palais de Chaillot, Paris.

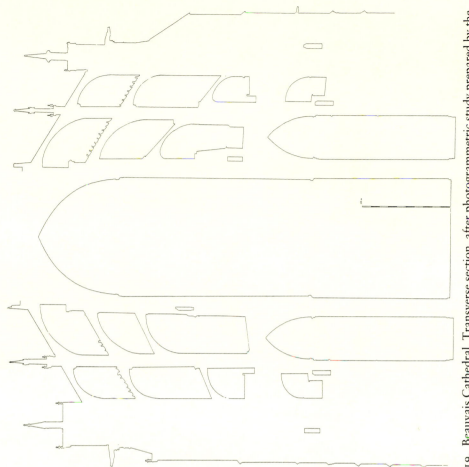

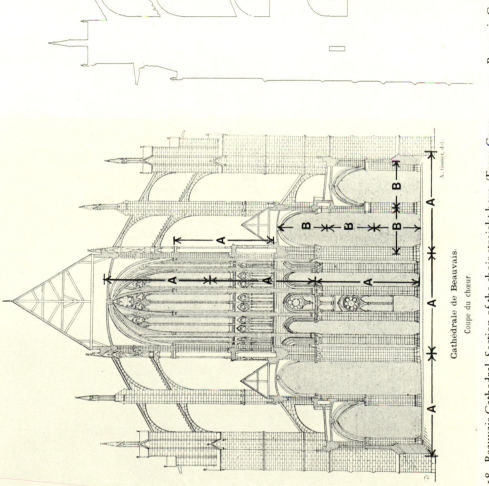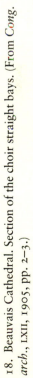

Cathédrale de Beauvais.

Coupe du chœur.

A. Gossit, del.

18. Beauvais Cathedral. Section of the choir straight bays. (From *Cong. arch.*, LXII, 1905, pp. 2–3.)

19. Beauvais Cathedral. Transverse section, after photogrammetric study prepared by the *Institut Géographique National*.

CATHÉDRALE DE BEAUVAIS

COUPE TRANSVERSALE
ECHELLE: 0,01 P.M.

NOTA: LA TOITURE DU DÉAMBULATOIRE, REPRÉSENTÉE ICI
EN TRAITS FINS, N'EXISTE PLUS. ELLE A ÉTÉ REM-
-PLACÉE PAR LA DALLE EN BÉTON ARMÉ, FIGURANT
EN TRAIT DE COUPE POCHÉ EN NOIR.

20. Beauvais Cathedral. Choir, section of hemicycle.

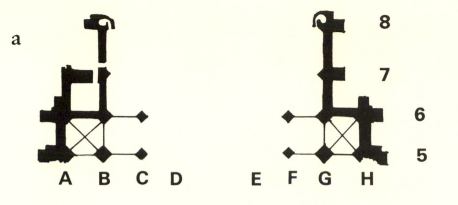

a

8

7

6

5

A B C D   E F G H

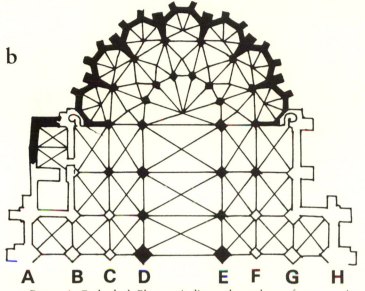

b

A   B   C   D   E   F   G   H

21. Beauvais Cathedral. Plans to indicate chronology of construction. (a) Cathedral of Bishop Miles of Nanteuil, 1225–1232; (b) Cathedral of Bishops Robert of Cressonsac and William of Grez, 1238–1272.

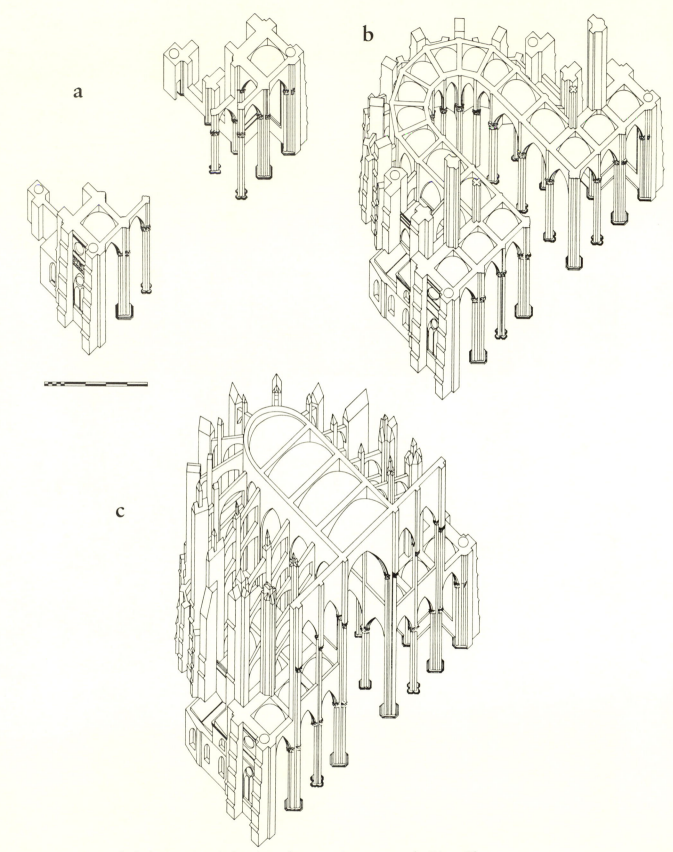

a

b

c

22. Beauvais Cathedral. Axonometric drawings of construction sequence, by Diego Oleas.
(a) Cathedral of Bishop Miles of Nanteuil, 1225–1232; (b) Cathedral of Bishop Robert of
Cressonsac, 1238–1240s; (c) Cathedral of Bishop William of Grez, 1250s–1260s.
(Note: upper east wall of transept is shown, although status is uncertain.)

COUPE SUR LA 1ᵉ CHAPELLE RAYONNANTE
DU BAS-COTÉ SUD.

ETAT ACTUEL.

CATHEDRALE DE BEAUVAIS.
REPRISE D'UN PILIER DU BAS-COTÉ SUD

23. Beauvais Cathedral. Drawing of buckled pier F 8, by Sauvageot, 1887.

24. Beauvais Cathedral. Section of buttressing system in hemicycle, by Viollet-le-Duc. (From Viollet-le-Duc, *Dictionnaire*, IV, p. 178.)

25. Beauvais Cathedral. View of the high altar with altar of Notre-Dame-de-la-Paix. (Bucquet-aux Cousteaux Collection.)

26. Beauvais Cathedral. State of the cathedral in 1464.
(From Desjardins, *Histoire*, p. 25.)

27. Beauvais Cathedral. State in 1530, from a tapestry in the series *Histoire fabuleuse des premiers rois des Gaules*, sixteenth century, in the Galerie Nationale de la Tapisserie, Beauvais.

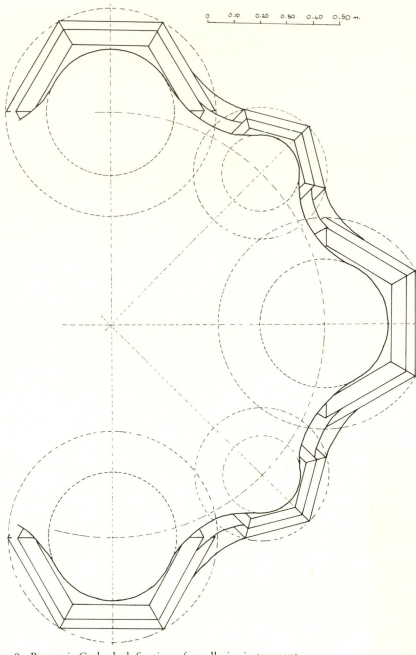

0   0.10   0.20   0.30   0.40   0.50 m.

28. Beauvais Cathedral. Section of small pier in transept.

29. Beauvais Cathedral. State in 1569 with crossing tower. (From Desjardins, *Histoire*, frontispiece.)

30a, b. Beauvais Cathedral. Bases of intermediary uprights of flying buttresses of hemicycle seen under the chapel roofs.

31. Beauvais Cathedral. Exterior, general view from the west with *Basse-Œuvre* in foreground.

32. Beauvais Cathedral. Exterior, general view from north.

33. Beauvais Cathedral. Exterior, choir, from northeast.

34. Beauvais Cathedral. Exterior, choir, upper parts, from northeast.

35. Beauvais Cathedral. Exterior, choir, lower parts, from east.

36. Beauvais Cathedral. Exterior, choir, from southeast.

37. Beauvais Cathedral. Exterior, choir, from south.

38. Beauvais Cathedral. Exterior, transept and choir, lower parts, from south.

39. Beauvais Cathedral. Exterior, transept and choir, upper parts, from south.

40. Beauvais Cathedral. Exterior, *Basse-Œuvre*, south side, Gothic portal.

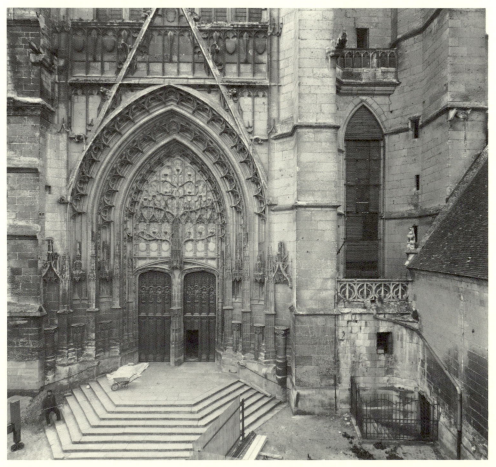

41. Beauvais Cathedral. Exterior, north transept portal.

42. Beauvais Cathedral. Exterior, north transept façade, east aisle, A 5 6.

43. Beauvais Cathedral. Exterior, north transept façade, east aisle, A 5 6, detail of lower window.

44. Beauvais Cathedral. Exterior, south transept façade, east aisle, H 5 6.

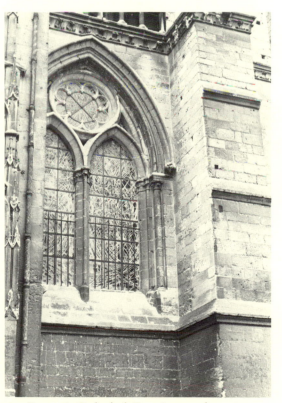

45. Beauvais Cathedral. Exterior, south transept façade, east aisle, H 5 6, detail of lower window.

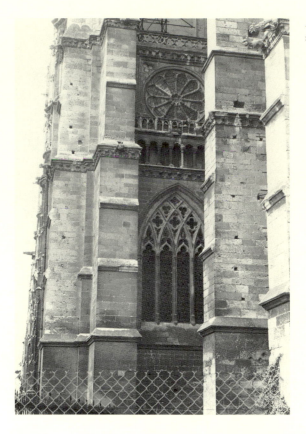

46. Beauvais Cathedral. Exterior, south transept, east side.

47. Beauvais Cathedral. Exterior, choir, north side, sacristy/treasury complex.

48. Beauvais Cathedral. Exterior,
north side of choir, buttress B 8
at base of hemicycle.

49. Beauvais Cathedral. Exterior choir,
north side, buttress B 8 from northeast.

50. Beauvais Cathedral. Exterior choir, south side, lower parts.

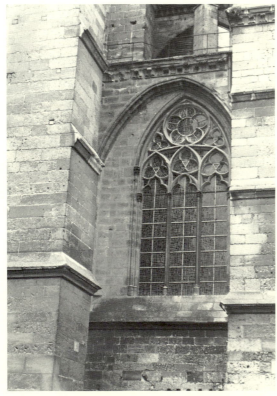

51. Beauvais Cathedral. Exterior choir, south side, chapel window G 6 7.

52. Beauvais Cathedral. Exterior choir, south side, buttress G 7 from southeast.

53. Beauvais Cathedral. Exterior choir, south side,
chapel window G 7 8.

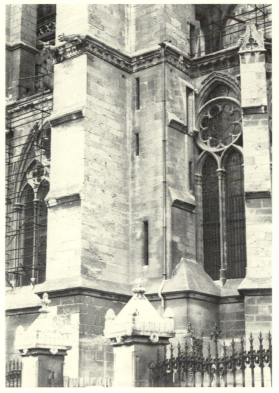

54. Beauvais Cathedral. Exterior choir, south side,
buttress G 8.

55. Beauvais Cathedral. Exterior choir and
transept, south side, hatched to show
phases of construction.

☐	1225–1232
▨	1238–1250
▧	1250–1272
⫼	1284–1350
✛	16th century
∘	18th–19th century

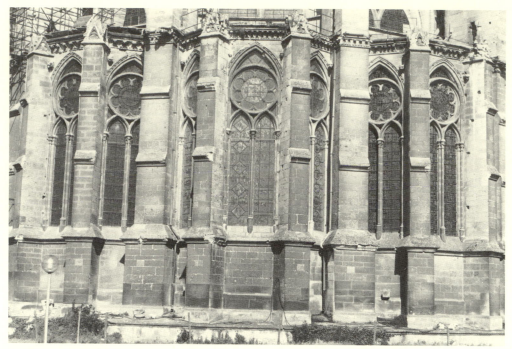

56. Beauvais Cathedral. Exterior choir, radiating chapels.

57. Beauvais Cathedral. Exterior choir, radiating chapels, axial chapel.

58. Beauvais Cathedral. Exterior, upper choir and transept, north side, flying buttress uprights at B 6 and C 6.

59. Beauvais Cathedral. Exterior, upper transept and choir, north side, flying buttress uprights at B 6 and C 6.

60. Beauvais Cathedral. Exterior, upper choir, north side, flying buttresses, divisions 7, 8 and hemicycle.

61. Beauvais Cathedral. Exterior, upper choir, north side, flying buttress upright at B 8.

62. Beauvais Cathedral. Exterior, upper transept and choir, south side, flying buttress upright at G 6.

63. Beauvais Cathedral. Exterior, upper choir, south side, flying buttress upright at F 6.

64. Beauvais Cathedral. Exterior, upper choir, south side, flying buttress at division 7.

65. Beauvais Cathedral. Exterior, upper choir, south side, flying buttress upright at G 7.

66. Beauvais Cathedral. Exterior, upper choir, south side, flying buttress upright at G 8.

67. Beauvais Cathedral. Exterior, upper hemicycle, north side, flying buttresses with C 8 and D 8 in foreground.

68. Beauvais Cathedral. Exterior, upper hemicycle, flying buttresses.

69. Beauvais Cathedral. Exterior, upper hemicycle, flying buttresses.

70. Beauvais Cathedral. Exterior, upper hemicycle, triforium.

71. Beauvais Cathedral. Exterior, upper hemicycle, detail of triforium.

72. Beauvais Cathedral. Exterior, upper choir, south side, clerestory at E 7-E 7/8-E 8.

73. Beauvais Cathedral. Exterior, upper hemicycle, south side, clerestory.

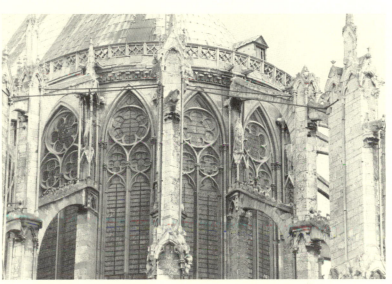

74. Beauvais Cathedral. Exterior, upper hemicycle, general view.

75. Beauvais Cathedral. Interior, transept.

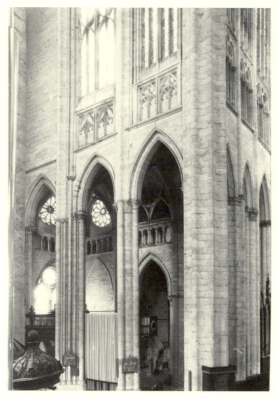

76. Beauvais Cathedral. Interior, north transept, east side.

77. Beauvais Cathedral. Interior, south transept, east side.

78. Beauvais Cathedral. Interior, north transept, vault of chapel A B 3 4.

79. Beauvais Cathedral. Interior, south transept, vault of chapel G H 3 4.

80. Beauvais Cathedral. Interior, southwest crossing pier, E 4.

81. Beauvais Cathedral. Interior, north transept, pier C 4.

82. Beauvais Cathedral. Interior, north transept, east aisle.

83. Beauvais Cathedral. Interior, north transept, base of pier B 5.

84. Beauvais Cathedral. Interior, north transept, base of pier C 6.

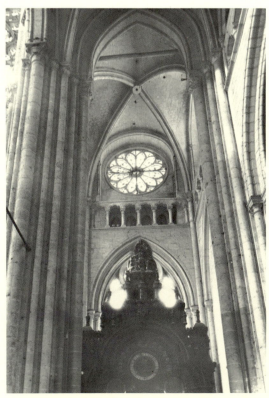

85. Beauvais Cathedral. Interior, north transept, east aisle, terminal bay.

86. Beauvais Cathedral. Interior, north transept, east aisle, terminal bay.

87. Beauvais Cathedral. Interior, north transept, east aisle, capital at B 6.

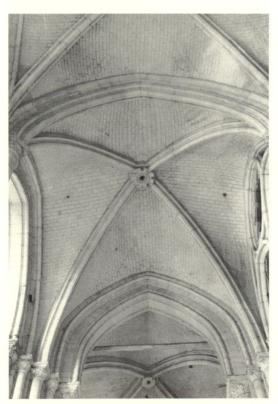

88. Beauvais Cathedral. Interior, north transept, east aisle, vaults at A B 5 6 and B C 5 6.

89. Beauvais Cathedral. Interior, north transept, east aisle, triforium, and clerestory at B C 6.

90. Beauvais Cathedral. Interior, north transept, east aisle and north aisle of choir.

91. Beauvais Cathedral. Interior, north transept, east aisle, capital at C 6.

92. Beauvais Cathedral. Interior, south transept, east aisle, terminal bay.

93. Beauvais Cathedral. Interior, south transept, capital at H 5.

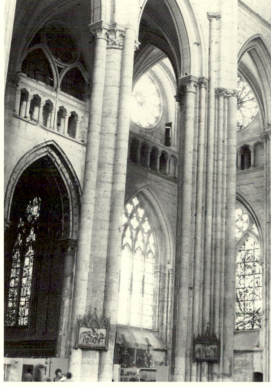

94. Beauvais Cathedral. Interior, south transept,
east aisle, terminal bay.

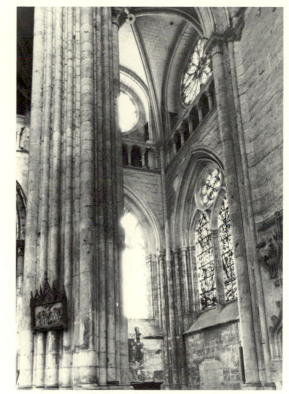

95. Beauvais Cathedral. Interior, south transept,
east aisle, terminal bay, southeast corner, H 6.

96. Beauvais Cathedral. Interior, south transept,
east aisle, bay F G 5 6.

97. Beauvais Cathedral. Interior, south transept, east aisle,
capital at F 6.

98. Beauvais Cathedral. Interior, north choir aisles, outer aisle, general view to the east.

99. Beauvais Cathedral. Interior, north choir aisles, outer aisle, general view to the east.

100. Beauvais Cathedral. Interior, north choir aisles, inner aisle, general view to the east.

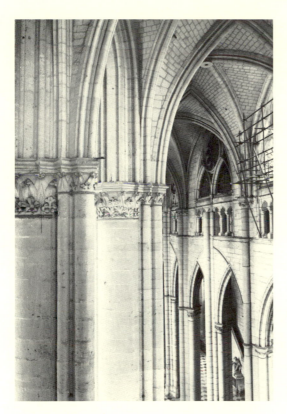

102. Beauvais Cathedral. Interior, north choir aisles, outer aisle, base at B 7.

101. Beauvais Cathedral. Interior, north choir aisles, inner aisle, general view to the west.

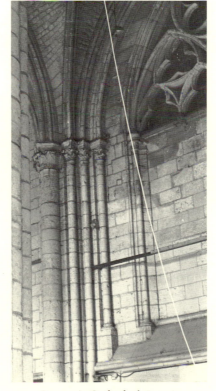

103. Beauvais Cathedral. Interior, north choir aisles, outer aisle, division B 7.

104. Beauvais Cathedral. Interior, north choir aisles, outer aisle, division B 7, from southeast.

105. Beauvais Cathedral. Interior, north choir aisles, outer aisle, capital at B 7.

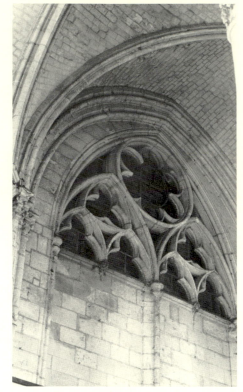

106. Beauvais Cathedral. Interior, north choir aisles, outer aisle, "window" at B 7 8.

107. Beauvais Cathedral. Interior, south choir aisles, inner aisle, general view, looking east.

108. Beauvais Cathedral. Interior, south choir aisles, outer aisle window at G 6 7.

110. Beauvais Cathedral. Interior, south choir aisles, base at F 7.

109. Beauvais Cathedral. Interior, south choir aisles, outer aisle, base at G 7.

111. Beauvais Cathedral. Interior, south choir aisles, outer aisle, window at G 7 8.

112. Beauvais Cathedral. Interior, south choir aisles, outer aisle, terminal wall F G 8.

113. Beauvais Cathedral. Interior, south choir aisles, outer aisle, terminal wall at G 8.

114. Beauvais Cathedral. Interior, south choir aisles, outer aisle, base at G 8.

115. Beauvais Cathedral. Interior, ambulatory, general view.

116. Beauvais Cathedral. Interior, ambulatory,
general view.

118. Beauvais Cathedral. Interior, radiating
chapels f and g.

117. Beauvais Cathedral. Interior, ambulatory,
detail of capital of transverse arch.

119. Beauvais Cathedral. Interior, east sacristy chamber, south wall.

120. Beauvais Cathedral. Interior, choir central vessel and north transept.

121. Beauvais Cathedral. Interior, choir central vessel and south transept.

122. Beauvais Cathedral. Interior, choir central vessel, general view.

123. Beauvais Cathedral. Interior, choir central vessel, north side.

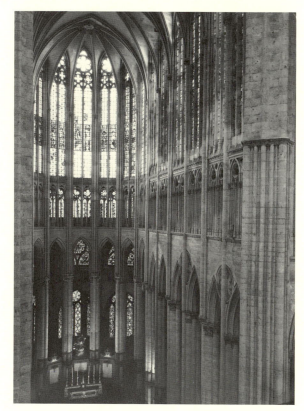

124. Beauvais Cathedral, choir, central vessel, south side.

125. Beauvais Cathedral. Interior, choir central vessel, main arcade, capital D 6.

127. Beauvais Cathedral. Interior, choir central vessel, main arcade, capital D 8.

126. Beauvais Cathedral. Interior, choir central vessel, main arcade, capital D 7.

128. Beauvais Cathedral. Interior, choir, base of hemicycle.

129. Beauvais Cathedral. Interior, choir, south side, at base of hemicycle.

130. Beauvais Cathedral. Interior, choir, central vessel, upper parts, hemicycle, triforium at D 8.

131. Beauvais Cathedral. Interior, choir, central vessel, upper parts, hemicycle, detail of triforium.

132. Beauvais Cathedral. Interior, choir, central vessel, upper parts, hemicycle, interior of triforium.

133. Beauvais Cathedral. Interior, choir, central vessel, upper parts, capital D 5/6.

134. Beauvais Cathedral. Interior, choir, central vessel, upper parts, capital D 6.

135. Beauvais Cathedral. Interior, choir, central vessel, upper parts, capital D 8.

136. Beauvais Cathedral. Interior, choir, central vessel, upper parts, hemicycle capitals.

137. Beauvais Cathedral. Interior, choir, central vessel, upper parts, capital E 8.

138. Beauvais Cathedral. Interior, choir, central vessel, upper parts, capital E 6.

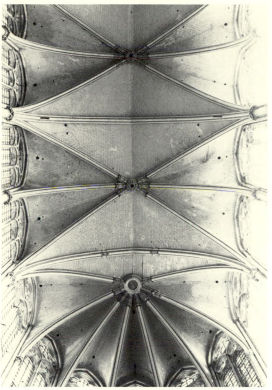

139. Beauvais Cathedral. Interior, choir, central vessel, high vaults.

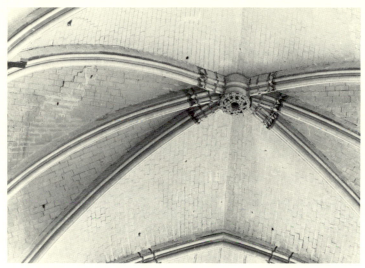

140. Beauvais Cathedral. Interior, choir, central vessel, vault 7 8.

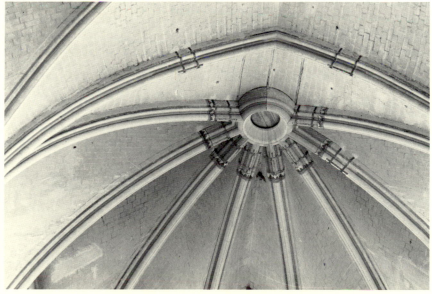

141. Beauvais Cathedral. Interior, choir, central vessel, vault of hemicycle.

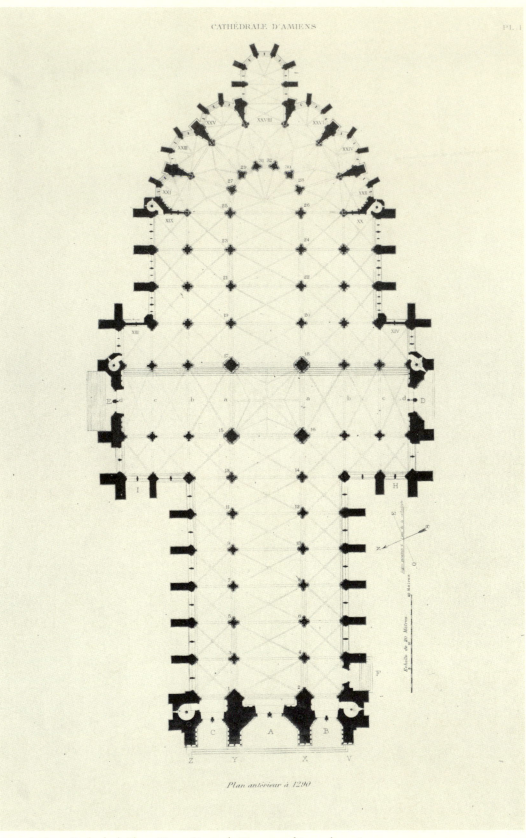

Plan antérieur à 1290

142. Amiens Cathedral. Plan. (From Durand, *Monographie*, I, plate I.)

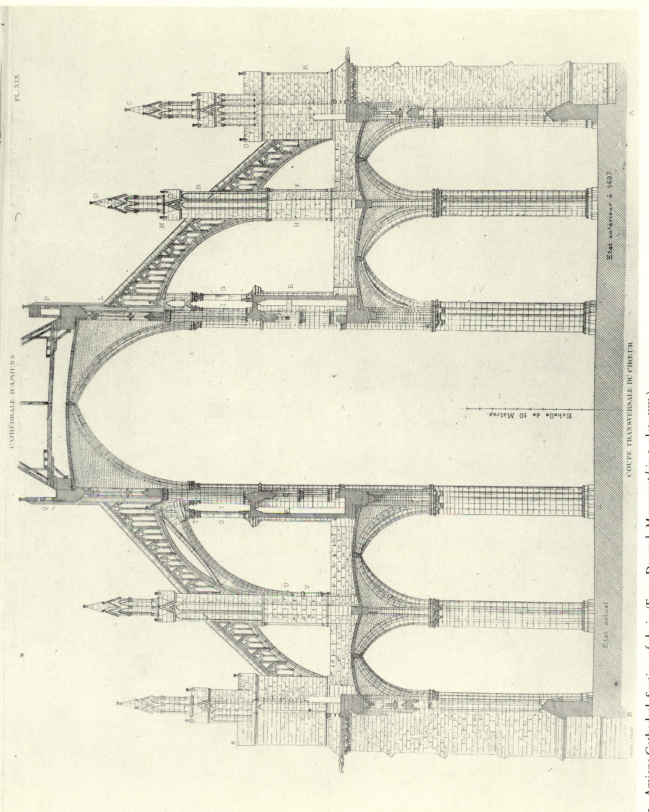

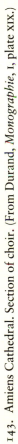

143. Amiens Cathedral. Section of choir. (From Durand, *Monographie*, I, plate XIX.)

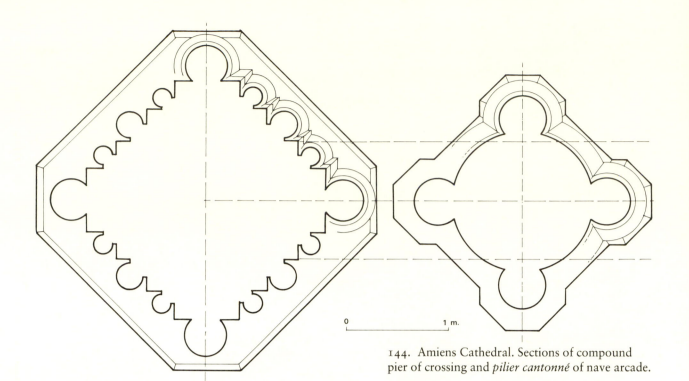

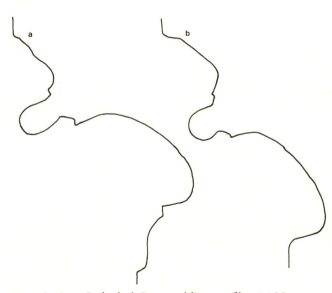

0   1 m.

144. Amiens Cathedral. Sections of compound pier of crossing and *pilier cantonné* of nave arcade.

145. Amiens Cathedral. Base molding profiles. (a) Nave pier; (b) Choir pier.

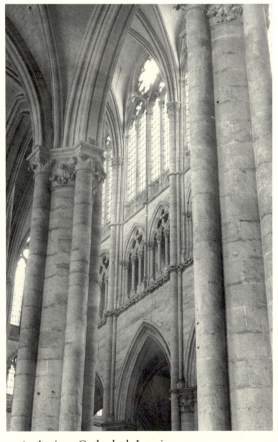

146. Amiens Cathedral. Interior, nave.

147. Amiens Cathedral. Exterior, choir, radiating chapels.

148. Amiens Cathedral. Interior, choir, ambulatory and radiating chapels.

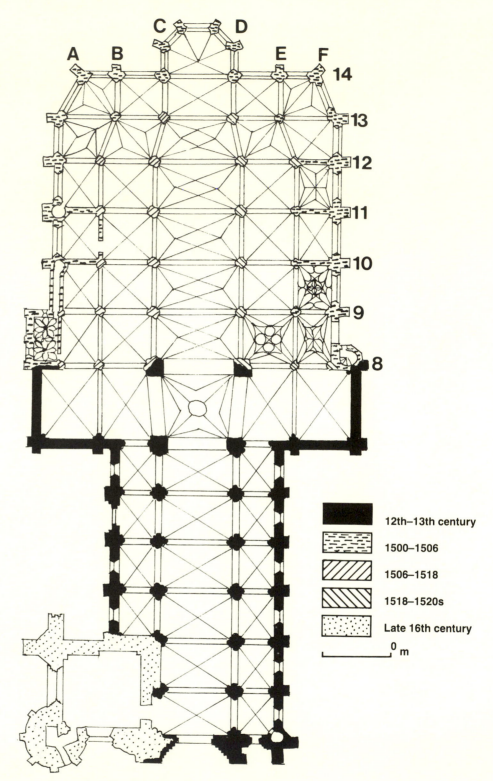

149. Beauvais, Saint-Etienne, plan.

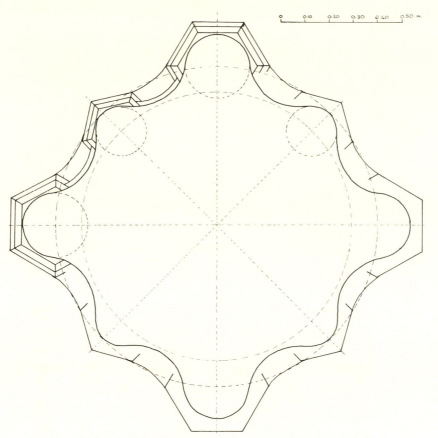

150. Beauvais, Saint-Etienne. Choir, section of main arcade pier.

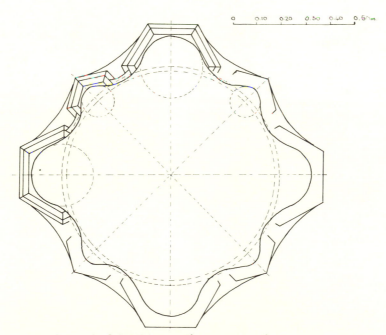

151. Beauvais, Saint-Etienne. Choir, section of aisle pier.

152. Beauvais, Saint-Etienne. Interior, choir, central vessel.

153. Beauvais, Saint-Etienne. Interior, choir, pier type I.

154. Beauvais, Saint Etienne. Interior, choir, pier type II.

155. Beauvais, Saint-Etienne. Interior, choir, pier type III.

156. Beauvais, Saint-Etienne. Interior, choir, vault of sepulchre chapel.

157. Beauvais, Saint-Etienne. Interior, choir, south aisle, decorative vaults.

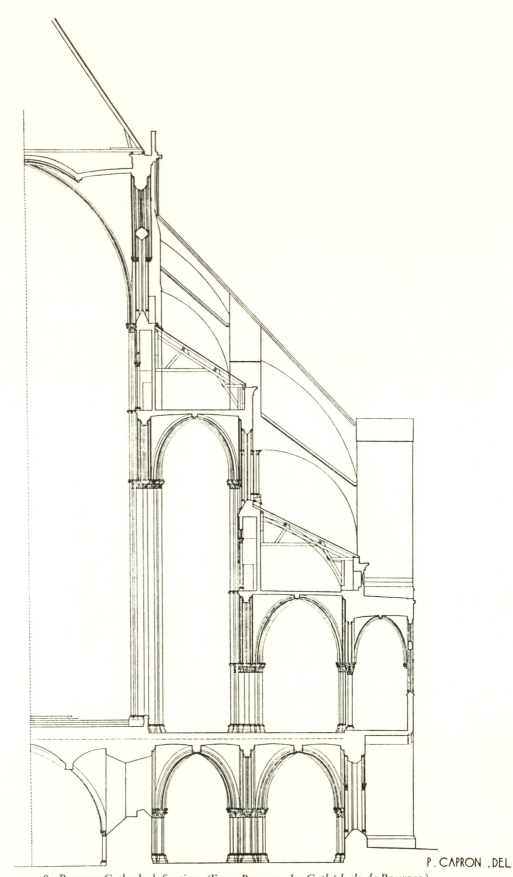

P. CAPRON .DEL

158. Bourges Cathedral. Section. (From Branner, *La Cathédrale de Bourges*.)

159. Bourges Cathedral. Interior, general view.

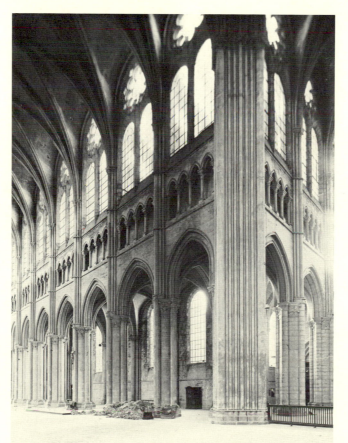

160. Chartres Cathedral. Interior, nave.

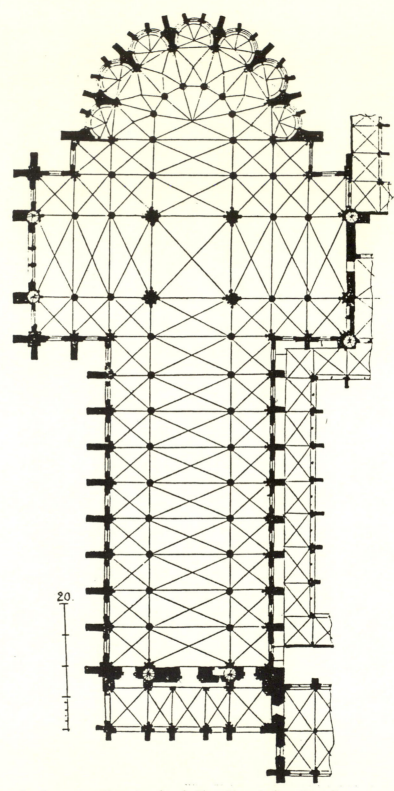

20.

161. Longpont. Cistercian church. Plan. (From Lefèvre-Pontalis, "Abbaye de Longpont," opp. p. 422.)

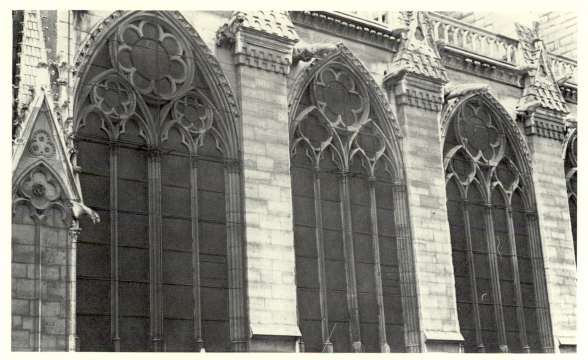

162. Paris, Notre-Dame. Exterior, nave, north side, three eastern chapels.

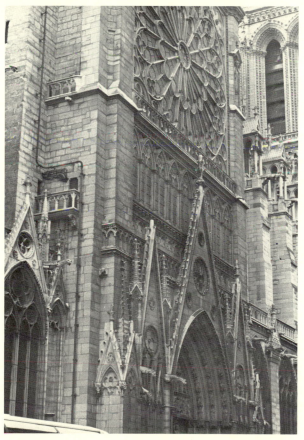

163. Paris, Notre-Dame. Exterior, north transept façade.

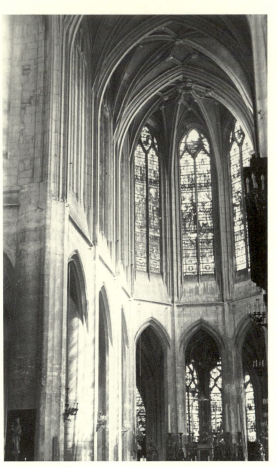

164. Paris, Saint-Germain-des-Prés, plan of monastic complex. (From Archives Nationales, Paris, III, Seine 84, 3.)

166. Paris, Saints-Gervais-et-Protais. Interior, choir.

165. Paris, Saint-Germain-des-Prés. Virgin chapel, reassembled elements of dado and tracery.

PLANS DE LA SAINTE-CHAPELLE

Chapelle basse   *Chapelle haute*

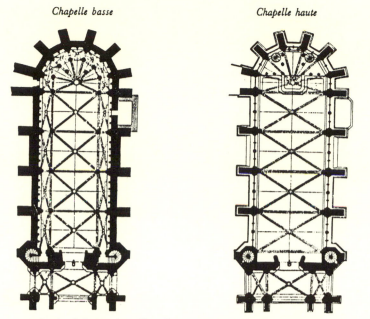

167. Paris, Sainte-Chapelle. Plan. (From Grodecki, *Sainte-Chapelle*, p. 42.)

168. Paris, Sainte-Chapelle. Exterior, south side.

169. Paris, Sainte-Chapelle. Interior, lower chapel.

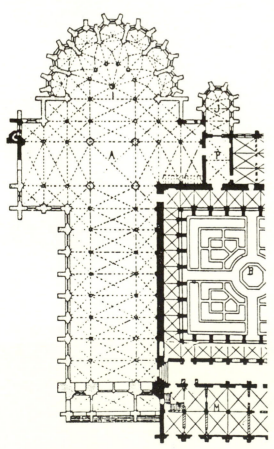

171. Royaumont. Cistercian church. Plan. (From Branner, *Saint Louis and the Court Style*, p. 34.)

170. Paris, Sainte-Chapelle. Interior, upper chapel.

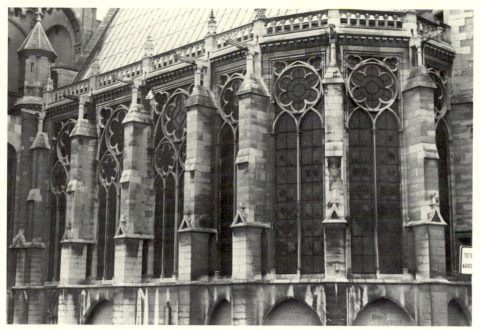

172. Saint-Germain-en-Laye. Chapel. Exterior, southeast side.

173. Saint-Germain-en-Laye. Chapel. Interior, east end.

174. Saint-Leu-d'Esserent. Interior, choir, base of compound pier. (Note: the diamond points here belong to restoration work. The same motif also exists in the unrestored parts of the choir, however.)

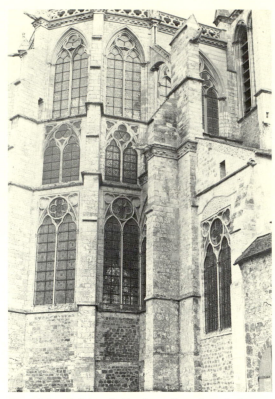

175. Saint-Sulpice-de-Favières. Exterior, choir, from northeast.

177. Saint-Sulpice-de-Favières. Interior, choir, south side.

176. Saint-Sulpice-de-Favières. Exterior, choir, window at east end of south choir aisle.

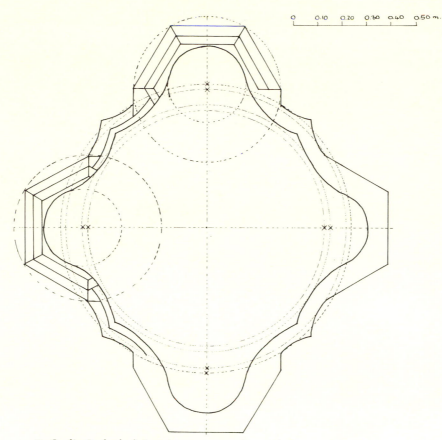

0   0.10   0.20   0.30   0.40   0.50 m.

178. Senlis Cathedral. Interior, transept, pier section.

179. Senlis Cathedral. Interior, transept, pier.

180. Troyes, Saint-Jean-au-Marché. Interior, choir.